The Marketing Firm

The Marketing Firm

Economic Psychology of Corporate Behaviour

Kevin J. Vella and Gordon R. Foxall

Cardiff Business School, Cardiff University, UK

Edward Elgar
Cheltenham, UK • Northampton, MA, USA

Published by
Edward Elgar Publishing Limited
The Lypiatts
15 Lansdown Road
Cheltenham
Glos GL50 2JA
UK

Edward Elgar Publishing, Inc.
William Pratt House
9 Dewey Court
Northampton
Massachusetts 01060
USA

A catalogue record for this book
is available from the British Library

Library of Congress Control Number: 2011925780

MIX
Paper from
responsible sources
FSC
www.fsc.org   FSC® C018575

ISBN 978 1 84844 415 7

Typeset by Servis Filmsetting Ltd, Stockport, Cheshire
Printed and bound by MPG Books Group, UK

Contents

Preface   vi

Introduction   1

1. The marketing firm   5
2. From consumer behaviour to corporate response   30
3. Methodology and measurement   40
4. Specification and interpretation   52
5. Corporate behaviour: the supply of wrapped impulse ice-cream   65
6. Reflections on 'the marketing firm'   103
7. Conclusions   118

Appendix 1.   *Pre-structured case outline*   125
Appendix 2.   *The case study protocol*   126
Appendix 3.   *Coding scheme*   136
Appendix 4.   *Data tables and commentary*   247
Appendix 5.   *Reflections on 'the marketing firm'*   286

References   297
Index   305

Preface

The 'theory of the marketing firm' (Foxall 1999a) draws upon operant psychology, economic theory, marketing and consumer research to propose an embryonic theory of the firm. Its distinctiveness lies in the argument that all firms exist to market, i.e., to acquire and retain customers. The theory assumes the Coasean notion that the reduction of transaction costs involved in such customer-related endeavours is central to the *raison d'être* of the firm. From the theory's operant perspective, firm behaviour, the sole focus of inquiry, is assumed to be a function of the consequences it produces in the environment. Behaviour is directly manifest in the marketing mix variables deposited and optimised by marketers to encourage favourable customer and supplier behaviour and to compete effectively. The second incorporated Coasean notion is that of firms being a system of contracts or interdependent relationships characterised by associated bilateral expectations and behaviour between parties. However, operant theory goes beyond, suggesting that parties to relationships are interlocked in mutually reinforcing relationships where the behaviour of one party acts as a stimulus to the other by signalling the positive and negative consequences contingent upon certain actions within that relationship. Firms shape and maintain favourable behaviour within the relationships by deploying marketing stimuli to compel behaviour in a given direction and/or to signal rewarding and punishing consequences contingent upon favourable and unfavourable actions. These stimuli, however, take meaning only in the presence of a learning history and/or through a process of deliberation.

Employing the strengths of case study design and utilising secondary data published by the UK Competition Commission in connection with Birds Eye Wall's Limited (BEW), this book seeks to establish an appropriate methodology by which to operationalise the central constructs of the theory of the marketing firm to evaluate its explanatory power in an early bout of empirical research. The findings support the central propositions on firm action and provide insights valuable in expanding theory.

KJV
GRF
30 November 2010

Introduction

Modern theories of the firm, which have emerged from criticisms of neo-classical microeconomics, are now subsumed in the domain called Economics of Organisation. This discipline includes the *purpose or existence of firms*, their *internal organisation* and their *boundaries* among its explananda (Douma and Schreuder 2008). The first to ask why firms exist was Ronald Coase, now widely recognised as the founder of modern theories of the firm. Coase (1937) believed that firms emerge under entrepreneurial coordination as a system of incomplete contractual relationships circumventing markets to organise exchange transactions more efficiently. Contrary to the neo-classical view, there *are* costs involved in operating a market, for example, the costs of searching for contracting parties, of negotiating and monitoring contracts and so on. Hence, firms emerge to reduce 'marketing costs' (Coase 1937, p. 392) (according to Klaes (2000), the first to coin the term 'transaction costs' was Marschak (1950)). Foxall (1999a) starts from Coase's work, focusing primarily on the purpose of firms, with the main contributions being: (a) the critical emphasis on customer acquisition and retention *and* transaction costs and (b) the introduction and use of an explicit operant psychology framework within which to analyse and explain the dynamics of contracts or firm relationships. Despite Coase's reference to the importance of marketing costs as being the onset for firms, most conceptualisations of the firm, including the dominant view (transaction costs economics), relegate customers to passive sources of demand.

In contrast, the theory of the marketing firm proposes that firms emerge to acquire and retain customers *in parallel* to economising on transaction costs. And, correctly so, for the most persistent memory of the first author's two-decade experience in industry as a marketing practitioner is the constant preoccupation with customer acquisition, retention, market share and improving return on marketing investment.

Similar to his approach in consumer behaviour, Foxall (1999a) addresses the existence and purpose of firms from an operant psychology perspective, or the approach within psychology that regards the study of human behaviour as determined by the context within which it occurs. Operant psychology assumes that an individual emits behaviour that operates (hence the term 'operant') on the environment to produce positive and negative outcomes or consequences which, in turn, as stimuli, determine the future rate of emission of that behaviour (Foxall 1990). For example, the purchase of a particular brand of ice-cream has utilitarian benefits (a refreshing confection on a hot day) and symbolic benefits (Birds Eye Wall's ice-cream freezer cabinets in current use depict a hip young tanned lad with 'cool shades' symbolising a particular life-style). Purchasing premium ice-cream comes at a price or negative consequence: the surrender of money in exchange for the product. Such positive and negative outcomes impinge on a consumer's behaviour over her learning history – the consequences of buying ice-cream are (a) reinforcing when the rate of purchase and consumption increases the likelihood of the consumer buying and eating ice-cream again in future, and (b) punishing when the likelihood of buying ice-cream in future decreases. Marketers deposit programmed stimuli in the environment to signal the positive outcomes of purchasing and consuming ice-cream. These stimuli come to control consumer behaviour by virtue of learning history within the purchase and consumption situation (Foxall 1997a).

From this perspective, therefore, understanding firm behaviour requires focusing on its observed function: What has behaviour accomplished? What are the consequences produced upon the environment? Which stimuli signal these outcomes and, thus, influence behaviour because of learning history (Baum 1994; Foxall 1997a)? If firms do exist to market, then firm behaviour of import is evident in the firm's marketing strategies embodied in the marketing mix, and its consequences are inexorably linked to consumer behaviour and, in turn, to the outcomes of such consumer behaviour. Marketers and consumers are thus linked by deep interdependent and reciprocal relationships that are mutually reinforcing. Such reciprocal relationships are known as bilateral contingencies and are not limited to Supplier↔Customer[1] relationships: in fact, the theory of the marketing firm holds that all firm individual relationships, including those held with competitors, are bilateral contingencies. Mutual reinforcement, in Supplier↔Customer relationships, is primarily contingent upon literal economic exchange, i.e. the exchange of products or services for money (Foxall 1999a).

Running counter to Coase (1937), Foxall claims that firms *circumscribe* marketing relationships and lock buyers and sellers in bilateral contingency relationships to render exchange transactions more predictable, more stable and, hence, more controllable. This idea of predictability and controllability does not simply stem from the theory's underlying operant paradigm:[2] economists have already contemplated this notion, for example, emphasising how firms seek to better forecast their production runs. Trading partners cement their cooperation through goodwill, contracts or some degree of shareholding (Richardson 1972, p. 884). This position appears to imply circumscription through informal or formal relationships for stability.

The theory of the marketing firm proposes two central strategic functions of firm behaviour within these mutually reinforcing relationships: (a) managing the consumer behaviour environment through elements of the marketing mix to control the behaviour alternatives available to consumers insofar as compelling them to act in particular ways; and (b) creating marketing programmes that signal and highlight the instrumental and symbolic benefits of purchase and consumption. Both strategies encourage consumer behaviour that is advantageous to the marketer and, naturally, detrimental to competition (Foxall 1999a).

The theory of the marketing firm remains largely an interpretation and requires an empirical investigation to evaluate critically its explanatory power by substantiating, or otherwise, its central claims: this research is such an investigative evaluation. It is a methodological piece that assumes the operant paradigm to accomplish its objective: *to generate an empirically based evaluation and resultant insights into the theory of the marketing firm through the construction of adequate operational measures and the application of such measures to qualitative data.* The research is positivist *and* qualitative, embracing the position that the term 'qualitative' simply refers to a method for collecting particular kinds of data useful and appropriate irrespective of worldviews (Guba and Lincoln 1994; Miles and Huberman 1994; Myers 1997). A case study design is adopted and populated by secondary data obtained from the UK Competition Commission in the form of a publicly available inquiry report entitled *The Supply of Impulse Ice Cream: A Report on the Supply in the UK of Ice Cream Purchased for Immediate Consumption* published in January 2000. The report is an in-depth investigation into the existence of a monopoly situation in the UK impulse ice-cream market. The dataset was chosen because of its immediate availability and its relatively extensive and exhaustive description of firm behaviour.

The focus is on three sets of bilateral contingencies:

- Manufacturer↔Distributor (Supplier↔Customer);
- Manufacturer↔Retailer (Supplier↔Customer); and
- Manufacturer↔Rival (Supplier↔Supplier).

Hence, the central research question is: *How adequately does the theory of the marketing firm explain the marketing behaviour of premium brand manufacturers in their bilateral contingency relationships with rivals, distributors and retailers, vis-à-vis the supply of wrapped impulse ice-cream in the United Kingdom?*

Our principal contribution is to extend the theory of the marketing firm through an empirically-based critical evaluation and the development of a case study methodology appropriate for an operant approach. The full rationale for this approach and the research programme within which our analysis of the marketing firm takes place can be found in Foxall (2007, 2010), which explicate the reasons for initially adopting a behaviourist paradigm and the subsequent roles of intentional and cognitive explanations. This book is concerned with the translation of that methodology from the analysis of consumer behaviour to the associated analysis of the corporation. It is confined to the initial stage of explanation based on operant analysis. This enables us to propose a methodology, which we understand as an epistemological device that incorporates a theoretical position, the technical measures it requires, and the relationships between them, which others, we urge, might use to analyse both our data and similar case histories to generate comparative evaluations of both theory and method.

Chapter 1 reproduces the original paper on the marketing firm (Foxall 1999a), slightly revised, as a point of reference for the remainder of the book. Chapter 2 explains the theoretical background to the theory of the marketing firm, bringing to bear its main concepts in an attempt to deepen the otherwise current 'broad brush image' presented in that paper (Foxall 1999c, p. 245) of the marketing firm. Since the aim of the book is to develop a methodology for evaluating the theory of the marketing firm, this chapter focuses on specifying a model of the firm in the light of the Behavioural Perspective Model of consumer choice as a prelude to the operational measurement of the theory in terms of the selected data (see also Chapters 3 and 4). The evaluation is a backdrop for the derived research propositions that guide the operationalisation of the construct (Chapter 4). The data is analysed in Chapter 5 and discussed in Chapter 6. Chapter 7 points out some limitations, areas for further research and general conclusions.

NOTES

1. The notation '↔' denotes a bilateral contingency.
2. Operant behaviourism is the philosophy of science undergirding operant psychology and is examined in Chapter 3. Suffice it to say, the operant paradigm seeks to explain behaviour for prediction and control (Baum 1994).

1. The marketing firm[1]

Firms exist in order to market. Understanding their nature thus requires an account of consumer behaviour as well as one of managerial response. Consumer and marketer behaviours are mutually reinforced and necessarily entail literal exchange. The marketing firm exists in order to reduce the transaction costs involved in finding and retaining customers. The analysis transcends the Coasean approach by portraying the complexity of the marketing firm and the marketing relationships which it facilitates. Research into relationship marketing elucidates the nature of the firm as a marketing entity, an organisation established to economise the transaction costs of creating and maintaining long-term marketing and quasi-marketing relationships.

INTRODUCTION

Objectives

This chapter undertakes a functional analysis of marketing, conceived as the intersecting activities of customers and marketers; i.e. it explores what marketing does. In the process of doing this, it defines the nature of the marketing firm. It has four interlinked objectives:

1. *To draw attention to the role of marketing in the corporation, thereby emphasising the need for consideration of consumer behaviour as the starting point for a theory of the firm.* The point that all firms market may appear trivial but this frequently overlooked aspect of the behaviour of business organisations is central to their definition and analysis. Indeed, it is only through an awareness of what marketing management does – the essence of its relationship with consumer behaviour – that the nature of the marketing firm can be appreciated.
2. *To understand what the marketing firm does, the nature and scope of marketing management, and the functions of marketing-orientated management.* The paper shows that the explanation of consumer behaviour presented in the Behavioural Perspective Model (Foxall 1990)

can be extended to cover the behaviour of marketing management and thereby gives valuable insight into the essence of economic exchange. The concept of reciprocally reinforced behaviours lays the basis of an analysis of marketing relationships.

3. *To consider the nature of marketing relationships and thereby to define genuine marketing and differentiate it from pseudo-marketing.* The analysis of consumer behaviour and marketing activity in similar terms, notably the mutual qualification of behaviour setting scope and reciprocal management of reinforcement, facilitates a clearer understanding of the essential content of marketing relationships which serves to distinguish marketing behaviour from other real and important economic and social activities which must be classified otherwise (as non-marketing).

4. *To note in conclusion that marketing management can be construed as behaviouristic.* And to invite consideration of the managerial and public policy implications of this.

AN ECONOMIC PSYCHOLOGY OF MARKETING

Economic psychologists have not usually been concerned with the nature of marketing activity, especially the role of marketing management in affluent consumer-orientated economies. One reason for this is that marketing studies appear to be adequately catered for in business schools where they often seem to acquire an ideological or technological bias in favour of the producer which does not fit with the pursuit of social science. But economic psychology can contribute uniquely to the understanding of marketing behaviour by virtue of its integration of both psychology and economic analysis. There are three principal reasons for this.

First, marketer behaviour is a legitimate sphere of human economic activity for scientific analysis and ought to be of special interest to economic psychologists whose wider knowledge of economic behaviour, especially that of consumers, can provide an integrative framework for a broader analysis of market exchange than is feasible in economics, psychology or marketing studies alone. Secondly, marketing studies in particular cannot attain the disciplinary depth which economics and psychology, notably when in tandem, can bring to the analysis of customer–firm interactions. Marketing is not a discipline but an application area for social science and other disciplines. As such, marketing provides a programme for social scientists by describing a field of human behaviour which they should be able to comprehend and explain. And, marketing behaviour is too important a facet of human activity to be left to the ideologues, whether they are found shoring up the business schools from within or, on the outside, trying to tear them down. Thirdly, the current challenge for economic psychologists lies in the fact that marketing behaviour and its analysis at the business school level are becoming increasingly complex. Economic psychology is required in order to unravel the actual nature of 'consumer-orientated management' and the structural circumstances of the economy in which it arises. This involves defining what is meant by 'marketing' as opposed to 'marketing management' and 'marketing-orientated management'. And that requires definitions in turn of 'consumer behaviour', 'consumer choice' and 'consumer-orientated management'.

These terms, which are extensively employed in marketing studies, lack the precise delineation which can come only from a disciplinary analysis such as economic psychology can provide. But economic psychology is also central to understanding and evaluating new developments in marketing thought and practice: 'relationship marketing', 'internal marketing' and 'social marketing', for instance. These terms are currently used, within and beyond marketing, with a degree of flexibility and sophistry that social scientists ought to be wary of and to whose clarification they should be willing to contribute. Above all, economic psychology can contribute to the understanding of what marketing is and what it does. Of all the disciplines available it is best placed to illuminate the nature of marketing behaviour and its significance to the theory of the firm, the mutual dependencies of consumer and managerial behaviour and the policy issues likely to arise from them. This paper pursues a particular approach to the economic psychology of marketing, one based on an extension of an existing model of consumer behaviour to the consideration of marketing behaviour as a whole. As the paper argues, it is important that the analysis of consumer behaviour and the marketing firm proceed in common terms and the Behavioural Perspective Model (Foxall 1990, 1994, 1997c) is particularly suited to achieving this integration. Its extension to the marketing firm also emphasises the need for an integrated psychological and economic perspective if marketing exchanges and relationships are to be adequately understood.

The operant behaviourist paradigm within which this analysis is pursued is, despite some contemporary accounts, far from anachronistic. Although psychology would like to present itself as a mature science in the Kuhn (1962) sense, and to portray the behaviouristic era as having been superseded by the cognitive revolution, it is unlikely that social science progresses through paradigmatic succession of this kind. Certainly, the critical juxtaposition of alternative explanations (Feyerabend 1970) is central to the BPM research programme of which this paper forms part (Foxall 1997c). Operant behaviourism is alive and well and concerned with the contextual explication of cognitive phenomena (e.g. Hayes and Chase 1991; Hayes and Hayes 1992; Hayes *et al.* 1993, 1994). It is, moreover, particularly appropriate for the analysis of microeconomic behaviour (Rosenberg 1976; Alhadeff 1982; Foxall 1997a).

THE NATURE OF THE MARKETING FIRM

'The marketing firm' does not designate a particular kind of business organisation, to be distinguished from other, presumably 'non-marketing', firms. Rather, it emphasises a characteristic of all firms by alluding to the central purpose of business as opposed to other organisations: to create and retain customers by serving them profitably in a competitive market context. But the origin of firms is usually traced, following Coase (1937, 1988a, 1988c, 1988d), to another set of market transactions, those previously undertaken exclusively within the external marketplace but now executed by employees of an entrepreneurial organisation.[2] However, a functional analysis of the firm must begin with the behaviour of its key stakeholder, that which calls it into existence and rationalises its use of resources; that is, with consumer behaviour. A theory of the firm will thus be a theory of an entity that engages in marketing because any firm is inescapably and essentially embedded in networks of marketing relationships; its nature and function cannot be understood if this point is neglected. 'The marketing firm' is a tautology but one that is necessary in view of the tendency of many social scientists to overlook marketing relationships as a defining characteristic of the firm. All firms market. Marketing has to be understood as the *raison d'être* of firms, the reason they come into existence, not an optional extra that firms can adopt if they feel like it or just under certain market conditions. The word 'marketing' ought, therefore, to be redundant as an adjective to describe the firm. I tried to emphasise this by describing 'the marketing firm' as a tautology. I described the term marketing firm in this way to make it clear that I understand 'firms' as entities that market, i.e., effect mutually reinforcing transactions with customers in the competitive marketplace. I chose the word tautology carefully to make this central point, an emphasis that goes decisively beyond the notions of the firm as Knight, Coase, Schumpeter, Demsetz, Hart, Williamson and others have conceived it, i.e., generally consumer-less and not, therefore, a marketing entity. However, because the subtlety of my point seems to have eluded some readers, 'truism' might have been a safer choice.

Marketing firms exist under particular economic-structural conditions, those which induce consumer-orientated management by the business as a whole. Consumer-orientation is a contingent behaviour appropriate to a particular external economic structure which generates consumer choice. This requires high levels of discretionary income among consumers and competition among suppliers. It also depends upon a situation in which the quantity of a good supplied or capable of being supplied exceeds demand (Foxall 1981). The managerial style of the marketing firm facilitates, economises and maintains marketing relationships in these conditions. By contrast, economic theories of the firm often adopt an intra-organisational perspective which stresses relationships based on production rather than the firm's external publics. At worst, they deal with apparently consumer-less economies from which many aspects of marketing are absent.[3] But intra-firm behaviour is comprehensible only in relation to the external institutions that control the organisation. That environment provides the reinforcement on which the continuance of the firm depends and for which it was established.

The behaviour of members of the firm, its managers and other employees and additional stakeholders such as its owners and those who invest in its shares cannot be understood in ignorance of the contingent relationships that bind firm and marketplace together. It follows that the function of the firm inheres uniquely within the management of marketing transactions and relationships, both 'internal' and 'external'. This includes, first, marketing management, which is responsible for using the marketing mix to manage consumer behaviour setting scope and to control the reinforcers that maintain consumer choice. Second, it involves the management of intra-firm quasi-marketing relationships, those which, on a Coasean understanding of the origin of the firm, were previously undertaken entirely within the market but have been integrated within the organisational boundaries of the firm. By tracing the interlocking environmental contingencies at these levels, the theory of the marketing firm shows how these contingencies and the behaviours they control encourage organisational responsiveness to the market. We can now describe what the marketing firm does: that is, the nature of the relationships (i) between the marketing firm and its consumers/suppliers, and (ii) between the firm's entrepreneurial function and its other members. These actions necessarily involve behaviour setting scope management and/or the management of reinforcers ('mutuality relationships') and market transactions which are characterised by literal exchange of property rights ('marketing relationships').

The firm also develops relationships with various parties that are not based on market (exchange) transactions and which are not therefore marketing relationships, e.g. public relations to consumers, internal communications (which is not 'internal marketing'), maintaining long-term relationships with customers or suppliers (which is not 'relationship marketing'). These non-market activities involve mutual reinforcement (those who claim they involve exchange use this term metaphorically). Hence, it is impossible to understand marketing management, social marketing, internal marketing or relationship marketing without making the distinction between relationships that inhere in mutual setting scope restriction and/or mutual reinforcement, and those which additionally involve real exchange in a marketing-oriented economic system.

This analysis contributes the recognition that the management of market relationships is the essence of firms; firms come into existence because they make marketing relationships possible/more economic. They make it possible to enclose market transactions and thereby to make them more predictable; this is circumscribing market relationships rather than circumventing the market. Production and selling are independent of firms in the sense of being functions whose execution does not require firms; the creation and management of marketing and quasi-marketing relationships, however, are the very essence of the firm's existence. They are what it is for.

WHAT MARKETING DOES

Economic Behaviour as Operant Response

To ask why the firm exists is to ask what it does. This is to enquire of the consequences of its behaviour (Lee 1988). Operant psychology is therefore particularly relevant to our task since economic behaviour is instrumentally conditioned. Thus its analysis in operant terms – i.e., as behaviour that operates on the environment to produce consequences that determine its future rate of emission – can elucidate the nature of consumer and corporate behaviour in affluent market-orientated societies. The operant behaviourist paradigm is summarised by the three-term contingency,

$$S^D: R \rightarrow S^{R/A},$$

where S^D is a discriminative (antecedent or setting) stimulus, R is a response, and $S^{R/A}$ is a positive or aversive (consequent) stimulus contingent upon the performance of R and controlling its future rate of emission.[4]

This formulation summarises the contingencies of reinforcement and punishment which comprise the operant approach to explanation. The application of this paradigm in the present context stems from the fact that economic behaviour is operant: it is emitted rather than reflexive behaviour the outcomes of which influence its rate. The consequences which strengthen it, making similar responses (R) more probable in similar circumstances, are known as reinforcers (S^R). Other consequences, which reduce the frequency of occurrence of the behaviour that produces them, are known as punishers, which consist of aversive consequences (S^A) which are accepted by the individual.

Antecedent, discriminative stimuli (S^D) signal the reinforcement contingent on the performance of specific behaviours. In their presence, the individual performs only those behaviours previously reinforced (Skinner 1974). The explanatory mode of the three-term contingency thus concentrates on the ways in which behaviour can be predicted and controlled through manipulation of the environmental contingencies that determine its rate.

Consumer Behaviour in Operant Perspective

The behaviour of human consumers can be comprehended within the general methodological orientation of operant analysis. But the complexity of such activity, in comparison with the simpler economic behaviour of infra-humans which is readily amenable to experimental analysis (Kagel 1988), requires two qualifications. First, the influence of environmental contingencies on behaviour is held to vary with the scope of the setting within which the behaviour occurs. This scope for behaving is determined by the nature of the social, physical, temporal and rule-based discriminative stimuli that compose the setting. Second, reinforcement in humans has two functions, utilitarian (incentive) and informational (feedback), which exert differential influences on the rate of response.[5]

Hence, in place of the unitary constructs of discriminative stimuli and reinforcement, our model of consumer behaviour incorporates two variables: a continuum of (relatively) open/(relatively) closed behaviour settings; and the degree to which reinforcement functions informationally and/or via the provision of utilitarian benefits (Figure 1.1).[6] In summary, the operant analysis of marketing proposes that: consumer behaviour consists of economic purchasing and consumption activities which are reinforced via utility and informationally, i.e., which recur because of the instrumental and expressive consequences contingent upon them. It provides the fundamental datum of operant consumer research. Consumer choice is any behaviour which reduces the aversive consequences of facing a number of apparently functionally equivalent options, i.e., those which have similar response strength for the individual.

It may involve or be preceded by private deliberation but this is not the cause of the ensuing behaviour; that behaviour is under the control of

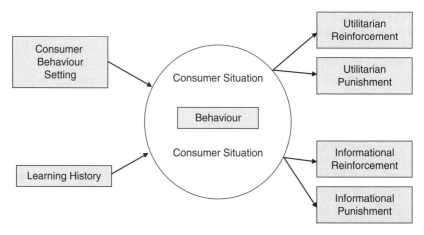

Figure 1.1   Summative Behavioural Perspective Model

the consumer's learning history and the current behaviour setting. Such choice is constrained therefore in two ways: by learning history (involving a particular pattern and structure of reinforcement) and by the pattern of reinforcement signalled by the discriminative stimuli that constitute the current behaviour setting as contingent upon performing particular behaviours in the setting.

Marketing Management in Operant Perspective

From this account of consumer choice emerges a novel interpretation of how marketing management works. For, if consumer behaviour settings actually influence choice, then marketing management ought logically to be found attempting to engineer the components of such settings to increase the probability that consumer behaviour advantageous to the firm will emerge. Those components are the social, physical, temporal and regulatory discriminative stimuli that signal the outcomes of specific behaviours in the setting. Moreover, if consumer behaviour is influenced by the pattern of utilitarian and informational reinforcement thus signalled, marketing management ought to be found arranging the contingencies which shape and maintain such behaviour. The extension of the Behavioural Perspective Model to the activities of the firm suggests that a great deal of marketing activity is, in fact, concerned with modifying two main variables that influence consumer behaviour. The first involves managing the scope of the consumer behaviour setting to increase its attractiveness for the individual and thus reducing the propensity to avoid or leave it without purchasing or consuming. The second is the management of the ways in which utilitarian and informational reinforcers are made available to the consumer.

Marketing management thus appears to be based upon a behaviouristic understanding of consumer behaviour and the operation of the marketing system. First, a considerable amount of managerial action in marketing can be viewed as the attempt to influence the scope of behaviour settings, making the purchase of whatever the marketer doers more likely (whether this refers to spending on buying a product or consuming a service such as depositing money in a savings account) and making other responses (such as leaving the store, buying or consuming an alternative offering) less probable. Obvious examples are the provision of credit facilities for consumers who cannot afford the full cash outlay immediately, changing consumers' moods through in-store music, using advertising to promise desirable reinforcers contingent upon buying and using the item, and so on. Nor is this strategy of closure necessarily manipulative (in the worse sense of the word), especially in a competitive environment. Presenting the consumer with a more pleasant retail environment, for instance, or with clearer way-finding aids and more legible shopping mall designs encourages the potential buyer to stay in the marketing environment and to become an actual consumer. Second, marketers manage the reinforcements available to consumers; they do so in three ways: enhancing the electiveness of reinforcers, controlling the schedules on which reinforcers are presented, and increasing the quantity or quality of reinforcers. These are, according to an operant analysis of buyer behaviour, the sole means by which such activity can be regulated (Alhadeff 1982). In summary, marketing management is a function of the firm which involves managing the marketing relationships between the firm and its customers and suppliers (through behaviour setting scope modification and the use of reinforcers). As will be shown, marketing management is but one activity of the marketing firm, which is additionally concerned with managing intra-firm (quasi-)marketing relationships (e.g. with employees) and extra-firm mutuality relationships (e.g. with stakeholders). We can also define consumer-orientated management as the activity of the firm that involves the creation and implementation of marketing mixes which reinforce consumers for purchasing the marketing organisation's brand (i.e., ensures that they are sufficiently satisfied to show some degree of loyalty for the firm's brand), as a result of which the firm is reinforced (i.e., keeps developing and offering marketing mixes of this kind which maintain consumer behaviour). In short, it requires the creation of conditions most conducive to consumers buying the brand of the marketing organisation using not only price but promotion, place/time and product utilities.

THE FIRM REVISITED

Origins

This analysis of the marketing function leads naturally to a consideration of the nature of the organisation responsible for marketing management. Why do such business organisations exist within a market framework which presumably could undertake these functions in the absence of firms? This is of course related to the question raised by Coase (1937): why do firms come into being? Our question is more complex, however: why do marketing firms exist?

Answering this question requires a more detailed examination of the nature of the marketing relationships that bind the firm to its publics. At the heart of the definition of economic behaviour is the idea of the transaction, a term which requires precise delineation in order to be analytically useful. It is not sufficient to point out that economic behaviour is that in which revenues and costs play a part, yielding a profit or loss since all operant behaviour can be loosely cast in these terms. Economic behaviour is simultaneously reinforced and punished and its probability in any specific instance can be represented as a vector quantity derived from the strength of the individual's history of reinforcement for similar behaviour in the past and that of a history of punishment stemming from the same source. Alhadeff (1982) notes that consumer behaviour, for example, is determined at the intersection of two response strengths: that for approach (a function of the benefit likely to result from purchase and/ or consumption) and that for avoidance (a function of the costs of that purchase/consumption). Each of these response strengths is the product of the reinforcement schedule on which it was acquired, the quality and quantity of reinforcement, and reinforcer delay. However, despite the centrality of this phenomenon to the analysis of economic behaviour, these 'contingencies of reinforcement' and even the presence of approach vs. avoidance response strengths are not definitive thereof.

Social relationships entail mutually reinforced actions. The behaviour of A (or its effects) reinforces that of B, while B's behaviour reinforces that of A. These behaviours are mutually contingent: each occurs only if the other is present to act as a discriminative stimulus for its enactment. Although social behaviours of this sort (say, two people waving to each other) are said to constitute exchanges, this usage is entirely metaphorical and does not apply to the economic behaviour of the marketing firm. An essential characteristic of an economic transaction is exchange. A bilateral economic exchange is marked by mutual reinforcement, achieved through swapping or trading entities; for analytic purposes, its essence lies in its constituting genuine exchange, i.e., the literal swapping of things rather than the symbolic or metaphorical interaction that occurs when people are said to 'exchange glances'.[7]

In operant terms, an exchange transaction is marked by mutual reinforcement, though in each case what is received is as reinforcing as or more reinforcing than the retention of what is given up. Some part of an economic exchange must be actual barter or pecuniary interchange. The reason for insisting on literal exchange is that the marketing firm cannot function in its absence. In economic behaviour, the actions of A (or B) provide both utilitarian and informational reinforcement for those of B (or A). Supplier A provides goods for customer B; in return B provides A with money and market intelligence. The goods are utilitarian in that they provide utility, and informational in that they provide economic capital (if the customer is a firm) or social status (if a final consumer). The money is utilitarian for the supplier (who extracts profits from it) and informational as well (as it is recorded in the supplier's accounts). Market intelligence is an informational reinforcer since it provides data on what consumers have bought, what they have paid, which allows the supplier to behave rationally with respect to future production decisions (what to make, what to charge). The reduction of transaction costs requires that marketing intelligence of this kind be available to the firm. But such information is available only if transactions include literal exchange.[8]

However, the question of what is exchanged needs further clarification, else the insistence on simple, literal exchange as integral to the definition of economic behaviour will become problematic on occasion, e.g. where services, which are intangible, are concerned. What is exchanged is legal title to the outcome of a service performed: the benefits of say a haircut or insurance policy. As Coase (1988b, p. 11) puts it, 'Lawyers . . . habitually think of what is bought and sold as consisting of a bundle of rights. It is easy to see why I was led to adopt the same approach in dealing with the radio frequency spectrum, since it is difficult to treat the use of the right to emit electrical radiations solely in physical terms . . .' (cf. Commons 1924). Economic exchange usually involves the parties' entering into an implicit or explicit contract to obtain or be recompensed for giving up goods under specified terms; the contract is enforceable either by process of law or by coercion. A transaction involves the exchange of two bundles of property rights (Demsetz 1967; Posner 1992; Dnes 1996). Legal entitlement and contractual provisions are part of the contingencies of reinforcement and punishment by which behaviour is shaped and maintained. Another source of such contingencies (and the environmental control of behaviour which they signify) is the market. A market is in essence a set of contingent relationships among discriminative stimuli (e.g. contracts of employment), responses (e.g. working practices) and reinforcing/punishing consequences (e.g. wages, being fired). Market transactions denote competitive pressures on both buyer and seller: the former may purchase elsewhere; the latter, sell to someone else. The definition of economic exchange also has an institutional component since the behaviour it entails is reinforced and punished by deliberately established and maintained institutions in society: social, economic, political, legal. The structural requirement of marketing-orientated management that there be numerous consumers with the discretionary income to allow them choice and competition among a multiplicity of suppliers means that the entities exchanged (legal rights) must be generally transferable through market transactions. The marketing firm is not engaged in a single bilateral relationship between itself and a buyer or supplier: if the property rights involved in a transaction are not for any reason exchanged, the structure of the market is such that another buyer or seller can be readily found. Market transactions are, therefore, general, though the marketing relationships that the firm engages in are specific to a given dyadic association.

Relationships
These considerations permit a clearer picture to be drawn of the marketing firm and its contrasts with certain notions of economic behaviour prevalent in marketing and economics. First, exchange theory (e.g. Homans 1974) does not capture economic exchange understood in this way. By assuming mutual reinforcement of the parties, it goes some way towards recognising mutuality; but it shows no appreciation of the necessity for economic exchange to be literal. Second, the market firm operates within markets which via the price mechanism signal what is to be produced, the amount to be produced, and its exchange value. Marketing as understood here necessarily involves economic exchanges. Third, the full complement of marketing mix elements is necessary in order to function as such a firm: hence, much 'social marketing' – the transmission of ideas, such as that of contraception in third world countries threatened by over-population, rather than goods – which relies on moral obligation and symbolic exchange is excluded on these criteria. Neither marketing relationships nor the economic behaviour of suppliers and customers can be understood if this is not grasped. Marketing requires the reciprocally reinforcing literal exchanges identified here as the sine qua non of economic behaviour. Marketing exchanges of this kind are usually accompanied by additional, social relationships, i.e., relationships characterised by reciprocally contingent reinforcement but not involving literal exchange. Although such mutuality relationships are a frequent accompaniment of marketing relationships, however, they do not of themselves constitute economic behaviour or marketing exchanges.

Hence, although the phenomena labelled social marketing undoubtedly exist, they are not marketing in the sense developed in this paper. Social marketing is not marketing for three reasons. First, it does not involve literal exchange, nor any transfer of property rights; it depends upon no price mechanism, nor therefore any idea of how much to produce. In the absence of these it could be a waste of corporate resources if conceived as marketing. Second, it does not use all of the marketing mix: it is fundamentally communication; the idea is a metaphor: no product, price, distribution. Third, it therefore consists of mutuality rather than exchange relationships. This is not to say these things are not useful and legitimate, only that it is inapt to apply the term marketing, as we have defined it here, to them. In practice, social marketing consists primarily of communication activities which are then rationalised as 'marketing' by saying that the message is the Product; the audience has to be somewhere or read the message somewhere, so this is said to represent 'Place'; the recipient of the message has to attend to it (rather than to something else), process the information it contains, act upon it, all of which are said to exact 'costs' and therefore to represent a Price. However, when nothing is literally exchanged, this is nonsense: lacking any logic of price and value, it gives no indication of what should be produced (why Product A which results in three smiles from 'consumers' rather than B which results in only two? How are smiles to be equated?), or how much, or for whom. So a figurative notion of exchange is substituted. In doing this, authors go entirely beyond the conceptualisation of marketing with which they began. This is fine as far as it goes: non-economic aspects of life cannot be measured with the accuracy that money/barter provides. But it should be conceptualised in terms of mutuality rather than exchange: i.e., reciprocal reinforcement that does not involve literal exchange.

In summary, marketing, the intersecting behaviours of consumers/ suppliers and marketers, requires mutual reinforcement, some or all of which involves a literal exchange of economic property rights. It therefore involves price (whether pecuniary or value expressed in whatever is exchanged for goods) which acts as a signal to firms with respect to what they should produce and in what quantity, and to consumers with respect to what and how much to buy. In a consumer-orientated economy, the exchange relationships which are the essence of this definition are usually accompanied by non-exchange relationships which consist in mutual reinforcement without literal exchange. Literal economic exchange relationships are necessary and sufficient to marketing; the conceptually distinct mutuality relationships, however, are never sufficient but may, in practice, be necessary, to marketing. Similar marketing relationships also exist between the firm and its suppliers.

The marketing firm

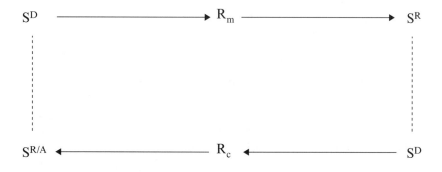

Figure 1.2   Bilateral contingency (1)

Other relationships, this time within the marketing firm, also involve literal, economic exchange, e.g. entrepreneur/employee interactions; other stakeholders in the marketing firm are linked to it only by mutuality relationships.

Bilateral Contingency

Economic transactions are represented in an operant account as a pattern of bilateral contingency (Figure 1.2). The behaviour of the consumer, say making a purchase, is preceded by the discriminative stimulus (say a store logo) provided as a consequence of the marketer's behaviour. The behaviour of the consumer has consequences (e.g. repeat purchase rate, market research opinions) which are proximal causes of further action by the marketer. In general terms, marketer behaviour, R_m, is an S^D for consumer behaviour.

The marketing firm also behaves in such a way as to provide and/or control S^Ds in the consumer behaviour setting so as to increase the probability of specific consumer responses (R_c). This is done in two ways. First, by altering those setting elements under whose direct control consumer behaviour falls, i.e., generalisation of stimulus control. Second, by ensuring that those S^Ds that signal reinforcement contingent on R_c are primed to do so effectively. Both of these are concerned with consumer behaviour setting scope management: they are designed to influence/shape momentary behaviour, i.e., consumer behaviour in this setting. Firms also attempt to shape streams of consumer behaviour over time by managing

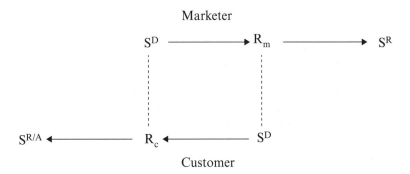

Figure 1.3 Bilateral contingency (2)

reinforcement over a period, thereby shifting from a concentration on transactions to one on relationships.

The bilateral contingency can be depicted at a more complex level in which the behaviours of each party rather than the consequences of those behaviours act as discriminative stimuli (Figure 1.3). R_c is an S^D for firm behaviour. It informs market research, for instance. R_c also determines $S^{R/A}$ (profit or loss) of the firm. In this case, firms are actively and deliberately involved in the manipulation of consumer behaviour setting scope and in reinforcement manipulation. Consumers also, collectively, control the behaviour of the firm and the reinforcement and/or punishment it receives (its profit or loss, and thus its future marketing offerings. But consumers rarely do this 'deliberately'; exceptions are organised consumer boycotts. Competitors deliberately influence another firm's setting scope and the consequences of its actions, just by competing in the normal way for consumers' attention, but also by fixing test markets, sabotage, espionage.

A similar pattern of contingencies exists when two firms, a customer and a supplier, are involved. This time, both organisations are actively and deliberately involved in setting management and reinforcer management.

Firm Behaviour: Mutual Qualification of Behaviour Setting Scope

The concept of behaviour setting scope, applied earlier to the circumstances which immediately determine consumer choice, can be extended to the understanding of marketer behaviour. The closedness of a behaviour setting again refers to the extent to which the determinants of behaviour are under the control of the individual who performs it. Consumers have a central role in reducing the behaviour setting scope of marketers by requiring quality control, value in exchange. So does the action of rival firms in an economic system characterised by high levels of discretionary income and minimal governmental control lead to the closure of the behaviour settings of those with whom they compete. The marketer behaviour setting comprises physical constraints (need for extensive distribution), social constraints (other competitors and publics/stakeholders), regulatory constraints (social norms, state laws) and temporal considerations (again largely affecting distribution). Many of these basic requirements are beyond the control of the marketer; some but not all of them are under the control of consumers, not necessarily individually, not necessarily in an organised manner, but in the aggregate. The concept of managerial behaviour setting scope underlies the analysis of organisational slack or X-inefficiency (Leibenstein 1966).

Similarly, the pattern of reinforcement (defined by relative utilitarian and relative informational reinforcement) is a concept applicable to the understanding of marketer behaviour. Utilitarian reinforcement again consists in the utilitarian consequences of behaviour which in the consumer example refers to the basic requirements of maintaining the self as a biological and social entity: it is exemplified most obviously in the corporate sphere by revenue and profit; informational reinforcement consists again in performance feedback: data on return on investment, comparative performance in new product development.

Coase (1988b, p.8) emphasises the need to analyse market structure in terms of 'the influence of the social institutions which facilitate exchange', i.e., the contingencies of reinforcement and punishment, the environmental factors that make exchange behaviours more or less probable. This is precisely what marketing institutions are. Within the operant purview, these contingencies consist in the scope of the setting in which behaviour takes place and the pattern of utilitarian and informational reinforcement that maintains such behaviour. Marketer behaviour is constrained by the scope of its settings just as consumer behaviour is. This is true not only of markets known to be severely circumscribed say by government regulations; speaking of stock exchanges and commodity exchanges as markets often used to exemplify perfect competition, Coase (1988b, pp.8–9) points out that 'All exchanges regulate in great detail the activities of those who trade in these markets (the times at which transactions can be made, what can be traded, the responsibilities of the parties, the terms of settlement), and they all provide machinery for the settlement of disputes and impose sanctions against those who infringe the rules of exchange...' In other words, transacting takes place within a framework of physical, social, temporal and regulatory discriminative stimuli, and is simultaneously reinforced by the benefits it brings and punished by the costs it imposes. Quoting Adam Smith, Coase notes that regulations may either 'widen the market' or 'narrow the competition', i.e., modify the scope of the marketer behaviour setting.

The basis of bilateral contingency is the mutual (partial) closure of the parties' behaviour settings, i.e., the restriction of their room for manoeuvre. In a market economy characterised by minimal state intervention, transactions occur when two parties (consumer and marketer; industrial supplier and industrial buyer; employee and employer; marketing department and production department) simultaneously effect a degree of closure of one another's behaviour setting. Consider the case of marketer and consumer. Alpha, a marketer, attempts to reduce consumer discretion by making its marketing mix more attractive or less escapable than those of competing marketers. This reduction in choice is acceptable to Beta, the consumer, because (given a learning history) it reduces her transactions costs, i.e., it becomes easier for the consumer to obtain the benefits of the product class by selecting the brand provided by Alpha. The consumer is willing to have the scope of her behaviour setting reduced in order to minimise such marketing costs as search and evaluation. In turn, consumers act to reduce the scope of the marketer's behaviour setting by demanding high levels of quality control, lower prices. This is accepted by the marketer because it allows it to reduce transactions costs: Alpha's brand can be economically tailored to the buying propensities of a known and reliable market segment. The relationships so formed are 'by consent', but only because the consequences of behaving in this way are positively reinforced by the acquisition of benefits of trade (obtaining the product or the money) and negatively reinforced by avoidance of costs.

Bilateral contingency of this kind can occur only in a marketing-orientated economic system, i.e., one which allows consumer choice based on competition among marketers, and buyers' discretionary income. The result of these structural factors is consumer-orientated marketing management; the bilateral contingency discussed earlier makes clear that it is equally marketer-orientated consumption on the part of the buyer.

The array of marketing and non-marketing relationships in which the firm is embedded is topographically of two kinds: those which extend between the marketing firm and external organisations/groups, which give rise to consideration of 'relationship marketing', and those which are internal to the marketing firm, which relate to 'internal marketing'. The content and function of these external and internal relationships define the nature of the marketing firm.

Marketing Relationships

As has been argued, the firm is engaged in marketing relationships with its customers and suppliers. Marketing relationships consist of literal exchange relations, and are often but not essentially accompanied by mutuality, i.e., bonds consisting in reciprocated qualification of behaviour setting scope and/or reciprocated reinforcement. Marketing relationships plus accompanying mutuality are essential components of relationship marketing, a term which requires careful consideration in view of its uncritical proliferation.

Several marketing authors have in recent years advocated the substitution of a relationship marketing paradigm for the traditional view of marketing mix management in which a relatively passive consumer is the target of product, price, promotion and distribution strategies and tactics launched by a relatively active marketer (Gronroos 1994). Within the relationship marketing framework of analysis, transactions – one-off deals – are contrasted with relationships – long-term mutually satisfying associations involving considerations of customer service, quality, trust and commitment (Webster 1992; Payne 1995). The aim is to retain customers by developing alliances which transcend commercial exchanges rather than simply dealing with them afresh every time a transaction looms. The counterpart work of economists on relational contracting includes Macaulay (1963) and Macneil (1978). To the extent that this is a descriptive account of relationships in marketing, it has engendered research conducted in a genuine spirit of enquiry with no axe to grind by way of proposing preordained guidelines for practical management. Much of the 'markets as networks' literature certainly falls into this camp. However, some writing on relationship marketing is more closely concerned with prescription. Barnes (1994), for instance, emphasises that relationship marketing is about 'caring for consumers'. Barnes thus rules out the erection of exit barriers such as the imposition of product switching costs from genuine relationship marketing. Such prescription militates against the positive investigation of the nature of the relationships that bind the marketing firm to its stakeholders. Until we have an idea of the actual content and effects of marketing relationships, know what sustains them and the ways in which pressures to dissolve them are overcome, we shall have no grounds for judging how far such prescriptions are realistic or naif. Exit barriers exist and need to be studied in the overall context of the marketing relationship to which they belong; they may make the sort of sense in that framework as does the retention of 'dogs' in a portfolio of interactive products: no dogs, no cash cows or stars. Relationships depend upon mutual contingency, and contingencies involve aversive consequences (or discriminative stimuli that threaten them) as well as positive reinforcers. Until the effects of the potential and real aversive consequences of a relationship can be ascertained, the notion of bond strength is meaningless. The reciprocity of marketing relationships cannot be ignored.

The other external relationships, those between the firm and those of its stakeholders other than customers and suppliers (unions, shareholders, owners, government and competitors) are non-marketing relationships because they do not (usually) involve literal exchange; they are, however, long-term relationships that are maintained over time by reciprocated behaviour setting qualification and reciprocated reinforcement. In order to distinguish them from marketing relationships, we shall refer to them as mutuality relationships. Note that relationship marketing consists of both types of relationship, though what has here been termed the mutuality component has attracted most of the recent attention of those who have written on this theme (Gronroos 1994; Morgan and Hunt 1994; Perrien and Ricard 1995).

The argument can be summarised thus. Market transactions are literal exchanges. They take place in the market before firms come into existence (whether or not one accepts the historicity of this Coasean sequence, it remains a useful analytical device; see Medema 1994). Marketing relationships consist of literal exchanges plus mutuality (i.e., reciprocal qualification of behaviour setting scope and/or reciprocal reinforcement). Firms come into existence to add mutuality to market relationships, i.e., to make relationships more stable and predictable through contracts. Marketing relationships are market relationships plus. They are bonds between the firm and its customers/suppliers. Relationship marketing is genuine marketing as defined in this paper as long as it includes the literal exchange identified as the essential component of marketing relationships. It cannot consist solely in mutuality relationships and will usually be part of a business strategy that employs the full marketing mix in response to the conditions requiring marketing-oriented management.

Quasi-Marketing Relationships

It is equally legitimate to speak of market transactions in the analysis of intra-firm behaviour as to do so in exploring the nature of transactions in external markets. Moreover, market transactions can be conceptualised and analysed in terms identical to those used in the examination of consumer markets: i.e., conceptualised as literal exchange subject to mutual reinforcement, and analysed as bilateral contingency. This is so despite the apparent contention of transaction cost economists that the firm exists only as a means to circumvent the market and thereby replace market transactions with administrative decision making (Williamson 1985). There is no argument with Coase's (1937) insight that firms come into being in order to economise transaction costs (he calls them, revealingly, 'marketing costs'). These are the costs of finding out with whom one wishes to or is able to deal, informing prospective co-transactors that one is available to deal and on what terms, negotiating a bargain, drawing up a contract and policing it, and so on (Coase 1960, p. 15). But two caveats are in order. First, firms appear when the transaction costs of both parties who would otherwise trade in the market are thereby reduced; and secondly, integration does not supersede or circumvent the market: it circumscribes the market by placing additional, usually contractual, contingencies alongside those that constitute the market; market relationships are thereby limited by contractual considerations but not removed (Alchian and Demsetz 1972; Jensen and Meckling 1976; Hart 1989).

As Coase (1988b, pp. 7–8) puts it 'Markets are institutions that exist to facilitate exchange, that is, they exist in order to reduce the cost of carrying out exchange transactions . . . The provision of markets is an entrepreneurial activity.'[9] Firms involve organisation, rules, customs which are brought into being to reduce transaction costs beyond what the market can accomplish. He goes on to say that the identifying character of the firm is its 'supersession of the price mechanism' (p. 36). But this surely cannot imply that the firm is not subject to the market, nor that the relationships it contains are free from ultimate market control (Alchian and Demsetz 1972; Jensen and Meckling 1976; Hart 1989; Medema 1994). Indeed, Coase acknowledges that the firm will continue to grow only until its marginal transaction can be more economically undertaken by the market. This stage will inevitably come: it is unlikely that the firm's long-term cost curve will decline indefinitely; only if this is so and if there is a single global firm could its expansion continue unremittingly. Firms are a mechanism for closing the setting, a means of coordinating/managing parts of the economics system in a less costly way than would be achieved without firms. The market is still there and remains the ultimate supplier of resources and arbiter of commercial success. Hence the firm is just a means of trying to control part of the price mechanism by closing the setting (e.g. through contracts of employment) for both parties. That is how firms reduce transaction costs. If this supersedes the price mechanism at all it does so temporarily and provisionally.[10]

In the terminology of an operant approach to economic behaviour, firms economise on transaction costs by restricting the scope of behaviour settings. That is, the firm is a mechanism for closing the behaviour settings of the parties in mutually acceptable ways, for circumscribing the more costly effects of the market in order that both parties may prosper: in fact, not only by economising transaction costs but by increasing the surplus of their revenues over all costs including those of open market transacting (or, in Coase's terms, marketing costs). The firm is subject nevertheless to the reinforcing and punishing consequences of behaviour in the marketplace. Competitors cannot be ignored whether they are alternative sources of supply to Alpha or rivalrous sellers to Alpha's customers.

A major cost of using the market is discovering the rules under which it is operating (e.g. price/quantity relationships offered by a number of suppliers). Some of this cost is removed if transactions are carried out within the firm on the basis of rules worked out between entrepreneur and producer. Closing the setting is a means of predicting and controlling the behaviour of others. Each party enters this relationship only because it reduces transaction costs and will remain in it for only as long as it reduces transaction costs (the control is 'by consent', meaning it brings economic benefits to both parties).

A special kind of internal relationship is that between the entrepreneur and the other members of the organisation. This is a marketing relationship in the sense that it involves genuine exchange (work done for wages), but it is severely modified by its incorporation within the firm. The firm exists in order to protect the relationship between entrepreneur and firm members from the day-to-day ravages of the market, and thereby to economise transaction costs by facilitating planning and prediction. The market is always there, of course, and will ultimately exert its influence on, for instance, how work is valued in wage terms. But because of the intervention of the firm it does not exercise this control on a continual basis: contracts of employment restrict it by providing that Alpha can only fire an employee, Epsilon, by giving a period of notice, Epsilon can only take up another offer of employment at the end of such a period, and wages may be adjustable in line with competitive conditions at a specific time of the year. Employment contracts vary of course and Epsilon may have more or less favourable terms than those of Beta, Gamma and Delta. A highly rated employee may force an immediate pay rise if he threatens to leave the firm in order to work for a competitor, and this capacity to use the external market severely modifies Alpha's authority over him.[11]

This kind of modified market/contractual agreement is the essence of the marketing firm. Indeed, the firm comes into being for the purpose of circumscribing the competitive vicissitudes of the market in order that production can take place in a framework of stable and predictable relationships. The function of the marketing firm is to introduce mutuality into the relationships between entrepreneur and employer/supplier/customer, to modify market relationships by turning them into marketing relationships. The marketing firm economises transaction costs that would otherwise be incurred by individuals transacting in the marketplace in the absence of firms. But, by engaging in marketing relationships, the firm incurs new transaction costs: costs of keeping in touch with suppliers and customers, as well as firm members and other stakeholders, ensuring that the long-term relationship endures, and so on. These are the costs of mutuality relationships, essential as we have seen to relationship marketing. Thus, as Coase points out, the marketing firm does not eliminate transactions costs; nor does it simply reduce those costs which are contingent upon trading in the open market. Rather, it changes the composition of the transaction cost structure that the firm encounters in order to receive the additional revenue and profit benefits of extending its marketing relationships.

Intra-firm marketing of this kind is far from coterminous with so-called 'internal marketing'; however, internal marketing refers to at least three essential functions of management: (i) ensuring that the entire organisation is focused on the marketing-orientated goal of ensuring that consumers receive the levels of service and quality necessary to retain their goodwill and patronage; (ii) internal communication of the aims and methods of the marketing function to other members of the organisation, especially those with responsibility for carrying out the marketing programme; and (iii) marketing within the firm, i.e., promoting the marketing philosophy and function as components of the organisation deserving of further resource allocation (Payne 1995). All of these things need to be done but it is a misnomer to refer to them as 'marketing' for, like so much 'social marketing', they lack the definitive component of marketing which is literal exchange. At most, therefore, they consist of mutuality relationships. We may sum up the argument as follows. An entrepreneur and the members of the firm are linked by quasi-marketing relationships: they depend upon modified market relationships plus mutuality. They are the reason for the firm's existence and their establishment and maintenance constitute its essential function. Mutuality relationships may consist of reciprocity alone (i.e., unaccompanied by market relationships); as such they characterise relationships between the firm and other organisations (especially the firm's stakeholders) where there is no (literal) exchange. Often, treatments of social, internal and relationship marketing deal only in mutuality relationships; thus defined, they are not genuine marketing relationships as understood here. True relationship marketing and internal marketing consist of marketing relationships, though the tendency has been to concentrate on the mutuality component and to embrace some non-market relationships under these terminologies. Thus, in summary, marketing-orientated management is the management of marketing relationships with suppliers, customers and employees in order to produce mutual reinforcement; it is an activity of the marketing firm involving both marketing and mutuality relationships. It is enjoined upon the firm by external conditions of competitiveness and consumer choice: the environmental contingencies that determine 'marketing-orientated management' on the part of the firm are discretionary income and competitiveness of supply/purchase, giving rise to 'consumer choice' and 'managerial scope for entrepreneurship'. Marketing-orientated management does not belong where there is monopoly: e.g. nationalised industries. It is these external contingencies that bring the (marketing) firm into being and sustain its operations.

SUMMARY AND CONCLUSION

All mutual social interaction involves reciprocal reinforcement. This is not exchange. The hallmark of economic behaviour is that the reciprocally reinforcing relationship involves literal exchange at some point. An employment transaction includes the exchange of labour for wages; a marketing relationship, goods for other goods or pecuniary recompense. The matching involved in marketing transactions is usually characterised by mutuality relationships in addition to literal exchange. While relationship marketing is genuinely so-called (despite a tendency to concentrate on the mutuality relationships rather than exchange), internal marketing and social marketing do not qualify. Table 1.1 summarises the differences.

Marketing management consists in the qualification of consumer behaviour setting scope and the management of reinforcers. This recognition that marketing management is de facto a behaviouristic pursuit has far-reaching implications for academic research and policy.[12] The marketing firm acts as though consumer behaviour were environmentally controlled. Manipulating the scope of consumer behaviour settings and managing reinforcer effectiveness attest to this. There are implications here for the ethics of marketing and for policy: as long as the principal concern of the operant analysis of economic behaviour was to propose an alternative (operant) explanation of consumer choice, ethical considerations did not arise. Marketers' behaviour might raise ethical considerations, but the operant interpretation of itself did not. However, the extension of the

Table 1.1   Marketing and pseudo-marketing

	Genuine marketing	Pseudo-marketing
Exchange	Literal	Symbolic
Use of marketing mix	All elements used or capable of incorporation	Principally communication
Nature of relationships	Exchange/economic and mutuality	Mutuality

model's sphere of applicability to marketer behaviour plus the conclusion that marketers act as if consumer behaviour were environmentally controlled has ethical and policy implications.

But marketing is not the only influence on consumers (so other groups than marketers are under ethical scrutiny, too). The fact that marketing takes place within a competitive context – at least in affluent societies that ensure high levels of discretionary income, an excess of marketing capacity over demand, and thus consumer choice – means that closure strategies are limited by firms' resources and the actions of their rivals. Furthermore, the analysis suggests that the control is mutual and by consent, at least in economic systems whose structures require consumer-orientated management. The implications of this finding require exploration of the interactive relationships of marketers and customers. Whether this is an exclusive interpretation of marketing management remains to be seen, but it is certainly a legitimate one which may suggest intriguing managerial and policy recommendations.

NOTES

1. Foxall (1999a). Reproduced with permission of the publisher, and slightly revised, from the *Journal of Economic Psychology*, 20, 1999, pp. 207–234.
2. Note that, while I am using Coase's approach to the nature of the firm as a reference point, several other accounts of the origin of firms and their function exist (e.g. Williamson 1975, 1985; Easterbrook and Fischel 1991; Demsetz 1995; Hart 1995). Unfortunately, all treat consumers as a passive source of demand which apparently requires no complementary analysis with that of the firm.
3. It is astonishing, for instance, that marketing-orientated management, the creation and implementation of marketing mixes to satisfy consumers profitably, is not considered one of the 'economic institutions of capitalism' by Williamson (1985), who also omits, therefore, to deal with the industrial structures that compel this managerial approach, and the demands it makes on the structure and functions of business organisations.
4. This notation differs slightly from that adopted in later chapters, where 'p' is used to denote aversive consequences rather than 'A'. The notation is also slightly different from that used in the original paper: here, the use of a colon emphasises the correlational relationship between antecedent stimulus and behaviour (see Foxall 1990, Chapter 2).
5. A third emphasis is that behaviour is explicitly held to have non-initiating causes which are found in that part of the environment enclosed within the skin. These proximal causes include private verbal and non-verbal discriminative stimuli such as rules; the ascription of a non-initiating nature to proximal causes indicates that they rely ultimately on the distal causes located in the external environment.
6. For full exposition of the model, see Foxall (1990, 1994, 1996).
7. Note that such exchange need not imply a market clearing price or that supply and demand are equated in some way by the transaction. The mutual reinforcement inherent in exchange signifies that the seller's opportunity costs of relinquishing the commodity are lower than the reinforcement he receives via the price he obtains. Similarly, the buyer's costs of surrendering that price are outweighed for him by the reinforcing consequences of owning and using the commodity.

8. The insistence on literalness of exchange may exclude from economic analysis some of the themes adopted by certain economics of law schools (see Duxbury 1995, Chapter 5).

9. Hence the identification of entrepreneurship with functional marketing and/or marketing-oriented management (Foxall and Minkes 1996).

10. Suppose Alpha is a widget entrepreneur who, instead of continuing to buy in widgets from Epsilon, a widget craftsman, employs Epsilon to produce widgets as a hired member of Alpha Enterprises. (The term 'entrepreneur' denotes the cadre of managers concerned with the strategic scope of the organisation (Foxall and Minkes 1996), especially in its relationships to other members of the firm.) The contractual arrangement thereby created economises the transactions costs of both Alpha and Epsilon. Alpha no longer has to search the market daily for the cheapest widgets; Epsilon no longer has to find a buyer for each day's production. But the market is still there as surely as before: if Epsilon cannot produce widgets of the required quality or quantity, he can be replaced (perhaps only at the expiration of his contract, rather than immediately: that is an extra contingency brought about by circumscribing the market). If Epsilon is a superb widgeter, his prowess is likely to come to the attention of Beta Enterprises, Alpha's rival, which will offer Epsilon higher remuneration than Alpha provides. Epsilon can move (again at the expiry of his contract). Moreover, our analysis is not confined to any particular world: Epsilon can leave Alpha and set up as a widget entrepreneur in his own right.

11. It seems clear that what distinguishes the quasi-marketing relationships of the intra-firm arrangement from the marketing relationships discussed above is that the former is based upon the authority of the entrepreneur which is not absolute but which circumscribes the market (Alchian and Demsetz 1972; Jensen and Meckling 1976; Foxall 1988; Hart 1989). Marketing relationships between suppliers and firms may also rest upon a degree of authority when there is quasi-vertical integration (cf. Blois 1972; Monteverde and Teece 1982).

12. Compare Posner's (1990) conclusions with respect to the operation of common law as a behaviouristic process.

2. From consumer behaviour to corporate response

INTRODUCTION

The theory of the marketing firm is an interpretation of operant and economic principles applied to create an explanation of firm marketing behaviour. With its critical origins (Baum 1994) and application to consumer behaviour (Foxall et al. 2007; Foxall 2009, 2010), operant theory has much to contribute to our understanding of the nature and behaviour of the firm.[1]

An operant inquiry into the essence of firms is equivalent to an inquiry into their behaviour as behaviour is environmentally influenced, i.e., shaped by the consequences of corporate action that increase or decrease the rate of emission of such behaviour in future. Yet, as firms are dependent on several forms of relationships, their behaviour and its consequences must be understood by examining these firm↔stakeholder (especially supplier↔consumer and competitor) relationships. In other words, a proper account of firm behaviour requires looking at (a) how both firms and consumers behave in their context-dependent inter-relationships and (b) how this behaviour affects rivals. The theory of the marketing firm locates firm behaviour within markets characterised by vigorous competition vying for the attention of a large number of consumers who have a discrete amount of disposable income and by minimal government intervention (Foxall 1999a).

THE THREE–TERM CONTINGENCY

Behaviour, the sole focus of inquiry, is environmentally determined (Baum 1994). An individual operates on her environment producing reinforcing and/or punishing consequences which respectively increase or decrease the rate of future emission of that behaviour. Economic behaviour is concurrently reinforced and punished (Foxall 1990) – when an individual purchases an item, he gains legal title to that item and related benefits. However, the associated cost is the surrender of money (Alhadeff 1982). The environment, antecedent events or stimuli, does not directly 'cause' behaviour; rather, some events may come to 'control' operant responses (Delprato and Midgely 1992) or modify them (Pierce and Cheney 2008) from the more or less frequent pairing with signals of reinforcing/punishing consequences (Foxall 1990). The individual's learning history, comprising the reinforcing/punishing consequences of past behaviour, primes these events into discriminative stimuli (S^D). S^D signal the likelihood and the intensity of reinforcement/punishment ($S^{r/p}$) contingent on the emission of a particular response (R): hence, the three-term contingency S^D: R→$S^{r/p}$ as a summary framework for these relationships.

The theory of the marketing firm describes the mutually reinforcing relationships between the firm and several of its stakeholders including customers and suppliers. In the management of its customer relationships, which are central to the existence of the firm, marketers leverage the full extent of marketing mix variables to influence, shape and maintain consumer (operant) behaviour by offering products/services which provide utilitarian and informational reinforcement.

Customers, on the other hand, through their expenditure and some measure of repeat purchase, provide firms with revenues, profits and market information signalling what to produce, at what quantity, at what price and where to supply the product.

Consumer Behaviour in Operant Perspective

Consumer behaviour is cast in operant terms, and such an account is embodied in the rich philosophical, theoretical (Foxall 2009, 2010) and empirical literature (Foxall 2005, 2007) which extends the three-term contingency to propose the Behavioural Perspective Model (BPM) as an interpretive and research framework. The BPM (see Figure 2.1) suggests an explanation of the entire sequence of pre-purchase, purchase, consumption and other post-purchase behaviour in natural settings at the marketing level of analysis (Foxall 1990, 1992b).

The consumer behaviour setting is composed of antecedent physical (point-of-purchase displays), social (fellow shoppers), regulatory (rules that specify relationships among stimuli, responses and their outcomes) and temporal (shopping times) stimuli that signal the reinforcement and/or punishment contingent upon performing certain responses (and not others). Marketer-controlled stimuli are embodied in the various marketing mix elements of price, product, promotion and place (Foxall 1990, 1997a) and are the observable products of marketing behaviour. Otherwise neutral stimuli acquire discriminative (Foxall 1990) or motivational function[2] (Fagerstrøm *et al.* 2010) in the presence of a person's learning and evolutionary history to form a consumer situation: a specific

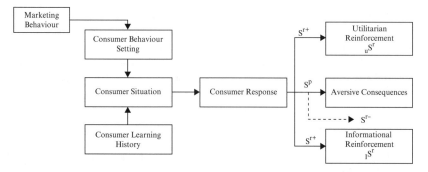

Note: S^{r+}, S^{r-} and S^p relate to the processes of positive and negative reinforcement and of punishment respectively.

Source: Adapted from Foxall (1997b, p. 103).

Figure 2.1   The Behavioural Perspective Model

physical context within which an individual with her history of reinforced and punished responses in similar circumstances, her state of deprivation and spending power and her biological inheritance responds (Foxall 1992a) through approach (window-shopping, purchase) or avoidance/ escape (buying a rival brand, exiting without purchase) (Foxall 1990). The setting activates this learning history and is also primed by it (Foxall 1997a). Through her learning history, the individual interprets the setting accurately and is able to predict the most likely outcomes resulting from her behaviour within that setting (Foxall *et al.* 2006). Hence, the capacity of the behaviour setting stimuli to control behaviour is not inherent to the stimuli themselves but from the individual's learning history (Foxall 2001). In the absence of such, the consumer deliberates (as private verbal behaviour) based on instructions given by marketers and/or others, her history of following others' rules, and any self-rules established/derived from her purchase/consumption history in unrelated settings and from her observations of choice outcomes of others as well as any other implicit self-rules (Foxall 1999b). The consumer situation is an observable and measurable event and is, thus, the critical explanatory instrument of the BPM (Foxall 1998).[3]

Consumer behaviour settings vary in the number and range of responses available to marketers and consumers on a continuum from relatively open to relatively closed reflecting who is in control of the contingencies of reinforcement and/or punishment (Foxall 1990). The more closed the setting, the greater the control by others (e.g., marketers) and the greater the extent to which consumers will be found following a pattern of

Table 2.1   Operant classes of behaviour contemplated in the BPM

| | | Utilitarian reinforcement | |
		High	Low
Informational reinforcement	High	*Accomplishment:* high incentive esteem/ status (e.g cultural achievements, gambling)	*Accumulation:* incremental acquisition (e.g. saving, collecting)
	Low	*Hedonism:* pleasure, amelioration of suffering (e.g popular entertainment, aspirin)	*Maintenance:* routine and mandatory (e.g grocery shopping, paying taxes)

Source: Adapted from Foxall (1997b, p. 103).

behaviour predetermined by these others (Foxall 1997a). Setting scope is a powerful independent variable in the analysis of consumer and marketer behaviour (Buttle 1984; Foxall 1998; Kearney *et al.* 2007).

Behaviour produces consequences that may consistently increase the probability of that or similar behaviour being emitted in future (reinforcement) or decrease it (punishment). Consumer behaviour analysis contemplates a bifurcation of reinforcement and punishment: reinforcing consequences of consumer behaviour include utilitarian (mediated by the technical and economic features of products/services) and informational (mediated, primarily, by others; symbolic non-monetary aspects) benefits (Foxall 1990, 1997a, 1998). Purchase is punished through the surrender of money (utilitarian aversive consequences) and may be socially punished (informational aversive consequences). Informational reinforcement and/ or punishment may include positive/negative self-feedback on one's performance as a consumer (Foxall 1997a). Within the BPM, utilitarian and informational reinforcement are assumed orthogonal (Foxall 1990), and empirical evidence supports such an assumption (Foxall 1998).

The BPM identifies four classes of purchase/consumption behaviour consequences (Table 2.1) based on the combination of consequential cues signalling the probability of relative levels of high-versus-low utilitarian reinforcement and high-versus-low informational reinforcement (Foxall 1992a, 1992b).

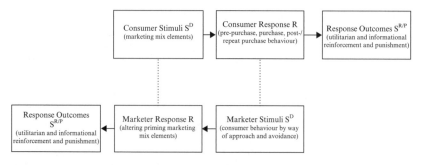

Source: Adapted from Foxall (1999a).

Figure 2.2   Marketer–customer bilateral contingency relationships

Marketer Behaviour in Operant Perspective

Relationships as bilateral contingencies of reinforcement

In economics, inter-firm relationships are characterised by associated bilateral expectations and behaviour between parties (Hart 1989). From an operant theory of the marketing firm perspective, the behaviour of each of the parties mutually reinforces the other, which transcends the common notion of interdependence and emphasises the interlocking nature of the two behaviour sets. Marketer behaviour operates on the environment, producing consequences which determine the rate of the future emission of such behaviour. Marketers deposit a configuration of reinforcing and punishing stimuli within the behaviour setting. The stimuli (e.g. brand features) are designed to signal utilitarian and information reinforcement and/or punishment and funnel purchase behaviour. Customers discriminate these stimuli on the basis of their learning history and purchase a particular brand if the net outcomes are relatively favourable (reinforcing) rather than aversive (punishing). Marketing, as firm behaviour, thus acts as a discriminative stimulus to consumers to emit purchase and consumption behaviour. However, in aggregate, consumer behaviour also acts as a discriminative stimulus to marketers: if a sufficient volume of purchases occur within the behaviour setting, marketers are reinforced through sales and profit and resulting market intelligence. Marketers maintain their practices and attempt to improve upon the effectiveness of their strategies in increasing the probability of customer acquisition and retention within given settings. Given respective learning histories, marketer behaviour and consumer behaviour are, thus, inextricably linked in a sequence of mutually reinforcing behaviours, with marketer behaviour acting as a stimulus for consumer action and vice versa (Foxall 1990). This mutual interdependence is epitomised in the concept of a bilateral contingency (see Figure 2.2). (Chapter 6 applies this framework and depicts the intricate web of stimulus–response outcomes with data emerging from the case study.)

Firms reside in a complex and dynamic network of bilateral contingencies (Foxall 1999a; Xiao and Nicholson 2010) with social, political, legal and economic dimensions. The behaviour within and the outcomes of Supplier↔Customer relationships act as cues to competitor response. The mutual dependence of rivals is recognised in strategic management literature: firm behaviour is determined by industry structure and strategy is formulated through the observation of rivals (Porter 1980). However, the theory of the marketing firm transcends simple interdependence through the introduction of mutual reinforcement thus adding explanatory power. For example, competitive mimicry or strategic isomorphism may emerge if one or more firms are successful enough (Johnson and Scholes 2002). If competitor A has a history of sales and profit (utilitarian and informational rewards) in following the strategies adopted by market leader B, then a new strategy by B signals reinforcement for A. Mimicry ensues. For B, mimicry may signal eventual punishment arising from reduced sales because of several rivals using the same strategy. B's history of reinforcement (innovative strategic behaviour in times of shrinking sales rates and isomorphism) allows it to interpret the setting and emit differentiated strategic behaviour. It is in this sense that competitive relationships are mutually contingent. Similarly, the actions of a single or a number of rivals may act as a stimulus for regulatory intervention (Xiao and Nicholson 2010) reinforcing and/or punishing it.

Marketing and mutuality relationships
Two principal forms of firm relationships may be discerned:

1. *Marketing (exchange) relationships*: The existence of the marketing firm is dependent on economic transactions, i.e. on literal exchange or the 'exchange of two bundles of property rights' (Foxall 1997a, p. 153). Literal exchange is mutually reinforcing: both customers and firms derive utilitarian and informational reinforcement, as long as, on the balance, what is received in exchange is just as or more reinforcing than keeping what is surrendered (Foxall 1999a).
2. *Mutuality (non-exchange) relationships* are relationships that a firm holds with other stakeholders (competitors, government) where mutual reinforcement does not arise from literal economic exchange.

Exchange relationships may hold an element of mutuality – mutuality-plus-exchange and mutuality (non-exchange) relationships (Foxall 1999a).

Business-to-business bilateral contingencies would typically be characterised by both unless intermediaries are involved.

The theory of the marketing firm does not address the role of intermediaries; nonetheless, the framework remains useful for generating an
interpretation of the more complex relationships found in the distribution
of fast-moving consumer goods where manufacturers do not engage in
exchange relationships with the final consumer. Exchange occurs between
parties at the different tiers of the channel (Kotler et al. 2001).[4]

Manufacturers hold mutuality relationships with consumers where reinforcement, for consumers, occurs through the various elements of the marketing mix (e.g. the brand, advertising) and, for manufacturers, through
aggregate demand for their brands and, consequently, market share and
scale economies of production, distribution, marketing and growth (Penrose
1959). Manufacturers' behaviour is also reinforced through their mutuality-
plus-exchange relationships with distributors and, in some cases, mutuality
relationships with retailers. Distributors' behaviour is similarly reinforced
while retailers hold direct exchange relations with consumers (see Figure
2.3).

The settings for marketer behaviour
It is useful to distinguish among three behaviour settings: (a) the consumer behaviour setting; (b) the marketer behaviour setting delineated by
the temporal, physical, social and regulatory stimuli outside the firm that
influence marketers at its intersection with consumer behaviour (Foxall
1997a) and, (c) the managerial behaviour setting which Foxall does not
define (Foxall 1999a, p. 223). By inference from consumer behaviour
analysis, this setting is now defined as incorporating temporal, physical,
social and regulatory stimuli *within* the firm that comes to control its
behaviour. The managerial behaviour setting, therefore, comprises the
learning and evolutionary history of the organisation as well as internal
deliberating behaviour, both of which are, to a large extent, directly
observable.[5] The former embodies the history of reinforced and punished
behaviour in similar circumstances and 'biological inheritance' incorporated, for example, in physical distribution networks. Deliberating
behaviour of firms is observable in explicit self-rules (objectives, targets,
operational and marketing plans) and other internal rules (profit targets
set by a mother company). The managerial behaviour setting, therefore,
is what determines which elements in the marketer and consumer behaviour setting act as reinforcers and punishers, and the behaviour required
to produce the likelihood of such outcomes. The firm will act only if the
setting contains the relevant signals of reinforcing and punishing outcomes. The extent of others' control is also reflected in the scope of the

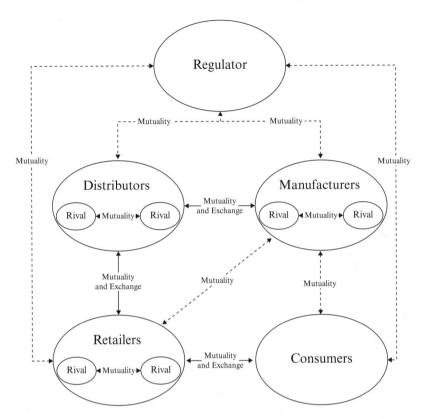

Figure 2.3 Diverse relationship forms within the distribution channel

managerial behaviour setting, i.e. the impact on behaviour of the reinforcing and punishing referents of the discriminative stimuli and motivating operations that it includes (Foxall 1997a).

Sources of reinforcement and punishment
Firm behaviour is contingent on utilitarian reinforcement (revenues and profits), utilitarian punishment (transaction costs of acquisition and retention, loss of income) and informational reinforcement and/or punishment (positive/negative feedback on performance) (Foxall 1999a). The extent to which relationships are predictable and stable has a reinforcing/punishing influence on firms. If firms exist to economise on the transaction costs of finding and retaining customers, then firms are also reinforced by the pursuit of scale economies in the acquisition and retention of customers and punished by diseconomies.

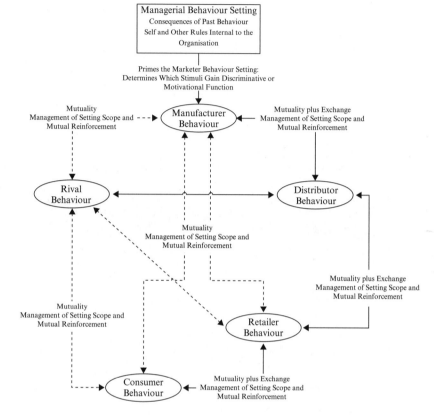

Note: Marketer Behaviour Setting encompasses Manufacturer↔Distributor, Manufacturer↔Retailer, and Manufacture↔Rivals relationships.

Figure 2.4   Conceptual framework with various bilateral contingencies between different actors in the industry

Marketing strategies: a functional analysis

According to the theory of the marketing firm, marketers, across all their mutuality and mutuality-plus-exchange relationships, will deliberately utilise the various elements of the marketing mix and optimise their effectiveness to engineer behaviour setting scopes and manage patterns of reinforcement to increase the likelihood of purchasing in such a way as to profitably encourage approach, discourage avoidance and deter escape (Foxall 1999a). This implies that as firms economise on customer acquisition and retention costs (implied attempts at cost leadership) and optimise their acquisition and retention strategies (implied attempts at leadership through differentiation) they would appear to follow both Porter's (1980) long-term generic strategies simultaneously, i.e. they outpace (Gilbert and Strebel 1989).

A conceptual framework is presented in Figure 2.4 highlighting the assumed typologies of the existing bilateral contingencies between the various actors.

NOTES

1. Operant behaviourism, the philosophy of science undergirding the theory of the marketing firm, is explained in Chapter 3. Here, we concentrate on the economic psychology that derives from this approach.
2. A stimulus with motivational function or motivating operation (MO) is defined as 'an environmental event that first establishes (or abolishes) the reinforcing or punishing effect of another event and second, evokes (or abates) behaviours associated with that event'. This type of stimulus function is in contrast to discriminative stimuli which signal the availability of reinforcement (given learning history) (Fagerstrøm *et al.* 2010, p. 110). Motivating operations are further explored in the light of the evidence in Chapter 6.
3. This is true not only of the extensional (operant) portrayal of the BPM employed here but also of the intentional and cognitive portrayals (Foxall 2007, 2011) which form part of the extended consumer behaviour analysis research programme (Foxall 2002).
4. Kotler *et al.* (2001) provide thorough descriptions of intermediary relationships and related marketing (place) strategies.
5. This is in sharp contrast to individual consumer behaviour where deliberation occurs privately and is not directly observable except through verbal reports of the individuals themselves (Foxall 1997c).

3. Methodology and measurement

INTRODUCTION

Deriving from the evaluative nature of the research and the aim of designing a case study methodology for analysing firm behaviour from an operant perspective, Chapter 3 explicitly articulates and follows a pre-structured research design framework (Miles and Huberman 1994).

Undergirding the entire project is a research strategy nested deeply within a set of ontological, epistemological and methodological a priori assumptions (Guba and Lincoln 1994) out of which flow all subsequent research decisions from design to interpretation (Bryman and Bell 2007). These assumptions allow for greater analytical depth (Nightingale 2008), amplify the range of questions that may be asked (Foxall 2009) and lead to greater theoretical cohesion. This study embraces operant behaviourism as its research paradigm, and this chapter aims to account for all the research decisions taken to conduct research from such a perspective. Such explicit formulations throughout enhance the credibility of the study (Miles and Huberman 1994), ensure its plausibility (Foxall 2009) and minimise error and bias (Yin 2003) by exposing, as transparently as possible, the entire framework used for collecting, analysing and interpreting the data. By documenting each stage and related considerations or decisions explicitly, a full audit trail is created (Mason 2002; Yin 2003), cementing validity and reliability (Yin 2003).

OPERANT BEHAVIOURISM

Founded and developed by B.F. Skinner (1904–90), mainly as a critique and alternative to realist methodological behaviourism, operant behaviourism is the philosophy of science supporting operant psychology (or behaviour analysis), which is the (natural) science of human behaviour. The purpose of such a science is the explanation, prediction and control of behaviour.

As the unique focus of attention, behaviour is conceived as a physical natural event (Delprato and Midgely 1992) and is defined as the 'action of the whole organism' to include private occurrences (e.g. deliberating, knowing) as well as public occurrences (e.g. consumption), thus rejecting Cartesian dualism, with no distinction between the mind and body (Foxall 2009). The proximate causes of behaviour are to be found *outside* the individual within the immediate environment and in her reinforcement history (Baum 1994). Behaviour operates on the environment to produce positive and negative consequences which, in turn, as stimuli, determine the future rate of emission of that behaviour (Foxall 1990). Operant behaviourism completely avoids making mentalist references as the ultimate causes of behaviour – such references are hypothetical, are completely hidden from direct observation and, therefore, hinder proper scientific inquiry.

Heavily influenced by Ernst Mach's positivism,[1] Skinner distanced himself from methodological behaviourism and focused on finding 'useful', comprehensible and economical concepts and terms to describe behaviour observations and linking these observations to make sense of experiences, i.e. to yield *explanations* (Baum 1994). Therefore, the primary effort of behaviour analysis is a focus on the most useful ways of describing observed phenomena and in uncovering reliable relations (i.e. laws) that govern behaviour for prediction and control (Delprato and Midgely 1992; Baum 1994; Foxall 2009). Whereas realist explanations start with a topographical description of behaviour and subsequently attempt to uncover mechanisms of causation, operant explanations focus on the observed function (consequences) of such behaviour. A *functional analysis* of behaviour lies at the core of operant methodology, and its central explanatory framework is the three-term contingency (Pierce and Cheney 2008).[2]

Operant methodology establishes that only through quantitative methods, in particular experimental methods, may the laws governing behaviour be uncovered, fully explained, predicted and ultimately controlled (Skinner 1953; Foxall 2009). Behaviour is explained once the researcher reliably establishes that changes in behaviour correlate with the changes in the environment in which it occurs. In the absence of such methods, behaviour explanations cannot be put forward – *reliable* functional relations between the independent (the environment) and dependent (behaviour) variables cannot be established. Therefore, analysis proceeds through interpretation, one which is rigorously based on the operant principles and assuming the continuity of such principles. Only in this way is interpretation plausible and valid. Further, interpretations are 'interim' explanations and must ultimately be tested by quantitative analysis (Foxall 2001, 2009).

EVALUATIVE CRITERIA

Few behaviourists have considered the criteria for evaluating such interpretations but the following are important.

First, the *plausibility* of the interpretation requires consistency and coherence to operant behaviourist principles and the assumption that such are applicable to the present analysis (Foxall 1998, 2009). Secondly, a *detailed knowledge of the subject matter* (in this case, marketing and economics) adds to plausibility by ensuring that the wrong conclusions are not drawn. Thirdly, there is the pragmatist criterion of *usefulness of concepts* or concepts that are epistemologically well founded, credible, relevant, reliable and normatively driven (Kelemen and Rumens 2008). These concepts are the foundation of explanation (Baum 1994). A final set of criteria emergent from the literature relates to *objectivity* that requires neutrality, precision, clarity and replication. The view of the objective researcher has been challenged (Guba and Lincoln 1994) and, while the research recognises that all research is theory- and value-laden (Foxall 1990), all attempts will be made to achieve this goal within these reasonable limits.

Researchers within the tradition have followed the general requirements of validity and reliability of positivist research when conducting their work (e.g. Yani Soriano and Foxall 2002). Therefore, this research gives full attention to the concepts as applicable to positivist qualitative case studies and the relevant suggestions found (e.g. Patton 1987, 1990; Potter and Levine-Donnerstein 1999; Mason 2002; Bryman and Bell 2007; Yin 2009). One recurring suggestion is the need to adopt a theory-led approach to ensure validity and reliability (e.g. Potter and Levine-Donnerstein 1999; Yin 2009). This study strives for analytic or theoretical generalisation (e.g. Hammersley and Gomm 2000; Yin 2003) even though replication to other cases is not attempted owing to time constraints.

PRELIMINARY DESIGN CONSIDERATIONS

Qualitative versus Quantitative Routes to Knowledge

Our study is founded on the belief that interpretive work of this kind requires both quantitative and qualitative approaches based on the view that the two terms simply refer to methods for collecting particular kinds of data that are useful and appropriate to all researchers irrespective of their worldviews (Guba and Lincoln 1994; Miles and Huberman 1994; Myers 1997). Qualitative research is not necessarily interpretivistic: it may be of a different sort depending upon philosophical assumptions (Myers 1997). Despite the preference of economic theorists for quantitative methods (Foss and Klein 2008), qualitative research appears useful to the domain especially when certain concepts have important non-quantifiable dimensions (Dnes 1992). Hence, the research methodology is positivist *and* qualitative. The qualitative route was chosen because of: (a) time constraints and (b) the historical richness and investigative depth of the data contained in the report to be analysed (consequently, its capacity to best meet the research objectives). Qualitative data have two potentially limiting disadvantages: the report itself is voluminous; and the techniques for data analysis are not sufficiently developed (Miles and Huberman 1994), especially in the application of behaviour analysis to firm behaviour.[3]

Case Study Research Design

Since much debate surrounds the meaning of the term 'case study' (Hammersley and Gomm 2000), our analysis takes the following position: case studies are a research design, i.e. a framework (Bryman and Bell 2007) within which both quantitative and qualitative (Hakim 2000; Hammersley and Gomm 2000; Yin 2003) data collection and analysis techniques are marshalled around a research strategy to suitably meet research objectives (Bryman and Bell 2007). Other designs, such as surveys and experiments (Hammersley and Gomm 2000; Yin 2003), were discarded on the basis that the data generated by these designs would not have been as rich as the secondary data used. Further, when planned carefully and theoretically informed, case studies are among the most robust designs within which to conduct rigorous research that investigates 'complex social phenomena' with the aim of bringing to the fore 'meaningful characteristics of real-life events' (Yin 2009, p. 4).

The Role of Theory

Opinion also seems divided on the extent to which theory should lead the case study process (Eisenhardt 1989; Miles and Huberman 1994; Gummesson 2000). The present study assumes that an initial concentration on theory ensures that the design is interlaced with theoretical concepts to become an advanced and robust blueprint for the entire research process. Such a theoretical framework creates the strongest context within which research propositions, questions and hypotheses are developed and within which data may be analysed and interpreted (Yin 2003). Existing theory also allows researchers to define concepts and construct valid and reliable measures (Churchill 1979), identify the units of analysis, and select the method for data collection and strategies for analysis (Yin 2009). Further, the behaviourist requirement of plausibility underscores the need for starting with theory. Hence, our research moves back and forth between theory (deductively) and data (inductively), an approach that finds support in methodological literature (e.g. Babbie 1990; Parkhe 1993).

Generating precise hypotheses for empirical testing was not possible because the present state of the theory of the marketing firm is relatively too generic for the development of such and the data is of a qualitative nature. Therefore, the study relies on propositions as guides for achieving the stated research objectives. These, together with related sub-research questions, are discussed in Chapter 4.

Miles and Huberman (1994, p. 272) argue that hypotheses *may* be drawn and tested within a qualitative research environment. This contention, steeped in grounded theory, assumes however that the research process progresses through iterations where, after pausing the data collection to reflect and analyse the data collected so far, the researcher may tease out or refine hypotheses and test them in subsequent bouts of data collection. Therefore, even if one were to assume Miles and Huberman's arguments on the power of qualitative research for testing hypotheses (Miles and Huberman 1994, p. 147), their position still requires passing through the rigours of several cases. Being a single case study, this research does not have this flexibility. Further, the approach described by Miles and Huberman (which emerges from the literature reviewed as an extremely common approach to non-positivist work) does not regard the rejection of hypotheses in the same manner as positivist studies where statistical significance is of greatest import. For example, Miles and Huberman (1994, p. 148) talk about collecting data with the aim of 'lending greater confidence to the evolving hypothesis', whereas a positivist approach deals with establishing confidence on a pre-defined hypothesis through statistical significance. Therefore, it was deemed more appropriate to explore the 'essential qualities' (Miles and Huberman 1994) of firm behaviour and evaluate whether the propositions generated by the theory of the marketing firm are theoretically significant (Yin 2009) (as opposed to statistically significant). After all, only on the basis of this work, one that explores both structure and function of behaviour, may precise hypotheses be drawn, in future, for statistical testing.

Secondary Data: Considerations, Assumptions and Limitations

Selecting the most appropriate collection method depends upon the suitability and the capacity of the method to answer the research questions satisfactorily (Creswell 2003; Silverman 2010). Despite the various sources of evidence that may be used to populate a case study (Yin 2009) and the consensus within the literature on the need to triangulate (e.g. Miles and Huberman 1994; Yin 2009) across, at least, two sources of data, this research only makes use of a single source of (secondary) data. Single (data) case studies do, however, have distinct advantages: specifically the ability of having more time to extensively investigate the evidence, thus providing a richer account of the subject of interest, with the possibility of expanding the core theory further (Yin 2009).

For the fourth time within a 20-year period,[4] in December 1998 the Director General of Fair Trading (DGFT) referred a case to the Competition Commission requiring the latter to conduct an investigation and establish whether a monopoly situation existed in relation to the supply and distribution of impulse ice-cream in the UK.[5] In January 2000, the Commission published its findings and suggested remedial actions. This research analyses this report (covering 1998 and 1999) to provide a behaviour analytic interpretation of the marketing behaviour of firms, thus exploring the explanatory power of the theory of the marketing firm within the given context.

Besides being selected for its extensive description of the marketing behaviour of certain firms, the report indicates that the subjects appeared to be operating according to the behaviouristic principles postulated by theory. Characteristics similar to the general ambient of the theory to be evaluated may be sufficient reason to conduct an appropriate analysis in order to investigate the propositions and hypotheses derived from extant literature (Rose 1991). Eisenhardt (1989, p. 537) also argues in favour of the selection of cases where the 'process of interest is "transparently observable"'. Single case studies may be especially strong if the theory is well developed and, consequently, a critical case is chosen to test it (Miles and Huberman 1994; Yin 2009). To do this, the case testing conditions must be met: the subjects of interest *do* seem to be operating according to behaviouristic principles, and the industry has a rich history of government intervention owing to firms exhibiting monopolistic behaviour and not acting in the public interest. In this way, the single case has enormous potential to confirm or challenge theory as well as extend it, thereby making significant contributions to knowledge while providing directions for future research (Yin 2003).

A discrete level of triangulation appears in the report: this was deemed an essential element during the selection phase because, while it enhances the quality of the case study itself (Yin 2009), it greatly compensates for the use of a single source of evidence. The report also provides important market information that is not usually available within the public domain.[6]

Since the documents are retrospective and recount episodes happening ten years ago, the research does not capture how the industry has since evolved. Further, any monopolistic actions occurring then may have been purely circumstantial and may not necessarily reflect naturally recurring firm behaviour. The evidence is prone to any errors made by the authors and their commissioned researchers over which there is no control. Snippets of evidence which might have been useful for the analysis were removed by the original authors on the basis of confidentiality. The objectives and requirements of the intended audiences of the report are not the same as those of the researcher (Yin 2003; Atkinson and Coffey 2004). These documents are not 'literal recordings' of the events as they unfolded (Mason 2002; Yin 2003); rather they are reports of behaviour observed by the investigators through a particular 'value-lens' (Guba and Lincoln 1994) and, as evidence, also contain the biased opinions of many industry players (most of whom had a direct vested financial interest in the outcome of the investigation), and the subjective interpretation and assessment of this evidence by the authors of the report. By identifying the objectives of the various stakeholders within the investigation and distinguishing between actual events and opinions it should be more difficult to be put off-track by the evidence and should be easier to develop a critical interpretation of the evidence (Yin 2009). Further, the data may not completely answer the central research question, because the investigation carried out by the Commission was designed to address different objectives. Therefore, an incomplete picture may emerge. However, for the central purposes of the research this incomplete picture would suffice.

FURTHER DESIGN CONSIDERATIONS

From a theory-led approach, designing the case study requires: (a) precisely defining the propositions and related sub-research questions (Chapter 4) through an a priori conceptual framework (Chapter 2); (b) deciding upon whether to use a holistic or embedded single case design; (c) defining the focus and bounds of the case, including identifying the units of analysis; and (d) data analysis strategies and techniques (Miles and Huberman 1994; Yin 2009).

Case Focus, Units of Analysis and Embedded Designs

The case focus was defined as: *a study of the marketing behaviour of major premium ice-cream manufacturers in their bilateral contingency relationships with rivals, distributors and retailers in the supply of wrapped impulse ice-cream in the UK as described by the report published by the Competition Commission in 2000.*[7]

The main units of analysis are the bilateral contingencies:

- Manufacturer↔Distributor;
- Manufacturer↔Retailer; and
- Manufacturer↔Rival.

Embedded within these units of analysis and easily discernible from the report owing to their being the focus of the Commission's investigation are the relationships of Birds Eye Wall's (BEW) as a major ice-cream manufacturer, those of Wall's Direct as its distribution arm, and those of a significant group within the independent wholesale tier, BEW's ex-dedicated distributors which it sought to replace after the formation of Wall's Direct. According to the report, the ex-dedicated distributors bore a significant part of the brunt of BEW's anti-competitive and distortive practices.

Figure 3.1 outlines these units of analysis, with ellipses denoting the actors (ellipses with dotted outlines are peripheral to the embedded units). Dotted arrow-lines are used to denote these elements and assumed

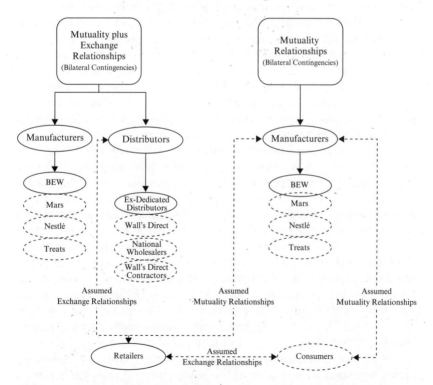

Figure 3.1   Embedded units of analysis within main unit of analysis

relationships. The relationships were presumed in this way to reflect non-conflicting-competitive tiers; in other words, the research purposely assumed that suppliers did not attempt to supplant their distributors and retailers by competing directly along each level of the channel.

Data Analysis Strategies and Techniques

A theory-led data analysis strategy that relies on conceptual propositions is deemed to provide the most powerful way for conducting good quality analysis (Yin 2009) and to enhance validity and reliability (Potter and Levine-Donnerstein 1999). In analysing the data, Yin (2009) emphasises the importance of attending to rival explanations where possible. As this study is a critical evaluation of *one* such possible explanation, rival theories are not fully examined and, hence, the study explicitly acknowledges that alternative interpretations are possible.

Three iterative data analytic steps are followed (Miles and Huberman 1994): data reduction (including within-case sampling and coding strategies), within-case analysis (data displays) and conclusion drawing.

Data reduction: Given that data reduction is that process which selects, focuses, simplifies, summarises, condenses and transforms large volumes of data into manageable chunks (Miles and Huberman 1994), the reduction technique used was the *pre-structured case outline* method.[8] It is based on the conceptual core of the research and is a most useful technique where time is of the essence, where there is a potentially large volume of data that needs to be examined and when the researcher is guided by a well-defined conceptual framework and an established sampling strategy as well as precisely specified research questions (Miles and Huberman 1994).

Within-case sampling: A popular within-case sampling strategy for qualitative studies is the sampling of subjects based on one or more characteristics deemed important by the researcher (Marshall 1996). Several types of such purposive techniques exist (Patton 1990), and selection from among these techniques results from the research questions (Miles and Huberman 1994; Marshall 1996), from the context of the research and practical considerations (Marshall 1996). Stratified purposeful sampling (Patton 1990) was used: premium brand ice-cream manufacturers were selected on the strength that they represented over 90 per cent (BEW alone accounted for 70 per cent) of total wrapped ice-cream sales in the UK, and were, thus, the subject of investigation by the Commission. The key dimension for distributor selection was the practical classification used by the report authors. The analytic procedures outlined by Miles and Huberman (1994) are based on several rounds of data collection. This study is finite in its capacity for generating new evidence, and this may be deemed a limiting factor since emergent themes cannot be explored further through follow-up. Yet the level of detail provided by the report is much deeper and broader than a number of rounds of interviews could accomplish.

Coding: Coding rests at the core of data analysis (Miles and Huberman 1994) and is useful in enhancing validity and reliability (Potter and Levine-Donnerstein 1999). The latter authors argue that the coding approach (whether developed prior to or during field work) depends upon where the 'locus of meaning' is assumed to lie, thus implying that the coding decision is also a function of the researcher's worldview. The prior or deductive approach assumes, as does the research, that meaning rests in the content itself but must be inferred (by the coder) through recognising elements that form a pattern (Potter and Levine-Donnerstein 1999) rather than resting with the coder. Besides, it was deemed necessary to derive the scheme directly from theory to evaluate its explanatory power. The inherent weakness of pre-structured coding is the possibility of an inconsistent application of coding rules, theory-ladenness, even though this is inescapable in any kind of research (Guba and Lincoln 1994; Foxall 2009), and similar reliability and validity trade-off to the inductive approach (Potter and Levine-Donnerstein 1999). The coding procedure (Appendix 3) establishes rules and instructions drawn directly from the operational definitions and research propositions to properly and effectively categorise the evidence (Yin 2009). A balance was maintained to ensure that the coding did not become too complex in such a way as to compromise ecological validity (Potter and Levine-Donnerstein 1999), and the scheme was constructed to ensure that any relevant snippet of text could be coded even if it was ambiguous. We separately tested the codes on a random sample of pages from the report and later refined these accordingly. Testing and validation by a third party could not be carried out; however, since the development of the codes and the coding process was carried out by the same person, such testing and validation was not considered to be an issue that affects reliability negatively. On the contrary, it was thought that reliability is positively enhanced, since the 'expert' and the 'coder' are the same individual and there is no need to transfer knowledge for coding appropriately and there is little risk in misinterpretation and/or inconsistent coding. Besides, having experience and knowledge of the (marketing/economics) subject matter is desirable in applied business analysis (Foxall 1998) and would reduce the risk of 'premature conclusion-drawing' (Miles and Huberman 1994).

Within-case analysis and conclusion drawing: This research follows the useful advice of Miles and Huberman (1994) for drawing up descriptive and explanatory case displays together with several strategies for drawing conclusions from the data, including clustering, counting, weighting of evidence and outlier analysis.

Managing the Research Process

Early in the research, a screening process identified and weeded out irrelevant, non-viable cases (Yin 2009) or cases without the main variables of interest (Bryman and Bell 2007) to select the current dataset. A case study protocol (Appendix 2) was also developed to increase reliability and overall analysis manageability (Dnes 1992; Yin 2009) by precisely decomposing the research propositions and questions into a focused range of sub-research questions reflecting the main and embedded units of analysis. A database of all the raw data including notes was created to maintain a chain of evidence aimed at improving reliability and construct validity (Yin 2009). NVivo 8 was used to manage the entire data analysis process.

ETHICAL CONSIDERATIONS

The researchers made every effort to report and analyse all the data fairly (Yin 2009). The study follows the standard professional ethics guidelines of conducting social science research.

There was always concern about the possible ethical implications of the findings, especially if the evidence did suggest that marketer behaviour is behaviouristic (see Foxall 1999a). According to operant methodology, any conclusions drawn from this type of study are 'interim' explanations that, ultimately, require scientific testing. Further, generalisability outside the case is not possible. Therefore, any useful policy recommendations are severely limited, if at all possible.[9] However, the most immediate task was to evaluate a theory rather than judge firm behaviour. Besides, it is the behaviour of firms that may have ethical implications, not an interpretation of it (Foxall 1999a).

NOTES

1. Ernst Mach was, in turn, influenced heavily by the pragmatism of William James. Hence, operant behaviourism is a pragmatist philosophy in contrast to other forms of realist behaviourism which Skinner dubbed methodological behaviourism (Baum 1994). Foxall (1990), Baum (1994) and Pierce and Cheney (2008) provide a short history of behaviourism. For philosophical and historical accounts of behaviourism, see Smith (1986) and Zuriff (1985).
2. See Chapter 2.
3. This chapter shows the approach taken to cushion these latter problems: by defining the case focus and the units of analysis and by giving specific regard to data analysis strategies and techniques including the decision to adopt the pre-structured case outline analysis method.

4. Similar investigations had already been reported in 1979 (covering 1976), 1994 (covering 1993) and, the most recent, 1998 (covering 1997). The 2000 report is publicly available at the Competition Commission website: http://www.competition-commission.org.uk/rep_pub/reports/2000/436ice.htm.

5. See also Appendix 4.1, which briefly outlines the timeline of events between 1979 and 1999.

6. Reference may be made to the About Us section in the Competition Commission website (http://www.competition-commission.org.uk), which clearly outlines its main aims to include ensuring healthy competition within UK industry.

7. According to Miles and Huberman (1994), the case focus is a first step towards data reduction because it defines what is to be studied and what will be disregarded. In this case, therefore, the Commission's recommendations by way of suggested remedies to the final investigation were not analysed, as these fell outside the scope of the study.

8. Refer to Appendix 1.

9. With respect to generalisability, however, the pragmatist criterion of prediction and control for emancipatory change (Kelemen and Rumens 2008) would suggest that policy makers maintain the level of intervention to ensure public interest: 'the very survival of a culture depends on the successful control over conditions that threaten it' (Delprato and Midgely 1992, p. 1510). Coase (1974) suggests that the threat of firms to the public interest lies in their bid to often gain 'monopolistic power', and hence government intervention is desirable.

4. Specification and interpretation

INTRODUCTION

Operant methodology requires the use of the three-term contingency (S^D: $R \rightarrow S^{r/p}$) as a framework of analysis. The BPM extends this framework to account for the complexities in natural behaviour settings. In the BPM, discriminative and motivational stimuli, as primed by the consumer's learning history, relate to the scope of the setting and $S^{r/p}$ to the patterns of utilitarian and informational reinforcement.

Antecedent scope stimuli are programmed to qualify the setting, whereas outcome or consequential stimuli are similarly programmed to signal reinforcement. These stimuli are designed to encourage approach and/or discourage avoidance (Foxall 1990, 1999a). The analysis of firm behaviour based on the BPM, therefore, requires the setting to be analysed to identify (a) antecedent scope stimuli that appear to channel approach/avoidance behaviour and (b) consequential stimuli that appear to signal the outcomes of the same behaviour. First, each antecedent scope stimulus, in the form of a marketing cue, is categorised according to the typical effect it appears to have been designed by marketers to produce on the setting scope (relatively open to relatively closed) according to the customer/supplier behaviour to be encouraged/discouraged.[1] Secondly, marketers appear to manage consequential stimuli in the behaviour setting to signal the positive consequences to be gained by customers from approaching them as well as the negative outcomes to be incurred for any avoidance. To show how this is done entails an examination of how each consequential stimulus, in the form of a marketing cue, appears to be managed by marketers to signal the positive and negative outcomes of customer/supplier approach and avoidance (Figure 4.1). The relationships between antecedent marketing cues and the behaviour they are designed to funnel, and the relationships between the outcomes of this same behaviour and the consequential cues designed to signal them, are inferred to produce the operant interpretation.

Therefore, it is important to first establish definitions (see ensuing sections) which will guide the coding procedure (see also Appendix 3) into categorising the text of the case appropriately.

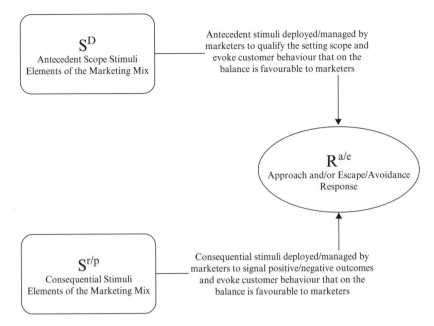

Figure 4.1   Analytic framework based on BPM – a basis for operational measures

RESEARCH PROPOSITIONS

Four sets of research propositions were formulated (see also Appendix 2).

The Antecedents Proposition

If firm behaviour is environmentally determined, then a number of key events in the marketer behaviour setting prior to the start of the investigation in December 1998 should be found 'controlling' firm behaviour. These stimuli, however, assume discriminative/motivational function only in the presence of the firm's managerial behaviour setting.

By inference from discussions on the managerial and marketer behaviour setting and the mutually reinforcing relationships existing between firms and their customers/suppliers and firms and the regulator, these events should include (a) a set of stimuli that, in the past, appear to have directly impinged on the behaviour of firms and that may still hold stimulus function and (b) a set of regulator-imposed rules by way of legally binding undertakings. These stimuli signal utilitarian and informational positive and aversive consequences contingent upon emitting certain behaviour.

Firms 'must always evolve and change in order to survive in a competitive market environment', and this evolutionary process requires behavioural selection (Xiao and Nicholson 2010, p. 247). Therefore, evidence should be found to directly associate some of these stimuli with emitted firm behaviour. In addition, if firms *do* attempt to increase monopolistic power (Coase 1974) and qualify the setting to make their relationships more predictable and stable (Foxall 1998, 1999a), then some of those same organisations negatively affected by the imposed undertakings will attempt to reaffirm their original position by opening the setting again in their favour. The resulting research proposition is, therefore, that

RP₁: Specific antecedent events including regulator intervention have, historically, come to control firm behaviour, with some of these stimuli maintaining stimulus control. In direct response to the regulator's intervention in 1998, firms immediately affected by the sanctions imposed upon them will attempt to close the behaviour setting.

The Reinforcement Management Proposition

The central claim of the theory of the marketing firm is that marketers will deploy consequential marketing stimuli to manage the patterns of reinforcement of their customers and suppliers, thereby ensuring favourable behaviour. The structure such behaviour takes is unknown. However, functionally, the behaviour is one of two opposing types, with the probability of purchase occurring at the intersection of two vectors, namely approach and avoidance(/escape[2]) (Alhadeff 1982): therefore, firms are expected to simultaneously deploy elements of the marketing mix that strengthen approach as well as weaken avoidance for the same customers or groups thereof. The topography of the mix elements used is similarly unknown. Hence,

RP₂: Behaviour within Manufacturer↔Distributor and Manufacturer ↔Retailer relationships is characterised by the management of patterns of reinforcement through marketing mix elements to encourage approach, discourage avoidance and bar escape of customers and suppliers.

RP₂.₁: Manufacturers manage patterns of reinforcement of their distribution customers through the marketing mix to simultaneously encourage approach, discourage avoidance and bar escape.

RP$_{2.2}$: Manufacturers manage patterns of reinforcement of their retail customers through the marketing mix to simultaneously encourage approach, discourage avoidance and bar escape.

RP$_{2.3}$: Distributors manage supplier patterns of reinforcement through the marketing mix to simultaneously encourage approach, discourage avoidance and bar escape.

RP$_{2.4}$: Retailers manage supplier patterns of reinforcement through the marketing mix to simultaneously encourage approach, discourage avoidance and bar escape.

The Scope Management Proposition

The second central claim of the theory of the marketing firm is that firms, within their customer/supplier relationships, manage behaviour setting scope to ensure that favourable behaviour emerges by depositing relevant marketing variables as scope stimuli. More precisely,

RP$_3$: The behaviour within Manufacturer↔Distributor and Manufacturer↔Retailer relationships is characterised by the management of behaviour setting scope through marketing mix elements to encourage approach, discourage avoidance and bar escape of customers and suppliers.

RP$_{3.1}$: Manufacturers manage the scope of the behaviour setting through marketing mix elements to simultaneously encourage approach, discourage avoidance and bar escape of their distribution customers.

RP$_{3.2}$: Manufacturers manage the scope of the behaviour setting through marketing mix elements to simultaneously encourage approach, discourage avoidance and bar escape of their retail customers.

RP$_{3.3}$: Distributors manage the scope of the behaviour setting through marketing mix elements to simultaneously encourage approach, discourage avoidance and bar escape of their suppliers.

RP$_{3.4}$: Retailers manage the scope of the behaviour setting through marketing mix elements to simultaneously encourage approach, discourage avoidance and bar escape of their suppliers.

The Competition Proposition

The theory of the marketing firm predicts how firms manage mutuality relationships with competitors engaging deliberately in strategies that fall within and outside the normal conduct of the business (Foxall 1999a). The strategies used in mutuality relationships are functionally identical to the ones described in the reinforcement and scope management propositions. Therefore,

$RP_{4.1}$: *The behaviour within Manufacturer↔Rival relationships is characterised by the management of patterns of reinforcement through marketing mix elements to produce behaviour on the part of rivals in a direction that is beneficial to the manufacturer.*

$RP_{4.2}$: *The behaviour within Manufacturer↔Rival relationships is characterised by the management of behaviour setting scope through marketing mix elements to produce behaviour on the part of rivals in a direction that is beneficial to the manufacturer.*

OPERATIONAL DEFINITIONS AND MEASURES

An *operant* is 'behaviour that operates on the environment to produce consequences which consistently effect its future rate of emission' (Pierce and Cheney 2008). Economic behaviour is operant behaviour in that the positive and negative consequences it generates affect its recurrence in future (Foxall 1990). *Reinforcement* is 'the process that strengthens the rate of responding over time', while *punishment* is 'a process that weakens the rate of responding to the extent of even extinguishing some such behaviour over time' (Pierce and Cheney 2008). Underlying these processes is the notion of a *consistent effect on the rate of responding*; otherwise behaviour is said to be simply rewarded or penalised (Foxall 1990). Purchase, consumption and marketing behaviour are assumed operant.

A *response class* is 'a set of behaviour responses that all have the same function irrespective of their topography'. Behaviour is composed of a single or a number of responses or even a set sequence in a chain (Pierce and Cheney 2008): for example, Foxall (1990) recounts the grocery shopping behaviour sequence, writing a list, driving to the supermarket and so on. Topographically, each response within this sequence is different; yet its function is the same. To purchase a particular brand an individual must emit a number of responses, the presentation of 250 pence to receive an ice-cream in exchange – 250 structurally identical responses obtain reinforcement.

Environmental Stimuli

From Foxall (1990) and Pierce and Cheney (2008) a definition of a *stimulus* may be formulated as: 'a physical, temporal, social or regulatory event that may produce a change in the rate of responding'. A *regulatory* stimulus is 'a rule that specifies relationships among stimuli, response and outcomes' (Foxall 1990). The *environment* or *behaviour setting* is defined as a 'context comprised of one or more of such events or stimuli marking the occasion for reinforcement and/or punishment contingent upon emitting certain behaviour' (Foxall 1990). A brand is conceived as 'an amalgam of stimuli (e.g. logo, packaging, product ingredients) that may come to produce a common effect on behaviour' and is, thus, a *stimulus class* (Pierce and Cheney 2008).

Antecedent stimuli in the behaviour setting, in the past, may have been repeatedly paired with the performance of behaviour and the outcomes of such behaviour. Over time, such antecedents tend to signal the occasion for the emission of such behaviour: if the response has been, on the balance, reinforced, then behaviour is emitted; if, on the other hand, the behaviour has been punished, such behaviour is weakened or extinguished (Foxall 1990). The events that mark the occasion for reinforcement and/ or punishment reliably preceding emitted or avoided responses acquire *discriminative function* and are known as *discriminative stimuli* – the stimuli predict reinforcement and/or punishment (Pierce and Cheney 2008). Given a learning history of reinforcement and punishment, these stimuli acquire their capacity to 'control' or 'regulate' behaviour (Foxall 1990).[3] The managerial behaviour setting functions in a similar way as consumer learning history and is, thus, defined as 'the consequences of past behaviour, i.e. any past outcomes of behaviour that would seem to impinge on the current situation, and/or any self or other rules (plus general economic and commercial rules) that are internal to the firm (including targets, objectives and plans) that appear to impinge on the current situation'.[4]

Behaviour and Its Consequences

Marketer behaviour is expressed in its product, 'the various elements of the marketing mix, namely price, product, promotion and place' (Kotler *et al.* 2001). Although varying extensively in their topography, these elements may be classed together by their function as scope or consequential stimuli according to the given context.

Outcomes of behaviour are classed as either reinforcing or punishing (Baum 1994; Pierce and Cheney 2008). *Reinforcers* are 'those consequences that function to strengthen behaviour, i.e. increase the future rate of emission of the operant', while *punishers* are 'those consequences that weaken behaviour, i.e. decrease the future rate of emission of the operant'. *Reinforcing stimuli* are 'events describing/signalling response-strengthening outcomes', and *punishing stimuli* are 'events describing/signalling response-weakening outcomes'.[5] Events are reinforcers or punishers *only* if the outcomes consistently influence the rate of emission of the response that produced them (Foxall 1990). Such relationships are assumed in this study.

The function of marketing

According to the theory of the marketing firm, the function of marketing is to attempt to influence, modify, shape and maintain the behaviour of the parties within relationships in such a way as to increase emitted behaviour favourable to the firm and/or to deter and bar unfavourable behaviour (Foxall 1999a). This involves: (a) identifying those stimuli which may have discriminative or motivational function for customers/suppliers or segments thereof and in which contexts (Foxall 1992b), and (b) optimising them to ensure effectiveness (Foxall 1999a).

Firms shape and maintain behaviour through reinforcement and punishment (Foxall 1990; Pierce and Cheney 2008):

1. *Positive reinforcement* is 'the process of increasing the probability of favourable behaviour occurring in future by presenting appetitive consequences or benefits (*positive reinforcers*)'.
2. *Negative reinforcement* is 'the process of strengthening favourable behaviour occurring in future by reducing or removing aversive consequences (*negative reinforcers*)'.
3. *Positive punishment* is 'the process of decreasing the probability of unfavourable behaviour occurring in future by presenting aversive consequences (*positive punishers*)'.
4. *Negative punishment* is 'the process of decreasing the probability of unfavourable behaviour occurring in future by removing positive consequences (*negative punishers*)'.

Contingency-shaped and rule-governed behaviour

Behaviour may be shaped either 'by direct exposure to the contingencies themselves, i.e. directly to the outcomes a particular response produces on the environment' (*contingency-shaped behaviour*) or 'by an indirect exposition established through rules or instructions that specify the contingencies' (*rule-governed behaviour*) (Foxall 1997a). The rules that specify behaviour may be found in contracts, advertisements, logos, marketing plans or firm objectives.

Figure 4.2   Approach and avoidance

Approach and avoidance

Approach and avoidance/escape are conceived as two separate but opposing response classes of behaviour (Figure 4.2). For the purposes of this study, *approach* is defined as 'any emitted behaviour which is advantageous to the firm'. *Avoidance* is defined as 'any emitted behaviour which is disadvantageous to the firm'. Escape is a more extreme form of avoidance, which for practical purposes is subsumed under avoidance unless there is clear evidence to the contrary (e.g. a refusal to sign a contract).[6]

Utilitarian and Informational Reinforcement

Utilitarian benefits or positive consequences are defined as 'those economic benefits or pay-offs or incentives arising directly from literal exchange akin to the economist notion of utility'. By analogy from consumer behaviour (Foxall 1997a), these benefits are related to the 'biological' survival of the firm. Hence, sales and profits are clear examples. *Utilitarian aversive consequences* are defined as the 'marketing or transaction costs of acquiring and retaining customers' (Foxall 1999a) and, hence, include a whole range of costs including the costs involved in finding customers, advertising, promotion, contracting and so on.

By inference (Foxall 1990, 1997a, 1999b), *informational benefits* or *positive consequences* are defined as 'positive other- and self-feedback on firm performance'. Positive feedback, for example, results from market information derived from the act of selling products. This information is not only recorded in the accounts of the firm (Foxall 1999a) but is contrasted to self-rules (sales and profit targets), market share percentages that help the firm assess its progress to date and its position versus rivals. Economies of scale are an informational measure indicating feedback on capacity utilisation across production, operations, distribution and marketing. Head-office provides top management with feedback on subsidiary performance, supplier relations involve progress reporting with manufacturers often demanding regular meetings and so on. *Informational aversive consequences* relate to 'nega- tive feedback on performance on the firm's behaviour by virtue of self- and other-rules'.

Utilitarian/informational positive reinforcement is 'the process that strengthens the rate of response that produced such consequences through the presentation of utilitarian/informational benefits (positive utilitarian/ informational reinforcers)'. *Utilitarian/informational negative reinforce- ment* is 'the process that strengthens the rate of response that produced such consequences through the removal of utilitarian/informational aversive consequences (negative utilitarian/informational reinforcers)'. *Utilitarian/informational positive punishment* is 'the process that weakens the rate of response that produced such consequences through the presentation of utilitarian/informational aversive consequences (positive utilitarian/informational punishers)'. *Utilitarian/informational negative punishment* is 'the process that weakens the rate of response that produced such consequences through the removal of utilitarian/informational ben- efits consequences (negative utilitarian/informational punishers)' (Pierce and Cheney 2008).

Managing Setting Scope

The criteria for recognising and establishing the degree to which the behaviour setting is open/closed (e.g. Foxall 1990, 1992b) are outlined below. It is assumed that scope stimuli compel the approach/avoidance behaviour for which they have been programmed. Although closed set- tings appear to typically engender approach, competing stimuli may be deployed to open the setting, providing customers with more behavioural alternatives, thereby attempting to entice them away from approaching the marketer who originally closed the setting.

1. *Availability and access to reinforcement and punishment:*
    a) The number of utilitarian and informational reinforcers avail- able. Closed settings are characterised by:
        i.   A limited number of reinforcers.
        ii. One or a few of these stimuli are especially prominent.
    b) The number of ways available to obtain these reinforcers. Closed settings are characterised by:
        i.   One or a relatively small number of responses available.
    c) The degree to which there are a certain number of tasks to be performed upon which reinforcers are contingent. Closed settings are characterised by:

    i.   The necessary tasks that need to be performed are clearly defined and precisely specified, typically through explicit rules or instructions imposed by others.

    ii.   The performance of the necessary tasks is reinforced.

    iii. Some tasks are interchangeable for the tasks to be reinforced.

2. *The external control of the situation:*

    a) The degree to which providers (a firm and its rivals) control access to these reinforcers. Closed settings are characterised by:

        i.   One or at the very best very few alternative providers are available.

        ii.   The marketer has some degree of control over the levels of deprivation.

    b) The degree to which contingencies of reinforcement and punishment appear to be largely arranged and controlled by marketers. Closed settings are characterised by:

        i.   Few or even one marketer arranging and controlling the contingencies of reinforcement and punishment.

    c) The degree to which marketers themselves are subject to these contingencies. Closed settings are characterised by:

        i.   Marketers not being subject to the contingencies.

    d) The degree to which there is easy access to alternatives to being in the particular situation. Closed settings are characterised by:

        i.   Limited or no alternative situations.

        ii.   Non-compliant responses (avoidance) are clearly punished to make the response less probable.

        iii. Compliant responses are, generally, negatively reinforced.

Managing Patterns of Reinforcement

Three broad techniques are available to marketers (Foxall 1990, 1992a, 1992b, 1997a) depending upon whether approach is to be encouraged and avoidance thwarted.

1. *Managing the effectiveness of a reinforcer or punisher* where *effectiveness* is 'a function of the level of deprivation and/or of whether stimuli are stated within a set of explicit rules, such as a contract' (Foxall 1997a). *Deprivation* refers to 'a state of not having access to some level of utilitarian and/or informational benefits and access to these benefits (especially utilitarian) is important'.[7]

2. *Increasing the quality and quantity of reinforcers and/or punishers.*

    (a) *Quality* refers to 'augmenting/improving or weakening the effect of present reinforcers or punishers'.

      i. Using quality to strengthen approach refers to 'increasing *the effect* of *present* utilitarian and informational benefits and/or decreasing or making less prominent the effect of *present* utilitarian and informational aversive consequences'.

     ii. Using quality to weaken avoidance refers to 'increasing *the effect* of *present* utilitarian and informational aversive consequences and/or decreasing or making less prominent the effect of *present* utilitarian and informational benefits'.

(b) *Quantity* refers to 'increasing or decreasing the number of, and therefore involves adding and/or removing, reinforcers and punishers'. The insistence on the idea of finding 'addition/removal' within the evidence stems from the need to demonstrate management of these stimuli.

     i. Using quantity to strengthen approach refers to 'adding to or increasing the number of utilitarian and informational benefits and/or decreasing or removing the number of utilitarian and informational aversive consequences'.

     ii. Using quantity to weaken avoidance refers to 'decreasing or removing the number of utilitarian and informational benefits and/or adding to or increasing the number of utilitarian and informational aversive consequences'.

3. *Managing schedules of reinforcement.* Underlying the patterns of reinforcement maintaining firm behaviour is 'the frequency with which a response is followed by a reinforcer (or punisher)', i.e. the *schedule of reinforcement* that is operating (Foxall 1990).

Schedules of reinforcement are precise arrangements of contingencies used in the controlled environs of operant laboratories where scientists have a large degree of control. Schedules are either continuous or intermittent, where continuous schedules provide reinforcement continuously and intermittent schedules provide reinforcement either according to specified time intervals (interval schedules) or according to numbers of responses (ratio schedules) (Pierce and Cheney 2008).[8] In natural human behaviour settings, a number of such schedules may be operating and interacting to exert complex and multiple effects (Foxall and Schrezenmaier 2003) that are difficult to identify/relate to behaviour with any degree of accuracy (Foxall 1990). The complex effects of the schedules may only be inferred from the responses and their outcomes (Foxall 1992a, 2009), and discussion proceeds by analogy. Such analogies provide a useful tool in interpreting economic behaviour (Foxall 1998).

MARKETING MIX ELEMENTS

The elements of the marketing mix are assigned to four topographical categories: price, product, promotion or place (Kotler *et al.* 2001) (see Table 4.1). Functionally, the various elements of the *marketing mix* are

Table 4.1 Non-exhaustive topography of marketing mix elements

Price	Retail price
	Distribution discounts
	Credit terms
	Rebates
Promotion	Personal selling
	Public relations
	Advertising
	Sales promotions
	Prizes
	Competitions
	Special incentive schemes
	Additional discounts
Product	Products and services
	Logo
	Product features
	Warranties
	Branding
	Customer service
	Product range, line and extension
	Product innovation/development
	Packing and labelling
Distribution	Merchandising
	Space allocation
	Point-of-sale material
	Special displays
	Freezers and cool cabinets
	Atmospherics
	Retail outlet
	Type
	Locational convenience
	Cold chain delivery
	Channel
	Length and breadth
	Integration
	Geographical coverage
	Organisation
	Warehousing
	Stocking

defined as 'physical, temporal, social and regulatory stimuli configured, programmed, deployed and optimised[9] by marketers to, individually and in combination, (a) qualify the setting scope, channelling approach and deterring avoidance, (b) establish and signal reinforcement and/or punishment contingent upon performing such behaviours, and (c) deliver such reinforcing and punishing consequences'. The effect of each element on the setting or on reinforcement management is dependent entirely on the situation (Foxall 1992a, 1997a).

NOTES

1. The underlying premise is that firms close the setting to increase the probability of purchase.
2. Escape is a more extreme form of avoidance.
3. Ice-cream manufacturers have learnt the negative effects seasonal fluctuations have on consumer demand and have attempted to routinise pure impulse purchasing through product development (DairyReporter.com 2003) to, most probably, streamline revenues and cash flows more evenly across the year. Without the intervening variable of learning history, these stimuli remain neutral. Conversely, learning history is activated in the setting, signalling the behaviour contingent for obtaining reinforcement (Foxall 1997a).
4. If a distributor has benefited by behaving in such a manner as to achieve economies of scale in distribution in the past, then it is reasonable to infer that (a) economies of scale are reinforcing outcomes of behaviour, (b) the firm may have some rule regarding the pursuit of such economies which would appear explicitly or, by inference, from the reasonable conduct of business, and (c) particular stimuli in the environment signal relevant scale outcomes or not.
5. While price is punishing because of the loss of spending power (Foxall 1997a), consumer discounts are reinforcing because the aversive consequences (the price) have been reduced by the amount of the discount.
6. Throughout the work, when reference is made to increasing/strengthening approach or decreasing/weakening avoidance, what is meant is increasing/strengthening or decreasing/weakening the probability or the likelihood of the response. In operant psychology, the dependent variable is the *rate* of response (Foxall 1997a).
7. If sales, profits or capacity utilisation are lower than planned, a firm may be said to be in a state of deprivation. Deprivation may also occur by not being able to gain access to distribution channel, a level of service or even a brand that is a commercial success.
8. Ratio schedules may be *fixed*, where 'reinforcement obtains after a certain fixed number of responses are performed', or *variable*, where 'the number of responses required changes from one reinforcer to the next'. Interval schedules may be *fixed*, where 'reinforcement is obtained according to a fixed time interval', or *variable*, where 'the amount of time elapsed between one reinforcer and the next is varied' (Pierce and Cheney 2008).
9. A distinction is appropriate between the real effects of these stimuli and the effects such stimuli are designed to produce. Learning history activates and transforms the programmed stimuli into actual discriminative stimuli (Foxall 1992b, 1997a) – marketers programme and deposit the stimuli in an attempt for firms to emit the favourable response.

5. Corporate behaviour: the supply of wrapped impulse ice-cream

ANTECEDENT STIMULI

Relationships as Routes to Market: 1979–98

The UK impulse ice-cream market has a history of regulatory intervention. Three investigations similar to the one published in 2000 were reported by the Competition Commission, namely in 1979 (investigating 1976), in 1994 (investigating 1993) and the most recent, the third, in 1998 (investigating 1997).[1]

Figures 5.1 and 5.2 show the industry channel landscape from manufacturers to retailers in 1998 (and before) and 1999 (and after) respectively.

Manufacturers engaged in a complex web of exchange-only, mutuality-only and mutuality-plus-exchange relationships (Figure 5.3), emitting behaviour resulting in utilitarian (sales volumes, revenues, profits, cash flow, marketing, distribution and operational costs) and informational (brand popularity, rates of brand sales, share of distribution market, retail penetration, market share, profitability, idle/excess capacity) benefits and costs. At the distribution tier, manufacturers used either of two intermediary services: pure logistics services which involved delivery from central storage to the retailer or wholesale services where distributors and/or wholesalers provided a range of value-added services including finding new customers. Access to the retail channel and, therefore, to final consumers was either direct (mutuality-plus-exchange relationships) circumventing wholesale services and delivering through integrated or outsourced logistical systems, or indirect (mutuality relationships) through either services.

Historically, some manufacturers used exclusive distribution agreements, placing obstacles to rivals en route to retail outlets. At the retail level, manufacturers barred access to retail outlets through outlet exclusivity and to space within that outlet through full or partial freezer exclusivity. These three main strategies were supported by generous programmes of relatively high/low levels of utilitarian/informational rewards for channel member approach and utilitarian/informational punishment for avoidance. Since such behaviour was emitted by several manufacturers

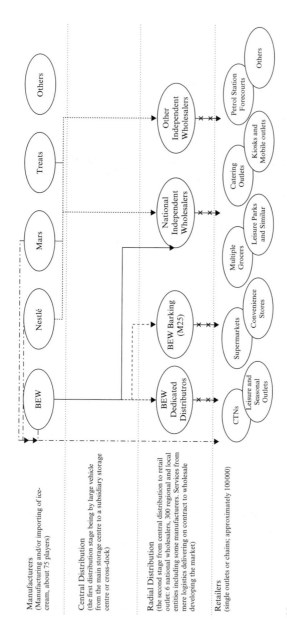

Manufacturers
(Manufacturing and/or importing of ice-cream, about 75 players)

Central Distribution
(the first distribution stage being by large vehicle from the main storage centre to a subsidiary storage centre or cross-dock)

Radial Distribution
(the second stage from central distribution to retail outlet: 6 national wholesalers, 300 regional and local entities including some manufacturers. Services from mere logistics delivering on contract to wholesale developing the market)

Retailers
(single outlets or chains; approximately 100000)

BEW · Nestlé · Mars · Treats · Others

Other Independent Wholesalers

National Independent Wholesalers

BEW Barking (M25)

BEW Dedicated Distributros

CTNs · Leisure and Seasonal Outlets · Supermarkets · Convenience Stores · Multiple Grocers · Leisure Parks and Similar · Catering Outlets · Kiosks and Mobile outlets · Petrol Station Forecourts · Others

Notes:

- CTNs are confectioners, tobacconists and newsagents.
- Black lines denote non-exclusive channels used by BEW; ------- are exclusive. Barking is a BEW contracted-out system that covers the area within the M25 London motorway. .... denote channels used by remaining majors. —✕—✕— denote retail routes to market. Dashed lines show manufacturer direct routes to retailers.
- Distribution from the main storage centre to the point of final sale: distribution carried out by the manufacturer (usually using a contractor), or by an independent wholesaler, or by the retailer (where the retailer has a nationwide chain of outlets, for example, supermarket chains). The distribution activity includes: physical delivery of the ice-cream; storage at regional centres to accommodate peaks and troughs in demand, and aggregation of orders from a number of outlets.

Figure 5.1   1998 industry landscape: main actors and routes to consumer market

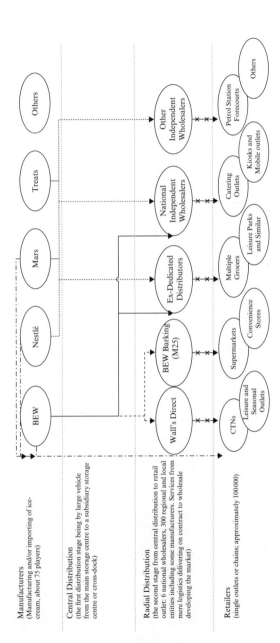

Manufacturers
(Manufacturing and/or importing of ice-cream, about 75 players)

Central Distribution
(the first distribution stage being by large vehicle from the main storage centre to a subsidiary storage centre or cross-dock)

Radial Distribution
(the second stage from central distribution to retail outlet: 6 national wholesalers, 300 regional and local entities including some manufacturers. Services from mere logistics delivering on contract to wholesale developing the market)

Retailers
(single outlets or chains; approximately 100 000)

Notes:

- CTNs are confectioners, tobacconists and newsagents.
- Black lines denote non-exclusive channels used by BEW; ------- are exclusive. Barking is a BEW contracted-out system that covers the area within the M25 London motorway. .... denote channels used by remaining majors. —✕—✕— denote retail routes to market. Dashed lines show manufacturer direct routes to retailers.
- Distribution from the main storage centre to the point of final sale: distribution carried out by the manufacturer (usually using a contractor), or by an independent wholesaler, or by the retailer (where the retailer has a nationwide chain of outlets, for example, supermarket chains). The distribution activity includes: physical delivery of the ice-cream; storage at regional centres to accommodate peaks and troughs in demand, and aggregation of orders from a number of outlets.

Figure 5.2   1999 Industry landscape: main actors and routes to consumer market

67

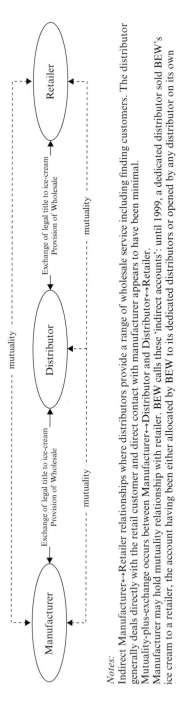

Notes:
Indirect Manufacturer↔Retailer relationships where distributors provide a range of wholesale service including finding customers. The distributor generally deals directly with the retail customer and direct contact with manufacturer appears to have been minimal.
Mutuality-plus-exchange occurs between Manufacturer↔Distributor and Distributor↔Retailer.
Manufacturer may hold mutuality relationship with retailer. BEW calls these 'indirect accounts': until 1999, a dedicated distributor sold BEW's ice cream to a retailer, the account having been either allocated by BEW to its dedicated distributors or opened by any distributor on its own initiative.

Panel 1: Indirect relationships with retailers

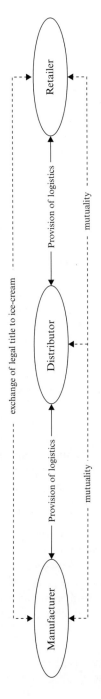

Notes:

Direct Manufacturer↔Retailer relationships where distributors may provide some wholesale services but typically simply deliver the ice-cream to the retailer. Both distributor and manufacturer deal directly with the retail customer. Contact with manufacturer still appears, in most cases, to have been of a lesser degree than that with distributor.

Exchange occurs between manufacturer and retailer. Manufacturer does not necessarily hold a mutuality relationship with the retailer.

Mutuality exists between Distributor↔Retailer and Manufacturer↔Distributor. Mutuality appears to be very important in this relationship with the retailer.

BEW calls these 'direct accounts': until the 1999 season, a direct account was defined as a retailer under which a dedicated distributor delivered BEW's wrapped ice-cream to a retailer, the retailer being invoiced by BEW.

Panel 2: Direct relationships with retailers

Figure 5.3   Exchange-only, mutuality-only and mutuality-plus-exchange relationships in the setting (distinction between direct and indirect accounts held by BEW, 1998)

over several years prior to the 1999 investigation it appears that these strategies were reinforced and/or punished rather than simply rewarded or penalised.

Distributors engaged in mutuality-plus-exchange relationships with manufacturers, as their suppliers, and retailers, as their customers. Mutuality-plus-exchange relationships with manufacturers took either of two forms. One was the provision of logistical services for a fee where legal title of the ice-cream remained with the manufacturer[2] and literal exchange of the ice-cream occurred between manufacturer and retailer. Alternatively, distributors assumed legal title and provided a series of value-added wholesale services including the acquisition and retention of retail customers, and delivery. The existence of distributors as stimuli in the setting signalled the utilitarian and informational reward and cost contingent upon using either of these services. Figure 5.3 describes the identified relationships with particular emphasis on BEW.

The Commission noted the importance of the distribution tier, including:

1. Distributors provided a capital-intensive delivery system that maintained the cold storage chain from manufacturer central depots to retailers that had limited outlet space for storing the product. In fact, retail freezers enhanced the usage of this limited space by providing required-quality cold storage and making the brands visible, prominent and available to store traffic.
2. Distributors also ensured that all freezers were stocked properly to maximise earnings potential.
3. At the radial distribution level of analysis, distribution was a key competitive arena, as intermediaries provided access to extensive retail penetration and thus had the potential of increasing manufacturer scale of operations, giving rise to significant production, distribution and marketing economies of scale, thus further reducing manufacturer transaction costs of customer acquisition and retention.

Consumer demand was seasonal and unstable because of unpredictable British weather.[3] To shape, maintain and strengthen retailer approach, distributors ensured that their physical set-up was such as to make the required timely delivery of stock, especially in the peak summer months. Distributors, therefore, had their own cold storage facilities and, in addition, relied on the manufacturer storage, production, ordering process/ times and delivery timings.

The aversive consequences of running a distribution business were a function of the interaction among such stimuli as: fleet size, the number of units[4] to be delivered to a given outlet (drop size), frequency of drops (drop frequency), distance travelled between outlets, overall number of outlets within a given territory (drop density) and travel time between one outlet and another. Drop density, size and frequency depended on the extent of retail penetration of a given brand within the distributor's territory. To achieve scale economies, distributors had proper incentive to broaden the scope of their business by carrying either the entire product ranges of a single manufacturer[5] or multiple rival products and brands (these latter distributors were called independent wholesalers). For example, as the scale of operation of a distributor increased, drop size and frequency to a given set of retail outlets grew – in addition, as the product range carried broadened, drop density increased purely from the wider variety of retail outlets that could be handled. This usually resulted in increases in revenues and decreases in per unit carriage costs (utilitarian benefits) and economies of scale, improved capacity planning and maintaining product quality (informational benefits). These factors, in turn, affected the ability of a distributor to achieve an economically viable business model and appear to have reinforced the behaviour emitted by certain distributors to carry multiple brands and products.

Typically, reciprocal reinforcement in Manufacturer↔Distributor mutuality-plus-exchange relationships was characterised by a set of utilitarian benefits, namely discounts (price) and bonuses/incentives (promotion) payable to distributors, on the one hand, and the provision of a range of services, as described, on the other. The utilitarian and informational benefits of the distribution channel for manufacturers as a route to market were a function of the interaction among several inter-related factors, including: (a) the quality of the distribution network in terms of the levels of service provided, the business volumes handled, the density of the network and the extent of coverage; and (b) the number of such distribution alternatives and their substitutes. The degree of setting closure that exclusivity had on the distribution setting depended upon the capability of barring rival access to the various alternatives and substitutes. The report shows how, as a single manufacturer increased its share of distribution through exclusivity arrangements, rivals had lesser access to quality distribution alternatives and the network of retailers these alternatives covered. Control was maintained through legally enforceable exclusivity tie-ins.

Throughout the 1980s and the 1990s, BEW built an extensive distribution system that included a group of entities entirely dedicated to the delivery and/or wholesale of its brands,[6] its vertically integrated Barking operation,[7] several non-exclusive national wholesalers and a host of independent wholesalers. BEW rewarded these routes to market differentially: to the highest strength of approach, BEW's exclusivity contracts were rewarded by significantly higher utilitarian (preferential discounts,

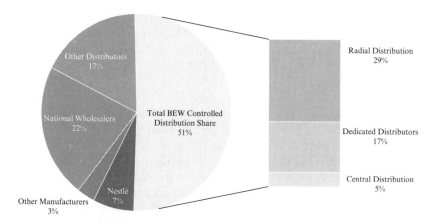

*Figure 5.4   Distribution market shares, 1998 (before Wall's Direct), by
           firm owning legal title to wrapped impulse ice-cream products*

incentive payments and performance-related bonus schemes) and informational (distribution economies) benefits to maintain dedicated custom.
National wholesalers typically traded over £7.5 million in BEW products
and were rewarded at a level between the strongest and weakest form
of approach, which was by the independent wholesalers whose business
model hinged on trading brands from multiple manufacturers. Differential
rewards contrasted the strongest forms of approach to the weakest forms
and, thus, acted as informational punishers, signalling rules with which to
shape the weaker approach of non-national independent wholesalers into
stronger behaviour favourable to BEW. The Commission claims that the
differential rewards system had seriously hurt wholesalers that were not
dedicated to BEW.

In parallel, BEW shaped and maintained retailer approach through the
superior level of service these distributors provided and through a host of
utilitarian rewards. The network of exclusivity contracts served to close
off important routes to market: the patterns of reinforcement managed by
BEW, on the whole, maintained strong distributor approach and punished
(or acted as a deterrent to) customer avoidance/escape and competitive
encroachment. By the end of 1998, BEW had more than a 50 per cent
share of the total distribution of wrapped impulse ice-cream in the UK[8]
(see Figure 5.4).

None of BEW's competitors had this extensive a distribution network,
and none appeared to have exclusivity contracts on such a scale. Nestlé
had also integrated downstream in radial distribution through contracted-
out distribution agreements: 74 per cent of its distribution was contracted

to a national independent wholesaler. Owing to considerably lower traded volumes, Nestlé and Mars (who used non-exclusive independent wholesalers) did not enjoy the same distribution or retail shares across all types of outlets as BEW[9] and, thus, lacked the scale of operation in manufacturing, distribution and marketing.

Retailers provided direct access to consumers, and competition for retailer attention was very strong among manufacturers. The routes to retailers were either indirect or direct.

Where distributors held mutuality-plus-exchange relationships with retailers, reciprocal reinforcement emerged directly from the exchange carried out: timely delivery of the legal title of the product (and other services, e.g. order taking) for trade in exchange for money. In these circumstances, manufacturers held (indirect) mutuality relationships with retailers and strengthened their approach through additional utilitarian reinforcers including additional discounts (price) and bonus schemes (promotion). On many occasions, manufacturers entered into freezer exclusivity (place) arrangements with retailers where the latter committed to allocate space within the outlet for an ice-cream freezer. Depending upon the arrangement, the retailer also agreed not to stock rival ice-cream brands within the freezer. Stocking of rival brands was, however, allowed in secondary (non-exclusive) freezers.[10] Where distributors held mutuality (only) relationships with retailers, and exchange of legal title was carried out between the manufacturer and the retailer directly, reciprocal reinforcement was contingent upon the utilitarian benefits of the relationship (the timely delivery of the product) and related informational benefits including personal contact, i.e. the account management function. The degree of personal contact between manufacturers and retailers varied. In general, it appears that, even though exchange might have been carried out between manufacturer and retailer, a good part of the mutuality relationship, in particular the social aspect, was retained by the distributor. In their direct mutuality-plus-exchange relationships, manufacturers strengthened retailer approach in ways similar to when the relationship was indirect. At times, manufacturers offered outlet exclusivity arrangements where the retailer exclusively sold a single manufacturer's brands. In outlet exclusivity, the patterns of reinforcement to shape and maintain retailer approach were the richest. Manufacturer↔Retailer relationships in the case of outlet exclusivity were always mutuality-plus-exchange relationships.

Generally, the range of impulse ice-cream products and brands within those ranges a manufacturer offered,[11] the demand for each of these brands and the individual brand rates of sales, together with the terms offered by manufacturers (directly or indirectly) and any additional distributor terms, determined the extent of utilitarian and informational benefits and costs contingent upon retailing a particular set of brands. These patterns of rein-forcement determined the strength of retailer approach.[12] Distributors, depending upon their strength of approach towards manufacturers, as stimuli in the retailer behaviour setting, signalled the variety of patterns of utilitarian and informational reinforcers/punishers contingent upon retail-ing a particular portfolio of brands. In combination, these factors also served as rules within the retailer managerial behaviour setting.

The utilitarian and informational benefits of the retail channel as a route to market were a function of the interaction among several interrelated stimuli, including:

1. Quality-related reinforcers: space allocated to the primary (and, more often than not, the only) freezer, outlet type and location, e.g. motorway service stations, leisure and entertainment, and seasonal beach outlets. Figure 5.5 depicts the percentage of wrapped impulse ice-cream sales by retail outlet type (see also Appendix 4.4). Figure 5.6 compares brand sales shares for manufacturers per outlet type.
2. Quantity-related reinforcers: store traffic per outlet and number of outlets within a chain, e.g. nationwide motorway and leisure chains.

The degree of setting closure that exclusivity brought about in the retail setting depended upon the manufacturer's capability of barring access to space within a retail outlet across a number and a variety of outlets across the nation. Freezer exclusivity partially contracted the setting at the retail spatial dimension, while outlet exclusivity worked to bar complete access of a given outlet to rivals. The greater the number of such relationships any manufacturer could muster, the more closed the setting would be, since a lesser number of retailing alternatives would be available to rivals. The utilitarian and informational benefits derived from such arrangements appeared to have reinforced such practices over several years.

BEW's Market Dominance

BEW dominated the market with 70 per cent market share of total retail sales value (£176 million) by the end of 1998 (see Table 5.1 and Appendix 4.4). Evidently market dominance allowed BEW a significant degree of control, and its brands, as business reinforcers, signalled significantly rich patterns of utilitarian and information reinforcement contingent upon trade. BEW's brands became 'must stock' items, while weaker manu-facturer brands diminished in their importance to distribution and retail channel members.

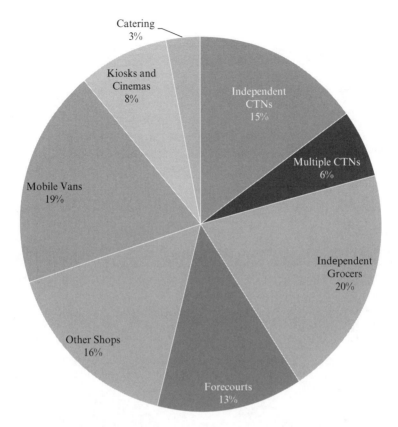

Note: CTNs are confectioners, newsagents and tobacconists.

Figure 5.5   Breakdown of wrapped impulse ice-cream sales by retail outlet type, 1998

Manufacturer Performance History

The sales performance of the major manufacturers was continually dismal in contrast to BEW's (see Figure 5.7).

Profitability[13] is a consequence of past behaviour, with higher revenues and trading profits encouraging a wider range of behaviours owing to an overall robust financial position. Profits resulted in a more open managerial setting and signalled the benefits from expansion behaviour. The report noted the overall healthy position of BEW to the extent that the firm increased sales and marketing expenditure by almost 10.5 per cent between 1996 and 1998, and, with £13.8 million net operating profit, BEW

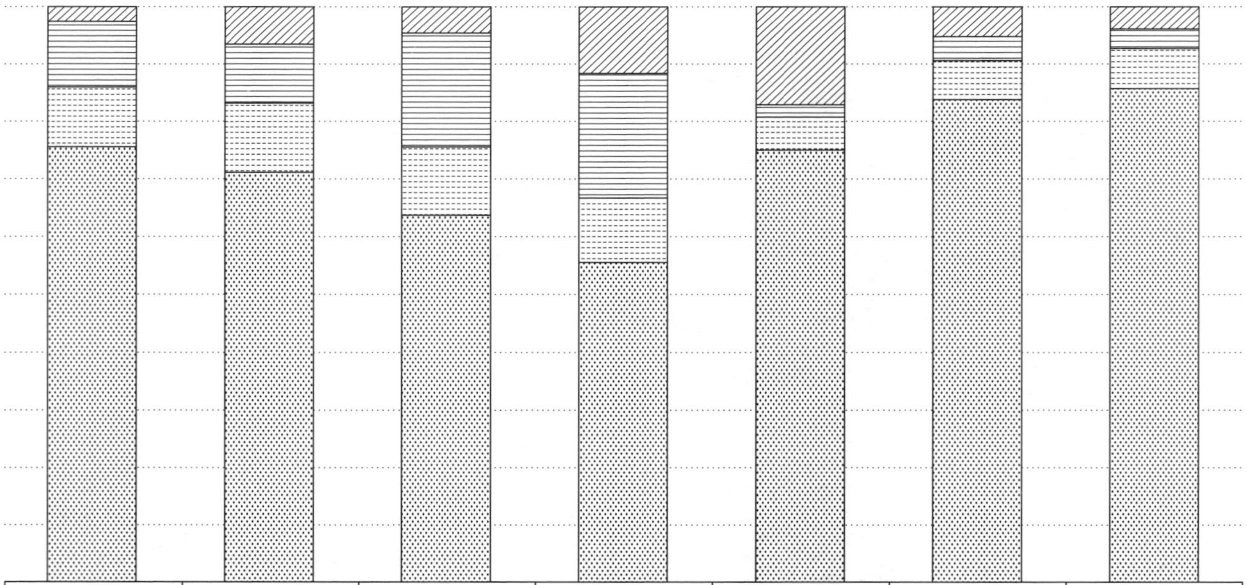

	All CTNs	Independent Grocers	Forecourts	Other Shops	Mobile Vans	Kiosks and Cinemas	Catering
Others	3.1%	7.0%	4.9%	11.8%	17.2%	5.7%	4.3%
Mars	11.3%	9.9%	19.9%	21.8%	2.1%	3.9%	3.2%
Nestlé	10.3%	12.3%	11.6%	11.0%	5.9%	6.7%	7.1%
BEW	75.3%	70.8%	63.6%	55.4%	74.8%	83.7%	85.4%

Figure 5.6 Wrapped impulse ice-cream market shares by retail outlet type – a comparison of manufacturers

Table 5.1   *Manufacturers' shares of consumer purchases at actual selling prices (1988–98)*

	1988	1989	1990	1991	1992	1993	1994	1995	1996	1997	1998
Wrapped singles (percentages)											
BEW	67	66	63	60	59	61	62	63	65	70	70
Nestlé/ Lyons Maid	23	21	21	18	13	9	11	11	11	10	10
Mars	N/A	1	6	7	8	11	13	15	11	9	10
Others	10	12	10	15	20	19	14	11	13	11	10
Total	100	100	100	100	100	100	100	100	100	100	100
Impulse (wrapped singles, scoop and soft) (percentages)											
BEW	48	49	49	49	47	49	52	51	54	57	53
Nestlé/ Lyons Maid	15	14	15	13	9	6	8	8	8	7	7
Mars	N/A	1	4	5	6	8	10	11	9	7	7
Others	37	36	32	33	38	37	30	30	29	29	33
Total	100	100	100	100	100	100	100	100	100	100	100
Market size (RSP £ million at constant 1998 prices)											
Wrapped singles	251	322	335	327	300	307	375	411	353	358	299
Scoop	57	64	58	47	49	36	34	39	34	34	45
Soft	77	86	78	63	66	82	78	91	79	80	85
Total impulse	385	472	471	437	415	425	487	541	466	472	429
Multipack	140	178	194	188	185	181	210	235	252	249	272
Other take-home	310	330	338	330	338	355	342	370	359	352	324
Weather index*	99.3	120.8	123.7	104.7	103.1	94.9	102	117.3	98.6	102.7	94.7

Notes:
* A figure below 100 indicates cooler than average; a figure above 100 warmer than average.
RSP is retailers' actual selling price including VAT and denotes consumer purchases.
The table presents a weather index, which shows how ice-cream sales and changes to the weather are directly related.

Source: Competition Commission (2000, p. 107), originally from BEW, based on data from AC Nielsen and TN Sofres (formerly AGB).

was nimble enough to invest over £10 million in Wall's Direct within a six-month period. Consistently profitable performance (see Figure 5.8) signalled the utilitarian and informational reinforcement contingent upon emitting its past behaviour – in fact, the strategies followed by BEW had remained relatively unchanged since the 1960s.

In contrast, other major manufacturers were consistently unprofitable.

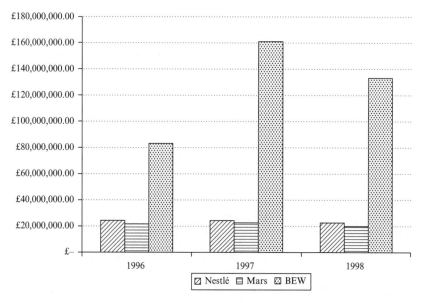

Source: Appendix A4.5.

Figure 5.7   Sales at gross sales value per manufacturer 1996–98

Both Mars (–1 per cent operating profit in 1998) and Nestlé (1 per cent operating profit in 1998) appeared to have had an incentive to reduce their overall (high) costs of operation while increasing their sales revenues through retail access and availability. These stimuli constrained, to a large extent, the behaviours of Nestlé and Mars:[14] neither had the financial muscle to mount a reasonable attack on BEW's market share; their behaviour was thus constrained.

Consumer Demand

The consumer surveys conducted by the Commission show how consumers selected from a full range of products within wrapped impulse ice-cream and tended to purchase alternative brands rather than visit other outlets if their preferred product was not available – it would appear that consumers viewed some brands as substitutes. They tended to purchase their wrapped impulse ice-creams from convenient locations and did not appear to have any specific brand preference, with product trial occurring only if it were available. The Commission noted how both advertising and promotional (including merchandising) expenditure had a significant

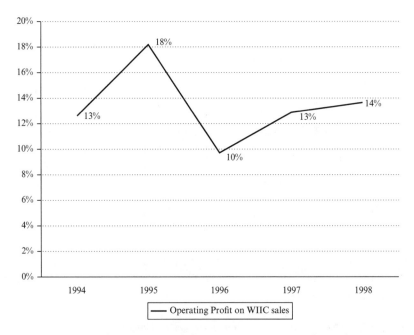

Figure 5.8   *BEW's operating profit as a ratio to wrapped impulse ice-cream (WIIC) sales 1994–98 (peak in 1995 marks unusually good summer in the UK)*

impact on consumer choice. Figure 5.9 contrasts manufacturer advertising spends between 1996 and 1998.

Retail Availability, Penetration and Market Share

Retailers stocked that product mix which gave them the best overall sales revenues and profit, i.e. the strength of retailer approach depended upon the overall richness of the patterns of utilitarian and informational benefits contingent upon selling a particular brand or set of brands over the aversive utilitarian and informational outcomes of operating. The richness of the overall patterns was a function of consumer demand, rate of brand sales and overall retail penetration and market share levels of the various manufacturers.

While advertising generated consumer demand, merchandising (freezer cabinets, related point-of-purchase materials and planograms for optimised use of freezer space) played a significant role in channelling consumer purchases by signalling the availability of the brands as reinforcers to consumers and shaping/maintaining the strength of their approach.

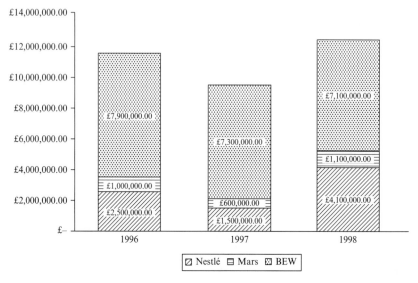

Note: See Appendix A4.5.

Figure 5.9   Manufacturer advertising spends (1996–98)

Given the patterns of consumer choice found by the Commission, merchandising appeared as the key determinant of the rate of sales of each
brand. Through freezer exclusivity, manufacturers were denied prominence and visibility in primary freezer space and, if the outlet had only one
freezer, even availability. Outlet exclusivity denied availability at the retail
level entirely.

Historically considerable manufacturer effort appeared to focus on
impeding brand visibility and availability at retail through exclusivity
arrangements. Figure 5.10 contrasts brand availability differences among
premium ice-cream brands at retail level.

If, in aggregate, consumers viewed brands as substitutes and purchased
only those brands that were available in their location, then the lack
of availability of a particular brand reduced consumers' demand for it,
increased that of the chosen available alternative and, hence, improved the
rate of sale of the available brand. Considerable manufacturer effort was
also invested in increasing retail acceptance/penetration through wholesalers and through field sales forces. The interaction of these factors on
a wide scale affected brand sales and, hence, retail market shares. Larger
market shares also commanded higher retail penetration, as more retailers readily accepted to trade in strong brands. As brands became stronger

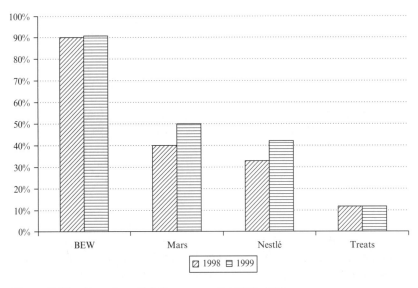

Figure 5.10   Brand availability at retail (1998–99)

and the utilitarian and informational benefits from retailing these brands became more predictable, retailers were more inclined to tie in exclusively to the manufacturer of the strong brands. Exclusivity tightened availability for the weaker brands. Stronger brands generated significant revenues, scale of operations and the profits for all who traded in them.

Regulatory Intervention

Over the years, regulatory intervention attempted to reverse the effects of anti-competitive behaviour and required legally binding undertakings for relevant changes in their strategies by those it found against.[15] The structure of the strategies used by manufacturers, however, did not change drastically despite these interventions. Manufacturers found ways to circumvent the precise undertakings instructed by the Commission.

DIRECT CONSEQUENCES OF THE 1998 GOVERNMENT INTERVENTION

BEW's history of dominance through exclusive or quasi-exclusive distribution/retail arrangements has been noted. The 1998 undertakings, therefore, acted as salient informational (negative) punishers: the regulator required a removal of BEW's ability to discriminate among dedicated and non-dedicated distributors through its terms. The evidence shows that BEW required this ability to set preferential terms to maintain the approach behaviour of some distributors and punish avoidance of the independent wholesalers or shape the emission of a stronger form of approach from among them. Although exposure to the contingencies was indirect, by March 1999, when these consequences were to take legal effect, BEW would be directly exposed to the aversive utilitarian and informational effects of not being able to shape and maintain the strength of distributor approach behaviour in ways most favourable to it. In other words, the undertakings were designed to break down the exclusive distribution system.

The creation of Wall's Direct was a direct response to the 1998 investigation and undertakings (see Table 5.2 for a summary of events leading up to its formation and Appendix A4.7). In late 1998, BEW terminated all dedicated distributor contracts,[16] laying the foundation for an entirely outsourced distribution system (Wall's Direct) that would handle its logistical requirements and which would eventually entirely replace its dependence on the non-national independent wholesale sector, thereby allowing it to engage solely in direct mutuality-plus-exchange relationships with retail customers. 'BEW has undermined the purpose of the 1998 undertakings . . . and deprived them of any real significance' (Competition Commission 2000, p. 24):

1. Midway through the 1998 investigation, BEW's management was already considering the impact the proposed undertakings would have on its business model and on the growth and distributional channel dominance objectives set by its mother company, Unilever.
2. The related plans proposed by management showed an explicit declaration of achieving these objectives through (a) circumscribing as many retailers as possible within mutuality-plus-exchange relationships and (b) eventually circumventing the independent non-national wholesale sector by a system of outsourced logistics. The system would be differentiated in the marketplace through a level of service superior to that provided by the dedicated distributors.
3. The system would enable the control *and* 'ownership of the point of retail purchase' (Competition Commission 2000, p. 173) by building stronger relationships with the existing 60 000 retail outlets and opening up access to an additional 40 000.
4. By 2002 the aversive consequences of related Wall's Direct investments[17] would have weakened, and BEW would return to profit by the following year.

Table 5.2   Summary of events leading to the formation of Wall's Direct

Mid-1988	The Competition Commission notes that BEW engaged the services of KPMG to investigate the possibilities of an alternative outsourced distribution system prior to the publication of the 1988 report. KPMG also makes its proposal.
July 1998	The Competition Commission publishes its report of the third inquiry covering 1997. BEW is found to supply ice-cream discriminating against non-dedicated wholesalers by supplying them with contractual terms (including additional benefits) less favourable than those offered to dedicated distributors. The Director General of Fair Trading seeks undertakings. BEW studies the situation to see how to respond.
August 1998 onwards	BEW management conduct a series of meetings internally and with Unilever's European office. BEW's management consider the impact of the proposed undertakings upon its business model and the growth and distributional channel dominance objectives set by its mother company, Unilever. Plans proposed by management show an explicit declaration of achieving these objectives through circumscribing as many retailers as possible within mutuality-plus-exchange relationships and eventually circumventing the independent non-national wholesale sector by a system of outsourced logistics. • The main differentiator in the marketplace of this system was the provision of a level of service superior to that provided by the dedicated distributors. • The system would enable the control *and* 'ownership of the point of retail purchase' (Competition Commission 2000, p. 173) by building stronger relationships with the existing 60 000 retail outlets and opening up access to an additional 40 000.
September 1998	BEW sends requests for information to a diverse range of possible service providers on 18 September, and the invitations to tender were also developed, followed by an evaluative and negotiation process.

Table 5.2   (continued)

	All the dedicated distributors are asked to tender, yet not all respond. Dedicated distributors would be able to participate as outsourcing partners, with the implied changes to their business model. Of those responding, a number were unsuccessful.
November 1998	BEW signs undertakings to the Secretary of State–the undertakings will come into force on 1 March 1999. It will not be able to discriminate between dedicated and non-dedicated distributors, and it must publish distribution terms. National wholesalers who trade more than £7.5 million in BEW products do not fall under these undertakings.
	On the same day, BEW gives a three-month contract termination notice to dedicated distributors. The termination of these contracts prior to their natural expiry was allowed by the relevant competition law in view of the undertakings just signed.
December 1998	The Director General of Fair Trading refers the ice-cream market case to the Competition Commission. The reference to the Commission is very broad, in contrast to earlier references that focused on a small number of practices by industry players.
January 1999	A group of ex-dedicated distributors form a buying entity called Ice-Cream World as a response to BEW terminating their contracts, which would now expire on 28 February 1999. Ice-Cream World starts operation around the end of January.
March 1999	Wall's Direct (WD) starts operations: • The system would eventually handle its logistical requirements, entirely removing its reliance on non-national independent wholesalers, to allow it, solely and directly, to engage in mutuality-plus-exchange relationships with retail customers. • By removing dependence on wholesaling, BEW would reduce the varying costs of distribution (outsourcing had the added utilitarian benefit of stabilising costs by capping contractor earnings), deploy a more manageable and predictable system of outsourced logistics contracts and, consequently, focus solely on the creation of demand.

Table 5.2 (continued)

- By 2002 the aversive consequences of related WD investments (£10 million-plus) would have weakened, and BEW would return to profit by the following year.
- The long-term utilitarian/informational rewards WD offered, the short-term aversive utilitarian/informational consequences and the Unilever-imposed 1999 growth rates acted as regulatory stimuli constraining BEW's behaviour: the WD objective was to capture at least 50 per cent of market share.

---

5. By removing dependence on wholesaling, BEW would reduce the varying transaction costs of distribution (outsourcing had the added utilitarian benefit of stabilising costs by capping contractor earnings), deploy a more manageable and predictable system of outsourced logistics contracts and, consequently, focus solely on the creation of demand.[18] Dedicated distributors would be able to participate as outsourcing partners, with the implied changes to their business model.
6. The long-term utilitarian and informational rewards Wall's Direct offered, the short-term aversive utilitarian and informational consequences, and the Unilever-imposed 1999 growth rates acted as regulatory stimuli constraining BEW's behaviour: the Wall's Direct objective was to capture at least 50 per cent of market share.

THE 1999 INVESTIGATION

To reach the scale of operations that would make Wall's Direct profitable and dominant at distribution, BEW had to regain the business lost by shedding its dedicated network,[19] acquire new business and channel all business through the new operation. However, in the short term, both BEW and its ex-dedicated distributors were mutually dependent: the ex-dedicated distributors of BEW held mutuality-plus-exchange relationships with the majority of retailers. BEW engaged in mutuality relationships with these retailers through provision of additional terms.[20] However, the ex-dedicated distributors maintained the important social aspect of that mutuality, essentially barring BEW from access to the full reinforcing consequences contingent upon holding a direct mutuality-plus-exchange. The setting appeared relatively closed purely by virtue of the BEW channel set-up.

The punishing consequences contingent upon allowing the ex-dedicated distributors to retain the social dimension of mutuality acquired discriminative function by virtue of the Unilever rules for growth and the punishing consequences of idle Wall's Direct capacity. BEW set in motion a programme of strategies geared towards regaining *complete* access to all the business previously flowing through its ex-dedicated distributors. To gain from the utilitarian and informational benefits contingent upon mutuality (in particular, the social dimensions therein), BEW entered a contract for outsourced sales teams, increasing its field force by 255 people.[21]

The 1999 investigation found several 'interlocking' marketing practices carried on by BEW and others that functioned to create and maintain a monopolistic hold on the market: the following sections discuss the evidence in the light of the reinforcer and scope management propositions (see Chapter 4).

Managing Distributor Patterns of Reinforcement and Setting Closure

BEW adopted a strategy deploying product, price, place and promotional reinforcers and punishers to:

1. Shape and maintain the strength and incidence of retailer approach through Wall's Direct, with particular emphasis on direct accounts[22] that, through service differentiation (a superior level of service of Wall's Direct at no extra charge) and other stimuli, were encouraged to abandon the ex-dedicated distributors.
2. Weaken and eliminate the strength and incidence of ex-dedicated distributors of BEW avoidance (sales arising from direct retail accounts).
3. Shape and maintain the strength and incidence of approach by BEW's ex-dedicated distributors (sales arising from indirect accounts).
4. Generally discriminate among independent (non-national) wholesalers, national independent wholesalers and outsourcing providers to punish the weakest forms of approach of the independent wholesalers (in particular the ex-dedicated distributors) and eventually reduce their importance by channelling them to abandon as many BEW retailer accounts as possible. By the time Wall's Direct started operating, the undertakings resulting from 1998 investigation had come into force: BEW could not discriminate among its intermediaries, with the exception of national wholesalers whose traded BEW volumes exceeded £7.5 million, where it was allowed to offer preferential terms. As Wall's Direct was designed on a model completely reliant on outsourced logistics contracts rather than conventional distribu-

tion arrangements, it fell outside the scope of the 1998 undertakings. Therefore, BEW could offer better terms to/through Wall's Direct. In keeping with the undertakings, BEW published standard distribution terms applicable to all intermediaries (ex-dedicated distributors included) that wanted to deal in BEW products. National wholesalers were allowed to remain on their previous preferential terms.

BEW shaped and maintained approach through setting closure and an intricate system of reinforcement management of distributors and retailers. Avoidance, or any behaviour not resulting in strong approach at the level of the national wholesalers or outsourcing providers, was punished.

BEW closed the setting by creating a requirement that all order taking, processing and fulfilment was to be carried out entirely through Wall's Direct. As business reinforcers, BEW's brands signalled the significant utilitarian and informational rewards contingent upon trading them. BEW's ex-dedicated distributors had no alternative to buying BEW products if they wanted to continue serving their retail customers. Their approach responses were reinforced through the standard distribution terms of supply. BEW was in full control of the contingencies and was not subject to them. Since BEW was the sole provider of these reinforcers, not placing an order was not an option for the ex-dedicated distributors, as that would have meant not serving retail customers, including the distinct probability of losing their custom.

By assigning differential values to pricing, promotional and place stimuli, the firm discriminated among providers according to the form of their approach. Avoidance was punished through reduction of benefits and increases in transaction costs. In this way, BEW managed the patterns of reinforcement of its intermediaries. On the balance, the patterns of utilitarian and informational reinforcement embodied in the terms offered previously to dedicated distributors were higher than those offered to independent wholesalers on standard terms: higher discounts on list price and incentive payments were made to the former, significantly improving their earnings potential. Further, BEW offered the dedicated distributors negative reinforcers in the form of allowances for additional delivery costs incurred (as a function of distance travelled).

By 1999, BEW had reduced the quality and quantity of utilitarian reinforcers by lowering standard terms applicable to its ex-dedicated distributors[23] to a fixed £1.10 deduction (9.8 per cent) on list price irrespective of the delivery distance travelled and removed the additional incentives payments they previously earned, severely reducing earnings power. The maximum any of the ex-dedicated distributors could earn, including top bonuses, was £2.08 per unit (18.3 per cent). As a positive punisher on approaching direct accounts, sales on these accounts were not included in bonus calculations. Comparatively, these terms were significantly lower than the per unit delivery costs of Wall's Direct (£3.33) and Barking (£1.78), both of which were calculated on significantly larger scales of operation. BEW, therefore, priced in such a way as to deprive those on standard terms of an economically viable business model revolving around independent wholesaling.[24] Further, by barring access to direct/indirect retail accounts through the interaction of setting closure (as explained above) and retailer reinforcer management (an aggressive push by the field sales force to promote Wall's Direct among retailers), the ex-dedicated distributors suffered significant losses in volumes as retailers defected to Wall's Direct (i.e. a loss in the quantity of reinforcers). The report shows how the ex-dedicated distributors entered a heightened state of deprivation: within five months of Wall's Direct starting operating, these firms had lost a significant proportion of business.[25] In parallel, as positive punishers, BEW also increased the costs associated with handling direct accounts: it required the ex-dedicated distributors to assume legal title of the ice-cream (previously BEW held legal title), thereby passing on associated administrative burdens of invoicing and debt collection and the burdens of credit risk and associated cash flow issues (Figure 5.11). In contrast, Wall's Direct contractor payments were based on the actual cost of the delivery plus a management fee and an enhanced capped management fee; thus, their BEW business was guaranteed at a profit. National independent wholesalers earned 25 per cent on list price including bonuses. These differential terms were potent informational stimuli indicating and regulating the strength of approach that was appropriate.

BEW further deployed discriminatory place positive punishers delaying reinforcement: it ceased overnight ordering facilities to distributors other than Wall's Direct contractors (this also had a regulatory dimension signalling the 'appropriate' strength of approach). Whereas such deliveries were previously made within 24 hours, there were now twice-weekly scheduled deliveries, or deliveries on 48 hours' notice. Thus, through Wall's Direct, BEW maintained ex-dedicated distributors (and all those who were not Wall's Direct contractors) at an increased level of deprivation, where such deprivation arose from the need to get products to satisfy demand at a usual superior level of service or 'when the sun came out' (Competition Commission 2000, p. 275).

BEW compounded its ex-dedicated distributors' punishment contingent on pursuing independent wholesaling by diluting the quality of per unit earnings, i.e. increasing the amount of their per unit delivery costs on any BEW business. While BEW allowed the ex-dedicated distributors to distribute rival brands, via standard terms, the firm imposed punishing

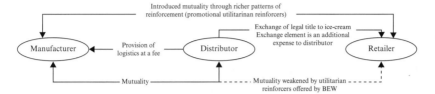

Notes:
Indirect account relationships did not change in structure even though there were changes to the terms involved. In contrast the structure of the direct account relationship was modified as shown in the figure.

In the 1999 season, BEW redefines direct accounts to build in a mutuality aspect, one that encourages direct engagement with Wall's Direct through richer patterns of reinforcement, effectively bypassing the distributor: a direct account is defined by BEW as a retailer which has been offered an off-invoice discount by BEW on its purchases of BEW's wrapped ice-cream, from a wholesaler and/or from Wall's Direct.

Exchange now occurs between distributor and retailer – some of the costs of carrying out transactions are passed on to distributor.

Mutuality exists between distributor and retailer, manufacturer and distributor, and also manufacturer and retailer.

Manufacturer offers a richer pattern of (supplementary) utilitarian reinforcement to reduce effect of mutuality aspect of the distributor–retailer relationship. The exchange element of the relationship carries an aversive consequence: the transaction costs incurred in directly managing the transaction, including invoicing and debt collection.

Figure 5.11   BEW's redefinition of direct account relationships enriching retailer patterns of reinforcement to retailers and souring ex-dedicated distributor patterns of reinforcement

obligations: distributors had to use Wall's Direct liveried vans, could not use those vans to carry the products of other manufacturers, and could not use those vans to deliver BEW products that were not ordered from Wall's Direct (this was also aimed at shaping ordering through Wall's Direct). Although the report does not explicitly state the full punishing consequences arising from not following these rules (for example, penalty clauses), the imposed punishing obligations clearly signalled important utilitarian and informational contingencies: wholesaling of rival brands would result in higher costs of operation and a reduction of the likelihood of achieving scale economies, since distribution economies were a function of drop size.

BEW managed retailer reinforcement through combinations of price, product, promotion and place utilitarian and informational reinforcers. BEW's consequential stimuli offered both qualitatively and quantitatively richer patterns[26] than those by the ex-dedicated distributors and considerable reduction in reinforcement delay. Utilitarian reinforcers used, for example, included the possibility of 24/7 ordering, with a 24-hour fulfilment promise even of a single unit (a box of wrapped impulse ice-cream singles) at no additional charge and free stock promotions. Informational reinforcers included the regulatory positive and negative stimuli of 'a discernible advantage in terms of service and profitability' (Competition Commission 2000, p. 447) derived from Wall's Direct. This level of service differentiation acted as an informational punisher further cordoning the ex-dedicated distributors away from retail accounts: the service could not be matched by the ex-dedicated distributors, since their given weakened per unit earnings potential (arising from standard terms) multiplied by the consistently declining volumes would not allow them to sustain extra costs. For example, the 24/7 promised delivery of a single unit at no extra charge created a negative informational regulatory punisher in the behaviour setting: the new service level had to be provided at no extra charge. Any ex-dedicated distributors of BEW that wanted to maintain its retail customer would have had to provide the same level of service or face the increased probability of the retailer switching to Wall's Direct. However, to provide such a level of service meant that unit delivery costs would increase considerably for the single unit. The standard terms offered by Wall's Direct for the supply of this order would ensure that the distributor would lose money. Moreover, the ex-dedicated distributors could not charge for a service which Wall's Direct offered free; and holding inventories cost money.[27] Even if ex-dedicated distributors had other rival brand orders to deliver to the retailer, they were precluded from doing so owing to the imposed obligations described earlier. Besides, the sales of rival brands appear to have been significantly slower.

Neither Nestlé nor Mars imposed distribution exclusivity. While Nestlé had an exclusive telesales centre, Mars did not. Both offered richer *per unit* patterns of utilitarian benefits to shape and strengthen independent wholesaler approach; Mars was more dependent on these types of wholesalers than Nestlé. However, the importance of BEW brands to independent wholesalers was such that the latter did not manage to compensate the loss of BEW business (–42 per cent volumes) with an equal or marginally smaller volume of sales from the other premium brands (+17 per cent volumes) – as Nestlé and Mars commented, the ex-dedicated distributors were induced to remain tied to BEW.

Managing Retailer Reinforcement: Manufacturers' Terms to Retailers

The patterns of reinforcement offered by manufacturers contingent upon retailer approach had utilitarian and informational function depending upon the quality of the benefits offered, the resulting aversive consequences and the potential sales volume of each brand. The effectiveness of

BEW-deployed patterns was enhanced by: (a) dominance of its brands in terms of market share, retail penetration and rates of sale, and (b) the firm's relatively high levels of performance granting it increased spending power to lavish upon retailers on a wider scale than its competitors.[28] Retailer patterns were richer when exchange was involved in the Manufacturer↔Retailer relationship and, in addition, these patterns served as punishers weakening retailer avoidance and deterring competitor encroachment.

Generally, manufacturers established retail terms that included standard or negotiated prices (discounts and supplementary retrospective discount schemes) and/or promotional elements[29] (monetary and non-monetary incentives, and performance-related bonuses). Additional informational reward contingent upon approach took the form of merchandising and marketing support. Standard or negotiated discounts were the inevitable aversive consequences, positive utilitarian punishers, retailers suffered in trading any given brand. Performance-related bonus scales were positive utilitarian reinforcers that provided retailers with an incentive to increase the volume of retail sales, thereby further strengthening their approach.

BEW constructed its bonus scales to punish rivals encroaching on its retail outlet shares: since BEW's rivals had weak brands, any of them that wanted to buy into part of the retailer's ice-cream annual sales would have had to make up for the inevitable losses in BEW bonuses incurred by the retailer through switching. The effectiveness of this positive punisher was enhanced by the strength of BEW brands across the entire market. If a rival wanted to buy into several retailers, the cost of doing so would increase significantly. The strength of BEW brand sales set two rules – a higher level of bonuses payable to individual retailers (informational reinforcer) and a higher cost of entry into that outlet (informational punisher). Thus, BEW created significant cost barriers, closing off bulk sections of the setting via reinforcer and punisher management. At times, BEW increased the effectiveness of these punishers by charging retailers a price for an additional BEW unit below the incremental cost of selling that unit. These negative punishers created a rule that weakened or barred encroachment, with direct exposure to the contingencies bringing utilitarian punishment into effect.

Bonus scheme effectiveness in maintaining retailer approach was enhanced through the retrospective application of discounts: when a particular level of purchases was realised, higher percentage bonuses were applied to the *full* value of purchases over the relevant period as additional discounts. These were negative utilitarian reinforcers because they reduced the aversive consequences of retailing a brand: the higher the discount, the less the aversive consequences contingent on buying that brand. The effectiveness of the reinforcer was enhanced through its retrospective application across *all* purchases. In the case of avoidance (e.g. low volumes), the aversive consequences to trading that brand were higher prices; in the case of escape (e.g. switching to a rival brand) the benefit was removed (negative punisher). BEW also applied higher discount rates irrespective of the volume of turnover, especially in the case of important retail outlets (the leisure sites) – this was a strong incentive towards continued retailer approach and, in addition, acted as another cost barrier to closing off the setting via reinforcer management to rival encroachment, to the extent that the ex-dedicated distributors were unanimous in their position that bonuses clearly had the effect of encouraging retailers to buy only from BEW.

BEW also utilised a variety of promotional positive reinforcers (free gifts, paid trips) that operated to weaken reinforcer delay – or the time and effort needed to gain the utilitarian benefits of bonus scales at the end of the year for a certain amount of responses (sales). Delay reduction was needed since there were competitors available with similar bonus schemes that could have stepped in to offer richer per unit patterns of reinforcement.

The evidence further suggests that retailer behaviour was shaped and maintained by high/low utilitarian/informational reinforcement (hedonism).

Freezer/Outlet Exclusivity Retail Setting Closure and Managing Patterns of Reinforcement

Freezer exclusivity and outlet exclusivity were place stimuli deployed by manufacturers circumscribing their relationships with retailers within legally enforceable contracts that precluded, to varying degrees, retailers from escaping and rivals from encroachment for, at least, the duration of such contracts (see Figure 5.12).

Exclusivity was pitched at retail level and supported by a combination of price, product, promotion and other place reinforcers and punishers that worked to (a) induce retailer approach in the form of being tied in exclusively to one manufacturer rather than rivals, (b) prevent retailer escape and/or bar competitive encroachment for the duration of the contract, (c) funnel the approach from as large a volume of consumers as possible at the retail outlet level to cultivate brand strength in the form of consumer demand and faster rates of brand sales, and (d) maintain retailers within the contracts upon expiry. The temporal dimensions of these contracts varied the degree to which the setting was kept in its relatively closed state and the duration of the contingent reinforcement patterns.[30] The Commission found that retailers expressed little concern about exclusivity practices, and most welcomed them.

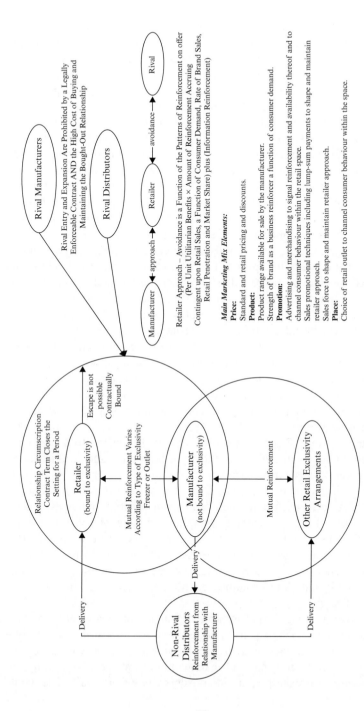

Figure 5.12 Circumscribing relationships through freezer and outlet exclusivity

While BEW claimed that outlet and freezer exclusivity practices inhered to the competitive arena, Nestlé and Mars claimed use in retaliation to BEW's anti-competitive behaviour. Another 30 manufacturers, including Treats, practised freezer exclusivity. The ex-dedicated distributors also practised freezer exclusivity, to a limited degree, by supplying retailers with freezers that were designed to showcase a variety of rival brands (industry versus standard freezers); their contracts prohibited retailers from getting their supply from rival distributors or manufacturers.

Freezer exclusivity functioned within a physical retail space, restricting or preventing entirely the primary freezer from being used to stock other manufacturers' brands. Retailers were permitted to allocate other retail space within the outlet to install other freezers to stock rival brands, and competition was additionally found tying additional freezer space in exclusivity arrangements – some retailers, however, left these freezers open for the remaining rival brands. Prominent placement of the primary freezers encouraged the approach of as much of the store's consumer traffic as possible to the brands showcased therein. Additional freezers were not usually placed as prominently. Outlet exclusivity[31] (including the franchising of mobile retail outlets[32]) operated to bar the availability of rival brands, eliminating consumer choice within the setting. Retailer reinforcement patterns contingent on freezer exclusivity appear to have been weaker than those patterns contingent on outlet exclusivity. Whereas freezer contracts lasted one year and had a 28-day opt-out clause thereafter, outlet contracts lasted for up to five years, during which time rival manufacturers are entirely 'precluded from supplying these outlets' (Competition Commission 2000, p. 59). Outlet exclusivity arrangements accounted for only 5 per cent of the market: however, BEW had clear plans to pursue exclusivity among certain high consumer traffic outlets and all other outlets wherever possible.

In general, reinforcement contingent upon manufacturers pitching and maintaining outlet exclusivity included benefits related to increasing scale of operations through greater geographic coverage of consumer traffic volumes, with the consequent increased retail penetration and market shares. The Commission notes how freezer and outlet exclusivity provided manufacturers with a relatively high degree of availability, consumer awareness, visibility and prominence within and across a whole range of retail settings.

Exclusivity was legally enforceable through contracts where manufacturers surrendered rich benefits[33] and required the imposition of sanctions in return for the mutual closure of behaviour setting scope, with the degree of closure being entirely closed for retailers but only relatively so for the manufacturer: for example, in outlet exclusivity, whereas a retailer could not sell rival brands, a manufacturer was permitted multiple exclusivity arrangements, including rival retailers.

Setting closure to retailers was affected because:

1. Availability and access to reinforcement were clearly demarcated by a small number of routes, including staying within the contract, ordering and retailing the products, maintaining adequate stock and, at times, achieving certain sales volumes. Product reinforcers defined which product ranges and brands were to be retailed, pricing reinforcers defined discounts, and promotional reinforcers included the incentives and bonuses contingent upon achieving various levels of sales. At times, these reinforcers were made more prominent, for example, through removal of the aversive consequences of purchasing and maintaining a freezer, or the presentation of additional utilitarian benefits (lump-sum payments on signing the contract) and informational benefits (merchandising and marketing support). Main prominence, however, was a function of the strength of the brands available for retail.

2. Outlet exclusivity contracts stipulated that reinforcement was contingent upon ordering from the manufacturer, while freezer exclusivity arrangements allowed retailers to obtain their stocks from any distributor dealing with the brand.

3. Contractual clauses probably defined retailer obligations explicitly. The use of standard discount and incentive schemes implied that ordering and achieving higher levels of sales were the responses to be reinforced negatively and positively.

4. Regarding the external control of the situation, ordering brands (business reinforcers) was routed through either the manufacturer or its agents. Although defection to rivals was possible to obtain ice-cream, within the exclusivity arrangement (here assumed to have been chosen on the basis of the patterns of reinforcement it signalled), only one manufacturer or its agents were available to supply the selected brand, making the supplier the sole source of supply of that brand. Consequently, the manufacturer came to control deprivation levels, becoming the sole route from which to derive the reinforcement contingent upon retail according to the terms established. Although outlet exclusivity contingencies of reinforcement and punishment were negotiable, the contingencies remained largely arranged and controlled by the marketer.[34]

5. Once the exclusivity contract was signed there were no alternatives available to retailers to being in the setting except without the punishment contingent upon escape.

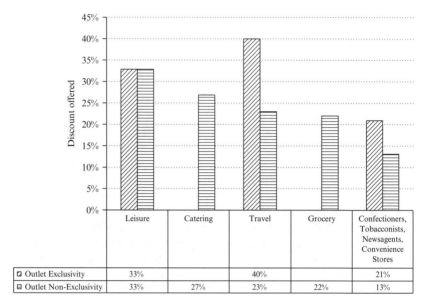

Figure 5.13   Exclusivity/non-exclusivity average total discounts per retail outlet type

The degree of setting closure in outlet exclusivity was far greater than in freezer exclusivity: in the latter cases, the retailer may have had a partially exclusive freezer arrangement or additional freezers occupied by competing brands, allowing the retailer access to a number of competing patterns of reinforcement contingent upon multiple rival brand retailing and a wider range of behaviour alternatives in any given instance. It comes as no surprise, therefore, that BEW's sales force tried dissuading retailers from having other freezers, enhancing the impact of BEW's exclusive (primary) freezers and/or installing BEW-exclusive secondary freezers.

The benefits offered appear to have been equitable enough to induce retailer approach with a high degree of competition for outlets of a certain type: this is visible from the average discounts awarded across retail types (Figure 5.13) which served in shaping and maintaining approach as well as in deterring rival encroachment. On lump-sum payments as approach inducements (reducing reinforcement delay), Nestlé lamented that competitors could not match BEW's pay-outs. The sales force appears to have been particularly instrumental in inducing and maintaining approach and in deterring avoidance and rival encroachment (including some cases of alleged malpractice).

Contracts are presumed to have described the contingencies of reinforcement, providing rules that specified the reinforcing outcomes of approach and the punishing outcome of avoidance. Direct exposure to the contingencies would have appeared to ultimately determine the duration of the exclusivity relationships. Generally, retailer approach within the contract, selling as much ice-cream as possible, was maintained through rewards which increased as the strength of approach increased – performance-related retrospective discounts directly reduced the aversive consequences of trade, while year-end bonus pay-outs (positive reinforcers) emphasised the positive effects of retailing a specific brand set. The reduction of benefits and increase in costs acted as positive and negative punishers, respectively, to sanction avoidance (slow sales) within the exclusivity contract. Although not specified within the report, penalties contingent upon breaching freezer contracts were probably lower than those relating to outlets. It is clear that the utilitarian and informational benefits of outlet exclusivity were higher than those with freezer exclusivity, which, in turn, were higher than the standard retailer terms.

Reinforcer effectiveness was managed through manipulating levels of deprivation and the quality and quantity of the reinforcers deployed. Retrospective bonuses, for example, acted to increase profits from ice-cream retail sales, consequently decreasing deprivation of profits from retailing such. Point-of-purchase materials, displays and merchandising advice acted to channel and optimise consumer traffic flow and purchase behaviour within a given retail setting, thereby reducing deprivation of sales and reinforcer delay by quickening rates of sale. The immediate provision of a free freezer signalled the probability of the exclusivity arrangement coming to quick action, thus reducing the wait for reinforcement contingent upon retailing. Reinforcement effectiveness was also managed through qualitative distinctions among the patterns of reinforcement contingent upon independent multiple brand retailing (standard terms), freezer exclusivity (standard terms plus) and outlet exclusivity (negotiated terms plus). And, within the latter, certain types of retail outlets by virtue of their size (e.g. chains of convenience stores) and ability to attract a high volume of consumer traffic owing to their location (e.g. leisure and entertainment outlets, motorway service stations) received even higher rewards.[35]

The effectiveness of brands as the ultimate source of retailer reinforcement was maintained qualitatively and quantitatively through effective investments in consumer demand (created and maintained through the reinforcement signalled by advertising), rates of brand sales (point-of-purchase displays and merchandising techniques signalling availability of reinforcers to consumers and the reinforcers communicated through advertising) and retail penetration (as a function of the utilitarian and

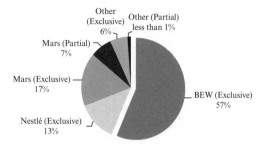

Figure 5.14 *Freezer exclusivity by the end of 1998, totalling 153,000 freezers across the UK*

informational reinforcement contingent upon outlet and exclusivity arrangements and general manufacturer terms to retailers). Underscoring these actions were manufacturer performance and the ability of each to invest in aspects of market development.

The evidence also suggests retailer behaviour being shaped and maintained by relatively high/low utilitarian/informational reinforcement.

Freezer and outlet exclusivity became rival-imposed barriers to product/ brand availability, consumer awareness, visibility and prominence within and across a whole range of retail spaces, decreasing the effective number of reinforcers (space within the stores and the number of outlets) available. Primary freezers, within a given retail space, were the only prominent reinforcers therein, since retailers placed them in conspicuous locations to encourage consumer approach. BEW's aggressive bid for freezer exclusivity (Figure 5.14) allowed it to reserve the best spaces for its brands and prominently signal their availability; in any case, BEW products were usually awarded this position by retailers because of their popularity and faster rates of sales.

Reserving space within already constrained retail capacity settings limited the ability of other manufacturers to compete in outlets with either no room for or no incentive to install additional freezers or, in the case of retail spaces with additional freezers, because secondary freezers were given reduced prominence and merchandising attention (some retailers even switched off these freezers during winter months). Manufacturers found it necessary to mimic freezer exclusivity since, as Mars pointed out, non-exclusive freezers could have been 'swamped with BEW's products' because of its wider range of brands/products and distribution together with various selling practices. BEW's market position allowed it to deprive manufacturers of high-quality visibility positions and, to a degree, manage the contingencies of reinforcement of its rivals. BEW was not entirely subject to these contingencies, because it was the owner of the strong brands and its financial stability was considerably stronger. Practising freezer exclusivity to such a wide extent allowed BEW to gain greater power in depriving its rivals of sales/profit and, therefore, in managing contingencies. The sheer investment required for increases in exclusive cabinet shares significantly penalised Nestlé and Mars. Despite increased freezer exclusivity investments, the availability of Nestlé and Mars brands remained poor.

The degree of setting closure with respect to outlets tied exclusively with a manufacturer was absolute – rivals were entirely precluded from encroachment by sheer force of legally binding contracts. Within an exclusive outlet only one manufacturer's brands were visible and available for consumer purchase. BEW's outlet exclusivity behaviour operated with effects similar to those of freezer exclusivity, including the deprivation of access to some of the more important/larger retail outlet chains.[36] Freezer and outlet exclusivity operated to quicken the pace of brand rates of sale, retail penetration and market share, with positive consequences on scale of operations.

Outlet exclusivity did not generally disadvantage distributors. The only apparent risk to the ex-dedicated distributors was that outlet exclusivity could operate to continue precluding them from serving certain types of outlets which now had direct relationships with the manufacturers. BEW outlet and freezer exclusivity practices fomented the position of Wall's Direct and Barking: as more outlets took up exclusivity, the scale of operations increased, as did production, distribution and marketing economies. Freezer exclusivity practised by manufacturers, however, appeared to endanger their position: an exclusive freezer (without additional freezers) signalled the aversive consequences of an inability to achieve the full utilitarian and informational benefits of their business model.

Therefore, the ex-dedicated distributors offered subsidised industry freezers on condition that the retailer would stock the freezers only from them: on the one hand, this would have allowed distributors to increase their multi-product and multi-brand drop sizes, while, on the other, retailers would have had the choice of several brands to stock at retail level and serve a wider range of consumer tastes. On the downside, subsidising a number of such freezers had aversive utilitarian and informational aversive consequences, including the higher cost of buying and maintaining industry (versus lower-cost standard) freezer cabinets. Moreover, their terms with BEW had significantly hurt their profitability, and the ability to sustain such practices appeared weak. With increased push for direct relationships with retailers, the ex-dedicated distributors were slowly being elbowed out of a significant market, and exclusivity arrangements endangered an already precarious position.

Distributor Responses: Ice-Cream World

The second and final instance of retaliatory behaviour by the ex-dedicated distributors was that of their forming a buying entity called Ice-Cream World (ICW) in January 1999 as a direct response to the formation of Wall's Direct. Until then, ICW members had a collective turnover of over £7.5 million and would have been able to negotiate significantly better terms with BEW while reinforcing it with a significant volume potential.

ICW signalled an important alternative to Wall's Direct with potential to open the setting by offering added choice to manufacturers and retailers alike. Given the cumulative volumes of business handled by the ex-dedicated distributors in early 1999, ICW was a potential threat to Wall's Direct: at the time of formation, the significantly large scale of ex-dedicated distributors of BEW operations signalled the possibility of passing on delivery cost savings to its customers via strong commercial terms. Further, ICW could have offered retailers the potential of carrying several manufacturer brands while gaining from volume discounts (some retailers preferred to concede stocking multiple brands to gain the higher volume discounts offered by BEW). The new entity had the potential to quicken sales rates, retail penetration and market share of the weaker brands. Not surprisingly, BEW refused to deal with ICW, thereby completely closing off opportunities to obtain the most important reinforcers for the ex-dedicated distributors – BEW's brands at better discounts for economic viability. In addition, this reduced the effectiveness of ICW's offering: the strength of retailer approach depended upon the brands ICW could distribute. On the other hand, the strength of manufacturer approach depended upon the number and quality of retailers participating as customers. Through its refusal, BEW deprived the ICW members, its prospective retail customers and, consequently, the major manufacturers of the full utilitarian benefits of network effects. Accepting ICW, as the Commission concludes, would have severely hit BEW's strong incentive to promote exclusive distribution through Wall's Direct.

NOTES

1. See Appendix A4.1 for a detailed timeline of events.
2. The distributor was simply a contractor to the manufacturer, e.g. 74 per cent of Nestlé's distribution was organised in this way.
3. See Appendix A4.2. For example, in the three summer months demand is (a) about five times higher than in the three winter months and (b) subject to large daily and weekly fluctuations. A string of related problems are outlined in Appendix A4.2, including possible erratic production runs when demand is particularly high, and the need to satisfy

retailer (as a function of consumer) demand immediately when stocks run out in good summers.

4. A unit was equal to a box of wrapped singles.
5. Most manufacturers dealt in several types of ice-cream products, and BEW manufactured non-ice-cream frozen products.
6. The dedicated distributors were not allowed to trade in rival manufacturer brands, while the non-exclusive national wholesalers distributed significant volumes of ice-cream and non-ice-cream products from BEW and were allowed to deal in rival brands.
7. The Barking operation was BEW's proprietary distribution operation covering the area within the M25 or the London Orbital motorway, which encompasses an area that has the highest population density in the UK (according to the UK Office for National Statistics). Within the M25, BEW sold direct to retailers. When, during 1998, four dedicated distributors ceased their relationship with BEW, the latter extended Barking to cover the territories previously handled by the former. Barking accounted for 10 per cent of BEW's distribution volumes.
8. See Appendix A4.3. The dedicated distributors effectively handled about 53 per cent of total BEW distribution volumes through either wholesaling or contracted-out logistical services.
9. See Appendix A4.4.
10. Freezer exclusivity appears to have further strengthened retailer approach by providing additional utilitarian positive reinforcers (free freezer or free stock) while removing related utilitarian negative reinforcers (maintenance/repair costs borne by the manufacturer).
11. While BEW and Nestlé offered a full range of impulse ice-cream, Mars and Treats offered only a part-range.
12. Typically, the wider the product ranges on offer, the stronger the approach.
13. Profitability is also a regulatory stimulus within the managerial behaviour setting that determines which stimuli signal profitable and loss-making outcomes and the behaviour to be emitted to achieve those positive or aversive outcomes. These rules are either self-imposed or imposed by others – the report shows how, for 1999, BEW had sales growth targets imposed by Unilever, its mother company, at 33 per cent. Chapter 5 of the report provides a detailed analysis of the performance of the major manufacturers. To an extent, comparisons are particularly difficult since many of the financials for Nestlé, Mars and Treats are purposely omitted by the Commission owing to confidentiality.
14. See Appendix A4.6.
15. It must be noted that, whereas previous investigations focused on specific aspects of alleged anti-competitive behaviour, by 1999 the DGFT had deemed it necessary to frame very broad terms of reference within which the Competition Commission would be able to conduct its inquiry (see also Appendix 4.1).
16. The termination of these contracts prior to their natural expiry was allowed by the relevant competition law in view of the undertakings then being finalised.
17. The total investment figure in Wall's Direct was undisclosed. Part of this investment, however, cost above £10 million.
18. These were stated objectives by BEW's management in its proposal to Unilever.
19. A considerable number of dedicated distributors either refused to become part of Wall's Direct or failed the tendering process BEW held in late 1998 for the outsourcing contracts under Wall's Direct. The extent of dedicated distributor avoidance was unexpected by BEW as stated in the report.
20. These additional terms, already noted, will be examined more fully in later sections. At this stage, suffice it to say that the terms were typically communicated to retailers via distributors – there appeared to be little social contact between BEW and such retailers. The evidence suggests the critical importance of sales relationships (the social dimension) with retailers.
21. In marketing mix terms, the sales force is a promotion variable.

22. See Figure 5.3, Figure 5.11 and Appendix A4.8. Direct accounts emerged as an important and significant source of revenue/profits for BEW and the ex-dedicated distributors, and the report shows that these were hotly contended. Prior to 1999, BEW held only exchange relationships with direct retail accounts, while the ex-dedicated distributors retained the mutuality *social* aspect, i.e. the personal contact with the retailer. This social aspect seems to have been important to BEW, as the evidence shows how (a) the ex-dedicated distributors lost considerably more sales to Wall's Direct than any of the other distributors and (b) the heaviest losses were from direct accounts.

23. See Appendix A4.8. The report shows that most ex-dedicated distributors stated they could not achieve their targets.

24. The rules of an economically viable business model exist in the managerial behaviour setting of all firms.

25. Total BEW sales handled by the ex-dedicated distributors fell 42 per cent, with an average decline of 21 per cent in indirect sales and an average decline of 59 per cent in direct sales.

26. (Differential) retail terms are discussed in later sections.

27. See Appendix A4.2. For example, each unit cost 1.4p to store in a central warehouse or 1.3 per cent of the standard deduction.

28. In one case, BEW was alleged to have paid the retailer a lump sum of £50 000 to gain outlet exclusivity. These lump-sum payments operated to reduce reinforcer delay.

29. Appendix A4.9 presents the retailer terms of supply of BEW, which are similar to the ones offered by Nestlé and Mars.

30. Appendices A4.10 and A4.11 describe the generic patterns of reinforcement that shape and maintain freezer and outlet exclusivity behaviour as gleaned from the report.

31. By virtue of the 1979 undertakings, manufacturers were only allowed to enter into outlet exclusivity arrangements at the request of the retailer.

32. See Appendix A4.9.1.

33. Appendix A4.9 shows the topography of benefits. BEW is used as an example since the report contains immense detail on its practices in contrast to the other manufacturers. The report shows how the policies used by rivals were very similar, including offering differential terms according to strengths of approach.

34. Certain types of retail outlets, by virtue of their size (e.g. chains of convenience stores) and ability to attract a high volume of consumer traffic, owing to their location (e.g. leisure and entertainment outlets, motorway service stations), were the subject of considerable competition because of the utilitarian benefits that would accrue from having them on exclusivity terms. In one case, BEW offered higher discounts to a retailer to offset the loss of sales resulting from that retailer not accepting exclusivity. Oddly, the Commission does not make mention of the possibility that, if outlets of certain importance were heavily contended for by the manufacturers, during negotiations retailers would have every incentive to behave opportunistically, pitting rivals against each other to squeeze out the best possible deals. This is an important factor contributing to the generous discounts paid out for exclusivity and that remained entirely unexplored by the Commission. It is not surprising that, overall, retailers did not comment negatively on freezer and outlet exclusivity.

35. Whereas non-exclusive outlets were offered total discounts/benefits of up to 13 to 33 per cent off list price, outlets with BEW exclusivity were offered total discounts of between 33 and 40 per cent (with some cases as high as 45 per cent and over).

36. The Commission notes how BEW secured the Granada Motorway Services contract, the largest chain of motorway retail outlets.

6. Reflections on 'the marketing firm'

THE ANTECEDENTS PROPOSITION

The preceding analysis shows that firms come under the control of several antecedent events. The formation of Wall's Direct was also a clear example of attempts to close the setting directly through scope stimuli but also through consequential stimuli, providing support for Foxall's (1997a) contention that managing reinforcement patterns does, at times, function in the same way as setting closure by channelling behaviour in a particular direction.

Discriminative Stimuli and Motivating Operations

A range of physical, regulatory, social and temporal antecedent stimuli were identified as residing in the actors' managerial behaviour setting and were found to be controlling behaviour over two decades.[1] These four dimensions of stimuli for consumer behaviour suggested by Foxall (1990, 1992a, 1992b, 1997a) provide an important framework within which to analyse antecedent events and their effects. Equally critical is the distinction in behaviourist literature (Michael 1982; Fagerstrøm et al. 2010) between discriminative stimuli and motivating operations.

Towards the end of 1998, the undertakings agreed with BEW were a regulatory stimulus designed by the Commission to constrain BEW's behaviour, thereby opening the behaviour setting. It appears that the Commission assumed that BEW, as it had done before, would comply with the undertakings. In addition, the Commission appears to have assumed that the *ability to discriminate* was the one strategy BEW sought to protect. By imposing punishment on BEW, the setting would be more open, as independent wholesalers, now unfettered by the aversive consequences the relativities in terms created, would be able to compete against the dedicated distributors on an identical rewards structure. However, the new rules set in motion a significant but unexpected outcome: the formation of Wall's Direct.[2]

The Commission's attempt at curbing specific behaviour on BEW's part through relevant punishment did not fail to garner the designed outcome because of some inattention or lack of rigour in research. Rather, from an operant perspective, the evidence suggests that these informational (punishing) stimuli had a motivating rather than discriminative function to BEW: such a distinction in the nature of stimuli appears to provide a deeper analytical frame within which BEW's subsequent behaviour (i.e. the formation of Wall's Direct and surrounding events) may be adequately explained.

A discriminative stimulus signals the availability of reinforcement and/ or punishment. A motivating operation, on the other hand, is an event that establishes or abolishes the reinforcing/punishing effects of other stimuli ('value-altering effects') and, independently but simultaneously, evokes or abates the responses associated with those stimuli ('behaviour-altering effects') (Fagerstrøm *et al.* 2010).

Until direct exposure to the contingency came into force (on 1 March 1999) the undertakings were informational negative punishers deployed by the Commission – the removal of benefits to weaken the differential pricing behaviour. The punishers signalled feedback on BEW's anti-competitive behaviour, the legally enforceable aversive utilitarian consequences that would come about if the firm continued on its route, and the loss of utilitarian benefits that BEW, in the past, had derived from price discrimination. Previously, BEW had been reinforced from the sheer utilitarian benefits derived from various strengths of approach across all channel tiers – from the strongest and most favourable dedicated distribution, to a weaker, but equally favourable, national wholesaling, to the least favourable independent wholesaling of multiple manufacturer brand distribution. BEW used discriminatory terms to create rules signalling the differential patterns of reinforcement and punishment contingent upon approach and avoidance. The firm, therefore, *shaped and maintained the strength and incidence of customer behaviour according to what was most favourable to it.*

The evidence is testament to the net positive outcomes generated over a history of shaping and maintaining extremely strong approach behaviour among its channel partners and increasing its incidence. The potential loss of utilitarian benefits was immense: from the reported discussions held by BEW's management, the punishers seemed to threaten the extensive distribution/retail/consumer market share, retail penetration and coverage it had built through its dedicated system. The evidence shows that BEW's learning history and, especially, the objectives (as rules) set by its mother company imbued the punishers defined in the undertakings with particular salience.

What the Commission failed to recognise was that the ability to present differential terms was a secondary reinforcer by virtue of its long-range association in the behaviour sequences emitted by BEW to derive the utilitarian and informational reinforcement contingent upon shaping and maintaining the strongest levels of approach from among its channel members (Alhadeff 1982). In other words, it was not the ability to discriminate that BEW wanted to retain but rather the ability to shape and maintain the approach strengths/incidence of its intermediaries. Over the years, BEW had simply used price discrimination as a highly effective tool to do just that. However, the punishers designed by the Commission simply removed the tool rather than extinguished the emission of the behaviour of direct import. Therefore, the informational punishers had both a value-altering effect and a behaviour-altering effect and were motivating operations.

1. The negative punishers signalled the distinct probability of lower utilitarian (e.g. the direct economic rewards) and informational (e.g. Unilever's rule of maintaining 'maximum control on the total distribution chain'; Competition Commission 2000, p. 447) reinforcers as a direct consequence of emitting compliant behaviour. Thus, the punishers changed the effectiveness of these reinforcers as reinforcers while precluding the behaviour which, historically, produced these reinforcers (value-altering).
2. The punishers increased the frequency of that behaviour that had been previously reinforced: not price discrimination behaviour but the ability to shape and maintain approach strength and incidence among its customers. This is the behaviour-altering effect. The evidence is irrefutable in this respect: the Commission notes how, as a direct consequence of the undertakings, BEW terminated its dedicated distributor contracts, replacing them with a fully outsourced, vertically integrated alternative that, by 2002, would completely replace independent wholesalers, avoiding the need to discriminate between dedicated and independent distributors by simply eliminating the exclusive third-party wholesaling system. In this way, price discrimination at the distribution tier was no longer necessary – through outsourced non-wholesaling, contractual relationships created stability and predictability, since the terms and obligations therein prescribed the exact strengths and incidence of approach and proscribed avoidance and escape for the duration of such. In fact, although the dedicated distributors were asked to form part of the Wall's Direct contractor relationships, they were also expected to change their business model.

Similarly, the termination of the dedicated distributor contracts appears to have achieved motivational function among at least some of the ex-dedicated distributors: the cancellation of the contract signalled the end to the significantly generous pattern of utilitarian and informational reinforcement contingent upon exclusivity, in particular volume discounts, performance-related bonuses and incentives, together with scale benefits. Impending termination (26 February 1999) also signalled the aversive consequences arising from investments made to support their dedicated relationship with BEW, from their previous obligation to pass on all customer information, and some who distributed only BEW brands. Such cancellation increased the effectiveness of previously available reinforcers, while it precluded access to them. This was the value-altering effect. If the formation of ICW is interpreted as an increased emission of behaviour the main outcomes of which were the utilitarian and informational benefits derived from trading in large volumes of BEW ice-cream, then this would be the behaviour-altering effect of the motivating operation. The preceding analysis shows how the ex-dedicated distributors were previously reinforced by the benefits of dealing in high volumes. BEW's special incentive to make Wall's Direct successful also seems to have acquired this motivational function.

The above discussion and the analysis in Chapter 5 provide strong support for RP_1.

MUTUALLY REINFORCING RELATIONSHIPS

Clearly, the relationships of mutuality, exchange and mutuality-plus-exchange among manufacturers, distributors and retailers were mutually reinforcing, with exchange playing an important role. The evidence provided details on the structure utilitarian and informational reinforcement took (Figure 6.1 to 6.3) and yielded insight on structural aspects of mutuality. Most importantly, the reinforcement patterns in mutuality appeared to include utilitarian benefits as discerned in the retailer terms offered by manufacturers even though exchange was carried out between distributor and retailer. Secondly, mutuality appears to have a social dimension, with BEW significantly extending its sales force through outsourced contracts to win back retail customers from the ex-dedicated distributors. Both these aspects do not emerge from the theory of the marketing firm.

The theory of the marketing firm proposes that exchange is a prerequisite to economic relationships (Foxall 1999a). However, a singular episode runs counter to some extent: BEW's redefinition of direct accounts to shift exchange away from its relationships with retailers towards the Distributor↔Retailer bilateral contingency. The preceding analysis interpreted this move as part of BEW's ex-dedicated distributors of BEW

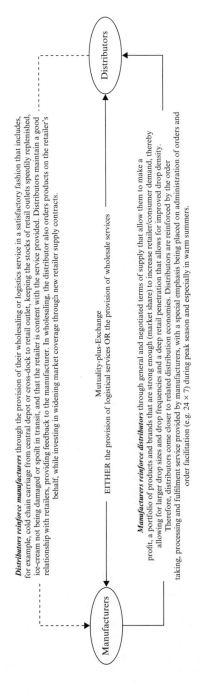

Distributors reinforce manufacturers through the provision of their wholesaling or logistics service in a satisfactory fashion that includes, for example, cold chain carriage from central depot or cross-dock to retail outlet, keeping the stocks of retail outlets speedily replenished, ice-cream not being damaged or spoilt in transit, and that the retailer is content with the service provided. Distributors maintain a good relationship with retailers, providing feedback to the manufacturer. In wholesaling, the distributor also orders products on the retailer's behalf, while investing in widening market coverage through new retailer supply contracts.

Mutuality-plus-Exchange

EITHER the provision of logistical services OR the provision of wholesale services

Manufacturers reinforce distributors through general and negotiated terms of supply that allow them to make a profit, a portfolio of products and brands that are strong enough (market share) to increase retailer/consumer demand, thereby allowing for larger drop sizes and drop frequencies and a deep retail penetration that allows for improved drop density.

Therefore, distributors come closer to related distribution economies. Distributors are reinforced by the order taking, processing and fulfilment service provided by manufacturers, with a special emphasis being placed on administration of orders and order facilitation (e.g. 24 × 7) during peak season and especially in warm summers.

Figure 6.1 Mutually reinforcing relationships: Manufacturer↔Distributor

Mutuality Relationships

Rivals reinforce each other through the extent to which they respond to each other's actions. In freezer exclusivity, for example, BEW's behaviour acted as a stimulus for retaliatory actions by Mars, Nestlé, Treats and 30 other manufacturers. Outlet exclusivity, in contrast, was only pursued by Nestlé and Mars again in retaliation. The nature of these competitor actions was also important, with BEW management asking its sales force to be its "eyes and ears" and reporting " any competitor activity of a new or unusual nature immediately". The quality and quantity of marketing stimuli deployed in the setting to attract customers away from each other also appear important. Rivals, generally, punished each other for encroachment on consumer, retailer and distributor market share. The degree of fair and unfair practice also appeared to have punishing effects.

Figure 6.2 Mutually reinforcing relationships: Manufacturer↔Rival

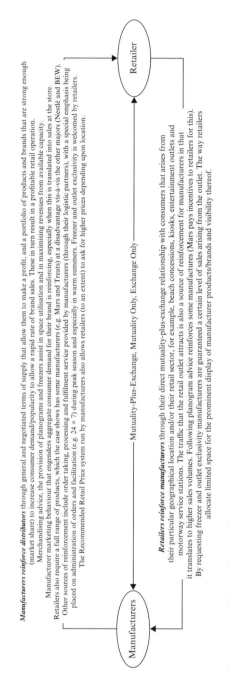

Manufacturers reinforce distributors through general and negotiated terms of supply that allow them to make a profit, and a portfolio of products and brands that are strong enough (market share) to increase consumer demand/popularity to allow a rapid rate of brand sales. These in turn result in a profitable retail operation.

Merchandising advice, the provision of planograms and freezers assist in space utilisation and in maximising revenues from available capacity.

Manufacturer marketing behaviour that engenders aggregate consumer demand for their brand is reinforcing, especially when this is translated into sales at the store.

Retailers also require a full range of products, which the case shows has some manufacturers (e.g. Mars and Treats) at a disadvantage vis-à-vis the other majors (Nestlé and BEW).

Other sources of reinforcement include order taking, processing and fulfilment service provided by manufacturers (through their logistic partners), with a special emphasis being placed on administration of orders and facilitation (e.g. 24 × 7) during peak season and especially in warm summers. Freezer and outlet exclusivity is welcomed by retailers.

The Recommended Retail Price system run by manufacturers also allows retailers (to an extent) to ask for higher prices depending upon location.

Mutuality-Plus-Exchange, Mutuality Only, Exchange Only

Retailers reinforce manufacturers through their direct mutuality-plus-exchange relationship with consumers that arises from their particular geographical location and/or their retail sector, for example, beach concessions, kiosks, entertainment outlets and motorway service stations. The traffic that the retail outlet attracts is also a source of reinforcement for manufacturers in that it translates to higher sales volumes. Following planogram advice reinforces some manufactures (Mars pays incentives to retailers for this).

By requesting freezer and outlet exclusivity manufacturers are guaranteed a certain level of sales arising from the outlet. The way retailers allocate limited space for the prominent display of manufacturer products/brands and visibility thereof.

Figure 6.3   Mutually reinforcing relationships: Manufacturer↔Retailer

reinforcement/punishment management programme – by increasing the transaction costs of Wall's Direct rivals (the ex-dedicated distributors) already in a weakened state, BEW could shape their independent whole-saling activities towards stronger approach or simply compel the surrender of direct accounts or both. This seems to imply that it is not important that literal exchange occurs within a particular relationship as long as it occurs somewhere downstream within the boundaries of other relationships connected to the manufacturer. This would also suggest that the boundaries of the firm are a function of the gamut of exchange and non-exchange contingency relationships. Coase (1937) suggests that firms decrease the number of transactions they handle (i.e. decrease in size) if they cannot organise them more efficiently than the market. However, BEW seems to have been better equipped than the ex-dedicated distributors to handle these transactions given its scale of operations.[3] On the other hand, it may simply have been a temporary measure, a form of shaping distributor behaviour towards abandoning the accounts so that BEW could later step in and again subsume exchange within the relationship, entrenching itself further at retail and shutting off the setting to distributors and rivals.[4]

Mutual interdependence among firms is strongly evident: reciprocity appeared across the entire channel including in Manufacturer↔Rival relationships. The dominance of one firm created a series of related behaviours side- and downstream. In support of Xiao and Nicholson's (2010) findings, the preceding analysis shows firms and regulator entwined in mutually reinforcing relationships. Figure 6.4, an adaptation from the relevant literature (Foxall 1990, 1999a), captures the complex inter-relatedness of supplier–customer relationships within the context of direct regulator intervention.

THE SCOPE AND REINFORCEMENT MANAGEMENT PROPOSITIONS

Approach, Avoidance and Escape

A functional analysis of economic behaviour identifies two response classes, approach and avoidance/escape. The operational definitions proved useful to a considerable extent in identifying the topographic forms of behaviour that suppliers and customers attempted to engender in the case.[5]

The analysis shows that the major manufacturers designed patterns of utilitarian and informational reinforcement of distributors and retailers to distinguish between various strengths of approach to shape and maintain such behaviour and weaken or extinguish avoidance/escape.

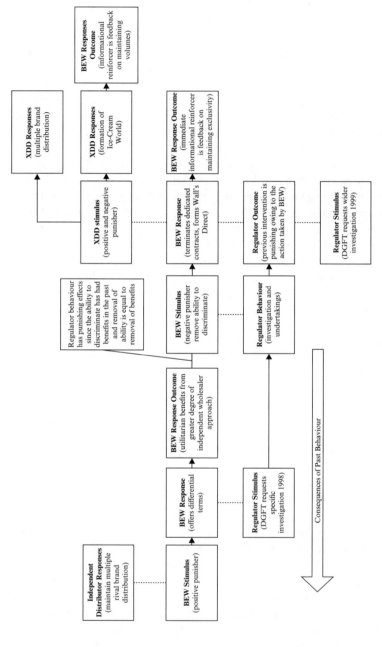

Figure 6.4   Dynamics of marketer–regulator interactions in the context of the 1998 undertakings

110

The strength of distributor and retailer approach to a manufacturer appears to have been a function of (a) the strength or potency of consumer approach behaviour to the manufacturer's brands in terms of demand and sold volumes, and (b) the incidence of this approach or the rate of occurrence, which, at the retail level of analysis, was seen to relate to the rate of brand sales. The analysis suggests that it is only within this frame that the patterns of reinforcement signalled by brands as business reinforcers would assume discriminative or motivational function and would come to influence approach/avoidance. The stronger and faster consumer approach behaviour towards a given brand at retail, the stronger distributor and retailer approach would be towards the owner of that brand. Moreover, faster rates of distributor and retailer approach result in higher levels of retail penetration and market shares.

The Commission's findings on consumer behaviour are reminiscent of academic research which suggests the functional substitutability of brands (Foxall *et al.* 2004) and multiple brand purchasing (Foxall *et al.* 2007), both phenomena underscoring the importance of brand availability in consumer choice. The literature also corroborates the Commission's remarks on the importance of merchandising (Buttle 1984) and 'locational convenience' (Kotler 1973) in channelling consumer behaviour at retail: from store traffic through merchandising and atmospherics to impulse purchases. Given these factors, it would seem only reasonable to find a high degree of marketing effort that utilises advertising to mould and strengthen aggregate consumer demand and quicken the incidence of this demand by rendering one set of brands more available than others. It also seems reasonable to find competitive action that impedes availability at store level across the entire retail sector through merchandising and other exclusivity arrangements – Buttle found setting closure tactics involving manufacturers supplying their own freezers to retailers (Buttle 1984, p. 111). The evidence also elucidates on the problem of 'double jeopardy' (Foxall 2005): consumers, perhaps, buy less of weaker brands owing to rival activity limiting their availability on a wide scale.

A descriptive framework is generated from the evidence and depicted in Figure 6.5 to show how, in aggregate, the various marketing variables work to encourage approach behaviour at all levels to foster retail penetration and market share.

Setting Scope and Reinforcement Management

Firms used price and non-price variables of the mix to shape and maintain customer behaviour. Marketer-controlled stimuli were embodied in the various marketing mix elements of price, product, promotion and place,

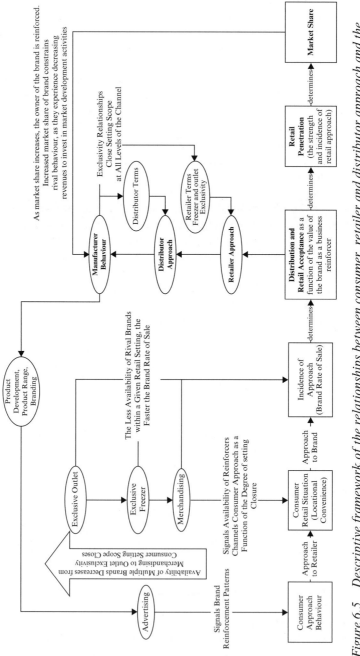

Figure 6.5   Descriptive framework of the relationships between consumer, retailer and distributor approach and the marketing stimuli used by manufacturers

and the stimuli were used as either reinforcers to strengthen behaviour or punishers to weaken it depending upon the situation.[6]

An operant account of firm economic behaviour is represented in a complex pattern of bilateral contingencies where the behaviour of one of the parties to the relationship acts as a discriminative stimulus to the other party. A complex sequence of contingencies emerges (Foxall 1999a), as is seen in Figure 6.4. To examine the central contentions of the theory of the marketing firm, those represented in RP_2 and RP_3, a set of research questions were designed to incorporate this reciprocity element.[7] Unfortunately, this is where the data failed the research project: there was very little data on how retailers and distributors managed manufacturer reinforcement patterns and setting scope. Thus, only six out of the eight sub-research propositions ($RP_{2.1}$ to $RP_{2.3}$ and $RP_{3.1}$ to $RP_{3.3}$) found direct empirical support. There are events implied in the data, however, that provide some support to $RP_{2.3}$ (retailers manage the patterns of reinforcement of manufacturers): for example, if outlets of certain importance were heavily contended by manufacturers, industry experience strongly suggests that during negotiations retailers would have every incentive to behave opportunistically, pitting rivals against each other to squeeze out the best possible deal. This could be plausibly interpreted as an indication of a degree of manufacturer reinforcement management on the part of such retailers. Therefore, on this basis, $RP_{2.3}$ is partially accepted. $RP_{3.3}$ (retailers manage the setting scope of manufacturers) is also partially accepted: it is plausible to assume that negotiated mobile franchising contracts allowed certain manufacturer behaviours (e.g. having several franchises) while proscribing others (e.g. the manufacturer is not allowed to have a second franchisee within the same territory). According to the theory of the marketing firm this is mutual qualification of setting scope.

The analysis demonstrates amply downstream reinforcement and setting scope management in Manufacturer↔Distributor and Manufacturer↔Retailer relationships. These two strategies were not mutually exclusive but used in tandem and designed to simultaneously strengthen the probability of approach and weaken the probability of avoidance. Topographically, the strategies have not changed over a 30-year period, providing support to similar findings cited by Hannan and Freeman (1989). Manufacturers were also found mimicking the dominant firm, with the implication that they too manage scope and consequential stimuli. BEW's dominance in the market is spectacular and appears to have enabled it to impose rules of engagement side- and downstream. The behaviour it emitted throughout 1999, clearly, had been reinforced over several decades in the UK ice-cream market. BEW was reinforced by the positive consequences of shaping, maintaining and strengthening favourable customer behaviour while reducing the aversive consequences arising from transaction costs of such (and transaction costs refer to the entire cost base of the firm). All industry behaviour seems to revolve around attempting both to increase custom and to decrease the resulting transaction costs.

The formation of ICW as a distributor response requires some attention. ICW's success hinged entirely upon two strengths of approach:

1. the strength of manufacturer approach, which depended on the net utilitarian and informational benefits contingent upon the strength and incidence of retailer approach, i.e. contingent upon the net rewards derived from having many retailers on board or sufficient retail penetration to generate higher volumes, revenues and profits; and
2. the strength of retailer approach, which depended on the net utilitarian and informational benefits contingent upon the strength and incidence of manufacturer approach, i.e. contingent upon the net rewards from having many manufacturers on board – opportunities to gain higher volume discounts and reduce the impact of the aversive consequences of distribution through further improvements in retailer pricing.

This is the 'chicken-and-egg' problem of 'two-sided' markets with network effects: the dilemma that relates to the need for businesses operating in such markets that require establishing simultaneously the buying and selling sides of the market to achieve a critical mass of revenues – similar to credit card networks, where banks need to ensure that a critical mass of merchants is available to accept credit cards and a critical mass of consumers is available to use the credit cards (Evans 2001, 2002). The network effects of ICW would occur when the increased usage of the distribution service offered increased its utilitarian and informational function: with a larger number of retailers approaching the system, higher retail penetration would be increasingly more probable. Through higher penetration would come the benefits of higher sales volumes and a larger scale of operations. As scale grew, improved terms could be offered to retailers. With a larger number of manufacturers approaching the system, the benefits of higher volume discounts across a wider range of rival brands would become more likely. By the sheer force of BEW's retail penetration and market share, ICW required the ability to offer the prized business reinforcers, BEW brands. Through its refusal (complete setting closure), BEW denied the ex-dedicated distributors their ability to sell the strongest brands in the market and gain from the full utilitarian and informational benefits of the network effects of the ICW system.

With the formation of Wall's Direct, BEW faced a similar dilemma. By directly owning the manufacturing system it guaranteed the strength of manufacturer approach. Yet such approach depended upon the strength of a sufficiently large scale of operations to offer strong terms to retailers. Therefore, it had to regain the sales volumes transacted by the ex-dedicated distributors and thus moved towards that direction, as shown in the previous analysis. On the retail side, BEW needed to ensure enough volumes to further increase and maintain its scale of operations. This is also evidenced in the preceding discussion. Such an analysis goes further than the one provided by the Commission, which completely disregarded this common economic problem. The dual-sided nature of the market in establishing a distribution system was a central determinant of BEW's behaviour and provides a deeper explanation of why it refused to acknowledge ICW. The theory of the marketing firm requires explicitly recognising the nature of the market as a rule within the managerial behaviour setting.

Patterns of Reinforcement

The theory of the marketing firm, by virtue of its operant foundations and direct influences from operant consumer behaviour studies, assumes that the rate of emission of behaviour by the firm is a function of utilitarian and informational reinforcement contingent upon such behaviour. The evidence provides support to this contention with, for example, retailers within their outlet and freezer exclusivity arrangements appearing to be maintained from relatively high/low levels of utilitarian/informational reinforcement.

The theory of the marketing firm makes no mention of which behaviour alternatives are chosen by the firm. Throughout the analysis, firms have been assumed to conform to *melioration* as contemplated in the matching law. Choice is assumed as the rate of manifest operant behaviour distributed over time. The matching law states that behaviour over time is allocated between activities in proportion to the benefits derived from each. Melioration underlies matching: whereas matching is a molar account dealing with overall relative rates over time, melioration is a molecular account that attempts an explanation of momentary behaviour. Melioration predicts that, at any point in time, given a choice of two mutually exclusive responses, the one with the higher local rate of reinforcement will be selected by the individual (Herrnstein 1997).[8]

The consumer behaviour literature suggests three broad techniques with which reinforcement patterns are managed. Certain difficulty was encountered in applying the last of these techniques to the data, that of managing the schedules of reinforcement.[9] Evidence of such management proved difficult to locate because of the complexities of behaviour in natural settings: yet two aspects of schedule management were of particular importance: (a) reinforcement delay and its manipulation, with shorter waiting times for reinforcement appearing to encourage approach, and (b) the manipulation of the number of responses to be emitted before obtaining reinforcement. For example, BEW changed the packaging of its units to increase the number of wrapped singles contained therein so that (a) distributors were delayed in obtaining reinforcement, since now retailers had to sell more singles before ordering an additional one unit, and (b) with per unit bonus levels remaining unchanged, distributors had to be more aggressive in their sales efforts to increase unit volumes (i.e. increased number of responses) to achieve previous bonus levels. The interaction of these two factors, the objectives of distribution scale economies and sales and the poorer patterns of reinforcement offered by BEW increased the effectiveness of BEW deployed punishers.

THE COMPETITION PROPOSITION

Competitive mutuality relationships are influenced by all other bilateral contingency relationships held by the firm (Foxall 1999a; Xiao and Nicholson 2010): when approach to a rival brand occurs, the firm is negatively influenced (positive punishment), while, when a rival brand is avoided, the firm is positively reinforced (only when that avoidance occurs in its favour). Foxall (1999a) proposed that managing rival behaviour entails scope and reinforcer management arising both as a sheer consequence of attracting customer approach and as a deliberate act (RP_4). Practices are both fair and unfair or distortive/anti-competitive. Empirical support in favour of RP_4 was amply found within the case, with punishment always involving deprivation through utilitarian positive/ negative punishers: a reduction of earnings capability and/or increasing the transaction costs of customer acquisition and retention. The problem, however, arose in finding an adequate descriptor to encompass the notions of 'behaviour in a direction that is beneficial/not beneficial to the manufacturer'. The evidence suggested *encroachment* as a term more suited than 'approach' or 'avoidance', with strategies designed to bar (outlet exclusivity) and punish (bonus scales designed by BEW) encroachment.

NOTES

1. Appendices A5.1 to A5.3 contrast a full topography of the stimuli identified as ante-cedent events in the managerial behaviour settings of manufacturers, distributors and retailers.
2. In its 1998 report, the Commission, however, had already claimed the possibility of BEW taking distribution in-house.
3. Chapter 5 showed how the standard terms offered to the ex-dedicated distributors (£1.10+£0.98) were significantly lower than the per unit delivery costs of Wall's Direct (£3.33) and Barking (£1.78), both of which were calculated on significantly larger scales of operation.
4. The potential risks on sales and profits of losing these accounts to rivals were not noted in the report.
5. Appendix A5.4 describes the structural form of approach and avoidance within Manufacturer↔Distributor and Manufacturer↔Retailer relationships.
6. Appendix A5.5 includes a complete topography of the marketing mix elements used.
7. The research questions drawn from the four propositions are laid out in Appendix 2 as the Case Study Protocol.
8. Maximisation theory arrives at a similar prediction even though matching does not indi-cate maximisation (Foxall and Schrezenmaier 2003; Foxall 2010): maximisation implies the highest returns on profits, while matching states average rates of reinforcement (Herrnstein 1997).
9. See also Chapter 4.

7. Conclusions

EMPIRICAL EVALUATION AND GENERAL RESEARCH DIRECTIONS

The study sought to evaluate the explanatory power of the theory of the marketing firm. The results of the case study suggest strong empirical support to the central propositions of the theory, confirming its potential as a rival theory of the firm despite being embryonic.

The application of operant psychology together with economic and applied disciplines provided a robust framework within which to generate an understanding of firm behaviour. The usefulness of the three-term contingency was augmented through the introduction of motivating operations (MO) and the use of the four-term contingency as a framework $MO:S^D:R \rightarrow S^{r/p}$ (Fagerstrøm *et al.* 2010). Although the concept requires further study within the context of firm behaviour, it emerged as instrumental in explaining why firms emitted certain behaviour and shows analytical and predictive promise. The analysis demonstrates how both price and non-price marketing mix variables were combined to operate at various levels, thereby confirming the importance of considering both demand elasticity and plasticity in an analysis of firm behaviour.

Scope and reinforcer management were not mutually exclusive strategies; rather they were used in combination and at various levels of the channel, down- and side-stream, simultaneously encouraging approach, deterring avoidance, punishing escape, imposing barriers and punishing/ deterring encroachment to reveal a complex tapestry of firm behaviour. The evidence runs counter to Foxall's (1997a, 1999a) suggestion that managing behaviour scope is a short-term behaviour modification strategy while reinforcement management is a longer-term approach. Both were equally viable in the short and long term and, in outlet exclusivity, the surrender of control by retailers was reinforced by generous patterns of reinforcement over periods of up to five years, suggesting that both strategies, when used jointly, are significantly more effective in shaping and maintaining long-term behaviour. As Foxall (1999a) suggests, by closing the setting the firm is able to predict and control the behaviour of others.

Further, the stability that mutuality is conceived to bring with it appears to arise directly from the attractiveness of the overall patterns of reinforcement contingent upon remaining within the relationship.

The notion of economising on transaction costs (Coase 1937) emerged as a very important element. However, neglecting customer acquisition and retention as a parallel ingredient to the firm's existence would not have resulted in a complete picture. It is only through consideration of both aspects that a full understanding of firm behaviour could be drawn out. Through its central claim that firms exist to acquire and retain customers *and* economise on related transaction costs, the theory of the marketing firm provided valuable insights to their behaviour within the case. A number of authors (e.g. Foss and Klein 2008; Pitelis and Teece 2009) argue that transaction costs are not sufficient to fully explain firms: the evidence seems to support these claims. Industry experience strongly suggests that practitioners juggle between the need to acquire and retain customers while increasing return on marketing investments. The evidence also suggests that the cost-minimisation and differentiation generic strategic choices pro-offered by Porter (1980) were not mutually exclusive alternatives to the industry incumbents, as his theory would suggest. Firms outpaced (Gilbert and Strebel 1989): in defending the formation of Wall's Direct to the Commission, BEW invoked innovation through service differentiation. It may be true that BEW's practices were distortive and anti-competitive; however, its reported behaviour shows a strong element of innovation across its entire scope of operations over the years. For example, BEW always provided a significantly higher quality of service in the marketplace, originally through the dedicated distributors and later through Wall's Direct.[1] Further, such innovative behaviour appeared critical to bar rival encroachment and manage retailer scope and consequential cues. In parallel, BEW strived for a large scale of operations to enjoy transaction cost economies across the board.

The concept of bilateral contingency relationships was equally useful: mutual reinforcement within supplier–customer relationships was evident even though the process of identifying which outcomes reinforced/punished which behaviour proceeded by inference from operant, economic and marketing principles. It was reasonable to assume, for example, that higher sales levels reinforced customer acquisition and retention. The analysis sheds more light on the concepts of mutuality and mutuality-plus-exchange relationships. However, a more complete picture would have emerged if the dataset placed greater importance on Retailer↔Consumer and Distributor↔Retailer relationships.

The analysis suggests that, while some relationships did not entail exchange, others did. Manufacturers depended entirely on the final exchange between retailer and consumer but not necessarily on whole-saling services. Retailers depended on the production and marketing of manufacturer brands but not necessarily on wholesaling services. Downstream and upstream integration circumventing some channel transactions occurred to get parties closer to these contingencies. This probably occurred to reduce the transaction costs of getting to market and/or simply to be closer to the contingencies to ensure some degree of predictability and control.

The analysis demonstrates how BEW circumvented the costs of han-dling exchange transactions by shifting legal title downstream, in so doing changing the relationship previously held with retailers from mutuality-plus-exchange to mutuality. Despite the interpretation given within the analysis, this action remains puzzling. One implication is that it would run counter to the theory of the marketing firm: perhaps such exchange does not need to occur within a particular relationship as long as it occurs further downstream within the relationship boundaries of the firm. Alternatively, it might simply have been a temporary ploy. Further study on the nature of mutuality needs to be carried out.

Approach, avoidance and escape were equally useful behaviour terms but required further elucidation through structural descriptions to provide deeper meaning to theory. This was especially evident in the rival bilateral contingency relationship. The theory of the marketing firm implies that firm boundaries are defined by the extent of the relationships held by the firm. The analysis adds the dimension that the basis of some of these boundaries is collaborative while the basis of others is competi-tive and shows how these boundaries evolved and changed. The theory needs to incorporate firm boundaries within its explanandum, with the collaborative/competitive distinctions, as this would appear to predict the form scope and reinforcer management could take: collaborative, as a weave of reinforcers and punishers the quality and quantity of which depend upon the strength of approach, and competitive, as generally a blanket of punishers for any form of rival encroachment. Further, the discussion on BEW's redefinition of the direct accounts (see Chapter 6) poses the question as to whether firm boundaries need to incorporate the firm directly: if exchange is being carried out on its behalf within other relationships, do these other relationships form part of the firm's boundaries?

The theory of the marketing firm does not explore learning history, and only cursory mention was made of the managerial behaviour setting, as the original 'Theory of the Marketing Firm' paper was focused on providing a sketch of how an operant theory of the firm from a mar-keting perspective would be structured. By the principle of continuity from consumer behaviour analysis (Foxall 2001, 2002, 2010), the study expanded on the concept, and evidence was found that the consequences of past action impinge on the present. Rules within the managerial behaviour setting, whether imposed by corporate headquarters or generated through planning, appeared equally important. Further expansion of this concept is critical. An explanation of the internal organisation of the firm incorporating the managerial behaviour setting from an operant perspective is needed.

The analysis demonstrates the importance of rule-setting and rule-following behaviour of the firms in the industry. This suggests that firm verbal behaviour is an extremely important aspect that requires considerable attention.

Retailer behaviour within exclusivity relationships emerged from the analysis to be shaped and maintained by high/low levels of utilitarian/informational reinforcement. Unfortunately, the data does not provide any conclusive evidence of the patterns (relatively high versus relatively low) of reinforcement that shape and maintain manufacturers and distributors. Generally, firm behaviour within the examined contexts appeared to fall under the hedonism operant class (see Table 2.1), with particular emphasis on relatively high utilitarian reinforcement. Yet, if most behaviour outcomes have both utilitarian and informational functions (Foxall 1997a), then the high levels of utilitarian reinforcement found certainly imply high levels of informational outcomes, which together would imply the accomplishment operant class. Further, as economics considers utilitarian benefits as the only source of reinforcement, informational reinforcement assumes a particular emphasis of interest that requires attention.

The theory of the marketing firm suggests that firms are generally limited in their control of the setting. Yet rivals appeared to be vying for control, with one company having achieved extensive control of the setting and with specific objectives for such. The formation of ICW may be plausibly interpreted as an attempt to reassert control on the part of the ex-dedicated distributors. Is this because firms are reinforced by the utilitarian and informational rewards contingent upon setting control? Or is it simply a common trait of firms investigated for anti-competitive conduct? Why do some firms seek (and obtain) market dominance?

In conclusion, the theory of the marketing firm with the suggested refinements introduced provides an interesting and useful explanation to most of the relationships of interest. The theory has promise, but requires much further attention, including an empirically based comparative analysis with rival theories.

METHODOLOGICAL LIMITATIONS

In designing and conducting the study, the authors gave full attention to developing a plausible, valid and reliable account of firm behaviour. In hindsight, the methodology followed was robust in its application. A number of issues and limitations did emerge:

1. One of the initial problems related to whether an inductive or deductive approach was to be followed. Without the combined inductive/deductive approach adopted, it would not have been possible to fully grasp the nuances of the literature and the data, and much would have been lost. For example, the concept of motivating operations, although mentioned in the literature review, was explored in depth late during the analysis; yet its introduction generated important insights that deepened the interpretation. It was not until most of the analysis was carried out that the explanatory significance of the concept emerged.

2. Reading the data carefully very early in the process also aided the analysis and provided a guide to outlining additional literature to review. The report is detailed and voluminous, and an appropriate coding method had to be established a priori (the three-term contingency framework was especially useful). This also involved extensive study of operant principles to ensure that inference proceeded according to specific patterns contemplated therein. Yet time constraints curtailed probing further and, hence, some elements might be missing.

3. Some methodological texts are correct to challenge the positivist notion of the researched not being affected by the researcher – the report clearly shows that the 1998 investigation was a catalyst that quickened the pace of the events that were analysed therein. This also suggests a limitation in that the reported behaviour of the firms was a one-off occurrence and, therefore, the support found in favour of the theory of the marketing firm propositions is purely circumstantial. Perhaps this is true; yet no claims to generalisability outside the case confines are being made or implied. Suffice it to say, the evidence suggests further study on several fronts within an operant theory of the marketing firm perspective. Further, this study should be replicated across a selection of similar reports published by the Commission and a cross-case analysis carried out.

4. Earlier, reference was made to the lack of data in attending to propositions under the reinforcement and scope management propositions. The method devised in operationalising the bilateral contingencies

does not seem to be the issue. Theory requires a patterned sequence of stimuli and responses that are closely connected. The data narrated aggregate strategies rather than chains of events. This mismatch between theory and data requires due attention in designing future research either as an acceptable trade-off or as unacceptable and, therefore, warranting primary data collection. Related to this problem was the omission of certain evidence because it was not deemed of public interest and more attention being given to BEW's behaviour – hence the data on BEW was considerably richer. Comparisons were thus difficult in some respects. The study recognises this limitation and considered this earlier in the research when defining the case focus. Also, the final proposed undertakings were disregarded, an acceptable and conscious omission resulting directly from the case focus (Miles and Huberman 1994). Also related to the data is the possibility that some of it contains considerable error (see Competition Commission 2000, p. 109, and Table A4.2). In this respect, the analysis proceeded, as much as possible, on relative descriptions and inferences rather than absolutes.

5. It was difficult to match actual instances of approach/avoidance/ escape to specific stimuli, and reliance had to be placed on the statements made by the Commission. Any misinterpretations of the direct evidence made by the Commission are, therefore, a limitation to this study. Whereas operant psychology deals with individual instances (e.g. it is clear that the undertakings were a significant determinant to the final formation of Wall's Direct), the study had to deal with aggregates and proceed through inference in some respects (e.g. BEW deployed several marketing stimuli and sales increased). The assumption made was that firms were expected to behave that way, as marketing and economic texts and personal experience imply.

6. One final issue was the need to demonstrate that all the data was attended to for the sake of reliability and validity. Given the time limit constraints this, admittedly, proved most challenging. Approximately two months was allocated to the iterative process of studying the report to ensure that all the main themes were attended to. Developing the case focus and dedicating appropriate time to data analysis techniques were critical in this respect.

The study we have described is an early foray into empirical research on the marketing firm and a stepping stone towards an applied behaviour analytic approach to firm behaviour or firm behaviour analysis.

NOTE

1. Interestingly, Stiglitz (2010) notes how, most recently, American banks innovated through the deployment of new financial instruments designed specifically to circumvent financial regulations and thus improve firm effective leverage.

Appendix 1.   Pre-structured case
outline

The pre-structured outline collects and organises the data around the following concepts drawn directly from the research propositions and research questions:

1. Antecedent stimuli prior to 1999 investigation and regulatory intervention
   - 1.1   Existing relationships and nature of reinforcement
   - 1.2   Antecedents in the managerial behaviour setting
   - 1.3   Regulatory intervention and related undertakings
   - 1.4   Undertakings as direct antecedents to behaviour
2. The 1999 investigation: behaviour in the setting
   - 2.1   Manufacturers managing scope and reinforcement of distributors
   - 2.2   Manufacturers managing scope and reinforcement of retailers
   - 2.3   Distributors managing scope and reinforcement of manufacturers
   - 2.4   Retailers managing scope and reinforcement of manufacturers
   - 2.5   Manufacturers managing scope and reinforcement of rivals

Appendix 2. The case study protocol

Research objective:	To generate an empirically based evaluation and resultant insights into the theory of the marketing firm through the construction of adequate operational measures and the application of such measures to qualitative data.
Research question:	How adequately does the theory of the marketing firm explain the marketing behaviour of premium brand manufacturers in their bilateral contingency relationships with rivals, distributors and retailers vis-à-vis the supply of wrapped impulse ice-cream in the United Kingdom?
Case focus:	A study of the marketing behaviour of major premium ice-cream manufacturers in their bilateral contingency relationships with rivals, distributors and retailers in the supply of wrapped impulse ice-cream in the UK as described by the report published by the Competition Commission in 2000.
Main unit of analysis:	Bilateral contingencies: Manufacturer↔Distributor Manufacturer↔Retailer Manufacturer↔Rivals
Embedded units (manufacturers): Embedded units (distributors):	BEW and Wall's Direct BEW ex-dedicated distributors
Research proposition 1: the antecedents proposition	RP$_1$: Specific antecedent events including regulator intervention have, historically, come to control firm behaviour, with some of these stimuli maintaining stimulus control. In direct response to the regulator's intervention in 1998, firms immediately affected by the sanctions imposed upon them will attempt to close the behaviour setting.

Research questions:

RQ$_{1a}$ What contingencies (S^D: $R \rightarrow S^{r/p}$ relationships) were in operation in the behaviour setting prior to the start of the December 1998 investigation?

RQ$_{1b}$ Why do these contingencies acquire stimulus function, i.e. what are the utilitarian and informational positive and aversive consequences that they appear to signal?

RQ$_{1c}$ What firm behaviour may be directly associated with the remedies suggested by the Commission in its 1998 report and the resultant undertakings with the Secretary of State?

Research proposition 2: the reinforcement management proposition

RP$_2$: The behaviour within Manufacturer$\leftrightarrow$Distributor and Manufacturer$\leftrightarrow$Retailer relationships is characterised by the management of patterns of reinforcement through marketing mix elements to encourage approach, discourage avoidance and bar escape of customers and suppliers.

RP$_{2.1}$: Manufacturers manage patterns of reinforcement of their distribution customers through the marketing mix to simultaneously encourage approach, discourage avoidance and bar escape.

RP$_{2.2}$: Manufacturers manage patterns of reinforcement of their retail customers through the marketing mix to simultaneously encourage approach, discourage avoidance and bar escape.

RP$_{2.3}$: Distributors manage supplier patterns of reinforcement through the marketing mix to simultaneously encourage approach, discourage avoidance and bar escape.

RP$_{2.4}$: Retailers manage supplier patterns of reinforcement through the marketing mix to simultaneously encourage approach, discourage avoidance and bar escape.

Research questions:

RQ$_2$ How do manufacturers, distributors and retailers in their Supplier$\leftrightarrow$Customer relationships manage patterns of reinforcement through the marketing mix to simultaneously encourage approach, discourage avoidance and bar escape?

Sub-research questions according to main unit of analysis

Manufacturer↔Distributor bilateral contingency

Manufacturer→

How do manufacturers manage the patterns of utilitarian and informational reinforcement of distributors through the marketing mix? Which strategies are designed for approach? Which for avoidance? Are these strategies simultaneously deployed?

Price

How do manufacturers manage the patterns of utilitarian and informational reinforcement of distributors through price? Which strategies are designed for approach? Which for avoidance? Are these strategies simultaneously deployed?

Product

How do manufacturers manage the patterns of utilitarian and informational reinforcement of distributors through product? Which strategies are designed for approach? Which for avoidance? Are these strategies simultaneously deployed?

Promotion

How do manufacturers manage the patterns of utilitarian and informational reinforcement of distributors through promotion? Which strategies are designed for approach? Which for avoidance? Are these strategies simultaneously deployed?

Place

How do manufacturers manage the patterns of utilitarian and informational reinforcement of distributors through place? Which strategies are designed for approach? Which for avoidance? Are these strategies simultaneously deployed?

Distributor→

How do distributors manage the patterns of utilitarian and informational reinforcement of suppliers through the marketing mix? Which strategies are designed for approach? Which for avoidance? Are these strategies simultaneously deployed?

Price

How do distributors manage the patterns of utilitarian and informational reinforcement of suppliers through price? Which strategies are designed for approach? Which for avoidance? Are these strategies simultaneously deployed?

Product

How do distributors manage the patterns of utilitarian and informational reinforcement of suppliers through the product? Which strategies are designed for approach? Which for avoidance? Are these strategies simultaneously deployed?

Promotion

How do distributors manage the patterns of utilitarian and informational reinforcement of suppliers through promotion? Which strategies are designed for approach? Which for avoidance? Are these strategies simultaneously deployed?

Place

How do distributors manage the patterns of utilitarian and informational reinforcement of suppliers through place? Which strategies are designed for approach? Which for avoidance? Are these strategies simultaneously deployed?

Manufacturer↔Retailer bilateral contingency

Manufacturer→

How do manufacturers manage the patterns of utilitarian and informational reinforcement of retailers through the marketing mix? Which strategies are designed for approach? Which for avoidance? Are these strategies simultaneously deployed?

Price

How do manufacturers manage the patterns of utilitarian and informational reinforcement of retailers through price? Which strategies are designed for approach? Which for avoidance? Are these strategies simultaneously deployed?

Product

How do manufacturers manage the patterns of utilitarian and informational reinforcement of retailers through product? Which strategies are designed for approach? Which for avoidance? Are these strategies simultaneously deployed?

Promotion

How do manufacturers manage the patterns of utilitarian and informational reinforcement of retailers through promotion? Which strategies are designed for approach? Which for avoidance? Are these strategies simultaneously deployed?

	Place
	How do manufacturers manage the patterns of utilitarian and informational reinforcement of retailers through place? Which strategies are designed for approach? Which for avoidance? Are these strategies simultaneously deployed?
	How do distributors manage the patterns of utilitarian and informational reinforcement of manufacturers through the marketing mix? Which strategies are designed for approach? Which for avoidance? Are these strategies simultaneously deployed?
Retailers→	*Price*
	How do retailers manage the patterns of utilitarian and informational reinforcement of manufacturers through price? Which strategies are designed for approach? Which for avoidance? Are these strategies simultaneously deployed?
	Product
	How do retailers manage the patterns of utilitarian and informational reinforcement of manufacturers through the product? Which strategies are designed for approach? Which for avoidance? Are these strategies simultaneously deployed?
	Promotion
	How do retailers manage the patterns of utilitarian and informational reinforcement of manufacturers through promotion? Which strategies are designed for approach? Which for avoidance? Are these strategies simultaneously deployed?
	Place
	How do retailers manage the patterns of utilitarian and informational reinforcement of manufacturers through place? Which strategies are designed for approach? Which for avoidance? Are these strategies simultaneously deployed?
Research proposition 3: the scope management proposition	RP₃: The behaviour within Manufacturer↔Distributor and Manufacturer↔Retailer relationships is characterised by the management of behaviour setting scope through marketing mix elements to encourage approach, discourage avoidance and bar escape of customers and suppliers.

RP$_{3.1}$: Manufacturers manage the scope of the behaviour setting through marketing mix elements to simultaneously encourage approach, discourage avoidance and bar escape of their distribution customers.

RP$_{3.2}$: Manufacturers manage the scope of the behaviour setting through marketing mix elements to simultaneously encourage approach, discourage avoidance and bar escape of their retail customers.

RP$_{3.3}$: Distributors manage the scope of the behaviour setting through marketing mix elements to simultaneously encourage approach, discourage avoidance and bar escape of their suppliers.

RP$_{3.4}$: Retailers manage the scope of the behaviour setting through marketing mix elements to simultaneously encourage approach, discourage avoidance and bar escape of their suppliers.

Research questions:

RQ$_3$

How do manufacturers, distributors and retailers in their Supplier↔Customer relationships manage the behaviour setting scope through the marketing mix to simultaneously encourage approach, discourage avoidance and bar escape?

Sub-research questions according to main unit of analysis

Manufacturer↔Distributor bilateral contingency

Manufacturer→

How do manufacturers manage the behaviour setting scope of distributors through the marketing mix? Which strategies are designed for approach? Which for avoidance? Are these strategies simultaneously deployed?

Price

How do manufacturers manage the behaviour setting scope of distributors through price? Which strategies are designed for approach? Which for avoidance? Are these strategies simultaneously deployed?

Product

How do manufacturers manage the behaviour setting scope of distributors through product? Which strategies are designed for approach? Which for avoidance? Are these strategies simultaneously deployed?

Promotion

How do manufacturers manage the behaviour setting scope of distributors through promotion? Which strategies are designed for approach? Which for avoidance? Are these strategies simultaneously deployed?

Place

How do manufacturers manage the behaviour setting scope of distributors through place? Which strategies are designed for approach? Which for avoidance? Are these strategies simultaneously deployed?

How do distributors manage the behaviour setting scope of suppliers through the marketing mix? Which strategies are designed for approach? Which for avoidance? Are these strategies simultaneously deployed?

Price

How do distributors manage the behaviour setting scope of suppliers through price? Which strategies are designed for approach? Which for avoidance? Are these strategies simultaneously deployed?

Product

How do distributors manage the behaviour setting scope of suppliers through the product? Which strategies are designed for approach? Which for avoidance? Are these strategies simultaneously deployed?

Promotion

How do distributors manage the behaviour setting scope of suppliers through promotion? Which strategies are designed for approach? Which for avoidance? Are these strategies simultaneously deployed?

Distributor→

Place

How do distributors manage the behaviour setting scope of suppliers through place? Which strategies are designed for approach? Which for avoidance? Are these strategies simultaneously deployed?

Manufacturer↔Retailer bilateral contingency

Manufacturer→

How do manufacturers manage the behaviour setting scope of retailers through the marketing mix? Which strategies are designed for approach? Which for avoidance? Are these strategies simultaneously deployed?

Price

How do manufacturers manage the behaviour setting scope of retailers through price? Which strategies are designed for approach? Which for avoidance? Are these strategies simultaneously deployed?

Product

How do manufacturers manage the behaviour setting scope of retailers through product? Which strategies are designed for approach? Which for avoidance? Are these strategies simultaneously deployed?

Promotion

How do manufacturers manage the behaviour setting scope of retailers through promotion? Which strategies are designed for approach? Which for avoidance? Are these strategies simultaneously deployed?

Place

How do manufacturers manage the behaviour setting scope of retailers through place? Which strategies are designed for approach? Which for avoidance? Are these strategies simultaneously deployed?

Retailers→

How do distributors manage the behaviour setting scope of manufacturers through the marketing mix? Which strategies are designed for approach? Which for avoidance? Are these strategies simultaneously deployed?

Price

How do retailers manage the behaviour setting scope of manufacturers through price? Which strategies are designed for approach? Which for avoidance? Are these strategies simultaneously deployed?

Product

How do retailers manage the behaviour setting scope of manufacturers through the product? Which strategies are designed for approach? Which for avoidance? Are these strategies simultaneously deployed?

Promotion

How do retailers manage the behaviour setting scope of manufacturers through promotion? Which strategies are designed for approach? Which for avoidance? Are these strategies simultaneously deployed?

Place

How do retailers manage the behaviour setting scope of manufacturers through place? Which strategies are designed for approach? Which for avoidance? Are these strategies simultaneously deployed?

Research proposition 4: the competition proposition

$RP_{4,1}$: The behaviour within Manufacturer→Rival relationships is characterised by the management of patterns of reinforcement through marketing mix elements to produce behaviour on the part of rivals in a direction that is beneficial to the manufacturer.

$RP_{4,2}$: The behaviour within Manufacturer→Rival relationships is characterised by the management of behaviour setting scope through marketing mix elements to produce behaviour on the part of rivals in a direction that is beneficial to the manufacturer.

Research questions:

$RQ_{4,1}$

How do manufacturers manage the patterns of reinforcement of rivals through elements of the marketing mix to produce behaviour response in rivals that is beneficial to the manufacturer?

$RQ_{4.2}$

How do manufacturers manage the behaviour setting scope of their rivals through elements of the marketing mix to produce behaviour response in rivals that is beneficial to the manufacturer?

Sub-research questions according to main unit of analysis

Manufacturer↔Rival bilateral contingency

Manufacturer→ Rivals→

How do manufacturers manage the patterns of reinforcement of rivals through elements of the marketing mix to produce behaviour response in rivals that is beneficial to the manufacturer?

Price

How do manufacturers manage the patterns of reinforcement of rivals through price to produce behaviour response in rivals that is beneficial to the manufacturer?

Product

How do manufacturers manage the patterns of reinforcement of rivals through product to produce behaviour response in rivals that is beneficial to the manufacturer?

Promotion

How do manufacturers manage the patterns of reinforcement of rivals through promotion to produce behaviour response in rivals that is beneficial to the manufacturer?

Place

How do manufacturers manage the patterns of reinforcement of rivals through price to place behaviour response in rivals that is beneficial to the manufacturer?

Appendix 3.   Coding scheme

The coding scheme revolves around the three main relationships of interest, Manufacturer↔Distributor, Manufacturer↔Retailer and Manufacturer ↔Rival. The coding reflects (a) the dyadic aspect of the relationships, (b) the four elements of the marketing mix, (c) a programme designed to strengthen approach and weaken avoidance, (d) the use of reinforcement and punishment for these behaviours, (e) a classification of stimuli according to operant theory, (f) whether each stimulus is used to qualify the setting or to manage reinforcement and (g) whether the exposure to the contingencies is direct, or indirect through a rule imposed by one party or implied in the managerial behaviour setting of the other.

So, for example, the tag 'Manufacturer → Avoidance → Price → Punishers → Negative → Reinforcement → Management → Informational → Distributor Rule' refers to 'Manufacturer deployed stimuli to weaken avoidance by removing negative (pricing) punishers that signal informational reinforcement. Exposure to the contingencies is indirect through a rule in the distributor managerial behaviour setting.' The intuitive tags are not abbreviated purposely to allow very rapid coding of the text.

Code	Description and rule

Manufacturer↔Distributor relationships (manufacturer-deployed stimuli)

Strengthening distributor approach (through reinforcement)

Price

Code	Description and rule
Manufacturer→Approach→Price→Reinforcers→Positive→ Scope Management→Setting→Direct Exposure to Contingency	Manufacturer-deployed stimuli to strengthen approach by presenting positive (Price) reinforcers that have an impact on the setting. Exposure to the contingencies is direct.
Manufacturer→Approach→Price→Reinforcers→Positive→ Scope Management→Setting→Manufacturer Rule	Manufacturer-deployed stimuli to strengthen approach by presenting positive (Price) reinforcers that have an impact on the setting. Exposure to the contingencies is indirect through a rule made by a manufacturer.
Manufacturer→Approach→Price→Reinforcers→Positive→ Scope Management→Setting→Distributor Rule	Manufacturer-deployed stimuli to strengthen approach by presenting positive (Price) reinforcers that have an impact on the setting. Exposure to the contingencies is indirect through a rule in the distributor managerial behaviour setting.
Manufacturer→Approach→Price→Reinforcers→Positive→ Reinforcement Management→Utilitarian→Direct Exposure to Contingency	Manufacturer-deployed stimuli to strengthen approach by presenting positive (Price) reinforcers that signal utilitarian reinforcement. Exposure to the contingencies is direct.
Manufacturer→Approach→Price→Reinforcers→Positive→ Reinforcement Management→Utilitarian→Manufacturer Rule	Manufacturer-deployed stimuli to strengthen approach by presenting positive (Price) reinforcers that signal utilitarian reinforcement. Exposure to the contingencies is indirect through a rule made by a manufacturer.
Manufacturer→Approach→Price→Reinforcers→Positive→ Reinforcement Management→Utilitarian→Distributor Rule	Manufacturer-deployed stimuli to strengthen approach by presenting positive (Price) reinforcers that signal utilitarian reinforcement. Exposure to the contingencies is indirect through a rule in the distributor managerial behaviour setting.

Code	Description and rule
Manufacturer→Approach→Price→Reinforcers→Positive→ Reinforcement Management→Informational→Direct Exposure to Contingency	Manufacturer-deployed stimuli to strengthen approach by presenting positive (Price) reinforcers that signal informational reinforcement. Exposure to the contingencies is direct.
Manufacturer→Approach→Price→Reinforcers→Positive→ Reinforcement Management→Informational→ Manufacturer Rule	Manufacturer-deployed stimuli to strengthen approach by presenting positive (Price) reinforcers that signal informational reinforcement. Exposure to the contingencies is indirect through a rule made by a manufacturer.
Manufacturer→Approach→Price→Reinforcers→Positive→ Reinforcement Management→Informational→Distributor Rule	Manufacturer-deployed stimuli to strengthen approach by presenting positive (Price) reinforcers that signal informational reinforcement. Exposure to the contingencies is indirect through a rule in the distributor managerial behaviour setting.
Manufacturer→Approach→Price→Reinforcers→Negative→ Scope Management→Setting→Direct Exposure to Contingency	Manufacturer-deployed stimuli to strengthen approach by removing negative (Price) reinforcers that have an impact on the setting. Exposure to the contingencies is direct.
Manufacturer→Approach→Price→Reinforcers→Negative→ Scope Management→Setting→Manufacturer Rule	Manufacturer-deployed stimuli to strengthen approach by removing negative (Price) reinforcers that have an impact on the setting. Exposure to the contingencies is indirect through a rule made by a manufacturer.
Manufacturer→Approach→Price→Reinforcers→Negative→ Scope Management→Setting→Distributor Rule	Manufacturer-deployed stimuli to strengthen approach by removing negative (Price) reinforcers that have an impact on the setting. Exposure to the contingencies is indirect through a rule in the distributor managerial behaviour setting.
Manufacturer→Approach→Price→Reinforcers→Negative→ Reinforcement Management→Utilitarian→Direct Exposure to Contingency	Manufacturer-deployed stimuli to strengthen approach by removing negative (Price) reinforcers that signal utilitarian reinforcement. Exposure to the contingencies is direct.

Manufacturer→Approach→Price→Reinforcers→Negative→Reinforcement Management→Utilitarian→Manufacturer Rule	Manufacturer-deployed stimuli to strengthen approach by removing negative (Price) reinforcers that signal utilitarian reinforcement. Exposure to the contingencies is indirect through a rule made by a manufacturer.
Manufacturer→Approach→Price→Reinforcers→Negative→Reinforcement Management→Utilitarian→Distributor Rule	Manufacturer-deployed stimuli to strengthen approach by removing negative (Price) reinforcers that signal utilitarian reinforcement. Exposure to the contingencies is indirect through a rule in the distributor managerial behaviour setting.
Manufacturer→Approach→Price→Reinforcers→Negative→Reinforcement Management→Informational→Direct Exposure to Contingency	Manufacturer-deployed stimuli to strengthen approach by removing negative (Price) reinforcers that signal informational reinforcement. Exposure to the contingencies is direct.
Manufacturer→Approach→Price→Reinforcers→Negative→Reinforcement Management→Informational→Manufacturer Rule	Manufacturer-deployed stimuli to strengthen approach by removing negative (Price) reinforcers that signal informational reinforcement. Exposure to the contingencies is indirect through a rule made by a manufacturer.
Manufacturer→Approach→Price→Reinforcers→Negative→Reinforcement Management→Informational→Distributor Rule	Manufacturer-deployed stimuli to strengthen approach by removing negative (Price) reinforcers that signal informational reinforcement. Exposure to the contingencies is indirect through a rule in the distributor managerial behaviour setting.
Product	
Manufacturer→Approach→Product→Reinforcers→Positive→Scope Management→Setting→Direct Exposure to Contingency	Manufacturer-deployed stimuli to strengthen approach by presenting positive (Product) reinforcers that have an impact on the setting. Exposure to the contingencies is direct.
Manufacturer→Approach→Product→Reinforcers→Positive→Scope Management→Setting→Manufacturer Rule	Manufacturer-deployed stimuli to strengthen approach by presenting positive (Product) reinforcers that have an impact on the setting. Exposure to the contingencies is indirect through a rule made by a manufacturer.

Code	Description and rule
Manufacturer→Approach→Product→Reinforcers→Positive→Scope Management→Setting→Distributor Rule	Manufacturer-deployed stimuli to strengthen approach by presenting positive (Product) reinforcers that have an impact on the setting. Exposure to the contingencies is indirect through a rule in the distributor managerial behaviour setting.
Manufacturer→Approach→Product→Reinforcers→Positive→Reinforcement Management→Utilitarian→Direct Exposure to Contingency	Manufacturer-deployed stimuli to strengthen approach by presenting positive (Product) reinforcers that signal utilitarian reinforcement. Exposure to the contingencies is direct.
Manufacturer→Approach→Product→Reinforcers→Positive→Reinforcement Management→Utilitarian→Manufacturer Rule	Manufacturer-deployed stimuli to strengthen approach by presenting positive (Product) reinforcers that signal utilitarian reinforcement. Exposure to the contingencies is indirect through a rule made by a manufacturer.
Manufacturer→Approach→Product→Reinforcers→Positive→Reinforcement Management→Utilitarian→Distributor Rule	Manufacturer-deployed stimuli to strengthen approach by presenting positive (Product) reinforcers that signal utilitarian reinforcement. Exposure to the contingencies is indirect through a rule in the distributor managerial behaviour setting.
Manufacturer→Approach→Product→Reinforcers→Positive→Reinforcement Management→Informational→Direct Exposure to Contingency	Manufacturer-deployed stimuli to strengthen approach by presenting positive (Product) reinforcers that signal informational reinforcement. Exposure to the contingencies is direct.
Manufacturer→Approach→Product→Reinforcers→Positive→Reinforcement Management→Informational→Manufacturer Rule	Manufacturer-deployed stimuli to strengthen approach by presenting positive (Product) reinforcers that signal informational reinforcement. Exposure to the contingencies is indirect through a rule made by a manufacturer.
Manufacturer→Approach→Product→Reinforcers→Positive→Reinforcement Management→Informational→Distributor Rule	Manufacturer-deployed stimuli to strengthen approach by presenting positive (Product) reinforcers that signal informational reinforcement. Exposure to the contingencies is indirect through a rule in the distributor managerial behaviour setting.

Manufacturer→Approach→Product→Reinforcers→Negative →Scope Management→Setting→Direct Exposure to Contingency	Manufacturer-deployed stimuli to strengthen approach by removing negative (Product) reinforcers that have an impact on the setting. Exposure to the contingencies is direct.
Manufacturer→Approach→Product→Reinforcers→Negative →Scope Management→Setting→Manufacturer Rule	Manufacturer-deployed stimuli to strengthen approach by removing negative (Product) reinforcers that have an impact on the setting. Exposure to the contingencies is indirect through a rule made by a manufacturer.
Manufacturer→Approach→Product→Reinforcers→Negative →Scope Management→Setting→Distributor Rule	Manufacturer-deployed stimuli to strengthen approach by removing negative (Product) reinforcers that have an impact on the setting. Exposure to the contingencies is indirect through a rule in the distributor managerial behaviour setting.
Manufacturer→Approach→Product→Reinforcers→Negative →Reinforcement Management→Utilitarian→Direct Exposure to Contingency	Manufacturer-deployed stimuli to strengthen approach by removing negative (Product) reinforcers that signal utilitarian reinforcement. Exposure to the contingencies is direct.
Manufacturer→Approach→Product→Reinforcers→Negative →Reinforcement Management→Utilitarian→Manufacturer Rule	Manufacturer-deployed stimuli to strengthen approach by removing negative (Product) reinforcers that signal utilitarian reinforcement. Exposure to the contingencies is indirect through a rule made by a manufacturer.
Manufacturer→Approach→Product→Reinforcers→Negative →Reinforcement Management→Utilitarian→Distributor Rule	Manufacturer-deployed stimuli to strengthen approach by removing negative (Product) reinforcers that signal utilitarian reinforcement. Exposure to the contingencies is indirect through a rule in the distributor managerial behaviour setting.
Manufacturer→Approach→Product→Reinforcers→Negative →Reinforcement Management→Informational→Direct Exposure to Contingency	Manufacturer-deployed stimuli to strengthen approach by removing negative (Product) reinforcers that signal informational reinforcement. Exposure to the contingencies is direct.
Manufacturer→Approach→Product→Reinforcers→Negative →Reinforcement Management→Informational→ Manufacturer Rule	Manufacturer-deployed stimuli to strengthen approach by removing negative (Product) reinforcers that signal informational reinforcement. Exposure to the contingencies is indirect through a rule made by a manufacturer.

Code	Description and rule
Manufacturer→Approach→Product→Reinforcers→Negative →Reinforcement Management→Informational→Distributor Rule	Manufacturer-deployed stimuli to strengthen approach by removing negative (Product) reinforcers that signal informational reinforcement. Exposure to the contingencies is indirect through a rule in the distributor managerial behaviour setting.
Promotion	
Manufacturer→Approach→Promotion→Reinforcers→ Positive→Scope Management→Setting→Direct Exposure to Contingency	Manufacturer-deployed stimuli to strengthen approach by presenting positive (Promotion) reinforcers that have an impact on the setting. Exposure to the contingencies is direct.
Manufacturer→Approach→Promotion→Reinforcers→ Positive→Scope Management→Setting→Manufacturer Rule	Manufacturer-deployed stimuli to strengthen approach by presenting positive (Promotion) reinforcers that have an impact on the setting. Exposure to the contingencies is indirect through a rule made by a manufacturer.
Manufacturer→Approach→Promotion→Reinforcers→ Positive→Scope Management→Setting→Distributor Rule	Manufacturer-deployed stimuli to strengthen approach by presenting positive (Promotion) reinforcers that have an impact on the setting. Exposure to the contingencies is indirect through a rule in the distributor managerial behaviour setting.
Manufacturer→Approach→Promotion→Reinforcers→ Positive→Reinforcement Management→Utilitarian→Direct Exposure to Contingency	Manufacturer-deployed stimuli to strengthen approach by presenting positive (Promotion) reinforcers that signal utilitarian reinforcement. Exposure to the contingencies is direct.
Manufacturer→Approach→Promotion→Reinforcers→ Positive→Reinforcement Management→Utilitarian→ Manufacturer Rule	Manufacturer-deployed stimuli to strengthen approach by presenting positive (Promotion) reinforcers that signal utilitarian reinforcement. Exposure to the contingencies is indirect through a rule made by a manufacturer.
Manufacturer→Approach→Promotion→Reinforcers→ Positive→Reinforcement Management→Utilitarian→ Distributor Rule	Manufacturer-deployed stimuli to strengthen approach by presenting positive (Promotion) reinforcers that signal utilitarian reinforcement. Exposure to the contingencies is indirect through a rule in the distributor managerial behaviour setting.

Manufacturer-deployed stimuli to strengthen approach by presenting positive (Promotion) reinforcers that signal informational reinforcement. Exposure to the contingencies is direct.

Manufacturer-deployed stimuli to strengthen approach by presenting positive (Promotion) reinforcers that signal informational reinforcement. Exposure to the contingencies is indirect through a rule made by a manufacturer.

Manufacturer-deployed stimuli to strengthen approach by presenting positive (Promotion) reinforcers that signal informational reinforcement. Exposure to the contingencies is indirect through a rule in the distributor managerial behaviour setting.

Manufacturer-deployed stimuli to strengthen approach by removing negative (Promotion) reinforcers that have an impact on the setting. Exposure to the contingencies is direct.

Manufacturer-deployed stimuli to strengthen approach by removing negative (Promotion) reinforcers that have an impact on the setting. Exposure to the contingencies is indirect through a rule made by a manufacturer.

Manufacturer-deployed stimuli to strengthen approach by removing negative (Promotion) reinforcers that have an impact on the setting. Exposure to the contingencies is indirect through a rule in the distributor managerial behaviour setting.

Manufacturer-deployed stimuli to strengthen approach by removing negative (Promotion) reinforcers that signal utilitarian reinforcement. Exposure to the contingencies is direct.

Manufacturer→Approach→Promotion→Reinforcers→ Positive→Reinforcement Management→Informational→ Direct Exposure to Contingency

Manufacturer→Approach→Promotion→Reinforcers→ Positive→Reinforcement Management→Informational→ Manufacturer Rule

Manufacturer→Approach→Promotion→Reinforcers→ Positive→Reinforcement Management→Informational→ Distributor Rule

Manufacturer→Approach→Promotion→Reinforcers→ Negative→Scope Management→Setting→Direct Exposure to Contingency

Manufacturer→Approach→Promotion→Reinforcers→ Negative→Scope Management→Setting→Manufacturer Rule

Manufacturer→Approach→Promotion→Reinforcers→ Negative→Scope Management→Setting→Distributor Rule

Manufacturer→Approach→Promotion→Reinforcers→ Negative→Reinforcement Management→Utilitarian→ Direct Exposure to Contingency

Code	Description and rule
Manufacturer→Approach→Promotion→Reinforcers→ Negative→Reinforcement Management→Utilitarian→| Manufacturer Rule	Manufacturer-deployed stimuli to strengthen approach by removing negative (Promotion) reinforcers that signal utilitarian reinforcement. Exposure to the contingencies is indirect through a rule made by a manufacturer.
Manufacturer→Approach→Promotion→Reinforcers→ Negative→Reinforcement Management→Utilitarian→ Distributor Rule	Manufacturer-deployed stimuli to strengthen approach by removing negative (Promotion) reinforcers that signal utilitarian reinforcement. Exposure to the contingencies is indirect through a rule in the distributor managerial behaviour setting.
Manufacturer→Approach→Promotion→Reinforcers→ Negative→Reinforcement Management→Informational→ Direct Exposure to Contingency	Manufacturer-deployed stimuli to strengthen approach by removing negative (Promotion) reinforcers that signal informational reinforcement. Exposure to the contingencies is direct.
Manufacturer→Approach→Promotion→Reinforcers→ Negative→Reinforcement Management→Informational→ Manufacturer Rule	Manufacturer-deployed stimuli to strengthen approach by removing negative (Promotion) reinforcers that signal informational reinforcement. Exposure to the contingencies is indirect through a rule made by a manufacturer.
Manufacturer→Approach→Promotion→Reinforcers→ Negative→Reinforcement Management→Informational→ Distributor Rule	Manufacturer-deployed stimuli to strengthen approach by removing negative (Promotion) reinforcers that signal informational reinforcement. Exposure to the contingencies is indirect through a rule in the distributor managerial behaviour setting.
Place	
Manufacturer→Approach→Place→Reinforcers→Positive→ Scope Management→Setting→Direct Exposure to Contingency	Manufacturer-deployed stimuli to strengthen approach by presenting positive (Place) reinforcers that have an impact on the setting. Exposure to the contingencies is direct.

Manufacturer→Approach→Place→Reinforcers→Positive→ Scope Management→Setting→Manufacturer Rule	Manufacturer-deployed stimuli to strengthen approach by presenting positive (Place) reinforcers that have an impact on the setting. Exposure to the contingencies is indirect through a rule made by a manufacturer.
Manufacturer→Approach→Place→Reinforcers→Positive→ Scope Management→Setting→Distributor Rule	Manufacturer-deployed stimuli to strengthen approach by presenting positive (Place) reinforcers that have an impact on the setting. Exposure to the contingencies is indirect through a rule in the distributor managerial behaviour setting.
Manufacturer→Approach→Place→Reinforcers→Positive→ Reinforcement Management→Utilitarian→Direct Exposure to Contingency	Manufacturer-deployed stimuli to strengthen approach by presenting positive (Place) reinforcers that signal utilitarian reinforcement. Exposure to the contingencies is direct.
Manufacturer→Approach→Place→Reinforcers→Positive→ Reinforcement Management→Utilitarian→Manufacturer Rule	Manufacturer-deployed stimuli to strengthen approach by presenting positive (Place) reinforcers that signal utilitarian reinforcement. Exposure to the contingencies is indirect through a rule made by a manufacturer.
Manufacturer→Approach→Place→Reinforcers→Positive→ Reinforcement Management→Utilitarian→Distributor Rule	Manufacturer-deployed stimuli to strengthen approach by presenting positive (Place) reinforcers that signal utilitarian reinforcement. Exposure to the contingencies is indirect through a rule in the distributor managerial behaviour setting.
Manufacturer→Approach→Place→Reinforcers→Positive→ Reinforcement Management→Informational→Direct Exposure to Contingency	Manufacturer-deployed stimuli to strengthen approach by presenting positive (Place) reinforcers that signal informational reinforcement. Exposure to the contingencies is direct.
Manufacturer→Approach→Place→Reinforcers→Positive→ Reinforcement Management→Informational→ Manufacturer Rule	Manufacturer-deployed stimuli to strengthen approach by presenting positive (Place) reinforcers that signal informational reinforcement. Exposure to the contingencies is indirect through a rule made by a manufacturer.

Code	Description and rule
Manufacturer→Approach→Place→Reinforcers→Positive→ Reinforcement Management→Informational→Distributor Rule	Manufacturer-deployed stimuli to strengthen approach by presenting positive (Place) reinforcers that signal informational reinforcement. Exposure to the contingencies is indirect through a rule in the distributor managerial behaviour setting.
Manufacturer→Approach→Place→Reinforcers→Negative→ Scope Management→Setting→Direct Exposure to Contingency	Manufacturer-deployed stimuli to strengthen approach by removing negative (Place) reinforcers that have an impact on the setting. Exposure to the contingencies is direct.
Manufacturer→Approach→Place→Reinforcers→Negative→ Scope Management→Setting→Manufacturer Rule	Manufacturer-deployed stimuli to strengthen approach by removing negative (Place) reinforcers that have an impact on the setting. Exposure to the contingencies is indirect through a rule made by a manufacturer.
Manufacturer→Approach→Place→Reinforcers→Negative→ Scope Management→Setting→Distributor Rule	Manufacturer-deployed stimuli to strengthen approach by removing negative (Place) reinforcers that have an impact on the setting. Exposure to the contingencies is indirect through a rule in the distributor managerial behaviour setting.
Manufacturer→Approach→Place→Reinforcers→Negative→ Reinforcement Management→Utilitarian→Direct Exposure to Contingency	Manufacturer-deployed stimuli to strengthen approach by removing negative (Place) reinforcers that signal utilitarian reinforcement. Exposure to the contingencies is direct.
Manufacturer→Approach→Place→Reinforcers→Negative→ Reinforcement Management→Utilitarian→Manufacturer Rule	Manufacturer-deployed stimuli to strengthen approach by removing negative (Place) reinforcers that signal utilitarian reinforcement. Exposure to the contingencies is indirect through a rule made by a manufacturer.
Manufacturer→Approach→Place→Reinforcers→Negative→ Reinforcement Management→Utilitarian→Distributor Rule	Manufacturer-deployed stimuli to strengthen approach by removing negative (Place) reinforcers that signal utilitarian reinforcement. Exposure to the contingencies is indirect through a rule in the distributor managerial behaviour setting.

Manufacturer-deployed stimuli to strengthen approach by removing negative (Place) reinforcers that signal informational reinforcement. Exposure to the contingencies is direct.

Manufacturer-deployed stimuli to strengthen approach by removing negative (Place) reinforcers that signal informational reinforcement. Exposure to the contingencies is indirect through a rule made by a manufacturer.

Manufacturer-deployed stimuli to strengthen approach by removing negative (Place) reinforcers that signal informational reinforcement. Exposure to the contingencies is indirect through a rule in the distributor managerial behaviour setting.

Manufacturer→Approach→Place→Reinforcers→Negative→Reinforcement Management→Informational→Direct Exposure to Contingency

Manufacturer→Approach→Place→Reinforcers→Negative→Reinforcement Management→Informational→Manufacturer Rule

Manufacturer→Approach→Place→Reinforcers→Negative→Reinforcement Management→Informational→Distributor Rule

Weakening distributor avoidance through punishment

Price

Manufacturer-deployed stimuli to weaken avoidance by presenting positive (Price) punishers that have an impact on the setting. Exposure to the contingencies is direct.

Manufacturer-deployed stimuli to weaken avoidance by presenting positive (Price) punishers that have an impact on the setting. Exposure to the contingencies is indirect through a rule made by a manufacturer.

Manufacturer-deployed stimuli to weaken avoidance by presenting positive (Price) punishers that have an impact on the setting. Exposure to the contingencies is indirect through a rule in the distributor managerial behaviour setting.

Manufacturer-deployed stimuli to weaken avoidance by presenting positive (Price) punishers that signal utilitarian reinforcement. Exposure to the contingencies is direct.

Manufacturer→Avoidance→Price→Punishers→Positive→Scope Management→Setting→Direct Exposure to Contingency

Manufacturer→Avoidance→Price→Punishers→Positive→Scope Management→Setting→Manufacturer Rule

Manufacturer→Avoidance→Price→Punishers→Positive→Scope Management→Setting→Distributor Rule

Manufacturer→Avoidance→Price→Punishers→Positive→Reinforcement Management→Utilitarian→Direct Exposure to Contingency

Code	Description and rule
Manufacturer→Avoidance→Price→Punishers→Positive→ Reinforcement Management→Utilitarian→Manufacturer Rule	Manufacturer-deployed stimuli to weaken avoidance by presenting positive (Price) punishers that signal utilitarian reinforcement. Exposure to the contingencies is indirect through a rule made by a manufacturer.
Manufacturer→Avoidance→Price→Punishers→Positive→ Reinforcement Management→Utilitarian→Distributor Rule	Manufacturer-deployed stimuli to weaken avoidance by presenting positive (Price) punishers that signal utilitarian reinforcement. Exposure to the contingencies is indirect through a rule in the distributor managerial behaviour setting.
Manufacturer→Avoidance→Price→Punishers→Positive→ Reinforcement Management→Informational→Direct Exposure to Contingency	Manufacturer-deployed stimuli to weaken avoidance by presenting positive (Price) punishers that signal informational reinforcement. Exposure to the contingencies is direct.
Manufacturer→Avoidance→Price→Punishers→Positive→ Reinforcement Management→Informational→ Manufacturer Rule	Manufacturer-deployed stimuli to weaken avoidance by presenting positive (Price) punishers that signal informational reinforcement. Exposure to the contingencies is indirect through a rule made by a manufacturer.
Manufacturer→Avoidance→Price→Punishers→Positive→ Reinforcement Management→Informational→Distributor Rule	Manufacturer-deployed stimuli to weaken avoidance by presenting positive (Price) punishers that signal informational reinforcement. Exposure to the contingencies is indirect through a rule in the distributor managerial behaviour setting.
Manufacturer→Avoidance→Price→Punishers→Negative→ Scope Management→Setting→Direct Exposure to Contingency	Manufacturer-deployed stimuli to weaken avoidance by removing negative (Price) punishers that have an impact on the setting. Exposure to the contingencies is direct.
Manufacturer→Avoidance→Price→Punishers→Negative→ Scope Management→Setting→Manufacturer Rule	Manufacturer-deployed stimuli to weaken avoidance by removing negative (Price) punishers that have an impact on the setting. Exposure to the contingencies is indirect through a rule made by a manufacturer.

148

Manufacturer→Avoidance→Price→Punishers→Negative→Scope Management→Setting→Distributor Rule

Manufacturer-deployed stimuli to weaken avoidance by removing negative (Price) punishers that have an impact on the setting. Exposure to the contingencies is indirect through a rule in the distributor managerial behaviour setting.

Manufacturer→Avoidance→Price→Punishers→Negative→Reinforcement Management→Utilitarian→Direct Exposure to Contingency

Manufacturer-deployed stimuli to weaken avoidance by removing negative (Price) punishers that signal utilitarian reinforcement. Exposure to the contingencies is direct.

Manufacturer→Avoidance→Price→Punishers→Negative→Reinforcement Management→Utilitarian→Manufacturer Rule

Manufacturer-deployed stimuli to weaken avoidance by removing negative (Price) punishers that signal utilitarian reinforcement. Exposure to the contingencies is indirect through a rule made by a manufacturer.

Manufacturer→Avoidance→Price→Punishers→Negative→Reinforcement Management→Utilitarian→Distributor Rule

Manufacturer-deployed stimuli to weaken avoidance by removing negative (Price) punishers that signal utilitarian reinforcement. Exposure to the contingencies is indirect through a rule in the distributor managerial behaviour setting.

Manufacturer→Avoidance→Price→Punishers→Negative→Reinforcement Management→Informational→Direct Exposure to Contingency

Manufacturer-deployed stimuli to weaken avoidance by removing negative (Price) punishers that signal informational reinforcement. Exposure to the contingencies is direct.

Manufacturer→Avoidance→Price→Punishers→Negative→Reinforcement Management→Informational→Manufacturer Rule

Manufacturer-deployed stimuli to weaken avoidance by removing negative (Price) punishers that signal informational reinforcement. Exposure to the contingencies is indirect through a rule made by a manufacturer.

Manufacturer→Avoidance→Price→Punishers→Negative→Reinforcement Management→Informational→Distributor Rule

Manufacturer-deployed stimuli to weaken avoidance by removing negative (Price) punishers that signal informational reinforcement. Exposure to the contingencies is indirect through a rule in the distributor managerial behaviour setting.

Code	Description and rule
Product	
Manufacturer→Avoidance→Product→Punishers→Positive→ Scope Management→Setting→Direct Exposure to Contingency	Manufacturer-deployed stimuli to weaken avoidance by presenting positive (Product) punishers that have an impact on the setting. Exposure to the contingencies is direct.
Manufacturer→Avoidance→Product→Punishers→Positive→ Scope Management→Setting→Manufacturer Rule	Manufacturer-deployed stimuli to weaken avoidance by presenting positive (Product) punishers that have an impact on the setting. Exposure to the contingencies is indirect through a rule made by a manufacturer.
Manufacturer→Avoidance→Product→Punishers→Positive→ Scope Management→Setting→Distributor Rule	Manufacturer-deployed stimuli to weaken avoidance by presenting positive (Product) punishers that have an impact on the setting. Exposure to the contingencies is indirect through a rule in the distributor managerial behaviour setting.
Manufacturer→Avoidance→Product→Punishers→Positive→ Reinforcement Management→Utilitarian→Direct Exposure to Contingency	Manufacturer-deployed stimuli to weaken avoidance by presenting positive (Product) punishers that signal utilitarian reinforcement. Exposure to the contingencies is direct.
Manufacturer→Avoidance→Product→Punishers→Positive→ Reinforcement Management→Utilitarian→Manufacturer Rule	Manufacturer-deployed stimuli to weaken avoidance by presenting positive (Product) punishers that signal utilitarian reinforcement. Exposure to the contingencies is indirect through a rule made by a manufacturer.
Manufacturer→Avoidance→Product→Punishers→Positive→ Reinforcement Management→Utilitarian→Distributor Rule	Manufacturer-deployed stimuli to weaken avoidance by presenting positive (Product) punishers that signal utilitarian reinforcement. Exposure to the contingencies is indirect through a rule in the distributor managerial behaviour setting.
Manufacturer→Avoidance→Product→Punishers→Positive →Reinforcement Management→Informational→Direct Exposure to Contingency	Manufacturer-deployed stimuli to weaken avoidance by presenting positive (Product) punishers that signal informational reinforcement. Exposure to the contingencies is direct.

Manufacturer→Avoidance→Product→Punishers→Positive→Reinforcement Management→Informational→Manufacturer Rule

Manufacturer-deployed stimuli to weaken avoidance by presenting positive (Product) punishers that signal informational reinforcement. Exposure to the contingencies is indirect through a rule made by a manufacturer.

Manufacturer→Avoidance→Product→Punishers→Positive →Reinforcement Management→Informational→Distributor Rule

Manufacturer-deployed stimuli to weaken avoidance by presenting positive (Product) punishers that signal informational reinforcement. Exposure to the contingencies is indirect through a rule in the distributor managerial behaviour setting.

Manufacturer→Avoidance→Product→Punishers→Negative →Scope Management→Setting→Direct Exposure to Contingency

Manufacturer-deployed stimuli to weaken avoidance by removing negative (Product) punishers that have an impact on the setting. Exposure to the contingencies is direct.

Manufacturer→Avoidance→Product→Punishers→Negative→Scope Management→Setting→Manufacturer Rule

Manufacturer-deployed stimuli to weaken avoidance by removing negative (Product) punishers that have an impact on the setting. Exposure to the contingencies is indirect through a rule made by a manufacturer.

Manufacturer→Avoidance→Product→Punishers→Negative→Scope Management→Setting→Distributor Rule

Manufacturer-deployed stimuli to weaken avoidance by removing negative (Product) punishers that have an impact on the setting. Exposure to the contingencies is indirect through a rule in the distributor managerial behaviour setting.

Manufacturer→Avoidance→Product→Punishers→Negative→Reinforcement Management→Utilitarian→Direct Exposure to Contingency

Manufacturer-deployed stimuli to weaken avoidance by removing negative (Product) punishers that signal utilitarian reinforcement. Exposure to the contingencies is direct.

Manufacturer→Avoidance→Product→Punishers→Negative→Reinforcement Management→Utilitarian→Manufacturer Rule

Manufacturer-deployed stimuli to weaken avoidance by removing negative (Product) punishers that signal utilitarian reinforcement. Exposure to the contingencies is indirect through a rule made by a manufacturer.

Code	Description and rule
Manufacturer→Avoidance→Product→Punishers→Negative→ Reinforcement Management→Utilitarian→Distributor Rule	Manufacturer-deployed stimuli to weaken avoidance by removing negative (Product) punishers that signal utilitarian reinforcement. Exposure to the contingencies is indirect through a rule in the distributor managerial behaviour setting.
Manufacturer→Avoidance→Product→Punishers→Negative →Reinforcement Management→Informational→Direct Exposure to Contingency	Manufacturer-deployed stimuli to weaken avoidance by removing negative (Product) punishers that signal informational reinforcement. Exposure to the contingencies is direct.
Manufacturer→Avoidance→Product→Punishers→Negative→ Reinforcement Management→Informational→ Manufacturer Rule	Manufacturer-deployed stimuli to weaken avoidance by removing negative (Product) punishers that signal informational reinforcement. Exposure to the contingencies is indirect through a rule made by a manufacturer.
Manufacturer→Avoidance→Product→Punishers→Negative→ Reinforcement Management→Informational→Distributor Rule	Manufacturer-deployed stimuli to weaken avoidance by removing negative (Product) punishers that signal informational reinforcement. Exposure to the contingencies is indirect through a rule in the distributor managerial behaviour setting.

Promotion

Code	Description and rule
Manufacturer→Avoidance→Promotion→Punishers→ Positive→Scope Management→Setting→Direct Exposure to Contingency	Manufacturer-deployed stimuli to weaken avoidance by presenting positive (Promotion) punishers that have an impact on the setting. Exposure to the contingencies is direct.
Manufacturer→Avoidance→Promotion→Punishers→Positive →Scope Management→Setting→Manufacturer Rule	Manufacturer-deployed stimuli to weaken avoidance by presenting positive (Promotion) punishers that have an impact on the setting. Exposure to the contingencies is indirect through a rule made by a manufacturer.
Manufacturer→Avoidance→Promotion→Punishers→Positive →Scope Management→Setting→Distributor Rule	Manufacturer-deployed stimuli to weaken avoidance by presenting positive (Promotion) punishers that have an impact on the setting. Exposure to the contingencies is indirect through a rule in the distributor managerial behaviour setting.

Manufacturer→Avoidance→Promotion→Punishers→Positive→Reinforcement Management→Utilitarian→Direct Exposure to Contingency

Manufacturer-deployed stimuli to weaken avoidance by presenting positive (Promotion) punishers that signal utilitarian reinforcement. Exposure to the contingencies is direct.

Manufacturer→Avoidance→Promotion→Punishers→Positive→Reinforcement Management→Utilitarian→Manufacturer Rule

Manufacturer-deployed stimuli to weaken avoidance by presenting positive (Promotion) punishers that signal utilitarian reinforcement. Exposure to the contingencies is indirect through a rule made by a manufacturer.

Manufacturer→Avoidance→Promotion→Punishers→Positive→Reinforcement Management→Utilitarian→Distributor Rule

Manufacturer-deployed stimuli to weaken avoidance by presenting positive (Promotion) punishers that signal utilitarian reinforcement. Exposure to the contingencies is indirect through a rule in the distributor managerial behaviour setting.

Manufacturer→Avoidance→Promotion→Punishers→Positive→Reinforcement Management→Informational→Direct Exposure to Contingency

Manufacturer-deployed stimuli to weaken avoidance by presenting positive (Promotion) punishers that signal informational reinforcement. Exposure to the contingencies is direct.

Manufacturer→Avoidance→Promotion→Punishers→Positive→Reinforcement Management→Informational→Manufacturer Rule

Manufacturer-deployed stimuli to weaken avoidance by presenting positive (Promotion) punishers that signal informational reinforcement. Exposure to the contingencies is indirect through a rule made by a manufacturer.

Manufacturer→Avoidance→Promotion→Punishers→Positive→Reinforcement Management→Informational→Distributor Rule

Manufacturer-deployed stimuli to weaken avoidance by presenting positive (Promotion) punishers that signal informational reinforcement. Exposure to the contingencies is indirect through a rule in the distributor managerial behaviour setting.

Manufacturer→Avoidance→Promotion→Punishers→Negative→Scope Management→Setting→Direct Exposure to Contingency

Manufacturer-deployed stimuli to weaken avoidance by removing negative (Promotion) punishers that have an impact on the setting. Exposure to the contingencies is direct.

Code	Description and rule
Manufacturer→Avoidance→Promotion→Punishers→Negative →Scope Management→Setting→Manufacturer Rule	Manufacturer-deployed stimuli to weaken avoidance by removing negative (Promotion) punishers that have an impact on the setting. Exposure to the contingencies is indirect through a rule made by a manufacturer.
Manufacturer→Avoidance→Promotion→Punishers→Negative →Scope Management→Setting→Distributor Rule	Manufacturer-deployed stimuli to weaken avoidance by removing negative (Promotion) punishers that have an impact on the setting. Exposure to the contingencies is indirect through a rule in the distributor managerial behaviour setting.
Manufacturer→Avoidance→Promotion→Punishers→ Negative→Reinforcement Management→Utilitarian→ Direct Exposure to Contingency	Manufacturer-deployed stimuli to weaken avoidance by removing negative (Promotion) punishers that signal utilitarian reinforcement. Exposure to the contingencies is direct.
Manufacturer→Avoidance→Promotion→Punishers→Negative →Reinforcement Management→Utilitarian→Manufacturer Rule	Manufacturer-deployed stimuli to weaken avoidance by removing negative (Promotion) punishers that signal utilitarian reinforcement. Exposure to the contingencies is indirect through a rule made by a manufacturer.
Manufacturer→Avoidance→Promotion→Punishers→ Negative→Reinforcement Management→Utilitarian→ Distributor Rule	Manufacturer-deployed stimuli to weaken avoidance by removing negative (Promotion) punishers that signal utilitarian reinforcement. Exposure to the contingencies is indirect through a rule in the distributor managerial behaviour setting.
Manufacturer→Avoidance→Promotion→Punishers→Negative →Reinforcement Management→Informational→Direct Exposure to Contingency	Manufacturer-deployed stimuli to weaken avoidance by removing negative (Promotion) punishers that signal informational reinforcement. Exposure to the contingencies is direct.
Manufacturer→Avoidance→Promotion→Punishers→Negative →Reinforcement Management→Informational→ Manufacturer Rule	Manufacturer-deployed stimuli to weaken avoidance by removing negative (Promotion) punishers that signal informational reinforcement. Exposure to the contingencies is indirect through a rule made by a manufacturer.

Manufacturer→Avoidance→Promotion→Punishers→Negative →Reinforcement Management→Informational→Distributor Rule

Manufacturer-deployed stimuli to weaken avoidance by removing negative (Promotion) punishers that signal informational reinforcement. Exposure to the contingencies is indirect through a rule in the distributor managerial behaviour setting.

Place

Manufacturer→Avoidance→Place→Punishers→Positive→ Scope Management→Setting→Direct Exposure to Contingency

Manufacturer-deployed stimuli to weaken avoidance by presenting positive (Place) punishers that have an impact on the setting. Exposure to the contingencies is direct.

Manufacturer→Avoidance→Place→Punishers→Positive→ Scope Management→Setting→Manufacturer Rule

Manufacturer-deployed stimuli to weaken avoidance by presenting positive (Place) punishers that have an impact on the setting. Exposure to the contingencies is indirect through a rule made by a manufacturer.

Manufacturer→Avoidance→Place→Punishers→Positive→ Scope Management→Setting→Distributor Rule

Manufacturer-deployed stimuli to weaken avoidance by presenting positive (Place) punishers that have an impact on the setting. Exposure to the contingencies is indirect through a rule in the distributor managerial behaviour setting.

Manufacturer→Avoidance→Place→Punishers→Positive→ Reinforcement Management→Utilitarian→Direct Exposure to Contingency

Manufacturer-deployed stimuli to weaken avoidance by presenting positive (Place) punishers that signal utilitarian reinforcement. Exposure to the contingencies is direct.

Manufacturer→Avoidance→Place→Punishers→Positive→ Reinforcement Management→Utilitarian→Manufacturer Rule

Manufacturer-deployed stimuli to weaken avoidance by presenting positive (Place) punishers that signal utilitarian reinforcement. Exposure to the contingencies is indirect through a rule made by a manufacturer.

Manufacturer→Avoidance→Place→Punishers→Positive→ Reinforcement Management→Utilitarian→Distributor Rule

Manufacturer-deployed stimuli to weaken avoidance by presenting positive (Place) punishers that signal utilitarian reinforcement. Exposure to the contingencies is indirect through a rule in the distributor managerial behaviour setting.

Code	Description and rule
Manufacturer→Avoidance→Place→Punishers→Positive→ Reinforcement Management→Informational→Direct Exposure to Contingency	Manufacturer-deployed stimuli to weaken avoidance by presenting positive (Place) punishers that signal informational reinforcement. Exposure to the contingencies is direct.
Manufacturer→Avoidance→Place→Punishers→Positive→ Reinforcement Management→Informational→ Manufacturer Rule	Manufacturer-deployed stimuli to weaken avoidance by presenting positive (Place) punishers that signal informational reinforcement. Exposure to the contingencies is indirect through a rule made by a manufacturer.
Manufacturer→Avoidance→Place→Punishers→Positive→ Reinforcement Management→Informational→Distributor Rule	Manufacturer-deployed stimuli to weaken avoidance by presenting positive (Place) punishers that signal informational reinforcement. Exposure to the contingencies is indirect through a rule in the distributor managerial behaviour setting.
Manufacturer→Avoidance→Place→Punishers→Negative→ Scope Management→Setting→Direct Exposure to Contingency	Manufacturer-deployed stimuli to weaken avoidance by removing negative (Place) punishers that have an impact on the setting. Exposure to the contingencies is direct.
Manufacturer→Avoidance→Place→Punishers→Negative→ Scope Management→Setting→Manufacturer Rule	Manufacturer-deployed stimuli to weaken avoidance by removing negative (Place) punishers that have an impact on the setting. Exposure to the contingencies is indirect through a rule made by a manufacturer.
Manufacturer→Avoidance→Place→Punishers→Negative→ Scope Management→Setting→Distributor Rule	Manufacturer-deployed stimuli to weaken avoidance by removing negative (Place) punishers that have an impact on the setting. Exposure to the contingencies is indirect through a rule in the distributor managerial behaviour setting.
Manufacturer→Avoidance→Place→Punishers→Negative→ Reinforcement Management→Utilitarian→Direct Exposure to Contingency	Manufacturer-deployed stimuli to weaken avoidance by removing negative (Place) punishers that signal utilitarian reinforcement. Exposure to the contingencies is direct.

Manufacturer→Avoidance→Place→Punishers→Negative→ Reinforcement Management→Utilitarian→Manufacturer Rule

Manufacturer-deployed stimuli to weaken avoidance by removing negative (Place) punishers that signal utilitarian reinforcement. Exposure to the contingencies is indirect through a rule made by a manufacturer.

Manufacturer→Avoidance→Place→Punishers→Negative→ Reinforcement Management→Utilitarian→Distributor Rule

Manufacturer-deployed stimuli to weaken avoidance by removing negative (Place) punishers that signal utilitarian reinforcement. Exposure to the contingencies is indirect through a rule in the distributor managerial behaviour setting.

Manufacturer→Avoidance→Place→Punishers→Negative→ Reinforcement Management→Informational→Direct Exposure to Contingency

Manufacturer-deployed stimuli to weaken avoidance by removing negative (Place) punishers that signal informational reinforcement. Exposure to the contingencies is direct.

Manufacturer→Avoidance→Place→Punishers→Negative→ Reinforcement Management→Informational→ Manufacturer Rule

Manufacturer-deployed stimuli to weaken avoidance by removing negative (Place) punishers that signal informational reinforcement. Exposure to the contingencies is indirect through a rule made by a manufacturer.

Manufacturer→Avoidance→Place→Punishers→Negative→ Reinforcement Management→Informational→Distributor Rule

Manufacturer-deployed stimuli to weaken avoidance by removing negative (Place) punishers that signal informational reinforcement. Exposure to the contingencies is indirect through a rule in the distributor managerial↔behaviour setting.

Distributor↔Manufacturer relationships (distributor-deployed stimuli)

Strengthening manufacturer approach (through reinforcement)

Price

Distributor→Approach→Price→Reinforcers→Positive→ Scope Management→Setting→Direct Exposure to Contingency

Distributor-deployed stimuli to strengthen approach by presenting positive (Price) reinforcers that have an impact on the setting. Exposure to the contingencies is direct.

Code	Description and rule
Distributor→Approach→Price→Reinforcers→Positive→ Scope Management→Setting→Distributor Rule	Distributor-deployed stimuli to strengthen approach by presenting positive (Price) reinforcers that have an impact on the setting. Exposure to the contingencies is indirect through a rule made by a manufacturer.
Distributor→Approach→Price→Reinforcers→Positive→ Scope Management→Setting→Manufacturer Rule	Distributor-deployed stimuli to strengthen approach by presenting positive (Price) reinforcers that have an impact on the setting. Exposure to the contingencies is indirect through a rule in the manufacturer managerial behaviour setting.
Distributor→Approach→Price→Reinforcers→Positive→ Reinforcement Management→Utilitarian→Direct Exposure to Contingency	Distributor-deployed stimuli to strengthen approach by presenting positive (Price) reinforcers that signal utilitarian reinforcement. Exposure to the contingencies is direct.
Distributor→Approach→Price→Reinforcers→Positive→ Reinforcement Management→Utilitarian→Distributor Rule	Distributor-deployed stimuli to strengthen approach by presenting positive (Price) reinforcers that signal utilitarian reinforcement. Exposure to the contingencies is indirect through a rule made by a manufacturer.
Distributor→Approach→Price→Reinforcers→Positive→ Reinforcement Management→Utilitarian→Manufacturer Rule	Distributor-deployed stimuli to strengthen approach by presenting positive (Price) reinforcers that signal utilitarian reinforcement. Exposure to the contingencies is indirect through a rule in the manufacturer managerial behaviour setting.
Distributor→Approach→Price→Reinforcers→Positive→ Reinforcement Management→Informational→Direct Exposure to Contingency	Distributor-deployed stimuli to strengthen approach by presenting positive (Price) reinforcers that signal informational reinforcement. Exposure to the contingencies is direct.
Distributor→Approach→Price→Reinforcers→Positive→ Reinforcement Management→Informational→Distributor Rule	Distributor-deployed stimuli to strengthen approach by presenting positive (Price) reinforcers that signal informational reinforcement. Exposure to the contingencies is indirect through a rule made by a manufacturer.

Distributor→Approach→Price→Reinforcers→Positive→Reinforcement Management→Informational→Manufacturer Rule

Distributor-deployed stimuli to strengthen approach by presenting positive (Price) reinforcers that signal informational reinforcement. Exposure to the contingencies is indirect through a rule in the manufacturer managerial behaviour setting.

Distributor→Approach→Price→Reinforcers→Negative→Scope Management→Setting→Direct Exposure to Contingency

Distributor-deployed stimuli to strengthen approach by removing negative (Price) reinforcers that have an impact on the setting. Exposure to the contingencies is direct.

Distributor→Approach→Price→Reinforcers→Negative→Scope Management→Setting→Distributor Rule

Distributor-deployed stimuli to strengthen approach by removing negative (Price) reinforcers that have an impact on the setting. Exposure to the contingencies is indirect through a rule made by a manufacturer.

Distributor→Approach→Price→Reinforcers→Negative→Scope Management→Setting→Manufacturer Rule

Distributor-deployed stimuli to strengthen approach by removing negative (Price) reinforcers that have an impact on the setting. Exposure to the contingencies is indirect through a rule in the manufacturer managerial behaviour setting.

Distributor→Approach→Price→Reinforcers→Negative→Reinforcement Management→Utilitarian→Direct Exposure to Contingency

Distributor-deployed stimuli to strengthen approach by removing negative (Price) reinforcers that signal utilitarian reinforcement. Exposure to the contingencies is direct.

Distributor→Approach→Price→Reinforcers→Negative→Reinforcement Management→Utilitarian→Distributor Rule

Distributor-deployed stimuli to strengthen approach by removing negative (Price) reinforcers that signal utilitarian reinforcement. Exposure to the contingencies is indirect through a rule made by a manufacturer.

Distributor→Approach→Price→Reinforcers→Negative→Reinforcement Management→Utilitarian→Manufacturer Rule

Distributor-deployed stimuli to strengthen approach by removing negative (Price) reinforcers that signal utilitarian reinforcement. Exposure to the contingencies is indirect through a rule in the manufacturer managerial behaviour setting.

Code	Description and rule
Distributor→Approach→Price→Reinforcers→Negative→Reinforcement Management→Informational→Direct Exposure to Contingency	Distributor-deployed stimuli to strengthen approach by removing negative (Price) reinforcers that signal informational reinforcement. Exposure to the contingencies is direct.
Distributor→Approach→Price→Reinforcers→Negative→Reinforcement Management→Informational→Distributor Rule	Distributor-deployed stimuli to strengthen approach by removing negative (Price) reinforcers that signal informational reinforcement. Exposure to the contingencies is indirect through a rule made by a manufacturer.
Distributor→Approach→Price→Reinforcers→Negative→Reinforcement Management→Informational→Manufacturer Rule	Distributor-deployed stimuli to strengthen approach by removing negative (Price) reinforcers that signal informational reinforcement. Exposure to the contingencies is indirect through a rule in the manufacturer managerial behaviour setting.
Product	
Distributor→Approach→Product→Reinforcers→Positive→Scope Management→Setting→Direct Exposure to Contingency	Distributor-deployed stimuli to strengthen approach by presenting positive (Product) reinforcers that have an impact on the setting. Exposure to the contingencies is direct.
Distributor→Approach→Product→Reinforcers→Positive→Scope Management→Setting→Manufacturer Rule	Distributor-deployed stimuli to strengthen approach by presenting positive (Product) reinforcers that have an impact on the setting. Exposure to the contingencies is indirect through a rule made by a manufacturer.
Distributor→Approach→Product→Reinforcers→Positive→Scope Management→Setting→Distributor Rule	Distributor-deployed stimuli to strengthen approach by presenting positive (Product) reinforcers that have an impact on the setting. Exposure to the contingencies is indirect through a rule in the manufacturer managerial behaviour setting.
Distributor→Approach→Product→Reinforcers→Positive→Reinforcement Management→Utilitarian→Direct Exposure to Contingency	Distributor-deployed stimuli to strengthen approach by presenting positive (Product) reinforcers that signal utilitarian reinforcement. Exposure to the contingencies is direct.

Distributor→Approach→Product→Reinforcers→Positive→ Reinforcement Management→Utilitarian→Manufacturer Rule

Distributor-deployed stimuli to strengthen approach by presenting positive (Product) reinforcers that signal utilitarian reinforcement. Exposure to the contingencies is indirect through a rule made by a manufacturer.

Distributor→Approach→Product→Reinforcers→Positive→ Reinforcement Management→Utilitarian→Distributor Rule

Distributor-deployed stimuli to strengthen approach by presenting positive (Product) reinforcers that signal utilitarian reinforcement. Exposure to the contingencies is indirect through a rule in the manufacturer managerial behaviour setting.

Distributor→Approach→Product→Reinforcers→Positive→ Reinforcement Management→Informational→Direct Exposure to Contingency

Distributor-deployed stimuli to strengthen approach by presenting positive (Product) reinforcers that signal informational reinforcement. Exposure to the contingencies is direct.

Distributor→Approach→Product→Reinforcers→Positive→ Reinforcement Management→Informational→ Manufacturer Rule

Distributor-deployed stimuli to strengthen approach by presenting positive (Product) reinforcers that signal informational reinforcement. Exposure to the contingencies is indirect through a rule made by a manufacturer.

Distributor→Approach→Product→Reinforcers→Positive→ Reinforcement Management→Informational→Distributor Rule

Distributor-deployed stimuli to strengthen approach by presenting positive (Product) reinforcers that signal informational reinforcement. Exposure to the contingencies is indirect through a rule in the manufacturer managerial behaviour setting.

Distributor→Approach→Product→Reinforcers→Negative→ Scope Management→Setting→Direct Exposure to Contingency

Distributor-deployed stimuli to strengthen approach by removing negative (Product) reinforcers that have an impact on the setting. Exposure to the contingencies is direct.

Distributor→Approach→Product→Reinforcers→Negative→ Scope Management→Setting→Manufacturer Rule

Distributor-deployed stimuli to strengthen approach by removing negative (Product) reinforcers that have an impact on the setting. Exposure to the contingencies is indirect through a rule made by a manufacturer.

Code	Description and rule
Distributor→Approach→Product→Reinforcers→Negative→Scope Management→Setting→Distributor Rule	Distributor-deployed stimuli to strengthen approach by removing negative (Product) reinforcers that have an impact on the setting. Exposure to the contingencies is indirect through a rule in the manufacturer managerial behaviour setting.
Distributor→Approach→Product→Reinforcers→Negative→Reinforcement Management→Utilitarian→Direct Exposure to Contingency	Distributor-deployed stimuli to strengthen approach by removing negative (Product) reinforcers that signal utilitarian reinforcement. Exposure to the contingencies is direct.
Distributor→Approach→Product→Reinforcers→Negative→Reinforcement Management→Utilitarian→Manufacturer Rule	Distributor-deployed stimuli to strengthen approach by removing negative (Product) reinforcers that signal utilitarian reinforcement. Exposure to the contingencies is indirect through a rule made by a manufacturer.
Distributor→Approach→Product→Reinforcers→Negative→Reinforcement Management→Utilitarian→Distributor Rule	Distributor-deployed stimuli to strengthen approach by removing negative (Product) reinforcers that signal utilitarian reinforcement. Exposure to the contingencies is indirect through a rule in the manufacturer managerial behaviour setting.
Distributor→Approach→Product→Reinforcers→Negative→Reinforcement Management→Informational→Direct Exposure to Contingency	Distributor-deployed stimuli to strengthen approach by removing negative (Product) reinforcers that signal informational reinforcement. Exposure to the contingencies is direct.
Distributor→Approach→Product→Reinforcers→Negative→Reinforcement Management→Informational→Manufacturer Rule	Distributor-deployed stimuli to strengthen approach by removing negative (Product) reinforcers that signal informational reinforcement. Exposure to the contingencies is indirect through a rule made by a manufacturer.
Distributor→Approach→Product→Reinforcers→Negative→Reinforcement Management→Informational→Distributor Rule	Distributor-deployed stimuli to strengthen approach by removing negative (Product) reinforcers that signal informational reinforcement. Exposure to the contingencies is indirect through a rule in the manufacturer managerial behaviour setting.

Promotion

Distributor→Approach→Promotion→Reinforcers→Positive→Scope Management→Setting→Direct Exposure to Contingency	Distributor-deployed stimuli to strengthen approach by presenting positive (Promotion) reinforcers that have an impact on the setting. Exposure to the contingencies is direct.
Distributor→Approach→Promotion→Reinforcers→Positive→Scope Management→Setting→Manufacturer Rule	Distributor-deployed stimuli to strengthen approach by presenting positive (Promotion) reinforcers that have an impact on the setting. Exposure to the contingencies is indirect through a rule made by a manufacturer.
Distributor→Approach→Promotion→Reinforcers→Positive→Scope Management→Setting→Distributor Rule	Distributor-deployed stimuli to strengthen approach by presenting positive (Promotion) reinforcers that have an impact on the setting. Exposure to the contingencies is indirect through a rule in the manufacturer managerial behaviour setting.
Distributor→Approach→Promotion→Reinforcers→Positive→Reinforcement Management→Utilitarian→Direct Exposure to Contingency	Distributor-deployed stimuli to strengthen approach by presenting positive (Promotion) reinforcers that signal utilitarian reinforcement. Exposure to the contingencies is direct.
Distributor→Approach→Promotion→Reinforcers→Positive→Reinforcement Management→Utilitarian→Manufacturer Rule	Distributor-deployed stimuli to strengthen approach by presenting positive (Promotion) reinforcers that signal utilitarian reinforcement. Exposure to the contingencies is indirect through a rule made by a manufacturer.
Distributor→Approach→Promotion→Reinforcers→Positive→Reinforcement Management→Utilitarian→Distributor Rule	Distributor-deployed stimuli to strengthen approach by presenting positive (Promotion) reinforcers that signal utilitarian reinforcement. Exposure to the contingencies is indirect through a rule in the manufacturer managerial behaviour setting.
Distributor→Approach→Promotion→Reinforcers→Positive→Reinforcement Management→Informational→Direct Exposure to Contingency	Distributor-deployed stimuli to strengthen approach by presenting positive (Promotion) reinforcers that signal informational reinforcement. Exposure to the contingencies is direct.

Code	Description and rule
Distributor→Approach→Promotion→Reinforcers→Positive→Reinforcement Management→Informational→Manufacturer Rule	Distributor-deployed stimuli to strengthen approach by presenting positive (Promotion) reinforcers that signal informational reinforcement. Exposure to the contingencies is indirect through a rule made by a manufacturer.
Distributor→Approach→Promotion→Reinforcers→Positive→Reinforcement Management→Informational→Distributor Rule	Distributor-deployed stimuli to strengthen approach by presenting positive (Promotion) reinforcers that signal informational reinforcement. Exposure to the contingencies is indirect through a rule in the manufacturer managerial behaviour setting.
Distributor→Approach→Promotion→Reinforcers→Negative →Scope Management→Setting→Direct Exposure to Contingency	Distributor-deployed stimuli to strengthen approach by removing negative (Promotion) reinforcers that have an impact on the setting. Exposure to the contingencies is direct.
Distributor→Approach→Promotion→Reinforcers→Negative→Scope Management→Setting→Manufacturer Rule	Distributor-deployed stimuli to strengthen approach by removing negative (Promotion) reinforcers that have an impact on the setting. Exposure to the contingencies is indirect through a rule made by a manufacturer.
Distributor→Approach→Promotion→Reinforcers→Negative→Scope Management→Setting→Distributor Rule	Distributor-deployed stimuli to strengthen approach by removing negative (Promotion) reinforcers that have an impact on the setting. Exposure to the contingencies is indirect through a rule in the manufacturer managerial behaviour setting.
Distributor→Approach→Promotion→Reinforcers→Negative→Reinforcement Management→Utilitarian→Direct Exposure to Contingency	Distributor-deployed stimuli to strengthen approach by removing negative (Promotion) reinforcers that signal utilitarian reinforcement. Exposure to the contingencies is direct.
Distributor→Approach→Promotion→Reinforcers→Negative →Reinforcement Management→Utilitarian→Manufacturer Rule	Distributor-deployed stimuli to strengthen approach by removing negative (Promotion) reinforcers that signal utilitarian reinforcement. Exposure to the contingencies is indirect through a rule made by a manufacturer.

Distributor→Approach→Promotion→Reinforcers→Negative→Reinforcement Management→Utilitarian→Distributor Rule	Distributor-deployed stimuli to strengthen approach by removing negative (Promotion) reinforcers that signal utilitarian reinforcement. Exposure to the contingencies is indirect through a rule in the manufacturer managerial behaviour setting.
Distributor→Approach→Promotion→Reinforcers→Negative→Reinforcement Management→Informational→Direct Exposure to Contingency	Distributor-deployed stimuli to strengthen approach by removing negative (Promotion) reinforcers that signal informational reinforcement. Exposure to the contingencies is direct.
Distributor→Approach→Promotion→Reinforcers→Negative→Reinforcement Management→Informational→Manufacturer Rule	Distributor-deployed stimuli to strengthen approach by removing negative (Promotion) reinforcers that signal informational reinforcement. Exposure to the contingencies is indirect through a rule made by a manufacturer.
Distributor→Approach→Promotion→Reinforcers→Negative→Reinforcement Management→Informational→Distributor Rule	Distributor-deployed stimuli to strengthen approach by removing negative (Promotion) reinforcers that signal informational reinforcement. Exposure to the contingencies is indirect through a rule in the manufacturer managerial behaviour setting.

Place

Distributor→Approach→Place→Reinforcers→Positive→Scope Management→Setting→Direct Exposure to Contingency	Distributor-deployed stimuli to strengthen approach by presenting positive (Place) reinforcers that have an impact on the setting. Exposure to the contingencies is direct.
Distributor→Approach→Place→Reinforcers→Positive→Scope Management→Setting→Manufacturer Rule	Distributor-deployed stimuli to strengthen approach by presenting positive (Place) reinforcers that have an impact on the setting. Exposure to the contingencies is indirect through a rule made by a manufacturer.

Code	Description and rule
Distributor→Approach→Place→Reinforcers→Positive→ Scope Management→Setting→Distributor Rule	Distributor-deployed stimuli to strengthen approach by presenting positive (Place) reinforcers that have an impact on the setting. Exposure to the contingencies is indirect through a rule in the manufacturer managerial behaviour setting.
Distributor→Approach→Place→Reinforcers→Positive→ Reinforcement Management→Utilitarian→Direct Exposure to Contingency	Distributor-deployed stimuli to strengthen approach by presenting positive (Place) reinforcers that signal utilitarian reinforcement. Exposure to the contingencies is direct.
Distributor→Approach→Place→Reinforcers→Positive→ Reinforcement Management→Utilitarian→Manufacturer Rule	Distributor-deployed stimuli to strengthen approach by presenting positive (Place) reinforcers that signal utilitarian reinforcement. Exposure to the contingencies is indirect through a rule made by a manufacturer.
Distributor→Approach→Place→Reinforcers→Positive→ Reinforcement Management→Utilitarian→Distributor Rule	Distributor-deployed stimuli to strengthen approach by presenting positive (Place) reinforcers that signal utilitarian reinforcement. Exposure to the contingencies is indirect through a rule in the manufacturer managerial behaviour setting.
Distributor→Approach→Place→Reinforcers→Positive→ Reinforcement Management→Informational→Direct Exposure to Contingency	Distributor-deployed stimuli to strengthen approach by presenting positive (Place) reinforcers that signal informational reinforcement. Exposure to the contingencies is direct.
Distributor→Approach→Place→Reinforcers→Positive→ Reinforcement Management→Informational→ Manufacturer Rule	Distributor-deployed stimuli to strengthen approach by presenting positive (Place) reinforcers that signal informational reinforcement. Exposure to the contingencies is indirect through a rule made by a manufacturer.
Distributor→Approach→Place→Reinforcers→Positive→ Reinforcement Management→Informational→Distributor Rule	Distributor-deployed stimuli to strengthen approach by presenting positive (Place) reinforcers that signal informational reinforcement. Exposure to the contingencies is indirect through a rule in the manufacturer managerial behaviour setting.

Distributor-deployed stimuli to strengthen approach by removing negative (Place) reinforcers that have an impact on the setting. Exposure to the contingencies is direct.

Distributor-deployed stimuli to strengthen approach by removing negative (Place) reinforcers that have an impact on the setting. Exposure to the contingencies is indirect through a rule made by a manufacturer.

Distributor-deployed stimuli to strengthen approach by removing negative (Place) reinforcers that have an impact on the setting. Exposure to the contingencies is indirect through a rule in the manufacturer managerial behaviour setting.

Distributor-deployed stimuli to strengthen approach by removing negative (Place) reinforcers that signal utilitarian reinforcement. Exposure to the contingencies is direct.

Distributor-deployed stimuli to strengthen approach by removing negative (Place) reinforcers that signal utilitarian reinforcement. Exposure to the contingencies is indirect through a rule made by a manufacturer.

Distributor-deployed stimuli to strengthen approach by removing negative (Place) reinforcers that signal utilitarian reinforcement. Exposure to the contingencies is indirect through a rule in the manufacturer managerial behaviour setting.

Distributor-deployed stimuli to strengthen approach by removing negative (Place) reinforcers that signal informational reinforcement. Exposure to the contingencies is direct.

Distributor-deployed stimuli to strengthen approach by removing negative (Place) reinforcers that signal informational reinforcement. Exposure to the contingencies is indirect through a rule made by a manufacturer.

Distributor→Approach→Place→Reinforcers→Negative→Scope Management→Setting→Direct Exposure to Contingency

Distributor→Approach→Place→Reinforcers→Negative→Scope Management→Setting→Manufacturer Rule

Distributor→Approach→Place→Reinforcers→Negative→Scope Management→Setting→Distributor Rule

Distributor→Approach→Place→Reinforcers→Negative→Reinforcement Management→Utilitarian→Direct Exposure to Contingency

Distributor→Approach→Place→Reinforcers→Negative→Reinforcement Management→Utilitarian→Manufacturer Rule

Distributor→Approach→Place→Reinforcers→Negative→Reinforcement Management→Utilitarian→Distributor Rule

Distributor→Approach→Place→Reinforcers→Negative→Reinforcement Management→Informational→Direct Exposure to Contingency

Distributor→Approach→Place→Reinforcers→Negative→Reinforcement Management→Informational→Manufacturer Rule

Code	Description and rule
Distributor→Approach→Place→Reinforcers→Negative→Reinforcement Management→Informational→Distributor Rule	Distributor-deployed stimuli to strengthen approach by removing negative (Place) reinforcers that signal informational reinforcement. Exposure to the contingencies is indirect through a rule in the manufacturer managerial behaviour setting.

Weakening manufacturer avoidance through punishment

Price

Code	Description and rule
Distributor→Avoidance→Price→Punishers→Positive→Scope Management→Setting→Direct Exposure to Contingency	Distributor-deployed stimuli to weaken avoidance by presenting positive (Price) punishers that have an impact on the setting. Exposure to the contingencies is direct.
Distributor→Avoidance→Price→Punishers→Positive→Scope Management→Setting→Distributor Rule	Distributor-deployed stimuli to weaken avoidance by presenting positive (Price) punishers that have an impact on the setting. Exposure to the contingencies is indirect through a rule made by a manufacturer.
Distributor→Avoidance→Price→Punishers→Positive→Scope Management→Setting→Manufacturer Rule	Distributor-deployed stimuli to weaken avoidance by presenting positive (Price) punishers that have an impact on the setting. Exposure to the contingencies is indirect through a rule in the manufacturer managerial behaviour setting.
Distributor→Avoidance→Price→Punishers→Positive→Reinforcement Management→Utilitarian→Direct Exposure to Contingency	Distributor-deployed stimuli to weaken avoidance by presenting positive (Price) punishers that signal utilitarian reinforcement. Exposure to the contingencies is direct.
Distributor→Avoidance→Price→Punishers→Positive→Reinforcement Management→Utilitarian→Distributor Rule	Distributor-deployed stimuli to weaken avoidance by presenting positive (Price) punishers that signal utilitarian reinforcement. Exposure to the contingencies is indirect through a rule made by a manufacturer.

Distributor→Avoidance→Price→Punishers→Positive→Reinforcement Management→Utilitarian→Manufacturer Rule

Distributor-deployed stimuli to weaken avoidance by presenting positive (Price) punishers that signal utilitarian reinforcement. Exposure to the contingencies is indirect through a rule in the manufacturer managerial behaviour setting.

Distributor→Avoidance→Price→Punishers→Positive→Reinforcement Management→Informational→Direct Exposure to Contingency

Distributor-deployed stimuli to weaken avoidance by presenting positive (Price) punishers that signal informational reinforcement. Exposure to the contingencies is direct.

Distributor→Avoidance→Price→Punishers→Positive→Reinforcement Management→Informational→Distributor Rule

Distributor-deployed stimuli to weaken avoidance by presenting positive (Price) punishers that signal informational reinforcement. Exposure to the contingencies is indirect through a rule made by a manufacturer.

Distributor→Avoidance→Price→Punishers→Positive→Reinforcement Management→Informational→Manufacturer Rule

Distributor-deployed stimuli to weaken avoidance by presenting positive (Price) punishers that signal informational reinforcement. Exposure to the contingencies is indirect through a rule in the manufacturer managerial behaviour setting.

Distributor→Avoidance→Price→Punishers→Negative→Scope Management→Setting→Direct Exposure to Contingency

Distributor-deployed stimuli to weaken avoidance by removing negative (Price) punishers that have an impact on the setting. Exposure to the contingencies is direct.

Distributor→Avoidance→Price→Punishers→Negative→Scope Management→Setting→Distributor Rule

Distributor-deployed stimuli to weaken avoidance by removing negative (Price) punishers that have an impact on the setting. Exposure to the contingencies is indirect through a rule made by a manufacturer.

Distributor→Avoidance→Price→Punishers→Negative→Scope Management→Setting→Manufacturer Rule

Distributor-deployed stimuli to weaken avoidance by removing negative (Price) punishers that have an impact on the setting. Exposure to the contingencies is indirect through a rule in the manufacturer managerial behaviour setting.

Code	Description and rule
Distributor→Avoidance→Price→Punishers→Negative→ Reinforcement Management→Utilitarian→Direct Exposure to Contingency	Distributor-deployed stimuli to weaken avoidance by removing negative (Price) punishers that signal utilitarian reinforcement. Exposure to the contingencies is direct.
Distributor→Avoidance→Price→Punishers→Negative→ Reinforcement Management→Utilitarian→Distributor Rule	Distributor-deployed stimuli to weaken avoidance by removing negative (Price) punishers that signal utilitarian reinforcement. Exposure to the contingencies is indirect through a rule made by a manufacturer.
Distributor→Avoidance→Price→Punishers→Negative→ Reinforcement Management→Utilitarian→Manufacturer Rule	Distributor-deployed stimuli to weaken avoidance by removing negative (Price) punishers that signal utilitarian reinforcement. Exposure to the contingencies is indirect through a rule in the manufacturer managerial behaviour setting.
Distributor→Avoidance→Price→Punishers→Negative→ Reinforcement Management→Informational→Direct Exposure to Contingency	Distributor-deployed stimuli to weaken avoidance by removing negative (Price) punishers that signal informational reinforcement. Exposure to the contingencies is direct.
Distributor→Avoidance→Price→Punishers→Negative→ Reinforcement Management→Informational→Distributor Rule	Distributor-deployed stimuli to weaken avoidance by removing negative (Price) punishers that signal informational reinforcement. Exposure to the contingencies is indirect through a rule made by a manufacturer.
Distributor→Avoidance→Price→Punishers→Negative→ Reinforcement Management→Informational→ Manufacturer Rule	Distributor-deployed stimuli to weaken avoidance by removing negative (Price) punishers that signal informational reinforcement. Exposure to the contingencies is indirect through a rule in the manufacturer managerial behaviour setting.
Product	
Distributor→Avoidance→Product→Punishers→Positive→ Scope Management→Setting→Direct Exposure to Contingency	Distributor-deployed stimuli to weaken avoidance by presenting positive (Product) punishers that have an impact on the setting. Exposure to the contingencies is direct.

Distributor→Avoidance→Product→Punishers→Positive→ Scope Management→Setting→Distributor Rule

Distributor-deployed stimuli to weaken avoidance by presenting positive (Product) punishers that have an impact on the setting. Exposure to the contingencies is indirect through a rule made by a manufacturer.

Distributor→Avoidance→Product→Punishers→Positive→ Scope Management→Setting→Manufacturer Rule

Distributor-deployed stimuli to weaken avoidance by presenting positive (Product) punishers that have an impact on the setting. Exposure to the contingencies is indirect through a rule in the manufacturer managerial behaviour setting.

Distributor→Avoidance→Product→Punishers→Positive→ Reinforcement Management→Utilitarian→Direct Exposure to Contingency

Distributor-deployed stimuli to weaken avoidance by presenting positive (Product) punishers that signal utilitarian reinforcement. Exposure to the contingencies is direct.

Distributor→Avoidance→Product→Punishers→Positive→ Reinforcement Management→Utilitarian→Distributor Rule

Distributor-deployed stimuli to weaken avoidance by presenting positive (Product) punishers that signal utilitarian reinforcement. Exposure to the contingencies is indirect through a rule made by a manufacturer.

Distributor→Avoidance→Product→Punishers→Positive→ Reinforcement Management→Utilitarian→Manufacturer Rule

Distributor-deployed stimuli to weaken avoidance by presenting positive (Product) punishers that signal utilitarian reinforcement. Exposure to the contingencies is indirect through a rule in the manufacturer managerial behaviour setting.

Distributor→Avoidance→Product→Punishers→Positive→ Reinforcement Management→Informational→Direct Exposure to Contingency

Distributor-deployed stimuli to weaken avoidance by presenting positive (Product) punishers that signal informational reinforcement. Exposure to the contingencies is direct.

Distributor→Avoidance→Product→Punishers→Positive→ Reinforcement Management→Informational→Distributor Rule

Distributor-deployed stimuli to weaken avoidance by presenting positive (Product) punishers that signal informational reinforcement. Exposure to the contingencies is indirect through a rule made by a manufacturer.

Code	Description and rule
Distributor→Avoidance→Product→Punishers→Positive→Reinforcement Management→Informational→Manufacturer Rule	Distributor-deployed stimuli to weaken avoidance by presenting positive (Product) punishers that signal informational reinforcement. Exposure to the contingencies is indirect through a rule in the manufacturer managerial behaviour setting.
Distributor→Avoidance→Product→Punishers→Negative→Scope Management→Setting→Direct Exposure to Contingency	Distributor-deployed stimuli to weaken avoidance by removing negative (Product) punishers that have an impact on the setting. Exposure to the contingencies is direct.
Distributor→Avoidance→Product→Punishers→Negative→Scope Management→Setting→Distributor Rule	Distributor-deployed stimuli to weaken avoidance by removing negative (Product) punishers that have an impact on the setting. Exposure to the contingencies is indirect through a rule made by a manufacturer.
Distributor→Avoidance→Product→Punishers→Negative→Scope Management→Setting→Manufacturer Rule	Distributor-deployed stimuli to weaken avoidance by removing negative (Product) punishers that have an impact on the setting. Exposure to the contingencies is indirect through a rule in the manufacturer managerial behaviour setting.
Distributor→Avoidance→Product→Punishers→Negative→Reinforcement Management→Utilitarian→Direct Exposure to Contingency	Distributor-deployed stimuli to weaken avoidance by removing negative (Product) punishers that signal utilitarian reinforcement. Exposure to the contingencies is direct.
Distributor→Avoidance→Product→Punishers→Negative→Reinforcement Management→Utilitarian→Distributor Rule	Distributor-deployed stimuli to weaken avoidance by removing negative (Product) punishers that signal utilitarian reinforcement. Exposure to the contingencies is indirect through a rule made by a manufacturer.
Distributor→Avoidance→Product→Punishers→Negative→Reinforcement Management→Utilitarian→Manufacturer Rule	Distributor-deployed stimuli to weaken avoidance by removing negative (Product) punishers that signal utilitarian reinforcement. Exposure to the contingencies is indirect through a rule in the manufacturer managerial behaviour setting.

Distributor→Avoidance→Product→Punishers→Negative→Reinforcement Management→Informational→Direct Exposure to Contingency

Distributor-deployed stimuli to weaken avoidance by removing negative (Product) punishers that signal informational reinforcement. Exposure to the contingencies is direct.

Distributor→Avoidance→Product→Punishers→Negative→Reinforcement Management→Informational→Distributor Rule

Distributor-deployed stimuli to weaken avoidance by removing negative (Product) punishers that signal informational reinforcement. Exposure to the contingencies is indirect through a rule made by a manufacturer.

Distributor→Avoidance→Product→Punishers→Negative→Reinforcement Management→Informational→Manufacturer Rule

Distributor-deployed stimuli to weaken avoidance by removing negative (Product) punishers that signal informational reinforcement. Exposure to the contingencies is indirect through a rule in the manufacturer managerial behaviour setting.

Promotion

Distributor→Avoidance→Promotion→Punishers→Positive→Scope Management→Setting→Direct Exposure to Contingency

Distributor-deployed stimuli to weaken avoidance by presenting positive (Promotion) punishers that have an impact on the setting. Exposure to the contingencies is direct.

Distributor→Avoidance→Promotion→Punishers→Positive→Scope Management→Setting→Distributor Rule

Distributor-deployed stimuli to weaken avoidance by presenting positive (Promotion) punishers that have an impact on the setting. Exposure to the contingencies is indirect through a rule made by a manufacturer.

Distributor→Avoidance→Promotion→Punishers→Positive→Scope Management→Setting→Manufacturer Rule

Distributor-deployed stimuli to weaken avoidance by presenting positive (Promotion) punishers that have an impact on the setting. Exposure to the contingencies is indirect through a rule in the manufacturer managerial behaviour setting.

Distributor→Avoidance→Promotion→Punishers→Positive→Reinforcement Management→Utilitarian→Direct Exposure to Contingency

Distributor-deployed stimuli to weaken avoidance by presenting positive (Promotion) punishers that signal utilitarian reinforcement. Exposure to the contingencies is direct.

Code	Description and rule
Distributor→Avoidance→Promotion→Punishers→Positive→ Reinforcement Management→Utilitarian→Distributor Rule	Distributor-deployed stimuli to weaken avoidance by presenting positive (Promotion) punishers that signal utilitarian reinforcement. Exposure to the contingencies is indirect through a rule made by a manufacturer.
Distributor→Avoidance→Promotion→Punishers→Positive→ Reinforcement Management→Utilitarian→Manufacturer Rule	Distributor-deployed stimuli to weaken avoidance by presenting positive (Promotion) punishers that signal utilitarian reinforcement. Exposure to the contingencies is indirect through a rule in the manufacturer managerial behaviour setting.
Distributor→Avoidance→Promotion→Punishers→Positive→ Reinforcement Management→Informational→Direct Exposure to Contingency	Distributor-deployed stimuli to weaken avoidance by presenting positive (Promotion) punishers that signal informational reinforcement. Exposure to the contingencies is direct.
Distributor→Avoidance→Promotion→Punishers→Positive→ Reinforcement Management→Informational→Distributor Rule	Distributor-deployed stimuli to weaken avoidance by presenting positive (Promotion) punishers that signal informational reinforcement. Exposure to the contingencies is indirect through a rule made by a manufacturer.
Distributor→Avoidance→Promotion→Punishers→Positive→ Reinforcement Management→Informational→ Manufacturer Rule	Distributor-deployed stimuli to weaken avoidance by presenting positive (Promotion) punishers that signal informational reinforcement. Exposure to the contingencies is indirect through a rule in the manufacturer managerial behaviour setting.
Distributor→Avoidance→Promotion→Punishers→Negative→ Scope Management→Setting→Direct Exposure to Contingency	Distributor-deployed stimuli to weaken avoidance by removing negative (Promotion) punishers that have an impact on the setting. Exposure to the contingencies is direct.
Distributor→Avoidance→Promotion→Punishers→Negative→ Scope Management→Setting→Distributor Rule	Distributor-deployed stimuli to weaken avoidance by removing negative (Promotion) punishers that have an impact on the setting. Exposure to the contingencies is indirect through a rule made by a manufacturer.

Distributor→Avoidance→Promotion→Punishers→Negative→Scope Management→Setting→Manufacturer Rule

Distributor-deployed stimuli to weaken avoidance by removing negative (Promotion) punishers that have an impact on the setting. Exposure to the contingencies is indirect through a rule in the manufacturer managerial behaviour setting.

Distributor→Avoidance→Promotion→Punishers→Negative→Reinforcement Management→Utilitarian→Direct Exposure to Contingency

Distributor-deployed stimuli to weaken avoidance by removing negative (Promotion) punishers that signal utilitarian reinforcement. Exposure to the contingencies is direct.

Distributor→Avoidance→Promotion→Punishers→Negative→Reinforcement Management→Utilitarian→Distributor Rule

Distributor-deployed stimuli to weaken avoidance by removing negative (Promotion) punishers that signal utilitarian reinforcement. Exposure to the contingencies is indirect through a rule made by a manufacturer.

Distributor→Avoidance→Promotion→Punishers→Negative→Reinforcement Management→Utilitarian→Manufacturer Rule

Distributor-deployed stimuli to weaken avoidance by removing negative (Promotion) punishers that signal utilitarian reinforcement. Exposure to the contingencies is indirect through a rule in the manufacturer managerial behaviour setting.

Distributor→Avoidance→Promotion→Punishers→Negative→Reinforcement Management→Informational→Direct Exposure to Contingency

Distributor-deployed stimuli to weaken avoidance by removing negative (Promotion) punishers that signal informational reinforcement. Exposure to the contingencies is direct.

Distributor→Avoidance→Promotion→Punishers→Negative→Reinforcement Management→Informational→Distributor Rule

Distributor-deployed stimuli to weaken avoidance by removing negative (Promotion) punishers that signal informational reinforcement. Exposure to the contingencies is indirect through a rule made by a manufacturer.

Distributor→Avoidance→Promotion→Punishers→Negative→Reinforcement Management→Informational→Manufacturer Rule

Distributor-deployed stimuli to weaken avoidance by removing negative (Promotion) punishers that signal informational reinforcement. Exposure to the contingencies is indirect through a rule in the manufacturer managerial behaviour setting.

Code	Description and rule
Place	
Distributor→Avoidance→Place→Punishers→Positive→Scope Management→Setting→Direct Exposure to Contingency	Distributor-deployed stimuli to weaken avoidance by presenting positive (Place) punishers that have an impact on the setting. Exposure to the contingencies is direct.
Distributor→Avoidance→Place→Punishers→Positive→Scope Management→Setting→Distributor Rule	Distributor-deployed stimuli to weaken avoidance by presenting positive (Place) punishers that have an impact on the setting. Exposure to the contingencies is indirect through a rule made by a manufacturer.
Distributor→Avoidance→Place→Punishers→Positive→Scope Management→Setting→Manufacturer Rule	Distributor-deployed stimuli to weaken avoidance by presenting positive (Place) punishers that have an impact on the setting. Exposure to the contingencies is indirect through a rule in the manufacturer managerial behaviour setting.
Distributor→Avoidance→Place→Punishers→Positive→Reinforcement Management→Utilitarian→Direct Exposure to Contingency	Distributor-deployed stimuli to weaken avoidance by presenting positive (Place) punishers that signal utilitarian reinforcement. Exposure to the contingencies is direct.
Distributor→Avoidance→Place→Punishers→Positive→Reinforcement Management→Utilitarian→Distributor Rule	Distributor-deployed stimuli to weaken avoidance by presenting positive (Place) punishers that signal utilitarian reinforcement. Exposure to the contingencies is indirect through a rule made by a manufacturer.
Distributor→Avoidance→Place→Punishers→Positive→Reinforcement Management→Utilitarian→Manufacturer Rule	Distributor-deployed stimuli to weaken avoidance by presenting positive (Place) punishers that signal utilitarian reinforcement. Exposure to the contingencies is indirect through a rule in the manufacturer managerial behaviour setting.
Distributor→Avoidance→Place→Punishers→Positive→Reinforcement Management→Informational→Direct Exposure to Contingency	Distributor-deployed stimuli to weaken avoidance by presenting positive (Place) punishers that signal informational reinforcement. Exposure to the contingencies is direct.

Distributor→Avoidance→Place→Punishers→Positive→Reinforcement Management→Informational→Distributor Rule	Distributor-deployed stimuli to weaken avoidance by presenting positive (Place) punishers that signal informational reinforcement. Exposure to the contingencies is indirect through a rule made by a manufacturer.
Distributor→Avoidance→Place→Punishers→Positive→Reinforcement Management→Informational→Manufacturer Rule	Distributor-deployed stimuli to weaken avoidance by presenting positive (Place) punishers that signal informational reinforcement. Exposure to the contingencies is indirect through a rule in the manufacturer managerial behaviour setting.
Distributor→Avoidance→Place→Punishers→Negative→Scope Management→Setting→Direct Exposure to Contingency	Distributor-deployed stimuli to weaken avoidance by removing negative (Place) punishers that have an impact on the setting. Exposure to the contingencies is direct.
Distributor→Avoidance→Place→Punishers→Negative→Scope Management→Setting→Distributor Rule	Distributor-deployed stimuli to weaken avoidance by removing negative (Place) punishers that have an impact on the setting. Exposure to the contingencies is indirect through a rule made by a manufacturer.
Distributor→Avoidance→Place→Punishers→Negative→Scope Management→Setting→Manufacturer Rule	Distributor-deployed stimuli to weaken avoidance by removing negative (Place) punishers that have an impact on the setting. Exposure to the contingencies is indirect through a rule in the manufacturer managerial behaviour setting.
Distributor→Avoidance→Place→Punishers→Negative→Reinforcement Management→Utilitarian→Direct Exposure to Contingency	Distributor-deployed stimuli to weaken avoidance by removing negative (Place) punishers that signal utilitarian reinforcement. Exposure to the contingencies is direct.
Distributor→Avoidance→Place→Punishers→Negative→Reinforcement Management→Utilitarian→Distributor Rule	Distributor-deployed stimuli to weaken avoidance by removing negative (Place) punishers that signal utilitarian reinforcement. Exposure to the contingencies is indirect through a rule made by a manufacturer.

Code	Description and rule
Distributor→Avoidance→Place→Punishers→Negative→ Reinforcement Management→Utilitarian→Manufacturer Rule	Distributor-deployed stimuli to weaken avoidance by removing negative (Place) punishers that signal utilitarian reinforcement. Exposure to the contingencies is indirect through a rule in the manufacturer managerial behaviour setting.
Distributor→Avoidance→Place→Punishers→Negative→ Reinforcement Management→Informational→Direct Exposure to Contingency	Distributor-deployed stimuli to weaken avoidance by removing negative (Place) punishers that signal informational reinforcement. Exposure to the contingencies is direct.
Distributor→Avoidance→Place→Punishers→Negative→ Reinforcement Management→Informational→Distributor Rule	Distributor-deployed stimuli to weaken avoidance by removing negative (Place) punishers that signal informational reinforcement. Exposure to the contingencies is indirect through a rule made by a manufacturer.
Distributor→Avoidance→Place→Punishers→Negative→ Reinforcement Management→Informational→ Manufacturer Rule	Distributor-deployed stimuli to weaken avoidance by removing negative (Place) punishers that signal informational reinforcement. Exposure to the contingencies is indirect through a rule in the manufacturer managerial behaviour setting.

Manufacturer↔Retailer relationships (manufacturer-deployed stimuli)

Strengthening retailer approach (through reinforcement)

Price

Manufacturer→Approach→Price→Reinforcers→Positive→ Scope Management→Setting→Direct Exposure to Contingency	Manufacturer-deployed stimuli to strengthen approach by presenting positive (Price) reinforcers that have an impact on the setting. Exposure to the contingencies is direct.
Manufacturer→Approach→Price→Reinforcers→Positive→ Scope Management→Setting→Manufacturer Rule	Manufacturer-deployed stimuli to strengthen approach by presenting positive (Price) reinforcers that have an impact on the setting. Exposure to the contingencies is indirect through a rule made by a manufacturer.

Manufacturer→Approach→Price→Reinforcers→Positive→ Scope Management→Setting→Retailer Rule

Manufacturer-deployed stimuli to strengthen approach by presenting positive (Price) reinforcers that have an impact on the setting. Exposure to the contingencies is indirect through a rule in the retailer managerial behaviour setting.

Manufacturer→Approach→Price→Reinforcers→Positive→ Reinforcement Management→Utilitarian→Direct Exposure to Contingency

Manufacturer-deployed stimuli to strengthen approach by presenting positive (Price) reinforcers that signal utilitarian reinforcement. Exposure to the contingencies is direct.

Manufacturer→Approach→Price→Reinforcers→Positive→ Reinforcement Management→Utilitarian→Manufacturer Rule

Manufacturer-deployed stimuli to strengthen approach by presenting positive (Price) reinforcers that signal utilitarian reinforcement. Exposure to the contingencies is indirect through a rule made by a manufacturer.

Manufacturer→Approach→Price→Reinforcers→Positive→ Reinforcement Management→Utilitarian→Retailer Rule

Manufacturer-deployed stimuli to strengthen approach by presenting positive (Price) reinforcers that signal utilitarian reinforcement. Exposure to the contingencies is indirect through a rule in the retailer managerial behaviour setting.

Manufacturer→Approach→Price→Reinforcers→Positive→ Reinforcement Management→Informational→Direct Exposure to Contingency

Manufacturer-deployed stimuli to strengthen approach by presenting positive (Price) reinforcers that signal informational reinforcement. Exposure to the contingencies is direct.

Manufacturer→Approach→Price→Reinforcers→Positive→ Reinforcement Management→Informational→ Manufacturer Rule

Manufacturer-deployed stimuli to strengthen approach by presenting positive (Price) reinforcers that signal informational reinforcement. Exposure to the contingencies is indirect through a rule made by a manufacturer.

Manufacturer→Approach→Price→Reinforcers→Positive→ Reinforcement Management→Informational→Retailer Rule

Manufacturer-deployed stimuli to strengthen approach by presenting positive (Price) reinforcers that signal informational reinforcement. Exposure to the contingencies is indirect through a rule in the retailer managerial behaviour setting.

Code	Description and rule
Manufacturer→Approach→Price→Reinforcers→Negative→ Scope Management→Setting→Direct Exposure to Contingency	Manufacturer-deployed stimuli to strengthen approach by removing negative (Price) reinforcers that have an impact on the setting. Exposure to the contingencies is direct.
Manufacturer→Approach→Price→Reinforcers→Negative→ Scope Management→Setting→Manufacturer Rule	Manufacturer-deployed stimuli to strengthen approach by removing negative (Price) reinforcers that have an impact on the setting. Exposure to the contingencies is indirect through a rule made by a manufacturer.
Manufacturer→Approach→Price→Reinforcers→Negative→ Scope Management→Setting→Retailer Rule	Manufacturer-deployed stimuli to strengthen approach by removing negative (Price) reinforcers that have an impact on the setting. Exposure to the contingencies is indirect through a rule in the retailer managerial behaviour setting.
Manufacturer→Approach→Price→Reinforcers→Negative→ Reinforcement Management→Utilitarian→Direct Exposure to Contingency	Manufacturer-deployed stimuli to strengthen approach by removing negative (Price) reinforcers that signal utilitarian reinforcement. Exposure to the contingencies is direct.
Manufacturer→Approach→Price→Reinforcers→Negative→ Reinforcement Management→Utilitarian→Manufacturer Rule	Manufacturer-deployed stimuli to strengthen approach by removing negative (Price) reinforcers that signal utilitarian reinforcement. Exposure to the contingencies is indirect through a rule made by a manufacturer.
Manufacturer→Approach→Price→Reinforcers→Negative→ Reinforcement Management→Utilitarian→Retailer Rule	Manufacturer-deployed stimuli to strengthen approach by removing negative (Price) reinforcers that signal utilitarian reinforcement. Exposure to the contingencies is indirect through a rule in the retailer managerial behaviour setting.
Manufacturer→Approach→Price→Reinforcers→Negative→ Reinforcement Management→Informational→Direct Exposure to Contingency	Manufacturer-deployed stimuli to strengthen approach by removing negative (Price) reinforcers that signal informational reinforcement. Exposure to the contingencies is direct.

Manufacturer→Approach→Price→Reinforcers→Negative→Reinforcement Management→Informational→Manufacturer Rule	Manufacturer-deployed stimuli to strengthen approach by removing negative (Price) reinforcers that signal informational reinforcement. Exposure to the contingencies is indirect through a rule made by a manufacturer.
Manufacturer→Approach→Price→Reinforcers→Negative→Reinforcement Management→Informational→Retailer Rule	Manufacturer-deployed stimuli to strengthen approach by removing negative (Price) reinforcers that signal informational reinforcement. Exposure to the contingencies is indirect through a rule in the retailer managerial behaviour setting.

Product

Manufacturer→Approach→Product→Reinforcers→Positive→Scope Management→Setting→Direct Exposure to Contingency	Manufacturer-deployed stimuli to strengthen approach by presenting positive (Product) reinforcers that have an impact on the setting. Exposure to the contingencies is direct.
Manufacturer→Approach→Product→Reinforcers→Positive→Scope Management→Setting→Manufacturer Rule	Manufacturer-deployed stimuli to strengthen approach by presenting positive (Product) reinforcers that have an impact on the setting. Exposure to the contingencies is indirect through a rule made by a manufacturer.
Manufacturer→Approach→Product→Reinforcers→Positive→Scope Management→Setting→Retailer Rule	Manufacturer-deployed stimuli to strengthen approach by presenting positive (Product) reinforcers that have an impact on the setting. Exposure to the contingencies is indirect through a rule in the retailer managerial behaviour setting.
Manufacturer→Approach→Product→Reinforcers→Positive→Reinforcement Management→Utilitarian→Direct Exposure to Contingency	Manufacturer-deployed stimuli to strengthen approach by presenting positive (Product) reinforcers that signal utilitarian reinforcement. Exposure to the contingencies is direct.
Manufacturer→Approach→Product→Reinforcers→Positive→Reinforcement Management→Utilitarian→Manufacturer Rule	Manufacturer-deployed stimuli to strengthen approach by presenting positive (Product) reinforcers that signal utilitarian reinforcement. Exposure to the contingencies is indirect through a rule made by a manufacturer.

Code	Description and rule
Manufacturer→Approach→Product→Reinforcers→Positive→ Reinforcement Management→Utilitarian→Retailer Rule	Manufacturer-deployed stimuli to strengthen approach by presenting positive (Product) reinforcers that signal utilitarian reinforcement. Exposure to the contingencies is indirect through a rule in the retailer managerial behaviour setting.
Manufacturer→Approach→Product→Reinforcers→Positive→ Reinforcement Management→Informational→Direct Exposure to Contingency	Manufacturer-deployed stimuli to strengthen approach by presenting positive (Product) reinforcers that signal informational reinforcement. Exposure to the contingencies is direct.
Manufacturer→Approach→Product→Reinforcers→Positive→ Reinforcement Management→Informational→ Manufacturer Rule	Manufacturer-deployed stimuli to strengthen approach by presenting positive (Product) reinforcers that signal informational reinforcement. Exposure to the contingencies is indirect through a rule made by a manufacturer.
Manufacturer→Approach→Product→Reinforcers→Positive→ Reinforcement Management→Informational→Retailer Rule	Manufacturer-deployed stimuli to strengthen approach by presenting positive (Product) reinforcers that signal informational reinforcement. Exposure to the contingencies is indirect through a rule in the retailer managerial behaviour setting.
Manufacturer→Approach→Product→Reinforcers→Negative →Scope Management→Setting→Direct Exposure to Contingency	Manufacturer-deployed stimuli to strengthen approach by removing negative (Product) reinforcers that have an impact on the setting. Exposure to the contingencies is direct.
Manufacturer→Approach→Product→Reinforcers→ Negative→Scope Management→Setting→Manufacturer Rule	Manufacturer-deployed stimuli to strengthen approach by removing negative (Product) reinforcers that have an impact on the setting. Exposure to the contingencies is indirect through a rule made by a manufacturer.
Manufacturer→Approach→Product→Reinforcers→ Negative→Scope Management→Setting→Retailer Rule	Manufacturer-deployed stimuli to strengthen approach by removing negative (Product) reinforcers that have an impact on the setting. Exposure to the contingencies is indirect through a rule in the retailer managerial behaviour setting.

Manufacturer→Approach→Product→Reinforcers→Negative→Reinforcement Management→Utilitarian→Direct Exposure to Contingency

Manufacturer→Approach→Product→Reinforcers→Negative→Reinforcement Management→Utilitarian→Manufacturer Rule

Manufacturer→Approach→Product→Reinforcers→Negative→Reinforcement Management→Utilitarian→Retailer Rule

Manufacturer→Approach→Product→Reinforcers→Negative→Reinforcement Management→Informational→Direct Exposure to Contingency

Manufacturer→Approach→Product→Reinforcers→Negative→Reinforcement Management→Informational→Manufacturer Rule

Manufacturer→Approach→Product→Reinforcers→Negative→Reinforcement Management→Informational→Retailer Rule

Promotion

Manufacturer→Approach→Promotion→Reinforcers→Positive→Scope Management→Setting→Direct Exposure to Contingency

Manufacturer-deployed stimuli to strengthen approach by removing negative (Product) reinforcers that signal utilitarian reinforcement. Exposure to the contingencies is direct.

Manufacturer-deployed stimuli to strengthen approach by removing negative (Product) reinforcers that signal utilitarian reinforcement. Exposure to the contingencies is indirect through a rule made by a manufacturer.

Manufacturer-deployed stimuli to strengthen approach by removing negative (Product) reinforcers that signal utilitarian reinforcement. Exposure to the contingencies is indirect through a rule in the retailer managerial behaviour setting.

Manufacturer-deployed stimuli to strengthen approach by removing negative (Product) reinforcers that signal informational reinforcement. Exposure to the contingencies is direct.

Manufacturer-deployed stimuli to strengthen approach by removing negative (Product) reinforcers that signal informational reinforcement. Exposure to the contingencies is indirect through a rule made by a manufacturer.

Manufacturer-deployed stimuli to strengthen approach by removing negative (Product) reinforcers that signal informational reinforcement. Exposure to the contingencies is indirect through a rule in the retailer managerial behaviour setting.

Manufacturer-deployed stimuli to strengthen approach by presenting positive (Promotion) reinforcers that have an impact on the setting. Exposure to the contingencies is direct.

Code	Description and rule
Manufacturer→Approach→Promotion→Reinforcers→ Positive→Scope Management→Setting→Manufacturer Rule	Manufacturer-deployed stimuli to strengthen approach by presenting positive (Promotion) reinforcers that have an impact on the setting. Exposure to the contingencies is indirect through a rule made by a manufacturer.
Manufacturer→Approach→Promotion→Reinforcers→ Positive→Scope Management→Setting→Retailer Rule	Manufacturer-deployed stimuli to strengthen approach by presenting positive (Promotion) reinforcers that have an impact on the setting. Exposure to the contingencies is indirect through a rule in the retailer managerial behaviour setting.
Manufacturer→Approach→Promotion→Reinforcers→ Positive→Reinforcement Management→Utilitarian→Direct Exposure to Contingency	Manufacturer-deployed stimuli to strengthen approach by presenting positive (Promotion) reinforcers that signal utilitarian reinforcement. Exposure to the contingencies is direct.
Manufacturer→Approach→Promotion→Reinforcers→ Positive→Reinforcement Management→Utilitarian→ Manufacturer Rule	Manufacturer-deployed stimuli to strengthen approach by presenting positive (Promotion) reinforcers that signal utilitarian reinforcement. Exposure to the contingencies is indirect through a rule made by a manufacturer.
Manufacturer→Approach→Promotion→Reinforcers→ Positive→Reinforcement Management→Utilitarian→ Retailer Rule	Manufacturer-deployed stimuli to strengthen approach by presenting positive (Promotion) reinforcers that signal utilitarian reinforcement. Exposure to the contingencies is indirect through a rule in the retailer managerial behaviour setting.
Manufacturer→Approach→Promotion→Reinforcers→ Positive→Reinforcement Management→Informational→ Direct Exposure to Contingency	Manufacturer-deployed stimuli to strengthen approach by presenting positive (Promotion) reinforcers that signal informational reinforcement. Exposure to the contingencies is direct.
Manufacturer→Approach→Promotion→Reinforcers→ Positive→Reinforcement Management→Informational→ Manufacturer Rule	Manufacturer-deployed stimuli to strengthen approach by presenting positive (Promotion) reinforcers that signal informational reinforcement. Exposure to the contingencies is indirect through a rule made by a manufacturer.

Manufacturer-deployed stimuli to strengthen approach by presenting positive (Promotion) reinforcers that signal informational reinforcement. Exposure to the contingencies is indirect through a rule in the retailer managerial behaviour setting.

Manufacturer-deployed stimuli to strengthen approach by removing negative (Promotion) reinforcers that have an impact on the setting. Exposure to the contingencies is direct.

Manufacturer-deployed stimuli to strengthen approach by removing negative (Promotion) reinforcers that have an impact on the setting. Exposure to the contingencies is indirect through a rule made by a manufacturer.

Manufacturer-deployed stimuli to strengthen approach by removing negative (Promotion) reinforcers that have an impact on the setting. Exposure to the contingencies is indirect through a rule in the retailer managerial behaviour setting.

Manufacturer-deployed stimuli to strengthen approach by removing negative (Promotion) reinforcers that signal utilitarian reinforcement. Exposure to the contingencies is direct.

Manufacturer-deployed stimuli to strengthen approach by removing negative (Promotion) reinforcers that signal utilitarian reinforcement. Exposure to the contingencies is indirect through a rule made by a manufacturer.

Manufacturer-deployed stimuli to strengthen approach by removing negative (Promotion) reinforcers that signal utilitarian reinforcement. Exposure to the contingencies is indirect through a rule in the retailer managerial behaviour setting.

Manufacturer→Approach→Promotion→Reinforcers→Positive→Reinforcement Management→Informational→Retailer Rule

Manufacturer→Approach→Promotion→Reinforcers→Negative→Scope Management→Setting→Direct Exposure to Contingency

Manufacturer→Approach→Promotion→Reinforcers→Negative→Scope Management→Setting→Manufacturer Rule

Manufacturer→Approach→Promotion→Reinforcers→Negative→Scope Management→Setting→Retailer Rule

Manufacturer→Approach→Promotion→Reinforcers→Negative→Reinforcement Management→Utilitarian→Direct Exposure to Contingency

Manufacturer→Approach→Promotion→Reinforcers→Negative→Reinforcement Management→Utilitarian→Manufacturer Rule

Manufacturer→Approach→Promotion→Reinforcers→Negative→Reinforcement Management→Utilitarian→Retailer Rule

Code	Description and rule
Manufacturer→Approach→Promotion→Reinforcers→ Negative→Reinforcement Management→Informational→ Direct Exposure to Contingency	Manufacturer-deployed stimuli to strengthen approach by removing negative (Promotion) reinforcers that signal informational reinforcement. Exposure to the contingencies is direct.
Manufacturer→Approach→Promotion→Reinforcers→ Negative→Reinforcement Management→Informational→ Manufacturer Rule	Manufacturer-deployed stimuli to strengthen approach by removing negative (Promotion) reinforcers that signal informational reinforcement. Exposure to the contingencies is indirect through a rule made by a manufacturer.
Manufacturer→Approach→Promotion→Reinforcers→ Negative→Reinforcement Management→Informational→ Retailer Rule	Manufacturer-deployed stimuli to strengthen approach by removing negative (Promotion) reinforcers that signal informational reinforcement. Exposure to the contingencies is indirect through a rule in the retailer managerial behaviour setting.
Place	
Manufacturer→Approach→Place→Reinforcers→Positive→ Scope Management→Setting→Direct Exposure to Contingency	Manufacturer-deployed stimuli to strengthen approach by presenting positive (Place) reinforcers that have an impact on the setting. Exposure to the contingencies is direct.
Manufacturer→Approach→Place→Reinforcers→Positive→ Scope Management→Setting→Manufacturer Rule	Manufacturer-deployed stimuli to strengthen approach by presenting positive (Place) reinforcers that have an impact on the setting. Exposure to the contingencies is indirect through a rule made by a manufacturer.
Manufacturer→Approach→Place→Reinforcers→Positive→ Scope Management→Setting→Retailer Rule	Manufacturer-deployed stimuli to strengthen approach by presenting positive (Place) reinforcers that have an impact on the setting. Exposure to the contingencies is indirect through a rule in the retailer managerial behaviour setting.

Manufacturer→Approach→Place→Reinforcers→Positive→Reinforcement Management→Utilitarian→Direct Exposure to Contingency	Manufacturer-deployed stimuli to strengthen approach by presenting positive (Place) reinforcers that signal utilitarian reinforcement. Exposure to the contingencies is direct.
Manufacturer→Approach→Place→Reinforcers→Positive→Reinforcement Management→Utilitarian→Manufacturer Rule	Manufacturer-deployed stimuli to strengthen approach by presenting positive (Place) reinforcers that signal utilitarian reinforcement. Exposure to the contingencies is indirect through a rule made by a manufacturer.
Manufacturer→Approach→Place→Reinforcers→Positive→Reinforcement Management→Utilitarian→Retailer Rule	Manufacturer-deployed stimuli to strengthen approach by presenting positive (Place) reinforcers that signal utilitarian reinforcement. Exposure to the contingencies is indirect through a rule in the retailer managerial behaviour setting.
Manufacturer→Approach→Place→Reinforcers→Positive→Reinforcement Management→Informational→Direct Exposure to Contingency	Manufacturer-deployed stimuli to strengthen approach by presenting positive (Place) reinforcers that signal informational reinforcement. Exposure to the contingencies is direct.
Manufacturer→Approach→Place→Reinforcers→Positive→Reinforcement Management→Informational→Manufacturer Rule	Manufacturer-deployed stimuli to strengthen approach by presenting positive (Place) reinforcers that signal informational reinforcement. Exposure to the contingencies is indirect through a rule made by a manufacturer.
Manufacturer→Approach→Place→Reinforcers→Positive→Reinforcement Management→Informational→Retailer Rule	Manufacturer-deployed stimuli to strengthen approach by presenting positive (Place) reinforcers that signal informational reinforcement. Exposure to the contingencies is indirect through a rule in the retailer managerial behaviour setting.
Manufacturer→Approach→Place→Reinforcers→Negative→Scope Management→Setting→Direct Exposure to Contingency	Manufacturer-deployed stimuli to strengthen approach by removing negative (Place) reinforcers that have an impact on the setting. Exposure to the contingencies is direct.

Code	Description and rule
Manufacturer→Approach→Place→Reinforcers→Negative→Scope Management→Setting→Manufacturer Rule	Manufacturer-deployed stimuli to strengthen approach by removing negative (Place) reinforcers that have an impact on the setting. Exposure to the contingencies is indirect through a rule made by a manufacturer.
Manufacturer→Approach→Place→Reinforcers→Negative→Scope Management→Setting→Retailer Rule	Manufacturer-deployed stimuli to strengthen approach by removing negative (Place) reinforcers that have an impact on the setting. Exposure to the contingencies is indirect through a rule in the retailer managerial behaviour setting.
Manufacturer→Approach→Place→Reinforcers→Negative→Reinforcement Management→Utilitarian→Direct Exposure to Contingency	Manufacturer-deployed stimuli to strengthen approach by removing negative (Place) reinforcers that signal utilitarian reinforcement. Exposure to the contingencies is direct.
Manufacturer→Approach→Place→Reinforcers→Negative→Reinforcement Management→Utilitarian→Manufacturer Rule	Manufacturer-deployed stimuli to strengthen approach by removing negative (Place) reinforcers that signal utilitarian reinforcement. Exposure to the contingencies is indirect through a rule made by a manufacturer.
Manufacturer→Approach→Place→Reinforcers→Negative→Reinforcement Management→Utilitarian→Retailer Rule	Manufacturer-deployed stimuli to strengthen approach by removing negative (Place) reinforcers that signal utilitarian reinforcement. Exposure to the contingencies is indirect through a rule in the retailer managerial behaviour setting.
Manufacturer→Approach→Place→Reinforcers→Negative→Reinforcement Management→Informational→Direct Exposure to Contingency	Manufacturer-deployed stimuli to strengthen approach by removing negative (Place) reinforcers that signal informational reinforcement. Exposure to the contingencies is direct.
Manufacturer→Approach→Place→Reinforcers→Negative→Reinforcement Management→Informational→Manufacturer Rule	Manufacturer-deployed stimuli to strengthen approach by removing negative (Place) reinforcers that signal informational reinforcement. Exposure to the contingencies is indirect through a rule made by a manufacturer.

Manufacturer→Approach→Place→Reinforcers→Negative→
Reinforcement Management→Informational→Retailer Rule

Manufacturer-deployed stimuli to strengthen approach by
removing negative (Place) reinforcers that signal informational
reinforcement. Exposure to the contingencies is indirect through
a rule in the retailer managerial behaviour setting.

Weakening retailer avoidance through punishment

Price

Manufacturer→Avoidance→Price→Punishers→Positive→
Scope Management→Setting→Direct Exposure to
Contingency

Manufacturer→Avoidance→Price→Punishers→Positive→
Scope Management→Setting→Manufacturer Rule

Manufacturer-deployed stimuli to weaken avoidance by
presenting positive (Price) punishers that have an impact on the
setting. Exposure to the contingencies is direct.

Manufacturer-deployed stimuli to weaken avoidance by
presenting positive (Price) punishers that have an impact on the
setting. Exposure to the contingencies is indirect through a rule
made by a manufacturer.

Manufacturer→Avoidance→Price→Punishers→Positive→
Scope Management→Setting→Retailer Rule

Manufacturer-deployed stimuli to weaken avoidance by
presenting positive (Price) punishers that have an impact on the
setting. Exposure to the contingencies is indirect through a rule
in the retailer managerial behaviour setting.

Manufacturer→Avoidance→Price→Punishers→Positive→
Reinforcement Management→Utilitarian→Direct Exposure
to Contingency

Manufacturer→Avoidance→Price→Punishers→Positive→
Reinforcement Management→Utilitarian→Manufacturer
Rule

Manufacturer-deployed stimuli to weaken avoidance by
presenting positive (Price) punishers that signal utilitarian
reinforcement. Exposure to the contingencies is direct.

Manufacturer-deployed stimuli to weaken avoidance by
presenting positive (Price) punishers that signal utilitarian
reinforcement. Exposure to the contingencies is indirect through
a rule made by a manufacturer.

Code	Description and rule
Manufacturer→Avoidance→Price→Punishers→Positive→Reinforcement Management→Utilitarian→Retailer Rule	Manufacturer-deployed stimuli to weaken avoidance by presenting positive (Price) punishers that signal utilitarian reinforcement. Exposure to the contingencies is indirect through a rule in the retailer managerial behaviour setting.
Manufacturer→Avoidance→Price→Punishers→Positive→Reinforcement Management→Informational→Direct Exposure to Contingency	Manufacturer-deployed stimuli to weaken avoidance by presenting positive (Price) punishers that signal informational reinforcement. Exposure to the contingencies is direct.
Manufacturer→Avoidance→Price→Punishers→Positive→Reinforcement Management→Informational→Manufacturer Rule	Manufacturer-deployed stimuli to weaken avoidance by presenting positive (Price) punishers that signal informational reinforcement. Exposure to the contingencies is indirect through a rule made by a manufacturer.
Manufacturer→Avoidance→Price→Punishers→Positive→Reinforcement Management→Informational→Retailer Rule	Manufacturer-deployed stimuli to weaken avoidance by presenting positive (Price) punishers that signal informational reinforcement. Exposure to the contingencies is indirect through a rule in the retailer managerial behaviour setting.
Manufacturer→Avoidance→Price→Punishers→Negative→Scope Management→Setting→Direct Exposure to Contingency	Manufacturer-deployed stimuli to weaken avoidance by removing negative (Price) punishers that have an impact on the setting. Exposure to the contingencies is direct.
Manufacturer→Avoidance→Price→Punishers→Negative→Scope Management→Setting→Manufacturer Rule	Manufacturer-deployed stimuli to weaken avoidance by removing negative (Price) punishers that have an impact on the setting. Exposure to the contingencies is indirect through a rule made by a manufacturer.
Manufacturer→Avoidance→Price→Punishers→Negative→Scope Management→Setting→Retailer Rule	Manufacturer-deployed stimuli to weaken avoidance by removing negative (Price) punishers that have an impact on the setting. Exposure to the contingencies is indirect through a rule in the retailer managerial behaviour setting.

Manufacturer→Avoidance→Price→Punishers→Negative→Utilitarian→Direct Exposure to Contingency

Manufacturer-deployed stimuli to weaken avoidance by removing negative (Price) punishers that signal utilitarian reinforcement. Exposure to the contingencies is direct.

Manufacturer→Avoidance→Price→Punishers→Negative→Utilitarian→Manufacturer Rule

Manufacturer-deployed stimuli to weaken avoidance by removing negative (Price) punishers that signal utilitarian reinforcement. Exposure to the contingencies is indirect through a rule made by a manufacturer.

Manufacturer→Avoidance→Price→Punishers→Negative→Utilitarian→Retailer Rule

Manufacturer-deployed stimuli to weaken avoidance by removing negative (Price) punishers that signal utilitarian reinforcement. Exposure to the contingencies is indirect through a rule in the retailer managerial behaviour setting.

Manufacturer→Avoidance→Price→Punishers→Negative→Informational→Direct Exposure to Contingency

Manufacturer-deployed stimuli to weaken avoidance by removing negative (Price) punishers that signal informational reinforcement. Exposure to the contingencies is direct.

Manufacturer→Avoidance→Price→Punishers→Negative→Informational→Manufacturer Rule

Manufacturer-deployed stimuli to weaken avoidance by removing negative (Price) punishers that signal informational reinforcement. Exposure to the contingencies is indirect through a rule made by a manufacturer.

Manufacturer→Avoidance→Price→Punishers→Negative→Informational→Retailer Rule

Manufacturer-deployed stimuli to weaken avoidance by removing negative (Price) punishers that signal informational reinforcement. Exposure to the contingencies is indirect through a rule in the retailer managerial behaviour setting.

Product

Manufacturer→Avoidance→Product→Punishers→Positive→Scope Management→Setting→Direct Exposure to Contingency

Manufacturer-deployed stimuli to weaken avoidance by presenting positive (Product) punishers that have an impact on the setting. Exposure to the contingencies is direct.

Code	Description and rule
Manufacturer→Avoidance→Product→Punishers→Positive→ Scope Management→Setting→Manufacturer Rule	Manufacturer-deployed stimuli to weaken avoidance by presenting positive (Product) punishers that have an impact on the setting. Exposure to the contingencies is indirect through a rule made by a manufacturer.
Manufacturer→Avoidance→Product→Punishers→Positive→ Scope Management→Setting→Retailer Rule	Manufacturer-deployed stimuli to weaken avoidance by presenting positive (Product) punishers that have an impact on the setting. Exposure to the contingencies is indirect through a rule in the retailer managerial behaviour setting.
Manufacturer→Avoidance→Product→Punishers→Positive→ Reinforcement Management→Utilitarian→Direct Exposure to Contingency	Manufacturer-deployed stimuli to weaken avoidance by presenting positive (Product) punishers that signal utilitarian reinforcement. Exposure to the contingencies is direct.
Manufacturer→Avoidance→Product→Punishers→Positive→ Reinforcement Management→Utilitarian→Manufacturer Rule	Manufacturer-deployed stimuli to weaken avoidance by presenting positive (Product) punishers that signal utilitarian reinforcement. Exposure to the contingencies is indirect through a rule made by a manufacturer.
Manufacturer→Avoidance→Product→Punishers→Positive→ Reinforcement Management→Utilitarian→Retailer Rule	Manufacturer-deployed stimuli to weaken avoidance by presenting positive (Product) punishers that signal utilitarian reinforcement. Exposure to the contingencies is indirect through a rule in the retailer managerial behaviour setting.
Manufacturer→Avoidance→Product→Punishers→Positive→ Reinforcement Management→Informational→Direct Exposure to Contingency	Manufacturer-deployed stimuli to weaken avoidance by presenting positive (Product) punishers that signal informational reinforcement. Exposure to the contingencies is direct.
Manufacturer→Avoidance→Product→Punishers→Positive→ Reinforcement Management→Informational→ Manufacturer Rule	Manufacturer-deployed stimuli to weaken avoidance by presenting positive (Product) punishers that signal informational reinforcement. Exposure to the contingencies is indirect through a rule made by a manufacturer.

Manufacturer→Avoidance→Product→Punishers→Positive→Informational→Reinforcement Management→Retailer Rule	Manufacturer-deployed stimuli to weaken avoidance by presenting positive (Product) punishers that signal informational reinforcement. Exposure to the contingencies is indirect through a rule in the retailer managerial behaviour setting.
Manufacturer→Avoidance→Product→Punishers→Negative→Scope Management→Setting→Direct Exposure to Contingency	Manufacturer-deployed stimuli to weaken avoidance by removing negative (Product) punishers that have an impact on the setting. Exposure to the contingencies is direct.
Manufacturer→Avoidance→Product→Punishers→Negative→Scope Management→Setting→Manufacturer Rule	Manufacturer-deployed stimuli to weaken avoidance by removing negative (Product) punishers that have an impact on the setting. Exposure to the contingencies is indirect through a rule made by a manufacturer.
Manufacturer→Avoidance→Product→Punishers→Negative→Scope Management→Setting→Retailer Rule	Manufacturer-deployed stimuli to weaken avoidance by removing negative (Product) punishers that have an impact on the setting. Exposure to the contingencies is indirect through a rule in the retailer managerial behaviour setting.
Manufacturer→Avoidance→Product→Punishers→Utilitarian→Reinforcement Management→Direct Exposure to Contingency	Manufacturer-deployed stimuli to weaken avoidance by removing negative (Product) punishers that signal utilitarian reinforcement. Exposure to the contingencies is direct.
Manufacturer→Avoidance→Product→Punishers→Negative→Utilitarian→Manufacturer Rule	Manufacturer-deployed stimuli to weaken avoidance by removing negative (Product) punishers that signal utilitarian reinforcement. Exposure to the contingencies is indirect through a rule made by a manufacturer.
Manufacturer→Avoidance→Product→Punishers→Utilitarian→Reinforcement Management→Retailer Rule	Manufacturer-deployed stimuli to weaken avoidance by removing negative (Product) punishers that signal utilitarian reinforcement. Exposure to the contingencies is indirect through a rule in the retailer managerial behaviour setting.

Code	Description and rule
Manufacturer→Avoidance→Product→Punishers→Negative→Reinforcement Management→Informational→Direct Exposure to Contingency	Manufacturer-deployed stimuli to weaken avoidance by removing negative (Product) punishers that signal informational reinforcement. Exposure to the contingencies is direct.
Manufacturer→Avoidance→Product→Punishers→Negative→Reinforcement Management→Informational→Manufacturer Rule	Manufacturer-deployed stimuli to weaken avoidance by removing negative (Product) punishers that signal informational reinforcement. Exposure to the contingencies is indirect through a rule made by a manufacturer.
Manufacturer→Avoidance→Product→Punishers→Negative→Reinforcement Management→Informational→Retailer Rule	Manufacturer-deployed stimuli to weaken avoidance by removing negative (Product) punishers that signal informational reinforcement. Exposure to the contingencies is indirect through a rule in the retailer managerial behaviour setting.

Promotion

Code	Description and rule
Manufacturer→Avoidance→Promotion→Punishers→Positive→Scope Management→Setting→Direct Exposure to Contingency	Manufacturer-deployed stimuli to weaken avoidance by presenting positive (Promotion) punishers that have an impact on the setting. Exposure to the contingencies is direct.
Manufacturer→Avoidance→Promotion→Punishers→Positive→Scope Management→Setting→Manufacturer Rule	Manufacturer-deployed stimuli to weaken avoidance by presenting positive (Promotion) punishers that have an impact on the setting. Exposure to the contingencies is indirect through a rule made by a manufacturer.
Manufacturer→Avoidance→Promotion→Punishers→Positive→Scope Management→Setting→Retailer Rule	Manufacturer-deployed stimuli to weaken avoidance by presenting positive (Promotion) punishers that have an impact on the setting. Exposure to the contingencies is indirect through a rule in the retailer managerial behaviour setting.
Manufacturer→Avoidance→Promotion→Punishers→Positive→Reinforcement Management→Utilitarian→Direct Exposure to Contingency	Manufacturer-deployed stimuli to weaken avoidance by presenting positive (Promotion) punishers that signal utilitarian reinforcement. Exposure to the contingencies is direct.

Manufacturer→Avoidance→Promotion→Punishers→Positive →Reinforcement Management→Utilitarian→Manufacturer Rule

Manufacturer-deployed stimuli to weaken avoidance by presenting positive (Promotion) punishers that signal utilitarian reinforcement. Exposure to the contingencies is indirect through a rule made by a manufacturer.

Manufacturer→Avoidance→Promotion→Punishers→ Positive→Reinforcement Management→Utilitarian→ Retailer Rule

Manufacturer-deployed stimuli to weaken avoidance by presenting positive (Promotion) punishers that signal utilitarian reinforcement. Exposure to the contingencies is indirect through a rule in the retailer managerial behaviour setting.

Manufacturer→Avoidance→Promotion→Punishers→Positive →Reinforcement Management→Informational→Direct Exposure to Contingency

Manufacturer-deployed stimuli to weaken avoidance by presenting positive (Promotion) punishers that signal informational reinforcement. Exposure to the contingencies is direct.

Manufacturer→Avoidance→Promotion→Punishers→Positive →Reinforcement Management→Informational→ Manufacturer Rule

Manufacturer-deployed stimuli to weaken avoidance by presenting positive (Promotion) punishers that signal informational reinforcement. Exposure to the contingencies is indirect through a rule made by a manufacturer.

Manufacturer→Avoidance→Promotion→Punishers→ Positive→Reinforcement Management→Informational→ Retailer Rule

Manufacturer-deployed stimuli to weaken avoidance by presenting positive (Promotion) punishers that signal informational reinforcement. Exposure to the contingencies is indirect through a rule in the retailer managerial behaviour setting.

Manufacturer→Avoidance→Promotion→Punishers→Negative →Scope Management→Setting→Direct Exposure to Contingency

Manufacturer-deployed stimuli to weaken avoidance by removing negative (Promotion) punishers that have an impact on the setting. Exposure to the contingencies is direct.

Manufacturer→Avoidance→Promotion→Punishers→Negative →Scope Management→Setting→Manufacturer Rule

Manufacturer-deployed stimuli to weaken avoidance by removing negative (Promotion) punishers that have an impact on the setting. Exposure to the contingencies is indirect through a rule made by a manufacturer.

Code	Description and rule
Manufacturer→Avoidance→Promotion→Punishers→Negative →Scope Management→Setting→Retailer Rule	Manufacturer-deployed stimuli to weaken avoidance by removing negative (Promotion) punishers that have an impact on the setting. Exposure to the contingencies is indirect through a rule in the retailer managerial behaviour setting.
Manufacturer→Avoidance→Promotion→Punishers→ Negative→Reinforcement Management→Utilitarian→ Direct Exposure to Contingency	Manufacturer-deployed stimuli to weaken avoidance by removing negative (Promotion) punishers that signal utilitarian reinforcement. Exposure to the contingencies is direct.
Manufacturer→Avoidance→Promotion→Punishers→Negative →Reinforcement Management→Utilitarian→Manufacturer Rule	Manufacturer-deployed stimuli to weaken avoidance by removing negative (Promotion) punishers that signal utilitarian reinforcement. Exposure to the contingencies is indirect through a rule made by a manufacturer.
Manufacturer→Avoidance→Promotion→Punishers→Negative →Reinforcement Management→Utilitarian→Retailer Rule	Manufacturer-deployed stimuli to weaken avoidance by removing negative (Promotion) punishers that signal utilitarian reinforcement. Exposure to the contingencies is indirect through a rule in the retailer managerial behaviour setting.
Manufacturer→Avoidance→Promotion→Punishers→Negative →Reinforcement Management→Informational→Direct Exposure to Contingency	Manufacturer-deployed stimuli to weaken avoidance by removing negative (Promotion) punishers that signal informational reinforcement. Exposure to the contingencies is direct.
Manufacturer→Avoidance→Promotion→Punishers→Negative →Reinforcement Management→Informational→ Manufacturer Rule	Manufacturer-deployed stimuli to weaken avoidance by removing negative (Promotion) punishers that signal informational reinforcement. Exposure to the contingencies is indirect through a rule made by a manufacturer.
Manufacturer→Avoidance→Promotion→Punishers→ Negative→Reinforcement Management→Informational→ Retailer Rule	Manufacturer-deployed stimuli to weaken avoidance by removing negative (Promotion) punishers that signal informational reinforcement. Exposure to the contingencies is indirect through a rule in the retailer managerial behaviour setting.

Place

Manufacturer→Avoidance→Place→Punishers→Positive→Scope Management→Setting→Direct Exposure to Contingency

Manufacturer-deployed stimuli to weaken avoidance by presenting positive (Place) punishers that have an impact on the setting. Exposure to the contingencies is direct.

Manufacturer→Avoidance→Place→Punishers→Positive→Scope Management→Setting→Manufacturer Rule

Manufacturer-deployed stimuli to weaken avoidance by presenting positive (Place) punishers that have an impact on the setting. Exposure to the contingencies is indirect through a rule made by a manufacturer.

Manufacturer→Avoidance→Place→Punishers→Positive→Scope Management→Setting→Retailer Rule

Manufacturer-deployed stimuli to weaken avoidance by presenting positive (Place) punishers that have an impact on the setting. Exposure to the contingencies is indirect through a rule in the retailer managerial behaviour setting.

Manufacturer→Avoidance→Place→Punishers→Positive→Reinforcement Management→Utilitarian→Direct Exposure to Contingency

Manufacturer-deployed stimuli to weaken avoidance by presenting positive (Place) punishers that signal utilitarian reinforcement. Exposure to the contingencies is direct.

Manufacturer→Avoidance→Place→Punishers→Positive→Reinforcement Management→Utilitarian→Manufacturer Rule

Manufacturer-deployed stimuli to weaken avoidance by presenting positive (Place) punishers that signal utilitarian reinforcement. Exposure to the contingencies is indirect through a rule made by a manufacturer.

Manufacturer→Avoidance→Place→Punishers→Positive→Reinforcement Management→Utilitarian→Retailer Rule

Manufacturer-deployed stimuli to weaken avoidance by presenting positive (Place) punishers that signal utilitarian reinforcement. Exposure to the contingencies is indirect through a rule in the retailer managerial behaviour setting.

Manufacturer→Avoidance→Place→Punishers→Positive→Reinforcement Management→Informational→Direct Exposure to Contingency

Manufacturer-deployed stimuli to weaken avoidance by presenting positive (Place) punishers that signal informational reinforcement. Exposure to the contingencies is direct.

Code	Description and rule
Manufacturer→Avoidance→Place→Punishers→Positive→ Reinforcement Management→Informational→ Manufacturer Rule	Manufacturer-deployed stimuli to weaken avoidance by presenting positive (Place) punishers that signal informational reinforcement. Exposure to the contingencies is indirect through a rule made by a manufacturer.
Manufacturer→Avoidance→Place→Punishers→Positive→ Reinforcement Management→Informational→Retailer Rule	Manufacturer-deployed stimuli to weaken avoidance by presenting positive (Place) punishers that signal informational reinforcement. Exposure to the contingencies is indirect through a rule in the retailer managerial behaviour setting.
Manufacturer→Avoidance→Place→Punishers→Negative→ Scope Management→Setting→Direct Exposure to Contingency	Manufacturer-deployed stimuli to weaken avoidance by removing negative (Place) punishers that have an impact on the setting. Exposure to the contingencies is direct.
Manufacturer→Avoidance→Place→Punishers→Negative→ Scope Management→Setting→Manufacturer Rule	Manufacturer-deployed stimuli to weaken avoidance by removing negative (Place) punishers that have an impact on the setting. Exposure to the contingencies is indirect through a rule made by a manufacturer.
Manufacturer→Avoidance→Place→Punishers→Negative→ Scope Management→Setting→Retailer Rule	Manufacturer-deployed stimuli to weaken avoidance by removing negative (Place) punishers that have an impact on the setting. Exposure to the contingencies is indirect through a rule in the retailer managerial behaviour setting.
Manufacturer→Avoidance→Place→Punishers→Negative→ Reinforcement Management→Utilitarian→Direct Exposure to Contingency	Manufacturer-deployed stimuli to weaken avoidance by removing negative (Place) punishers that signal utilitarian reinforcement. Exposure to the contingencies is direct.
Manufacturer→Avoidance→Place→Punishers→Negative→ Reinforcement Management→Utilitarian→Manufacturer Rule	Manufacturer-deployed stimuli to weaken avoidance by removing negative (Place) punishers that signal utilitarian reinforcement. Exposure to the contingencies is indirect through a rule made by a manufacturer.

Manufacturer→Avoidance→Place→Punishers→Negative→
Reinforcement Management→Utilitarian→Retailer Rule

Manufacturer-deployed stimuli to weaken avoidance by removing negative (Place) punishers that signal utilitarian reinforcement. Exposure to the contingencies is indirect through a rule in the retailer managerial behaviour setting.

Manufacturer→Avoidance→Place→Punishers→Negative→
Reinforcement Management→Informational→Direct
Exposure to Contingency

Manufacturer-deployed stimuli to weaken avoidance by removing negative (Place) punishers that signal informational reinforcement. Exposure to the contingencies is direct.

Manufacturer→Avoidance→Place→Punishers→Negative→
Reinforcement Management→Informational→
Manufacturer Rule

Manufacturer-deployed stimuli to weaken avoidance by removing negative (Place) punishers that signal informational reinforcement. Exposure to the contingencies is indirect through a rule made by a manufacturer.

Manufacturer→Avoidance→Place→Punishers→Negative→
Reinforcement Management→Informational→Retailer Rule

Manufacturer-deployed stimuli to weaken avoidance by removing negative (Place) punishers that signal informational reinforcement. Exposure to the contingencies is indirect through a rule in the retailer managerial behaviour setting.

Retailer↔Manufacturer relationships (retailer-deployed stimuli)

Strengthening manufacturer approach (through reinforcement)

Price

Retailer→Approach→Price→Reinforcers→Positive→Scope
Management→Setting→Direct Exposure to Contingency

Retailer-deployed stimuli to strengthen approach by presenting positive (Price) reinforcers that have an impact on the setting. Exposure to the contingencies is direct.

Retailer→Approach→Price→Reinforcers→Positive→Scope
Management→Setting→Retailer Rule

Retailer-deployed stimuli to strengthen approach by presenting positive (Price) reinforcers that have an impact on the setting. Exposure to the contingencies is indirect through a rule made by a manufacturer.

Code	Description and rule
Retailer→Approach→Price→Reinforcers→Positive→Scope Management→Setting→Manufacturer Rule	Retailer-deployed stimuli to strengthen approach by presenting positive (Price) reinforcers that have an impact on the setting. Exposure to the contingencies is indirect through a rule in the manufacturer managerial behaviour setting.
Retailer→Approach→Price→Reinforcers→Positive→ Reinforcement Management→Utilitarian→Direct Exposure to Contingency	Retailer-deployed stimuli to strengthen approach by presenting positive (Price) reinforcers that signal utilitarian reinforcement. Exposure to the contingencies is direct.
Retailer→Approach→Price→Reinforcers→Positive→ Reinforcement Management→Utilitarian→Retailer Rule	Retailer-deployed stimuli to strengthen approach by presenting positive (Price) reinforcers that signal utilitarian reinforcement. Exposure to the contingencies is indirect through a rule made by a manufacturer.
Retailer→Approach→Price→Reinforcers→Positive→ Reinforcement Management→Utilitarian→Manufacturer Rule	Retailer-deployed stimuli to strengthen approach by presenting positive (Price) reinforcers that signal utilitarian reinforcement. Exposure to the contingencies is indirect through a rule in the manufacturer managerial behaviour setting.
Retailer→Approach→Price→Reinforcers→Positive→ Reinforcement Management→Informational→Direct Exposure to Contingency	Retailer-deployed stimuli to strengthen approach by presenting positive (Price) reinforcers that signal informational reinforcement. Exposure to the contingencies is direct.
Retailer→Approach→Price→Reinforcers→Positive→ Reinforcement Management→Informational→Retailer Rule	Retailer-deployed stimuli to strengthen approach by presenting positive (Price) reinforcers that signal informational reinforcement. Exposure to the contingencies is indirect through a rule made by a manufacturer.
Retailer→Approach→Price→Reinforcers→Positive→ Reinforcement Management→Informational→ Manufacturer Rule	Retailer-deployed stimuli to strengthen approach by presenting positive (Price) reinforcers that signal informational reinforcement. Exposure to the contingencies is indirect through a rule in the manufacturer managerial behaviour setting.

Retailer→Approach→Price→Reinforcers→Negative→Scope Management→Setting→Direct Exposure to Contingency

Retailer-deployed stimuli to strengthen approach by removing negative (Price) reinforcers that have an impact on the setting. Exposure to the contingencies is direct.

Retailer→Approach→Price→Reinforcers→Negative→Scope Management→Setting→Retailer Rule

Retailer-deployed stimuli to strengthen approach by removing negative (Price) reinforcers that have an impact on the setting. Exposure to the contingencies is indirect through a rule made by a manufacturer.

Retailer→Approach→Price→Reinforcers→Negative→Scope Management→Setting→Manufacturer Rule

Retailer-deployed stimuli to strengthen approach by removing negative (Price) reinforcers that have an impact on the setting. Exposure to the contingencies is indirect through a rule in the manufacturer managerial behaviour setting.

Retailer→Approach→Price→Reinforcers→Negative→ Reinforcement Management→Utilitarian→Direct Exposure to Contingency

Retailer-deployed stimuli to strengthen approach by removing negative (Price) reinforcers that signal utilitarian reinforcement. Exposure to the contingencies is direct.

Retailer→Approach→Price→Reinforcers→Negative→ Reinforcement Management→Utilitarian→Retailer Rule

Retailer-deployed stimuli to strengthen approach by removing negative (Price) reinforcers that signal utilitarian reinforcement. Exposure to the contingencies is indirect through a rule made by a manufacturer.

Retailer→Approach→Price→Reinforcers→Negative→ Reinforcement Management→Utilitarian→Manufacturer Rule

Retailer-deployed stimuli to strengthen approach by removing negative (Price) reinforcers that signal utilitarian reinforcement. Exposure to the contingencies is indirect through a rule in the manufacturer managerial behaviour setting.

Retailer→Approach→Price→Reinforcers→Negative→ Reinforcement Management→Informational→Direct Exposure to Contingency

Retailer-deployed stimuli to strengthen approach by removing negative (Price) reinforcers that signal informational reinforcement. Exposure to the contingencies is direct.

Code	Description and rule
Retailer→Approach→Price→Reinforcers→Negative→Reinforcement Management→Informational→Retailer Rule	Retailer-deployed stimuli to strengthen approach by removing negative (Price) reinforcers that signal informational reinforcement. Exposure to the contingencies is indirect through a rule made by a manufacturer.
Retailer→Approach→Price→Reinforcers→Negative→Reinforcement Management→Informational→Manufacturer Rule	Retailer-deployed stimuli to strengthen approach by removing negative (Price) reinforcers that signal informational reinforcement. Exposure to the contingencies is indirect through a rule in the manufacturer managerial behaviour setting.

Product

Code	Description and rule
Retailer→Approach→Product→Reinforcers→Positive→Scope Management→Setting→Direct Exposure to Contingency	Retailer-deployed stimuli to strengthen approach by presenting positive (Product) reinforcers that have an impact on the setting. Exposure to the contingencies is direct.
Retailer→Approach→Product→Reinforcers→Positive→Scope Management→Setting→Manufacturer Rule	Retailer-deployed stimuli to strengthen approach by presenting positive (Product) reinforcers that have an impact on the setting. Exposure to the contingencies is indirect through a rule made by a manufacturer.
Retailer→Approach→Product→Reinforcers→Positive→Scope Management→Setting→Retailer Rule	Retailer-deployed stimuli to strengthen approach by presenting positive (Product) reinforcers that have an impact on the setting. Exposure to the contingencies is indirect through a rule in the manufacturer managerial behaviour setting.
Retailer→Approach→Product→Reinforcers→Positive→Reinforcement Management→Utilitarian→Direct Exposure to Contingency	Retailer-deployed stimuli to strengthen approach by presenting positive (Product) reinforcers that signal utilitarian reinforcement. Exposure to the contingencies is direct.

Retailer→Approach→Product→Reinforcers→Positive→ Reinforcement Management→Utilitarian→Manufacturer Rule	Retailer-deployed stimuli to strengthen approach by presenting positive (Product) reinforcers that signal utilitarian reinforcement. Exposure to the contingencies is indirect through a rule made by a manufacturer.
Retailer→Approach→Product→Reinforcers→Positive→ Reinforcement Management→Utilitarian→Retailer Rule	Retailer-deployed stimuli to strengthen approach by presenting positive (Product) reinforcers that signal utilitarian reinforcement. Exposure to the contingencies is indirect through a rule in the manufacturer managerial behaviour setting.
Retailer→Approach→Product→Reinforcers→Positive→ Reinforcement Management→Informational→Direct Exposure to Contingency	Retailer-deployed stimuli to strengthen approach by presenting positive (Product) reinforcers that signal informational reinforcement. Exposure to the contingencies is direct.
Retailer→Approach→Product→Reinforcers→Positive→ Reinforcement Management→Informational→ Manufacturer Rule	Retailer-deployed stimuli to strengthen approach by presenting positive (Product) reinforcers that signal informational reinforcement. Exposure to the contingencies is indirect through a rule made by a manufacturer.
Retailer→Approach→Product→Reinforcers→Positive→ Reinforcement Management→Informational→Retailer Rule	Retailer-deployed stimuli to strengthen approach by presenting positive (Product) reinforcers that signal informational reinforcement. Exposure to the contingencies is indirect through a rule in the manufacturer managerial behaviour setting.
Retailer→Approach→Product→Reinforcers→Negative→ Scope Management→Setting→Direct Exposure to Contingency	Retailer-deployed stimuli to strengthen approach by removing negative (Product) reinforcers that have an impact on the setting. Exposure to the contingencies is direct.
Retailer→Approach→Product→Reinforcers→Negative→ Scope Management→Setting→Manufacturer Rule	Retailer-deployed stimuli to strengthen approach by removing negative (Product) reinforcers that have an impact on the setting. Exposure to the contingencies is indirect through a rule made by a manufacturer.

Code	Description and rule
Retailer→Approach→Product→Reinforcers→Negative→Scope Management→Setting→Retailer Rule	Retailer-deployed stimuli to strengthen approach by removing negative (Product) reinforcers that have an impact on the setting. Exposure to the contingencies is indirect through a rule in the manufacturer managerial behaviour setting.
Retailer→Approach→Product→Reinforcers→Negative→Reinforcement Management→Utilitarian→Direct Exposure to Contingency	Retailer-deployed stimuli to strengthen approach by removing negative (Product) reinforcers that signal utilitarian reinforcement. Exposure to the contingencies is direct.
Retailer→Approach→Product→Reinforcers→Negative→Reinforcement Management→Utilitarian→Manufacturer Rule	Retailer-deployed stimuli to strengthen approach by removing negative (Product) reinforcers that signal utilitarian reinforcement. Exposure to the contingencies is indirect through a rule made by a manufacturer.
Retailer→Approach→Product→Reinforcers→Negative→Reinforcement Management→Utilitarian→Retailer Rule	Retailer-deployed stimuli to strengthen approach by removing negative (Product) reinforcers that signal utilitarian reinforcement. Exposure to the contingencies is indirect through a rule in the manufacturer managerial behaviour setting.
Retailer→Approach→Product→Reinforcers→Negative→Reinforcement Management→Informational→Direct Exposure to Contingency	Retailer-deployed stimuli to strengthen approach by removing negative (Product) reinforcers that signal informational reinforcement. Exposure to the contingencies is direct.
Retailer→Approach→Product→Reinforcers→Negative→Reinforcement Management→Informational→Manufacturer Rule	Retailer-deployed stimuli to strengthen approach by removing negative (Product) reinforcers that signal informational reinforcement. Exposure to the contingencies is indirect through a rule made by a manufacturer.
Retailer→Approach→Product→Reinforcers→Negative→Reinforcement Management→Informational→Retailer Rule	Retailer-deployed stimuli to strengthen approach by removing negative (Product) reinforcers that signal informational reinforcement. Exposure to the contingencies is indirect through a rule in the manufacturer managerial behaviour setting.

Promotion

Retailer→Approach→Promotion→Reinforcers→Positive→
Scope Management→Setting→Direct Exposure to
Contingency

Retailer-deployed stimuli to strengthen approach by presenting positive (Promotion) reinforcers that have an impact on the setting. Exposure to the contingencies is direct.

Retailer→Approach→Promotion→Reinforcers→Positive→
Scope Management→Setting→Manufacturer Rule

Retailer-deployed stimuli to strengthen approach by presenting positive (Promotion) reinforcers that have an impact on the setting. Exposure to the contingencies is indirect through a rule made by a manufacturer.

Retailer→Approach→Promotion→Reinforcers→Positive→
Scope Management→Setting→Retailer Rule

Retailer-deployed stimuli to strengthen approach by presenting positive (Promotion) reinforcers that have an impact on the setting. Exposure to the contingencies is indirect through a rule in the manufacturer managerial behaviour setting.

Retailer→Approach→Promotion→Reinforcers→Positive→
Reinforcement Management→Utilitarian→Direct Exposure
to Contingency

Retailer-deployed stimuli to strengthen approach by presenting positive (Promotion) reinforcers that signal utilitarian reinforcement. Exposure to the contingencies is direct.

Retailer→Approach→Promotion→Reinforcers→Positive→
Reinforcement Management→Utilitarian→Manufacturer
Rule

Retailer-deployed stimuli to strengthen approach by presenting positive (Promotion) reinforcers that signal utilitarian reinforcement. Exposure to the contingencies is indirect through a rule made by a manufacturer.

Retailer→Approach→Promotion→Reinforcers→Positive→
Reinforcement Management→Utilitarian→Retailer Rule

Retailer-deployed stimuli to strengthen approach by presenting positive (Promotion) reinforcers that signal utilitarian reinforcement. Exposure to the contingencies is indirect through a rule in the manufacturer managerial behaviour setting.

Retailer→Approach→Promotion→Reinforcers→Positive→
Reinforcement Management→Informational→Direct
Exposure to Contingency

Retailer-deployed stimuli to strengthen approach by presenting positive (Promotion) reinforcers that signal informational reinforcement. Exposure to the contingencies is direct.

Code	Description and rule
Retailer→Approach→Promotion→Reinforcers→Positive→Reinforcement Management→Informational→Manufacturer Rule	Retailer-deployed stimuli to strengthen approach by presenting positive (Promotion) reinforcers that signal informational reinforcement. Exposure to the contingencies is indirect through a rule made by a manufacturer.
Retailer→Approach→Promotion→Reinforcers→Positive→Reinforcement Management→Informational→Retailer Rule	Retailer-deployed stimuli to strengthen approach by presenting positive (Promotion) reinforcers that signal informational reinforcement. Exposure to the contingencies is indirect through a rule in the manufacturer managerial behaviour setting.
Retailer→Approach→Promotion→Reinforcers→Negative→Scope Management→Setting→Direct Exposure to Contingency	Retailer-deployed stimuli to strengthen approach by removing negative (Promotion) reinforcers that have an impact on the setting. Exposure to the contingencies is direct.
Retailer→Approach→Promotion→Reinforcers→Negative→Scope Management→Setting→Manufacturer Rule	Retailer-deployed stimuli to strengthen approach by removing negative (Promotion) reinforcers that have an impact on the setting. Exposure to the contingencies is indirect through a rule made by a manufacturer.
Retailer→Approach→Promotion→Reinforcers→Negative→Scope Management→Setting→Retailer Rule	Retailer-deployed stimuli to strengthen approach by removing negative (Promotion) reinforcers that have an impact on the setting. Exposure to the contingencies is indirect through a rule in the manufacturer managerial behaviour setting.
Retailer→Approach→Promotion→Reinforcers→Negative→Reinforcement Management→Utilitarian→Direct Exposure to Contingency	Retailer-deployed stimuli to strengthen approach by removing negative (Promotion) reinforcers that signal utilitarian reinforcement. Exposure to the contingencies is direct.
Retailer→Approach→Promotion→Reinforcers→Negative→Reinforcement Management→Utilitarian→Manufacturer Rule	Retailer-deployed stimuli to strengthen approach by removing negative (Promotion) reinforcers that signal utilitarian reinforcement. Exposure to the contingencies is indirect through a rule made by a manufacturer.

Retailer→Approach→Promotion→Reinforcers→Negative→Reinforcement Management→Utilitarian→Retailer Rule

Retailer-deployed stimuli to strengthen approach by removing negative (Promotion) reinforcers that signal utilitarian reinforcement. Exposure to the contingencies is indirect through a rule in the manufacturer managerial behaviour setting.

Retailer→Approach→Promotion→Reinforcers→Negative→Reinforcement Management→Informational→Direct Exposure to Contingency

Retailer-deployed stimuli to strengthen approach by removing negative (Promotion) reinforcers that signal informational reinforcement. Exposure to the contingencies is direct.

Retailer→Approach→Promotion→Reinforcers→Negative→Reinforcement Management→Informational→Manufacturer Rule

Retailer-deployed stimuli to strengthen approach by removing negative (Promotion) reinforcers that signal informational reinforcement. Exposure to the contingencies is indirect through a rule made by a manufacturer.

Retailer→Approach→Promotion→Reinforcers→Negative→Reinforcement Management→Informational→Retailer Rule

Retailer-deployed stimuli to strengthen approach by removing negative (Promotion) reinforcers that signal informational reinforcement. Exposure to the contingencies is indirect through a rule in the manufacturer managerial behaviour setting.

Place

Retailer→Approach→Place→Reinforcers→Positive→Scope Management→Setting→Direct Exposure to Contingency

Retailer-deployed stimuli to strengthen approach by presenting positive (Place) reinforcers that have an impact on the setting. Exposure to the contingencies is direct.

Retailer→Approach→Place→Reinforcers→Positive→Scope Management→Setting→Manufacturer Rule

Retailer-deployed stimuli to strengthen approach by presenting positive (Place) reinforcers that have an impact on the setting. Exposure to the contingencies is indirect through a rule made by a manufacturer.

Retailer→Approach→Place→Reinforcers→Positive→Scope Management→Setting→Retailer Rule

Retailer-deployed stimuli to strengthen approach by presenting positive (Place) reinforcers that have an impact on the setting. Exposure to the contingencies is indirect through a rule in the manufacturer managerial behaviour setting.

Code	Description and rule
Retailer→Approach→Place→Reinforcers→Positive→ Reinforcement Management→Utilitarian→Direct Exposure to Contingency	Retailer-deployed stimuli to strengthen approach by presenting positive (Place) reinforcers that signal utilitarian reinforcement. Exposure to the contingencies is direct.
Retailer→Approach→Place→Reinforcers→Positive→ Reinforcement Management→Utilitarian→Manufacturer Rule	Retailer-deployed stimuli to strengthen approach by presenting positive (Place) reinforcers that signal utilitarian reinforcement. Exposure to the contingencies is indirect through a rule made by a manufacturer.
Retailer→Approach→Place→Reinforcers→Positive→ Reinforcement Management→Utilitarian→Retailer Rule	Retailer-deployed stimuli to strengthen approach by presenting positive (Place) reinforcers that signal utilitarian reinforcement. Exposure to the contingencies is indirect through a rule in the manufacturer managerial behaviour setting.
Retailer→Approach→Place→Reinforcers→Positive→ Reinforcement Management→Informational→Direct Exposure to Contingency	Retailer-deployed stimuli to strengthen approach by presenting positive (Place) reinforcers that signal informational reinforcement. Exposure to the contingencies is direct.
Retailer→Approach→Place→Reinforcers→Positive→ Reinforcement Management→Informational→ Manufacturer Rule	Retailer-deployed stimuli to strengthen approach by presenting positive (Place) reinforcers that signal informational reinforcement. Exposure to the contingencies is indirect through a rule made by a manufacturer.
Retailer→Approach→Place→Reinforcers→Positive→ Reinforcement Management→Informational→Retailer Rule	Retailer-deployed stimuli to strengthen approach by presenting positive (Place) reinforcers that signal informational reinforcement. Exposure to the contingencies is indirect through a rule in the manufacturer managerial behaviour setting.
Retailer→Approach→Place→Reinforcers→Negative→Scope Management→Setting→Direct Exposure to Contingency	Retailer-deployed stimuli to strengthen approach by removing negative (Place) reinforcers that have an impact on the setting. Exposure to the contingencies is direct.

Retailer→Approach→Place→Reinforcers→Negative→Scope Management→Setting→Manufacturer Rule

Retailer-deployed stimuli to strengthen approach by removing negative (Place) reinforcers that have an impact on the setting. Exposure to the contingencies is indirect through a rule made by a manufacturer.

Retailer→Approach→Place→Reinforcers→Negative→Scope Management→Setting→Retailer Rule

Retailer-deployed stimuli to strengthen approach by removing negative (Place) reinforcers that have an impact on the setting. Exposure to the contingencies is indirect through a rule in the manufacturer managerial behaviour setting.

Retailer→Approach→Place→Reinforcers→Negative→ Reinforcement Management→Utilitarian→Direct Exposure to Contingency

Retailer-deployed stimuli to strengthen approach by removing negative (Place) reinforcers that signal utilitarian reinforcement. Exposure to the contingencies is direct.

Retailer→Approach→Place→Reinforcers→Negative→ Reinforcement Management→Utilitarian→Manufacturer Rule

Retailer-deployed stimuli to strengthen approach by removing negative (Place) reinforcers that signal utilitarian reinforcement. Exposure to the contingencies is indirect through a rule made by a manufacturer.

Retailer→Approach→Place→Reinforcers→Negative→ Reinforcement Management→Utilitarian→Retailer Rule

Retailer-deployed stimuli to strengthen approach by removing negative (Place) reinforcers that signal utilitarian reinforcement. Exposure to the contingencies is indirect through a rule in the manufacturer managerial behaviour setting.

Retailer→Approach→Place→Reinforcers→Negative→ Reinforcement Management→Informational→Direct Exposure to Contingency

Retailer-deployed stimuli to strengthen approach by removing negative (Place) reinforcers that signal informational reinforcement. Exposure to the contingencies is direct.

Retailer→Approach→Place→Reinforcers→Negative→ Reinforcement Management→Informational→ Manufacturer Rule

Retailer-deployed stimuli to strengthen approach by removing negative (Place) reinforcers that signal informational reinforcement. Exposure to the contingencies is indirect through a rule made by a manufacturer.

Code	Description and rule
Retailer→Approach→Place→Reinforcers→Negative→ Reinforcement Management→Informational→Retailer Rule	Retailer-deployed stimuli to strengthen approach by removing negative (Place) reinforcers that signal informational reinforcement. Exposure to the contingencies is indirect through a rule in the manufacturer managerial behaviour setting.

Weakening manufacturer avoidance through punishment

Price

Code	Description and rule
Retailer→Avoidance→Price→Punishers→Positive→Scope Management→Setting→Direct Exposure to Contingency	Retailer-deployed stimuli to weaken avoidance by presenting positive (Price) punishers that have an impact on the setting. Exposure to the contingencies is direct.
Retailer→Avoidance→Price→Punishers→Positive→Scope Management→Setting→Retailer Rule	Retailer-deployed stimuli to weaken avoidance by presenting positive (Price) punishers that have an impact on the setting. Exposure to the contingencies is indirect through a rule made by a manufacturer.
Retailer→Avoidance→Price→Punishers→Positive→Scope Management→Setting→Manufacturer Rule	Retailer-deployed stimuli to weaken avoidance by presenting positive (Price) punishers that have an impact on the setting. Exposure to the contingencies is indirect through a rule in the manufacturer managerial behaviour setting.
Retailer→Avoidance→Price→Punishers→Positive→ Reinforcement Management→Utilitarian→Direct Exposure to Contingency	Retailer-deployed stimuli to weaken avoidance by presenting positive (Price) punishers that signal utilitarian reinforcement. Exposure to the contingencies is direct.
Retailer→Avoidance→Price→Punishers→Positive→ Reinforcement Management→Utilitarian→Retailer Rule	Retailer-deployed stimuli to weaken avoidance by presenting positive (Price) punishers that signal utilitarian reinforcement. Exposure to the contingencies is indirect through a rule made by a manufacturer.

Retailer→Avoidance→Price→Punishers→Positive→ Reinforcement Management→Utilitarian→Manufacturer Rule

Retailer-deployed stimuli to weaken avoidance by presenting positive (Price) punishers that signal utilitarian reinforcement. Exposure to the contingencies is indirect through a rule in the manufacturer managerial behaviour setting.

Retailer→Avoidance→Price→Punishers→Positive→ Reinforcement Management→Informational→Direct Exposure to Contingency

Retailer-deployed stimuli to weaken avoidance by presenting positive (Price) punishers that signal informational reinforcement. Exposure to the contingencies is direct.

Retailer→Avoidance→Price→Punishers→Positive→ Reinforcement Management→Informational→Retailer Rule

Retailer-deployed stimuli to weaken avoidance by presenting positive (Price) punishers that signal informational reinforcement. Exposure to the contingencies is indirect through a rule made by a manufacturer.

Retailer→Avoidance→Price→Punishers→Positive→ Reinforcement Management→Informational→ Manufacturer Rule

Retailer-deployed stimuli to weaken avoidance by presenting positive (Price) punishers that signal informational reinforcement. Exposure to the contingencies is indirect through a rule in the manufacturer managerial behaviour setting.

Retailer→Avoidance→Price→Punishers→Negative→Scope Management→Setting→Direct Exposure to Contingency

Retailer-deployed stimuli to weaken avoidance by removing negative (Price) punishers that have an impact on the setting. Exposure to the contingencies is direct.

Retailer→Avoidance→Price→Punishers→Negative→Scope Management→Setting→Retailer Rule

Retailer-deployed stimuli to weaken avoidance by removing negative (Price) punishers that have an impact on the setting. Exposure to the contingencies is indirect through a rule made by a manufacturer.

Retailer→Avoidance→Price→Punishers→Negative→Scope Management→Setting→Manufacturer Rule

Retailer-deployed stimuli to weaken avoidance by removing negative (Price) punishers that have an impact on the setting. Exposure to the contingencies is indirect through a rule in the manufacturer managerial behaviour setting.

Code	Description and rule
Retailer→Avoidance→Price→Punishers→Negative→ Reinforcement Management→Utilitarian→Direct Exposure to Contingency	Retailer-deployed stimuli to weaken avoidance by removing negative (Price) punishers that signal utilitarian reinforcement. Exposure to the contingencies is direct.
Retailer→Avoidance→Price→Punishers→Negative→ Reinforcement Management→Utilitarian→Retailer Rule	Retailer-deployed stimuli to weaken avoidance by removing negative (Price) punishers that signal utilitarian reinforcement. Exposure to the contingencies is indirect through a rule made by a manufacturer.
Retailer→Avoidance→Price→Punishers→Negative→ Reinforcement Management→Utilitarian→Manufacturer Rule	Retailer-deployed stimuli to weaken avoidance by removing negative (Price) punishers that signal utilitarian reinforcement. Exposure to the contingencies is indirect through a rule in the manufacturer managerial behaviour setting.
Retailer→Avoidance→Price→Punishers→Negative→ Reinforcement Management→Informational→Direct Exposure to Contingency	Retailer-deployed stimuli to weaken avoidance by removing negative (Price) punishers that signal informational reinforcement. Exposure to the contingencies is direct.
Retailer→Avoidance→Price→Punishers→Negative→ Reinforcement Management→Informational→Retailer Rule	Retailer-deployed stimuli to weaken avoidance by removing negative (Price) punishers that signal informational reinforcement. Exposure to the contingencies is indirect through a rule made by a manufacturer.
Retailer→Avoidance→Price→Punishers→Negative→ Reinforcement Management→Informational→ Manufacturer Rule	Retailer-deployed stimuli to weaken avoidance by removing negative (Price) punishers that signal informational reinforcement. Exposure to the contingencies is indirect through a rule in the manufacturer managerial behaviour setting.

Product

Code	Description and rule
Retailer→Avoidance→Product→Punishers→Positive→Scope Management→Setting→Direct Exposure to Contingency	Retailer-deployed stimuli to weaken avoidance by presenting positive (Product) punishers that have an impact on the setting. Exposure to the contingencies is direct.

Retailer→Avoidance→Product→Punishers→Positive→Scope Management→Setting→Retailer Rule

Retailer-deployed stimuli to weaken avoidance by presenting positive (Product) punishers that have an impact on the setting. Exposure to the contingencies is indirect through a rule made by a manufacturer.

Retailer→Avoidance→Product→Punishers→Positive→Scope Management→Setting→Manufacturer Rule

Retailer-deployed stimuli to weaken avoidance by presenting positive (Product) punishers that have an impact on the setting. Exposure to the contingencies is indirect through a rule in the manufacturer managerial behaviour setting.

Retailer→Avoidance→Product→Punishers→Positive→Reinforcement Management→Utilitarian→Direct Exposure to Contingency

Retailer-deployed stimuli to weaken avoidance by presenting positive (Product) punishers that signal utilitarian reinforcement. Exposure to the contingencies is direct.

Retailer→Avoidance→Product→Punishers→Positive→Reinforcement Management→Utilitarian→Retailer Rule

Retailer-deployed stimuli to weaken avoidance by presenting positive (Product) punishers that signal utilitarian reinforcement. Exposure to the contingencies is indirect through a rule made by a manufacturer.

Retailer→Avoidance→Product→Punishers→Positive→Reinforcement Management→Utilitarian→Manufacturer Rule

Retailer-deployed stimuli to weaken avoidance by presenting positive (Product) punishers that signal utilitarian reinforcement. Exposure to the contingencies is indirect through a rule in the manufacturer managerial behaviour setting.

Retailer→Avoidance→Product→Punishers→Positive→Reinforcement Management→Informational→Direct Exposure to Contingency

Retailer-deployed stimuli to weaken avoidance by presenting positive (Product) punishers that signal informational reinforcement. Exposure to the contingencies is direct.

Retailer→Avoidance→Product→Punishers→Positive→Reinforcement Management→Informational→Retailer Rule

Retailer-deployed stimuli to weaken avoidance by presenting positive (Product) punishers that signal informational reinforcement. Exposure to the contingencies is indirect through a rule made by a manufacturer.

Code	Description and rule
Retailer→Avoidance→Product→Punishers→Positive→ Reinforcement Management→Informational→ Manufacturer Rule	Retailer-deployed stimuli to weaken avoidance by presenting positive (Product) punishers that signal informational reinforcement. Exposure to the contingencies is indirect through a rule in the manufacturer managerial behaviour setting.
Retailer→Avoidance→Product→Punishers→Negative→Scope Management→Setting→Direct Exposure to Contingency	Retailer-deployed stimuli to weaken avoidance by removing negative (Product) punishers that have an impact on the setting. Exposure to the contingencies is direct.
Retailer→Avoidance→Product→Punishers→Negative→Scope Management→Setting→Retailer Rule	Retailer-deployed stimuli to weaken avoidance by removing negative (Product) punishers that have an impact on the setting. Exposure to the contingencies is indirect through a rule made by a manufacturer.
Retailer→Avoidance→Product→Punishers→Negative→Scope Management→Setting→Manufacturer Rule	Retailer-deployed stimuli to weaken avoidance by removing negative (Product) punishers that have an impact on the setting. Exposure to the contingencies is indirect through a rule in the manufacturer managerial behaviour setting.
Retailer→Avoidance→Product→Punishers→Negative→ Reinforcement Management→Utilitarian→Direct Exposure to Contingency	Retailer-deployed stimuli to weaken avoidance by removing negative (Product) punishers that signal utilitarian reinforcement. Exposure to the contingencies is direct.
Retailer→Avoidance→Product→Punishers→Negative→ Reinforcement Management→Utilitarian→Retailer Rule	Retailer-deployed stimuli to weaken avoidance by removing negative (Product) punishers that signal utilitarian reinforcement. Exposure to the contingencies is indirect through a rule made by a manufacturer.
Retailer→Avoidance→Product→Punishers→Negative→ Reinforcement Management→Utilitarian→Manufacturer Rule	Retailer-deployed stimuli to weaken avoidance by removing negative (Product) punishers that signal utilitarian reinforcement. Exposure to the contingencies is indirect through a rule in the manufacturer managerial behaviour setting.

Retailer→Avoidance→Product→Punishers→Negative→Reinforcement Management→Informational→Direct Exposure to Contingency

Retailer-deployed stimuli to weaken avoidance by removing negative (Product) punishers that signal informational reinforcement. Exposure to the contingencies is direct.

Retailer→Avoidance→Product→Punishers→Negative→Reinforcement Management→Informational→Retailer Rule

Retailer-deployed stimuli to weaken avoidance by removing negative (Product) punishers that signal informational reinforcement. Exposure to the contingencies is indirect through a rule made by a manufacturer.

Retailer→Avoidance→Product→Punishers→Negative→Reinforcement Management→Informational→Manufacturer Rule

Retailer-deployed stimuli to weaken avoidance by removing negative (Product) punishers that signal informational reinforcement. Exposure to the contingencies is indirect through a rule in the manufacturer managerial behaviour setting.

Promotion

Retailer→Avoidance→Promotion→Punishers→Positive→Scope Management→Setting→Direct Exposure to Contingency

Retailer-deployed stimuli to weaken avoidance by presenting positive (Promotion) punishers that have an impact on the setting. Exposure to the contingencies is direct.

Retailer→Avoidance→Promotion→Punishers→Positive→Scope Management→Setting→Retailer Rule

Retailer-deployed stimuli to weaken avoidance by presenting positive (Promotion) punishers that have an impact on the setting. Exposure to the contingencies is indirect through a rule made by a manufacturer.

Retailer→Avoidance→Promotion→Punishers→Positive→Scope Management→Setting→Manufacturer Rule

Retailer-deployed stimuli to weaken avoidance by presenting positive (Promotion) punishers that have an impact on the setting. Exposure to the contingencies is indirect through a rule in the manufacturer managerial behaviour setting.

Retailer→Avoidance→Promotion→Punishers→Positive→Reinforcement Management→Utilitarian→Direct Exposure to Contingency

Retailer-deployed stimuli to weaken avoidance by presenting positive (Promotion) punishers that signal utilitarian reinforcement. Exposure to the contingencies is direct.

Code	Description and rule
Retailer→Avoidance→Promotion→Punishers→Positive→Reinforcement Management→Utilitarian→Retailer Rule	Retailer-deployed stimuli to weaken avoidance by presenting positive (Promotion) punishers that signal utilitarian reinforcement. Exposure to the contingencies is indirect through a rule made by a manufacturer.
Retailer→Avoidance→Promotion→Punishers→Positive→Reinforcement Management→Utilitarian→Manufacturer Rule	Retailer-deployed stimuli to weaken avoidance by presenting positive (Promotion) punishers that signal utilitarian reinforcement. Exposure to the contingencies is indirect through a rule in the manufacturer managerial behaviour setting.
Retailer→Avoidance→Promotion→Punishers→Positive→Reinforcement Management→Informational→Direct Exposure to Contingency	Retailer-deployed stimuli to weaken avoidance by presenting positive (Promotion) punishers that signal informational reinforcement. Exposure to the contingencies is direct.
Retailer→Avoidance→Promotion→Punishers→Positive→Reinforcement Management→Informational→Retailer Rule	Retailer-deployed stimuli to weaken avoidance by presenting positive (Promotion) punishers that signal informational reinforcement. Exposure to the contingencies is indirect through a rule made by a manufacturer.
Retailer→Avoidance→Promotion→Punishers→Positive→Reinforcement Management→Informational→Manufacturer Rule	Retailer-deployed stimuli to weaken avoidance by presenting positive (Promotion) punishers that signal informational reinforcement. Exposure to the contingencies is indirect through a rule in the manufacturer managerial behaviour setting.
Retailer→Avoidance→Promotion→Punishers→Negative→Scope Management→Setting→Direct Exposure to Contingency	Retailer-deployed stimuli to weaken avoidance by removing negative (Promotion) punishers that have an impact on the setting. Exposure to the contingencies is direct.
Retailer→Avoidance→Promotion→Punishers→Negative→Scope Management→Setting→Retailer Rule	Retailer-deployed stimuli to weaken avoidance by removing negative (Promotion) punishers that have an impact on the setting. Exposure to the contingencies is indirect through a rule made by a manufacturer.

Retailer→Avoidance→Promotion→Punishers→Negative→Scope Management→Setting→Manufacturer Rule

Retailer-deployed stimuli to weaken avoidance by removing negative (Promotion) punishers that have an impact on the setting. Exposure to the contingencies is indirect through a rule in the manufacturer managerial behaviour setting.

Retailer→Avoidance→Promotion→Punishers→Negative→Reinforcement Management→Utilitarian→Direct Exposure to Contingency

Retailer-deployed stimuli to weaken avoidance by removing negative (Promotion) punishers that signal utilitarian reinforcement. Exposure to the contingencies is direct.

Retailer→Avoidance→Promotion→Punishers→Negative→Reinforcement Management→Utilitarian→Retailer Rule

Retailer-deployed stimuli to weaken avoidance by removing negative (Promotion) punishers that signal utilitarian reinforcement. Exposure to the contingencies is indirect through a rule made by a manufacturer.

Retailer→Avoidance→Promotion→Punishers→Negative→Reinforcement Management→Utilitarian→Manufacturer Rule

Retailer-deployed stimuli to weaken avoidance by removing negative (Promotion) punishers that signal utilitarian reinforcement. Exposure to the contingencies is indirect through a rule in the manufacturer managerial behaviour setting.

Retailer→Avoidance→Promotion→Punishers→Negative→Reinforcement Management→Informational→Direct Exposure to Contingency

Retailer-deployed stimuli to weaken avoidance by removing negative (Promotion) punishers that signal informational reinforcement. Exposure to the contingencies is direct.

Retailer→Avoidance→Promotion→Punishers→Negative→Reinforcement Management→Informational→Retailer Rule

Retailer-deployed stimuli to weaken avoidance by removing negative (Promotion) punishers that signal informational reinforcement. Exposure to the contingencies is indirect through a rule made by a manufacturer.

Retailer→Avoidance→Promotion→Punishers→Negative→Reinforcement Management→Informational→Manufacturer Rule

Retailer-deployed stimuli to weaken avoidance by removing negative (Promotion) punishers that signal informational reinforcement. Exposure to the contingencies is indirect through a rule in the manufacturer managerial behaviour setting.

Code	Description and rule
Place	
Retailer→Avoidance→Place→Punishers→Positive→Scope Management→Setting→Direct Exposure to Contingency	Retailer-deployed stimuli to weaken avoidance by presenting positive (Place) punishers that have an impact on the setting. Exposure to the contingencies is direct.
Retailer→Avoidance→Place→Punishers→Positive→Scope Management→Setting→Retailer Rule	Retailer-deployed stimuli to weaken avoidance by presenting positive (Place) punishers that have an impact on the setting. Exposure to the contingencies is indirect through a rule made by a manufacturer.
Retailer→Avoidance→Place→Punishers→Positive→Scope Management→Setting→Manufacturer Rule	Retailer-deployed stimuli to weaken avoidance by presenting positive (Place) punishers that have an impact on the setting. Exposure to the contingencies is indirect through a rule in the manufacturer managerial behaviour setting.
Retailer→Avoidance→Place→Punishers→Positive→ Reinforcement Management→Utilitarian→Direct Exposure to Contingency	Retailer-deployed stimuli to weaken avoidance by presenting positive (Place) punishers that signal utilitarian reinforcement. Exposure to the contingencies is direct.
Retailer→Avoidance→Place→Punishers→Positive→ Reinforcement Management→Utilitarian→Retailer Rule	Retailer-deployed stimuli to weaken avoidance by presenting positive (Place) punishers that signal utilitarian reinforcement. Exposure to the contingencies is indirect through a rule made by a manufacturer.
Retailer→Avoidance→Place→Punishers→Positive→ Reinforcement Management→Utilitarian→Manufacturer Rule	Retailer-deployed stimuli to weaken avoidance by presenting positive (Place) punishers that signal utilitarian reinforcement. Exposure to the contingencies is indirect through a rule in the manufacturer managerial behaviour setting.
Retailer→Avoidance→Place→Punishers→Positive→ Reinforcement Management→Informational→Direct Exposure to Contingency	Retailer-deployed stimuli to weaken avoidance by presenting positive (Place) punishers that signal informational reinforcement. Exposure to the contingencies is direct.

Retailer→Avoidance→Place→Punishers→Positive→Reinforcement Management→Informational→Retailer Rule

Retailer-deployed stimuli to weaken avoidance by presenting positive (Place) punishers that signal informational reinforcement. Exposure to the contingencies is indirect through a rule made by a manufacturer.

Retailer→Avoidance→Place→Punishers→Positive→Reinforcement Management→Informational→Manufacturer Rule

Retailer-deployed stimuli to weaken avoidance by presenting positive (Place) punishers that signal informational reinforcement. Exposure to the contingencies is indirect through a rule in the manufacturer managerial behaviour setting.

Retailer→Avoidance→Place→Punishers→Negative→Scope Management→Setting→Direct Exposure to Contingency

Retailer-deployed stimuli to weaken avoidance by removing negative (Place) punishers that have an impact on the setting. Exposure to the contingencies is direct.

Retailer→Avoidance→Place→Punishers→Negative→Scope Management→Setting→Retailer Rule

Retailer-deployed stimuli to weaken avoidance by removing negative (Place) punishers that have an impact on the setting. Exposure to the contingencies is indirect through a rule made by a manufacturer.

Retailer→Avoidance→Place→Punishers→Negative→Scope Management→Setting→Manufacturer Rule

Retailer-deployed stimuli to weaken avoidance by removing negative (Place) punishers that have an impact on the setting. Exposure to the contingencies is indirect through a rule in the manufacturer managerial behaviour setting.

Retailer→Avoidance→Place→Punishers→Negative→Reinforcement Management→Utilitarian→Direct Exposure to Contingency

Retailer-deployed stimuli to weaken avoidance by removing negative (Place) punishers that signal utilitarian reinforcement. Exposure to the contingencies is direct.

Retailer→Avoidance→Place→Punishers→Negative→Reinforcement Management→Utilitarian→Retailer Rule

Retailer-deployed stimuli to weaken avoidance by removing negative (Place) punishers that signal utilitarian reinforcement. Exposure to the contingencies is indirect through a rule made by a manufacturer.

Code	Description and rule
Retailer→Avoidance→Place→Punishers→Negative→ Reinforcement Management→Utilitarian→Manufacturer Rule	Retailer-deployed stimuli to weaken avoidance by removing negative (Place) punishers that signal utilitarian reinforcement. Exposure to the contingencies is indirect through a rule in the manufacturer managerial behaviour setting.
Retailer→Avoidance→Place→Punishers→Negative→ Reinforcement Management→Informational→Direct Exposure to Contingency	Retailer-deployed stimuli to weaken avoidance by removing negative (Place) punishers that signal informational reinforcement. Exposure to the contingencies is direct.
Retailer→Avoidance→Place→Punishers→Negative→ Reinforcement Management→Informational→Retailer Rule	Retailer-deployed stimuli to weaken avoidance by removing negative (Place) punishers that signal informational reinforcement. Exposure to the contingencies is indirect through a rule made by a manufacturer.
Retailer→Avoidance→Place→Punishers→Negative→ Reinforcement Management→Informational→ Manufacturer Rule	Retailer-deployed stimuli to weaken avoidance by removing negative (Place) punishers that signal informational reinforcement. Exposure to the contingencies is indirect through a rule in the manufacturer managerial behaviour setting.

Manufacturer↔Rival relationships (manufacturer-deployed stimuli)

Strengthening rival favourable (approach) behaviour through reinforcement

Price

Manufacturer→Approach→Price→Reinforcers→Positive→ Scope Management→Setting→Direct Exposure to Contingency	Manufacturer-deployed stimuli reinforce the behaviour of rivals that is favourable to the manufacturer by presenting positive (Price) reinforcers that have an impact on the setting. Exposure to the contingencies is direct.

Manufacturer→Approach→Price→Reinforcers→Positive→Scope Management→Setting→Manufacturer Rule

Manufacturer-deployed stimuli reinforce the behaviour of rivals that is favourable to the manufacturer by presenting positive (Price) reinforcers that have an impact on the setting. Exposure to the contingencies is indirect through a rule made by a manufacturer.

Manufacturer→Approach→Price→Reinforcers→Positive→Scope Management→Setting→Rival Rule

Manufacturer-deployed stimuli reinforce the behaviour of rivals that is favourable to the manufacturer by presenting positive (Price) reinforcers that have an impact on the setting. Exposure to the contingencies is indirect through a rule in the rival managerial behaviour setting.

Manufacturer→Approach→Price→Reinforcers→Positive→Reinforcement Management→Utilitarian→Direct Exposure to Contingency

Manufacturer-deployed stimuli reinforce the behaviour of rivals that is favourable to the manufacturer by presenting positive (Price) reinforcers that signal utilitarian reinforcement. Exposure to the contingencies is direct.

Manufacturer→Approach→Price→Reinforcers→Positive→Reinforcement Management→Utilitarian→Manufacturer Rule

Manufacturer-deployed stimuli reinforce the behaviour of rivals that is favourable to the manufacturer by presenting positive (Price) reinforcers that signal utilitarian reinforcement. Exposure to the contingencies is indirect through a rule made by a manufacturer.

Manufacturer→Approach→Price→Reinforcers→Positive→Reinforcement Management→Utilitarian→Rival Rule

Manufacturer-deployed stimuli reinforce the behaviour of rivals that is favourable to the manufacturer by presenting positive (Price) reinforcers that signal utilitarian reinforcement. Exposure to the contingencies is indirect through a rule in the rival managerial behaviour setting.

Manufacturer→Approach→Price→Reinforcers→Positive→Reinforcement Management→Informational→Direct Exposure to Contingency

Manufacturer-deployed stimuli reinforce the behaviour of rivals that is favourable to the manufacturer by presenting positive (Price) reinforcers that signal informational reinforcement. Exposure to the contingencies is direct.

Code	Description and rule
Manufacturer→Approach→Price→Reinforcers→Positive→Reinforcement Management→Informational→Manufacturer Rule	Manufacturer-deployed stimuli reinforce the behaviour of rivals that is favourable to the manufacturer by presenting positive (Price) reinforcers that signal informational reinforcement. Exposure to the contingencies is indirect through a rule made by a manufacturer.
Manufacturer→Approach→Price→Reinforcers→Positive→Reinforcement Management→Informational→Rival Rule	Manufacturer-deployed stimuli reinforce the behaviour of rivals that is favourable to the manufacturer by presenting positive (Price) reinforcers that signal informational reinforcement. Exposure to the contingencies is indirect through a rule in the rival managerial behaviour setting.
Manufacturer→Approach→Price→Reinforcers→Negative→Scope Management→Setting→Direct Exposure to Contingency	Manufacturer-deployed stimuli reinforce the behaviour of rivals that is favourable to the manufacturer by removing negative (Price) reinforcers that have an impact on the setting. Exposure to the contingencies is direct.
Manufacturer→Approach→Price→Reinforcers→Negative→Scope Management→Setting→Manufacturer Rule	Manufacturer-deployed stimuli reinforce the behaviour of rivals that is favourable to the manufacturer by removing negative (Price) reinforcers that have an impact on the setting. Exposure to the contingencies is indirect through a rule made by a manufacturer.
Manufacturer→Approach→Price→Reinforcers→Negative→Scope Management→Setting→Rival Rule	Manufacturer-deployed stimuli reinforce the behaviour of rivals that is favourable to the manufacturer by removing negative (Price) reinforcers that have an impact on the setting. Exposure to the contingencies is indirect through a rule in the rival managerial behaviour setting.

Manufacturer→Approach→Price→Reinforcers→Negative→ Reinforcement Management→Utilitarian→Direct Exposure to Contingency

Manufacturer-deployed stimuli reinforce the behaviour of rivals that is favourable to the manufacturer by removing negative (Price) reinforcers that signal utilitarian reinforcement. Exposure to the contingencies is direct.

Manufacturer→Approach→Price→Reinforcers→Negative→ Reinforcement Management→Utilitarian→Manufacturer Rule

Manufacturer-deployed stimuli reinforce the behaviour of rivals that is favourable to the manufacturer by removing negative (Price) reinforcers that signal utilitarian reinforcement. Exposure to the contingencies is indirect through a rule made by a manufacturer.

Manufacturer→Approach→Price→Reinforcers→Negative→ Reinforcement Management→Utilitarian→Rival Rule

Manufacturer-deployed stimuli reinforce the behaviour of rivals that is favourable to the manufacturer by removing negative (Price) reinforcers that signal utilitarian reinforcement. Exposure to the contingencies is indirect through a rule in the rival managerial behaviour setting.

Manufacturer→Approach→Price→Reinforcers→Negative→ Reinforcement Management→Informational→Direct Exposure to Contingency

Manufacturer-deployed stimuli reinforce the behaviour of rivals that is favourable to the manufacturer by removing negative (Price) reinforcers that signal informational reinforcement. Exposure to the contingencies is direct.

Manufacturer→Approach→Price→Reinforcers→Negative→ Reinforcement Management→Informational→ Manufacturer Rule

Manufacturer-deployed stimuli reinforce the behaviour of rivals that is favourable to the manufacturer by removing negative (Price) reinforcers that signal informational reinforcement. Exposure to the contingencies is indirect through a rule made by a manufacturer.

Manufacturer→Approach→Price→Reinforcers→Negative→ Reinforcement Management→Informational→Rival Rule

Manufacturer-deployed stimuli reinforce the behaviour of rivals that is favourable to the manufacturer by removing negative (Price) reinforcers that signal informational reinforcement. Exposure to the contingencies is indirect through a rule in the rival managerial behaviour setting.

Code	Description and rule
Product	
Manufacturer→Approach→Product→Reinforcers→ Positive→Scope Management→Setting→Direct Exposure to Contingency	Manufacturer-deployed stimuli reinforce the behaviour of rivals that is favourable to the manufacturer by presenting positive (Product) reinforcers that have an impact on the setting. Exposure to the contingencies is direct.
Manufacturer→Approach→Product→Reinforcers→Positive→ Scope Management→Setting→Manufacturer Rule	Manufacturer-deployed stimuli reinforce the behaviour of rivals that is favourable to the manufacturer by presenting positive (Product) reinforcers that have an impact on the setting. Exposure to the contingencies is indirect through a rule made by a manufacturer.
Manufacturer→Approach→Product→Reinforcers→Positive→ Scope Management→Setting→Rival Rule	Manufacturer-deployed stimuli reinforce the behaviour of rivals that is favourable to the manufacturer by presenting positive (Product) reinforcers that have an impact on the setting. Exposure to the contingencies is indirect through a rule in the rival managerial behaviour setting.
Manufacturer→Approach→Product→Reinforcers→Positive→ Reinforcement Management→Utilitarian→Direct Exposure to Contingency	Manufacturer-deployed stimuli reinforce the behaviour of rivals that is favourable to the manufacturer by presenting positive (Product) reinforcers that signal utilitarian reinforcement. Exposure to the contingencies is direct.
Manufacturer→Approach→Product→Reinforcers→Positive→ Reinforcement Management→Utilitarian→Manufacturer Rule	Manufacturer-deployed stimuli reinforce the behaviour of rivals that is favourable to the manufacturer by presenting positive (Product) reinforcers that signal utilitarian reinforcement. Exposure to the contingencies is indirect through a rule made by a manufacturer.

Manufacturer→Approach→Product→Reinforcers→Positive→Reinforcement Management→Utilitarian→Rival Rule

Manufacturer-deployed stimuli reinforce the behaviour of rivals that is favourable to the manufacturer by presenting positive (Product) reinforcers that signal utilitarian reinforcement. Exposure to the contingencies is indirect through a rule in the rival managerial behaviour setting.

Manufacturer→Approach→Product→Reinforcers→Positive→Reinforcement Management→Informational→Direct Exposure to Contingency

Manufacturer-deployed stimuli reinforce the behaviour of rivals that is favourable to the manufacturer by presenting positive (Product) reinforcers that signal informational reinforcement. Exposure to the contingencies is direct.

Manufacturer→Approach→Product→Reinforcers→Positive→Reinforcement Management→Informational→Manufacturer Rule

Manufacturer-deployed stimuli reinforce the behaviour of rivals that is favourable to the manufacturer by presenting positive (Product) reinforcers that signal informational reinforcement. Exposure to the contingencies is indirect through a rule made by a manufacturer.

Manufacturer→Approach→Product→Reinforcers→Positive→Reinforcement Management→Informational→Rival Rule

Manufacturer-deployed stimuli reinforce the behaviour of rivals that is favourable to the manufacturer by presenting positive (Product) reinforcers that signal informational reinforcement. Exposure to the contingencies is indirect through a rule in the rival managerial behaviour setting.

Manufacturer→Approach→Product→Reinforcers→Negative→Scope Management→Setting→Direct Exposure to Contingency

Manufacturer-deployed stimuli reinforce the behaviour of rivals that is favourable to the manufacturer by removing negative (Product) reinforcers that have an impact on the setting. Exposure to the contingencies is direct.

Manufacturer→Approach→Product→Reinforcers→Negative→Scope Management→Setting→Manufacturer Rule

Manufacturer-deployed stimuli reinforce the behaviour of rivals that is favourable to the manufacturer by removing negative (Product) reinforcers that have an impact on the setting. Exposure to the contingencies is indirect through a rule made by a manufacturer.

Code	Description and rule
Manufacturer→Approach→Product→Reinforcers→Negative→Scope Management→Setting→Rival Rule	Manufacturer-deployed stimuli reinforce the behaviour of rivals that is favourable to the manufacturer by removing negative (Product) reinforcers that have an impact on the setting. Exposure to the contingencies is indirect through a rule in the rival managerial behaviour setting.
Manufacturer→Approach→Product→Reinforcers→Negative→Reinforcement Management→Utilitarian→Direct Exposure to Contingency	Manufacturer-deployed stimuli reinforce the behaviour of rivals that is favourable to the manufacturer by removing negative (Product) reinforcers that signal utilitarian reinforcement. Exposure to the contingencies is direct.
Manufacturer→Approach→Product→Reinforcers→Negative→Reinforcement Management→Utilitarian→Manufacturer Rule	Manufacturer-deployed stimuli reinforce the behaviour of rivals that is favourable to the manufacturer by removing negative (Product) reinforcers that signal utilitarian reinforcement. Exposure to the contingencies is indirect through a rule made by a manufacturer.
Manufacturer→Approach→Product→Reinforcers→Negative→Reinforcement Management→Utilitarian→Rival Rule	Manufacturer-deployed stimuli reinforce the behaviour of rivals that is favourable to the manufacturer by removing negative (Product) reinforcers that signal utilitarian reinforcement. Exposure to the contingencies is indirect through a rule in the rival managerial behaviour setting.
Manufacturer→Approach→Product→Reinforcers→Negative→Reinforcement Management→Informational→Direct Exposure to Contingency	Manufacturer-deployed stimuli reinforce the behaviour of rivals that is favourable to the manufacturer by removing negative (Product) reinforcers that signal informational reinforcement. Exposure to the contingencies is direct.

Manufacturer→Approach→Product→Reinforcers→ Negative→Reinforcement Management→Informational→ Manufacturer Rule

Manufacturer-deployed stimuli reinforce the behaviour of rivals that is favourable to the manufacturer by removing negative (Product) reinforcers that signal informational reinforcement. Exposure to the contingencies is indirect through a rule made by a manufacturer.

Manufacturer→Approach→Product→Reinforcers→ Negative→Reinforcement Management→Informational→ Rival Rule

Manufacturer-deployed stimuli reinforce the behaviour of rivals that is favourable to the manufacturer by removing negative (Product) reinforcers that signal informational reinforcement. Exposure to the contingencies is indirect through a rule in the rival managerial behaviour setting.

Promotion

Manufacturer→Approach→Promotion→Reinforcers→ Positive→Scope Management→Setting→Direct Exposure to Contingency

Manufacturer-deployed stimuli reinforce the behaviour of rivals that is favourable to the manufacturer by presenting positive (Promotion) reinforcers that have an impact on the setting. Exposure to the contingencies is direct.

Manufacturer→Approach→Promotion→Reinforcers→ Positive→Scope Management→Setting→Manufacturer Rule

Manufacturer-deployed stimuli reinforce the behaviour of rivals that is favourable to the manufacturer by presenting positive (Promotion) reinforcers that have an impact on the setting. Exposure to the contingencies is indirect through a rule made by a manufacturer.

Manufacturer→Approach→Promotion→Reinforcers→ Positive→Scope Management→Setting→Rival Rule

Manufacturer-deployed stimuli reinforce the behaviour of rivals that is favourable to the manufacturer by presenting positive (Promotion) reinforcers that have an impact on the setting. Exposure to the contingencies is indirect through a rule in the rival managerial behaviour setting.

Code	Description and rule
Manufacturer→Approach→Promotion→Reinforcers→ Positive→Reinforcement Management→Utilitarian→Direct Exposure to Contingency	Manufacturer-deployed stimuli reinforce the behaviour of rivals that is favourable to the manufacturer by presenting positive (Promotion) reinforcers that signal utilitarian reinforcement. Exposure to the contingencies is direct.
Manufacturer→Approach→Promotion→Reinforcers→ Positive→Reinforcement Management→Utilitarian→ Manufacturer Rule	Manufacturer-deployed stimuli reinforce the behaviour of rivals that is favourable to the manufacturer by presenting positive (Promotion) reinforcers that signal utilitarian reinforcement. Exposure to the contingencies is indirect through a rule made by a manufacturer.
Manufacturer→Approach→Promotion→Reinforcers→ Positive→Reinforcement Management→Utilitarian→Rival Rule	Manufacturer-deployed stimuli reinforce the behaviour of rivals that is favourable to the manufacturer by presenting positive (Promotion) reinforcers that signal utilitarian reinforcement. Exposure to the contingencies is indirect through a rule in the rival managerial behaviour setting.
Manufacturer→Approach→Promotion→Reinforcers→ Positive→Reinforcement Management→Informational→ Direct Exposure to Contingency	Manufacturer-deployed stimuli reinforce the behaviour of rivals that is favourable to the manufacturer by presenting positive (Promotion) reinforcers that signal informational reinforcement. Exposure to the contingencies is direct.
Manufacturer→Approach→Promotion→Reinforcers→ Positive→Reinforcement Management→Informational→ Manufacturer Rule	Manufacturer-deployed stimuli reinforce the behaviour of rivals that is favourable to the manufacturer by presenting positive (Promotion) reinforcers that signal informational reinforcement. Exposure to the contingencies is indirect through a rule made by a manufacturer.

Manufacturer-deployed stimuli reinforce the behaviour of rivals that is favourable to the manufacturer by presenting positive (Promotion) reinforcers that signal informational reinforcement. Exposure to the contingencies is indirect through a rule in the rival managerial behaviour setting.

Manufacturer→Approach→Promotion→Reinforcers→ Positive→Reinforcement Management→Informational→ Rival Rule

Manufacturer-deployed stimuli reinforce the behaviour of rivals that is favourable to the manufacturer by removing negative (Promotion) reinforcers that have an impact on the setting. Exposure to the contingencies is direct.

Manufacturer→Approach→Promotion→Reinforcers→ Negative→Scope Management→Setting→Direct Exposure to Contingency

Manufacturer-deployed stimuli reinforce the behaviour of rivals that is favourable to the manufacturer by removing negative (Promotion) reinforcers that have an impact on the setting. Exposure to the contingencies is indirect through a rule made by a manufacturer.

Manufacturer→Approach→Promotion→Reinforcers→ Negative→Scope Management→Setting→Manufacturer Rule

Manufacturer-deployed stimuli reinforce the behaviour of rivals that is favourable to the manufacturer by removing negative (Promotion) reinforcers that have an impact on the setting. Exposure to the contingencies is indirect through a rule in the rival managerial behaviour setting.

Manufacturer→Approach→Promotion→Reinforcers→ Negative→Scope Management→Setting→Rival Rule

Manufacturer-deployed stimuli reinforce the behaviour of rivals that is favourable to the manufacturer by removing negative (Promotion) reinforcers that signal utilitarian reinforcement. Exposure to the contingencies is direct.

Manufacturer→Approach→Promotion→Reinforcers→ Negative→Reinforcement Management→Utilitarian→ Direct Exposure to Contingency

Manufacturer-deployed stimuli reinforce the behaviour of rivals that is favourable to the manufacturer by removing negative (Promotion) reinforcers that signal utilitarian reinforcement. Exposure to the contingencies is indirect through a rule made by a manufacturer.

Manufacturer→Approach→Promotion→Reinforcers→ Negative→Reinforcement Management→Utilitarian→ Manufacturer Rule

Code	Description and rule
Manufacturer→Approach→Promotion→Reinforcers→ Negative→Reinforcement Management→Utilitarian→Rival Rule	Manufacturer-deployed stimuli reinforce the behaviour of rivals that is favourable to the manufacturer by removing negative (Promotion) reinforcers that signal utilitarian reinforcement. Exposure to the contingencies is indirect through a rule in the rival managerial behaviour setting.
Manufacturer→Approach→Promotion→Reinforcers→ Negative→Reinforcement Management→Informational→ Direct Exposure to Contingency	Manufacturer-deployed stimuli reinforce the behaviour of rivals that is favourable to the manufacturer by removing negative (Promotion) reinforcers that signal informational reinforcement. Exposure to the contingencies is direct.
Manufacturer→Approach→Promotion→Reinforcers→ Negative→Reinforcement Management→Informational→ Manufacturer Rule	Manufacturer-deployed stimuli reinforce the behaviour of rivals that is favourable to the manufacturer by removing negative (Promotion) reinforcers that signal informational reinforcement. Exposure to the contingencies is indirect through a rule made by a manufacturer.
Manufacturer→Approach→Promotion→Reinforcers→ Negative→Reinforcement Management→Informational→ Rival Rule	Manufacturer-deployed stimuli reinforce the behaviour of rivals that is favourable to the manufacturer by removing negative (Promotion) reinforcers that signal informational reinforcement. Exposure to the contingencies is indirect through a rule in the rival managerial behaviour setting.
Place Manufacturer→Approach→Place→Reinforcers→Positive→ Scope Management→Setting→Direct Exposure to Contingency	Manufacturer-deployed stimuli reinforce the behaviour of rivals that is favourable to the manufacturer by presenting positive (Place) reinforcers that have an impact on the setting. Exposure to the contingencies is direct.

Manufacturer→Approach→Place→Reinforcers→Positive→Scope Management→Setting→Manufacturer Rule

Manufacturer-deployed stimuli reinforce the behaviour of rivals that is favourable to the manufacturer by presenting positive (Place) reinforcers that have an impact on the setting. Exposure to the contingencies is indirect through a rule made by a manufacturer.

Manufacturer→Approach→Place→Reinforcers→Positive→Scope Management→Setting→Rival Rule

Manufacturer-deployed stimuli reinforce the behaviour of rivals that is favourable to the manufacturer by presenting positive (Place) reinforcers that have an impact on the setting. Exposure to the contingencies is indirect through a rule in the rival managerial behaviour setting.

Manufacturer→Approach→Place→Reinforcers→Positive→Reinforcement Management→Utilitarian→Direct Exposure to Contingency

Manufacturer-deployed stimuli reinforce the behaviour of rivals that is favourable to the manufacturer by presenting positive (Place) reinforcers that signal utilitarian reinforcement. Exposure to the contingencies is direct.

Manufacturer→Approach→Place→Reinforcers→Positive→Reinforcement Management→Utilitarian→Manufacturer Rule

Manufacturer-deployed stimuli reinforce the behaviour of rivals that is favourable to the manufacturer by presenting positive (Place) reinforcers that signal utilitarian reinforcement. Exposure to the contingencies is indirect through a rule made by a manufacturer.

Manufacturer→Approach→Place→Reinforcers→Positive→Reinforcement Management→Utilitarian→Rival Rule

Manufacturer-deployed stimuli reinforce the behaviour of rivals that is favourable to the manufacturer by presenting positive (Place) reinforcers that signal utilitarian reinforcement. Exposure to the contingencies is indirect through a rule in the rival managerial behaviour setting.

Manufacturer→Approach→Place→Reinforcers→Positive→Reinforcement Management→Informational→Direct Exposure to Contingency

Manufacturer-deployed stimuli reinforce the behaviour of rivals that is favourable to the manufacturer by presenting positive (Place) reinforcers that signal informational reinforcement. Exposure to the contingencies is direct.

Code	Description and rule
Manufacturer→Approach→Place→Reinforcers→Positive→Reinforcement Management→Informational→Manufacturer Rule	Manufacturer-deployed stimuli reinforce the behaviour of rivals that is favourable to the manufacturer by presenting positive (Place) reinforcers that signal informational reinforcement. Exposure to the contingencies is indirect through a rule made by a manufacturer.
Manufacturer→Approach→Place→Reinforcers→Positive→Reinforcement Management→Informational→Rival Rule	Manufacturer-deployed stimuli reinforce the behaviour of rivals that is favourable to the manufacturer by presenting positive (Place) reinforcers that signal informational reinforcement. Exposure to the contingencies is indirect through a rule in the rival managerial behaviour setting.
Manufacturer→Approach→Place→Reinforcers→Negative→Scope Management→Setting→Direct Exposure to Contingency	Manufacturer-deployed stimuli reinforce the behaviour of rivals that is favourable to the manufacturer by removing negative (Place) reinforcers that have an impact on the setting. Exposure to the contingencies is direct.
Manufacturer→Approach→Place→Reinforcers→Negative→Scope Management→Setting→Manufacturer Rule	Manufacturer-deployed stimuli reinforce the behaviour of rivals that is favourable to the manufacturer by removing negative (Place) reinforcers that have an impact on the setting. Exposure to the contingencies is indirect through a rule made by a manufacturer.
Manufacturer→Approach→Place→Reinforcers→Negative→Scope Management→Setting→Rival Rule	Manufacturer-deployed stimuli reinforce the behaviour of rivals that is favourable to the manufacturer by removing negative (Place) reinforcers that have an impact on the setting. Exposure to the contingencies is indirect through a rule in the rival managerial behaviour setting.
Manufacturer→Approach→Place→Reinforcers→Negative→Reinforcement Management→Utilitarian→Direct Exposure to Contingency	Manufacturer-deployed stimuli reinforce the behaviour of rivals that is favourable to the manufacturer by removing negative (Place) reinforcers that signal utilitarian reinforcement. Exposure to the contingencies is direct.

Manufacturer→Approach→Place→Reinforcers→Negative→ Reinforcement Management→Utilitarian→Manufacturer Rule

Manufacturer-deployed stimuli reinforce the behaviour of rivals that is favourable to the manufacturer by removing negative (Place) reinforcers that signal utilitarian reinforcement. Exposure to the contingencies is indirect through a rule made by a manufacturer.

Manufacturer→Approach→Place→Reinforcers→Negative→ Reinforcement Management→Utilitarian→Rival Rule

Manufacturer-deployed stimuli reinforce the behaviour of rivals that is favourable to the manufacturer by removing negative (Place) reinforcers that signal utilitarian reinforcement. Exposure to the contingencies is indirect through a rule in the rival managerial behaviour setting.

Manufacturer→Approach→Place→Reinforcers→Negative→ Reinforcement Management→Informational→Direct Exposure to Contingency

Manufacturer-deployed stimuli reinforce the behaviour of rivals that is favourable to the manufacturer by removing negative (Place) reinforcers that signal informational reinforcement. Exposure to the contingencies is direct.

Manufacturer→Approach→Place→Reinforcers→Negative→ Reinforcement Management→Informational→ Manufacturer Rule

Manufacturer-deployed stimuli reinforce the behaviour of rivals that is favourable to the manufacturer by removing negative (Place) reinforcers that signal informational reinforcement. Exposure to the contingencies is indirect through a rule made by a manufacturer.

Manufacturer→Approach→Place→Reinforcers→Negative→ Reinforcement Management→Informational→Rival Rule

Manufacturer-deployed stimuli reinforce the behaviour of rivals that is favourable to the manufacturer by removing negative (Place) reinforcers that signal informational reinforcement. Exposure to the contingencies is indirect through a rule in the rival managerial behaviour setting.

Code	Description and rule
Weakening rival unfavourable (avoidance) behaviour through punishment	
Price	
Manufacturer→Avoidance→Price→Punishers→Positive→ Scope Management→Setting→Direct Exposure to Contingency	Manufacturer-deployed stimuli punish the behaviour of rivals that is unfavourable to the manufacturer by presenting positive (Price) punishers that have an impact on the setting. Exposure to the contingencies is direct.
Manufacturer→Avoidance→Price→Punishers→Positive→ Scope Management→Setting→Manufacturer Rule	Manufacturer-deployed stimuli punish the behaviour of rivals that is unfavourable to the manufacturer by presenting positive (Price) punishers that have an impact on the setting. Exposure to the contingencies is indirect through a rule made by a manufacturer.
Manufacturer→Avoidance→Price→Punishers→Positive→ Scope Management→Setting→Rival Rule	Manufacturer-deployed stimuli punish the behaviour of rivals that is unfavourable to the manufacturer by presenting positive (Price) punishers that have an impact on the setting. Exposure to the contingencies is indirect through a rule in the rival managerial behaviour setting.
Manufacturer→Avoidance→Price→Punishers→Positive→ Reinforcement Management→Utilitarian→Direct Exposure to Contingency	Manufacturer-deployed stimuli punish the behaviour of rivals that is unfavourable to the manufacturer by presenting positive (Price) punishers that signal utilitarian reinforcement. Exposure to the contingencies is direct.
Manufacturer→Avoidance→Price→Punishers→Positive→ Reinforcement Management→Utilitarian→Manufacturer Rule	Manufacturer-deployed stimuli punish the behaviour of rivals that is unfavourable to the manufacturer by presenting positive (Price) punishers that signal utilitarian reinforcement. Exposure to the contingencies is indirect through a rule made by a manufacturer.

Manufacturer→Avoidance→Price→Punishers→Positive→Reinforcement Management→Utilitarian→Rival Rule

Manufacturer-deployed stimuli punish the behaviour of rivals that is unfavourable to the manufacturer by presenting positive (Price) punishers that signal utilitarian reinforcement. Exposure to the contingencies is indirect through a rule in the rival managerial behaviour setting.

Manufacturer→Avoidance→Price→Punishers→Positive→Reinforcement Management→Informational→Direct Exposure to Contingency

Manufacturer-deployed stimuli punish the behaviour of rivals that is unfavourable to the manufacturer by presenting positive (Price) punishers that signal informational reinforcement. Exposure to the contingencies is direct.

Manufacturer→Avoidance→Price→Punishers→Positive→Reinforcement Management→Informational→Manufacturer Rule

Manufacturer-deployed stimuli punish the behaviour of rivals that is unfavourable to the manufacturer by presenting positive (Price) punishers that signal informational reinforcement. Exposure to the contingencies is indirect through a rule made by a manufacturer.

Manufacturer→Avoidance→Price→Punishers→Positive→Reinforcement Management→Informational→Rival Rule

Manufacturer-deployed stimuli punish the behaviour of rivals that is unfavourable to the manufacturer by presenting positive (Price) punishers that signal informational reinforcement. Exposure to the contingencies is indirect through a rule in the rival managerial behaviour setting.

Manufacturer→Avoidance→Price→Punishers→Negative→Scope Management→Setting→Direct Exposure to Contingency

Manufacturer-deployed stimuli punish the behaviour of rivals that is unfavourable to the manufacturer by removing negative (Price) punishers that have an impact on the setting. Exposure to the contingencies is direct.

Manufacturer→Avoidance→Price→Punishers→Negative→Scope Management→Setting→Manufacturer Rule

Manufacturer-deployed stimuli punish the behaviour of rivals that is unfavourable to the manufacturer by removing negative (Price) punishers that have an impact on the setting. Exposure to the contingencies is indirect through a rule made by a manufacturer.

Code	Description and rule
Manufacturer→Avoidance→Price→Punishers→Negative→ Scope Management→Setting→Rival Rule	Manufacturer-deployed stimuli punish the behaviour of rivals that is unfavourable to the manufacturer by removing negative (Price) punishers that have an impact on the setting. Exposure to the contingencies is indirect through a rule in the rival managerial behaviour setting.
Manufacturer→Avoidance→Price→Punishers→Negative→ Reinforcement Management→Utilitarian→Direct Exposure to Contingency	Manufacturer-deployed stimuli punish the behaviour of rivals that is unfavourable to the manufacturer by removing negative (Price) punishers that signal utilitarian reinforcement. Exposure to the contingencies is direct.
Manufacturer→Avoidance→Price→Punishers→Negative→ Reinforcement Management→Utilitarian→Manufacturer Rule	Manufacturer-deployed stimuli punish the behaviour of rivals that is unfavourable to the manufacturer by removing negative (Price) punishers that signal utilitarian reinforcement. Exposure to the contingencies is indirect through a rule made by a manufacturer.
Manufacturer→Avoidance→Price→Punishers→Negative→ Reinforcement Management→Utilitarian→Rival Rule	Manufacturer-deployed stimuli punish the behaviour of rivals that is unfavourable to the manufacturer by removing negative (Price) punishers that signal utilitarian reinforcement. Exposure to the contingencies is indirect through a rule in the rival managerial behaviour setting.
Manufacturer→Avoidance→Price→Punishers→Negative→ Reinforcement Management→Informational→Direct Exposure to Contingency	Manufacturer-deployed stimuli punish the behaviour of rivals that is unfavourable to the manufacturer by removing negative (Price) punishers that signal informational reinforcement. Exposure to the contingencies is direct.
Manufacturer→Avoidance→Price→Punishers→Negative→ Reinforcement Management→Informational→ Manufacturer Rule	Manufacturer-deployed stimuli punish the behaviour of rivals that is unfavourable to the manufacturer by removing negative (Price) punishers that signal informational reinforcement. Exposure to the contingencies is indirect through a rule made by a manufacturer.

Manufacturer-deployed stimuli punish the behaviour of rivals that is unfavourable to the manufacturer by removing negative reinforcement. (Price) punishers that signal informational reinforcement. Exposure to the contingencies is indirect through a rule in the rival managerial behaviour setting.

Manufacturer→Avoidance→Price→Punishers→Negative→Reinforcement Management→Informational→Rival Rule

Product

Manufacturer-deployed stimuli punish the behaviour of rivals that is unfavourable to the manufacturer by presenting positive (Product) punishers that have an impact on the setting. Exposure to the contingencies is direct.

Manufacturer→Avoidance→Product→Punishers→Positive→Scope Management→Setting→Direct Exposure to Contingency

Manufacturer-deployed stimuli punish the behaviour of rivals that is unfavourable to the manufacturer by presenting positive (Product) punishers that have an impact on the setting. Exposure to the contingencies is indirect through a rule made by a manufacturer.

Manufacturer→Avoidance→Product→Punishers→Positive→Scope Management→Setting→Manufacturer Rule

Manufacturer-deployed stimuli punish the behaviour of rivals that is unfavourable to the manufacturer by presenting positive (Product) punishers that have an impact on the setting. Exposure to the contingencies is indirect through a rule in the rival managerial behaviour setting.

Manufacturer→Avoidance→Product→Punishers→Positive→Scope Management→Setting→Rival Rule

Manufacturer-deployed stimuli punish the behaviour of rivals that is unfavourable to the manufacturer by presenting positive (Product) punishers that signal utilitarian reinforcement. Exposure to the contingencies is direct.

Manufacturer→Avoidance→Product→Punishers→Positive→Reinforcement Management→Utilitarian→Direct Exposure to Contingency

Manufacturer-deployed stimuli punish the behaviour of rivals that is unfavourable to the manufacturer by presenting positive (Product) punishers that signal utilitarian reinforcement. Exposure to the contingencies is indirect through a rule made by a manufacturer.

Manufacturer→Avoidance→Product→Punishers→Positive→Reinforcement Management→Utilitarian→Manufacturer Rule

Code	Description and rule
Manufacturer→Avoidance→Product→Punishers→Positive→Reinforcement Management→Utilitarian→Rival Rule	Manufacturer-deployed stimuli punish the behaviour of rivals that is unfavourable to the manufacturer by presenting positive (Product) punishers that signal utilitarian reinforcement. Exposure to the contingencies is indirect through a rule in the rival managerial behaviour setting.
Manufacturer→Avoidance→Product→Punishers→Positive→Reinforcement Management→Informational→Direct Exposure to Contingency	Manufacturer-deployed stimuli punish the behaviour of rivals that is unfavourable to the manufacturer by presenting positive (Product) punishers that signal informational reinforcement. Exposure to the contingencies is direct.
Manufacturer→Avoidance→Product→Punishers→Positive→Reinforcement Management→Informational→Manufacturer Rule	Manufacturer-deployed stimuli punish the behaviour of rivals that is unfavourable to the manufacturer by presenting positive (Product) punishers that signal informational reinforcement. Exposure to the contingencies is indirect through a rule made by a manufacturer.
Manufacturer→Avoidance→Product→Punishers→Positive→Reinforcement Management→Informational→Rival Rule	Manufacturer-deployed stimuli punish the behaviour of rivals that is unfavourable to the manufacturer by presenting positive (Product) punishers that signal informational reinforcement. Exposure to the contingencies is indirect through a rule in the rival managerial behaviour setting.
Manufacturer→Avoidance→Product→Punishers→Negative→Scope Management→Setting→Direct Exposure to Contingency	Manufacturer-deployed stimuli punish the behaviour of rivals that is unfavourable to the manufacturer by removing negative (Product) punishers that have an impact on the setting. Exposure to the contingencies is direct.
Manufacturer→Avoidance→Product→Punishers→Negative→Scope Management→Setting→Manufacturer Rule	Manufacturer-deployed stimuli punish the behaviour of rivals that is unfavourable to the manufacturer by removing negative (Product) punishers that have an impact on the setting. Exposure to the contingencies is indirect through a rule made by a manufacturer.

Manufacturer→Avoidance→Product→Punishers→Negative→Scope Management→Setting→Rival Rule

Manufacturer-deployed stimuli punish the behaviour of rivals that is unfavourable to the manufacturer by removing negative (Product) punishers that have an impact on the setting. Exposure to the contingencies is indirect through a rule in the rival managerial behaviour setting.

Manufacturer→Avoidance→Product→Punishers→Negative→Reinforcement Management→Utilitarian→Direct Exposure to Contingency

Manufacturer-deployed stimuli punish the behaviour of rivals that is unfavourable to the manufacturer by removing negative (Product) punishers that signal utilitarian reinforcement. Exposure to the contingencies is direct.

Manufacturer→Avoidance→Product→Punishers→Negative→Reinforcement Management→Utilitarian→Manufacturer Rule

Manufacturer-deployed stimuli punish the behaviour of rivals that is unfavourable to the manufacturer by removing negative (Product) punishers that signal utilitarian reinforcement. Exposure to the contingencies is indirect through a rule made by a manufacturer.

Manufacturer→Avoidance→Product→Punishers→Negative→Reinforcement Management→Utilitarian→Rival Rule

Manufacturer-deployed stimuli punish the behaviour of rivals that is unfavourable to the manufacturer by removing negative (Product) punishers that signal utilitarian reinforcement. Exposure to the contingencies is indirect through a rule in the rival managerial behaviour setting.

Manufacturer→Avoidance→Product→Punishers→Negative→Reinforcement Management→Informational→Direct Exposure to Contingency

Manufacturer-deployed stimuli punish the behaviour of rivals that is unfavourable to the manufacturer by removing negative (Product) punishers that signal informational reinforcement. Exposure to the contingencies is direct.

Manufacturer→Avoidance→Product→Punishers→Negative→Reinforcement Management→Informational→Manufacturer Rule

Manufacturer-deployed stimuli punish the behaviour of rivals that is unfavourable to the manufacturer by removing negative (Product) punishers that signal informational reinforcement. Exposure to the contingencies is indirect through a rule made by a manufacturer.

Code	Description and rule
Manufacturer→Avoidance→Product→Punishers→Negative→ Reinforcement Management→Informational→Rival Rule	Manufacturer-deployed stimuli punish the behaviour of rivals that is unfavourable to the manufacturer by removing negative (Product) punishers that signal informational reinforcement. Exposure to the contingencies is indirect through a rule in the rival managerial behaviour setting.
Promotion	
Manufacturer→Avoidance→Promotion→Punishers→ Positive→Scope Management→Setting→Direct Exposure to Contingency	Manufacturer-deployed stimuli punish the behaviour of rivals that is unfavourable to the manufacturer by presenting positive (Promotion) punishers that have an impact on the setting. Exposure to the contingencies is direct.
Manufacturer→Avoidance→Promotion→Punishers→ Positive→Scope Management→Setting→Manufacturer Rule	Manufacturer-deployed stimuli punish the behaviour of rivals that is unfavourable to the manufacturer by presenting positive (Promotion) punishers that have an impact on the setting. Exposure to the contingencies is indirect through a rule made by a manufacturer.
Manufacturer→Avoidance→Promotion→Punishers→ Positive→Scope Management→Setting→Rival Rule	Manufacturer-deployed stimuli punish the behaviour of rivals that is unfavourable to the manufacturer by presenting positive (Promotion) punishers that have an impact on the setting. Exposure to the contingencies is indirect through a rule in the rival managerial behaviour setting.
Manufacturer→Avoidance→Promotion→Punishers→ Positive→Reinforcement Management→Utilitarian→Direct Exposure to Contingency	Manufacturer-deployed stimuli punish the behaviour of rivals that is unfavourable to the manufacturer by presenting positive (Promotion) punishers that signal utilitarian reinforcement. Exposure to the contingencies is direct.

Manufacturer→Avoidance→Promotion→Punishers→Positive→Reinforcement Management→Utilitarian→Manufacturer Rule

Manufacturer-deployed stimuli punish the behaviour of rivals that is unfavourable to the manufacturer by presenting positive (Promotion) punishers that signal utilitarian reinforcement. Exposure to the contingencies is indirect through a rule made by a manufacturer.

Manufacturer→Avoidance→Promotion→Punishers→Positive→Reinforcement Management→Utilitarian→Rival Rule

Manufacturer-deployed stimuli punish the behaviour of rivals that is unfavourable to the manufacturer by presenting positive (Promotion) punishers that signal utilitarian reinforcement. Exposure to the contingencies is indirect through a rule in the rival managerial behaviour setting.

Manufacturer→Avoidance→Promotion→Punishers→Positive→Reinforcement Management→Informational→Direct Exposure to Contingency

Manufacturer-deployed stimuli punish the behaviour of rivals that is unfavourable to the manufacturer by presenting positive (Promotion) punishers that signal informational reinforcement. Exposure to the contingencies is direct.

Manufacturer→Avoidance→Promotion→Punishers→Positive→Reinforcement Management→Informational→Manufacturer Rule

Manufacturer-deployed stimuli punish the behaviour of rivals that is unfavourable to the manufacturer by presenting positive (Promotion) punishers that signal informational reinforcement. Exposure to the contingencies is indirect through a rule made by a manufacturer.

Manufacturer→Avoidance→Promotion→Punishers→Positive→Reinforcement Management→Informational→Rival Rule

Manufacturer-deployed stimuli punish the behaviour of rivals that is unfavourable to the manufacturer by presenting positive (Promotion) punishers that signal informational reinforcement. Exposure to the contingencies is indirect through a rule in the rival managerial behaviour setting.

Manufacturer→Avoidance→Promotion→Punishers→Negative→Scope Management→Setting→Direct Exposure to Contingency

Manufacturer-deployed stimuli punish the behaviour of rivals that is unfavourable to the manufacturer by removing negative (Promotion) punishers that have an impact on the setting. Exposure to the contingencies is direct.

Code	Description and rule
Manufacturer→Avoidance→Promotion→Punishers→ Negative→Scope Management→Setting→Manufacturer Rule	Manufacturer-deployed stimuli punish the behaviour of rivals that is unfavourable to the manufacturer by removing negative (Promotion) punishers that have an impact on the setting. Exposure to the contingencies is indirect through a rule made by a manufacturer.
Manufacturer→Avoidance→Promotion→Punishers→ Negative→Scope Management→Setting→Rival Rule	Manufacturer-deployed stimuli punish the behaviour of rivals that is unfavourable to the manufacturer by removing negative (Promotion) punishers that have an impact on the setting. Exposure to the contingencies is indirect through a rule in the rival managerial behaviour setting.
Manufacturer→Avoidance→Promotion→Punishers→ Negative→Reinforcement Management→Utilitarian→ Direct Exposure to Contingency	Manufacturer-deployed stimuli punish the behaviour of rivals that is unfavourable to the manufacturer by removing negative (Promotion) punishers that signal utilitarian reinforcement. Exposure to the contingencies is direct.
Manufacturer→Avoidance→Promotion→Punishers→ Negative→Reinforcement Management→Utilitarian→ Manufacturer Rule	Manufacturer-deployed stimuli punish the behaviour of rivals that is unfavourable to the manufacturer by removing negative (Promotion) punishers that signal utilitarian reinforcement. Exposure to the contingencies is indirect through a rule made by a manufacturer.
Manufacturer→Avoidance→Promotion→Punishers→ Negative→Reinforcement Management→Utilitarian→Rival Rule	Manufacturer-deployed stimuli punish the behaviour of rivals that is unfavourable to the manufacturer by removing negative (Promotion) punishers that signal utilitarian reinforcement. Exposure to the contingencies is indirect through a rule in the rival managerial behaviour setting.
Manufacturer→Avoidance→Promotion→Punishers→ Negative→Reinforcement Management→Informational→ Direct Exposure to Contingency	Manufacturer-deployed stimuli punish the behaviour of rivals that is unfavourable to the manufacturer by removing negative (Promotion) punishers that signal informational reinforcement. Exposure to the contingencies is direct.

Manufacturer→Avoidance→Promotion→Punishers→
Negative→Reinforcement Management→Informational→
Manufacturer Rule

Manufacturer-deployed stimuli punish the behaviour of rivals that is unfavourable to the manufacturer by removing negative (Promotion) punishers that signal informational reinforcement. Exposure to the contingencies is indirect through a rule made by a manufacturer.

Manufacturer→Avoidance→Promotion→Punishers→
Negative→Reinforcement Management→Informational→
Rival Rule

Manufacturer-deployed stimuli punish the behaviour of rivals that is unfavourable to the manufacturer by removing negative (Promotion) punishers that signal informational reinforcement. Exposure to the contingencies is indirect through a rule in the rival managerial behaviour setting.

Place

Manufacturer→Avoidance→Place→Punishers→Positive→
Scope Management→Setting→Direct Exposure to
Contingency

Manufacturer-deployed stimuli punish the behaviour of rivals that is unfavourable to the manufacturer by presenting positive (Place) punishers that have an impact on the setting. Exposure to the contingencies is direct.

Manufacturer→Avoidance→Place→Punishers→Positive→
Scope Management→Setting→Manufacturer Rule

Manufacturer-deployed stimuli punish the behaviour of rivals that is unfavourable to the manufacturer by presenting positive (Place) punishers that have an impact on the setting. Exposure to the contingencies is indirect through a rule made by a manufacturer.

Manufacturer→Avoidance→Place→Punishers→Positive→
Scope Management→Setting→Rival Rule

Manufacturer-deployed stimuli punish the behaviour of rivals that is unfavourable to the manufacturer by presenting positive (Place) punishers that have an impact on the setting. Exposure to the contingencies is indirect through a rule in the rival managerial behaviour setting.

Manufacturer→Avoidance→Place→Punishers→Positive→
Reinforcement Management→Utilitarian→Direct Exposure
to Contingency

Manufacturer-deployed stimuli punish the behaviour of rivals that is unfavourable to the manufacturer by presenting positive (Place) punishers that signal utilitarian reinforcement. Exposure to the contingencies is direct.

Code	Description and rule
Manufacturer→Avoidance→Place→Punishers→Positive→ Reinforcement Management→Utilitarian→Manufacturer Rule	Manufacturer-deployed stimuli punish the behaviour of rivals that is unfavourable to the manufacturer by presenting positive (Place) punishers that signal utilitarian reinforcement. Exposure to the contingencies is indirect through a rule made by a manufacturer.
Manufacturer→Avoidance→Place→Punishers→Positive→ Reinforcement Management→Utilitarian→Rival Rule	Manufacturer-deployed stimuli punish the behaviour of rivals that is unfavourable to the manufacturer by presenting positive (Place) punishers that signal utilitarian reinforcement. Exposure to the contingencies is indirect through a rule in the rival managerial behaviour setting.
Manufacturer→Avoidance→Place→Punishers→Positive→ Reinforcement Management→Informational→Direct Exposure to Contingency	Manufacturer-deployed stimuli punish the behaviour of rivals that is unfavourable to the manufacturer by presenting positive (Place) punishers that signal informational reinforcement. Exposure to the contingencies is direct.
Manufacturer→Avoidance→Place→Punishers→Positive→ Reinforcement Management→Informational→ Manufacturer Rule	Manufacturer-deployed stimuli punish the behaviour of rivals that is unfavourable to the manufacturer by presenting positive (Place) punishers that signal informational reinforcement. Exposure to the contingencies is indirect through a rule made by a manufacturer.
Manufacturer→Avoidance→Place→Punishers→Positive→ Reinforcement Management→Informational→Rival Rule	Manufacturer-deployed stimuli punish the behaviour of rivals that is unfavourable to the manufacturer by presenting positive (Place) punishers that signal informational reinforcement. Exposure to the contingencies is indirect through a rule in the rival managerial behaviour setting.

Manufacturer→Avoidance→Place→Punishers→Negative→Scope Management→Setting→Direct Exposure to Contingency

Manufacturer-deployed stimuli punish the behaviour of rivals that is unfavourable to the manufacturer by removing negative (Place) punishers that have an impact on the setting. Exposure to the contingencies is direct.

Manufacturer→Avoidance→Place→Punishers→Negative→Scope Management→Setting→Manufacturer Rule

Manufacturer-deployed stimuli punish the behaviour of rivals that is unfavourable to the manufacturer by removing negative (Place) punishers that have an impact on the setting. Exposure to the contingencies is indirect through a rule made by a manufacturer.

Manufacturer→Avoidance→Place→Punishers→Negative→Scope Management→Setting→Rival Rule

Manufacturer-deployed stimuli punish the behaviour of rivals that is unfavourable to the manufacturer by removing negative (Place) punishers that have an impact on the setting. Exposure to the contingencies is indirect through a rule in the rival managerial behaviour setting.

Manufacturer→Avoidance→Place→Punishers→Negative→Reinforcement Management→Utilitarian→Direct Exposure to Contingency

Manufacturer-deployed stimuli punish the behaviour of rivals that is unfavourable to the manufacturer by removing negative (Place) punishers that signal utilitarian reinforcement. Exposure to the contingencies is direct.

Manufacturer→Avoidance→Place→Punishers→Negative→Reinforcement Management→Utilitarian→Manufacturer Rule

Manufacturer-deployed stimuli punish the behaviour of rivals that is unfavourable to the manufacturer by removing negative (Place) punishers that signal utilitarian reinforcement. Exposure to the contingencies is indirect through a rule made by a manufacturer.

Manufacturer→Avoidance→Place→Punishers→Negative→Reinforcement Management→Utilitarian→Rival Rule

Manufacturer-deployed stimuli punish the behaviour of rivals that is unfavourable to the manufacturer by removing negative (Place) punishers that signal utilitarian reinforcement. Exposure to the contingencies is indirect through a rule in the rival managerial behaviour setting.

Code	Description and rule
Manufacturer→Avoidance→Place→Punishers→Negative→Reinforcement Management→Informational→Direct Exposure to Contingency	Manufacturer-deployed stimuli punish the behaviour of rivals that is unfavourable to the manufacturer by removing negative (Place) punishers that signal informational reinforcement. Exposure to the contingencies is direct.
Manufacturer→Avoidance→Place→Punishers→Negative→Reinforcement Management→Informational→Manufacturer Rule	Manufacturer-deployed stimuli punish the behaviour of rivals that is unfavourable to the manufacturer by removing negative (Place) punishers that signal informational reinforcement. Exposure to the contingencies is indirect through a rule made by a manufacturer.
Manufacturer→Avoidance→Place→Punishers→Negative→Reinforcement Management→Informational→Rival Rule	Manufacturer-deployed stimuli punish the behaviour of rivals that is unfavourable to the manufacturer by removing negative (Place) punishers that signal informational reinforcement. Exposure to the contingencies is indirect through a rule in the rival managerial behaviour setting.

Appendix 4.   Data tables and commentary

A4.1   TIMELINE OF EVENTS LEADING UP TO THE 1999 INVESTIGATION

Table A4.1   Timeline of events leading up to the 2000 report based on the conclusions of the Competition Commission

Date	Description
1922	Wall's introduces factory ice-cream production in the UK and appears to have been the dominant brand since.
1960s	Wall's is the only national brand. Three companies merge to form Lyons Maid for national coverage.
August 1979	Publication of the first inquiry; period under investigation 1976, covering the entire ice-cream market (impulse and non-impulse).
	Impulse ice-cream market shares:
	• Wall's (forerunner of BEW) and Lyons Maid each had 45 per cent and were found to be scale monopolists.
	Main findings against public interest:
	• Outlet exclusivity or the supply of ice-cream to retail outlets under agreements stipulating the other manufacturers' ice-creams should not be stocked (PLACE[1]).
	• Marketing practices by Glacier Foods Ltd (then owning Lyons Maid) requiring:
	a) Wholesalers of its products not to sell competing brands (PLACE). This is a form of dedicated or exclusive distribution.
	b) Customers buying soft ice-cream from Lyons should also buy Lyons hard ice-cream (PRODUCT);
	c) Mobile van franchisees of Lyons to stock or sell only specified brands (PLACE).

Table A4.1 (continued)

Date	Description

- Wall's and Lyons supply contracts (PLACE) ran for periods longer than one year. Further bonuses (PROMOTION) accruing to retailers for having achieved or surpassed their sales targets ran on schedules that did not coincide with the contract renewal periods. Therefore, according to the Commission, these bonuses acted as 'inducing the retailers to stay with the same supplier' (Competition Commission, 2000, p. 377).

Findings not against public interest but restrictive:

- Freezer exclusivity or the supply to retailers of refrigerated cabinets on condition that they were used to stock for sale only the supplier's ice-cream (PLACE). Freezers were supplied either free of charge or at a nominal rent.

Undertakings given to the Secretary of State in May 1982:

- Manufacturers[2] were required not to enter into arrangements whereby retailers of their products should not sell other manufacturers' ice-cream. (Mars and Nestlé were not subject to these undertakings since they were not present in the market until later).
- In general, freezer exclusivity was somewhat relaxed to allow retailers the possibility of stocking competing brands in those situations where the supplier could not provide for the retailer's requirements.
- Wall's and Lyons undertook that contract periods required an expiry of at least 12 months, with one month's termination notice, and bonuses were to be kept in sync with contracts.
- Lyons undertook to stop practice (b) above as well as not requiring that wholesalers only stock Lyons brands. Lyons also relaxed its franchisee requirements.

Other practices/findings:

- BEW carried out its own distribution activities, and eventually formed a dedicated franchised distribution network consisting of 38 independent companies to serve areas outside the M25.[3] In the 1998 report these were referred to as dedicated distributors.

248

	• Within the M25, BEW continued selling direct.
	• Lyons carried out most of its distribution through its subsidiary Alpine.
1980s	BEW (comes into existence in 1981) market share increases to 52 per cent, that of Lyons Maid to 39 per cent, owing to a heavy investment by BEW (but not by Lyons Maid) in product and brand development as well as advertising. Investment in distribution is also maintained.
1989	Mars enters UK market.
1991	Treats is bought out by its management from Unilever.
1992	Lyons Maid is acquired by Nestlé.
	BEW's dedicated distributors now distribute about 63 per cent (60 per cent in 1995) of BEW's wrapped impulse ice-cream in terms of volume. BEW remains direct within the M25, and remaining sales are distributed through proprietary and independent mobile retailers, through wholesalers and direct delivery to a handful of national accounts.
1994	Publication of the second inquiry; period under investigation 1993, covering the supply of ice-cream for immediate consumption but limited to freezer exclusivity.

Impulse ice-cream market shares:

- BEW's share of wrapped impulse ice-cream was 67 per cent, and share of all impulse ice-cream was 49 per cent.
- Lyons Maid share had fallen to 11 per cent.
- Mars, with a limited higher-priced range, had a 14 per cent market share.

Main findings not against public interest:

- Freezer exclusivity was not against public interest to the extent that the Commission found that the phenomenon posed less of a threat than was originally found in 1979. There was 'insufficient evidence' to support contentions that freezer exclusivity, the conditions upon which freezers were so supplied or the charges for using exclusive freezers inhibited choice or competition or negatively affected pricing, innovation, efficiency or aspects related to public interest.

Table A4.1 (continued)

Date	Description
1994	• No evidence to suggest that overall sales would increase if freezer exclusivity was terminated. And competition was effective despite the existence of freezer exclusivity. Retailers did not need to rely on the provision of a single exclusive freezer. Several options were available, including (a) the acquisition of their own freezers, which would also mean improved discounts from manufacturers (differential terms by way of **PRICE**) and additional bonus payments (differential terms by way of **PROMOTION**); and (b) space permitting, the addition of a second, non-exclusive freezer.
	• A survey of small retailers by the Commission showed that 74 per cent of respondents had only one freezer for selling impulse ice-cream and 36 per cent were exclusive to a single manufacturer.
	• Advertising (**PROMOTION**) and the need to offer a freezer represented a cost of market entry, but neither constituted a barrier.
	Other practices/findings:
	• The report, as with all subsequent reports, found that **distribution played an extremely important role in the competition between manufacturers**: 'the limited space of many retailers for holding stock … require[s] products to be distributed … using a well-controlled capital-intensive system [from manufacturer to] regional cold stores [using] refrigerated vans, with delivery at short notice when demand is high' (Competition Commission 2000, p. 18).
	• BEW's dedicated distributors are now an established provider of very high-quality and dependable service to the manufacturer and its retail customers. The distribution arrangements were similar to the Lyons 1979 arrangements, but could not be fully investigated since they fell outside the Commission's terms of reference.
	• Relatively limited brand choice at point of sale, with the same survey finding 42 per cent of small retailers stocking products from a single manufacturer and 31 per cent stocking only BEW products.
	• Mars collaborates with Nestlé, with the latter distributing products for the former and stocking in own (outlet) freezers.
1996	Mars and Nestlé terminate their collaboration on distribution.

July 1998

Publication of third inquiry; period under investigation 1997, covering distribution practices by BEW on the supply of impulse ice-cream.[4]

Impulse ice-cream market shares:

- BEW's share of wrapped impulse ice-cream was 69 per cent, and share of all impulse ice-cream was 54 per cent.

Main findings against public interest:

- BEW refused to supply wrapped impulse ice-cream to non-dedicated wholesalers unless on contractual terms (PRICE) and/or additional benefits (PROMOTION) less favourable to those that were dedicated distributors.
- BEW granted additional discounts (PRICE) only to those retailers that purchased their BEW wrapped impulse ice-cream from dedicated distributors.

Undertakings given to the Secretary of State in November 1998:

- BEW undertook to offer dedicated and non-dedicated distributors the same standard terms on list prices and discounts. Further, these standard terms and any variations thereof would be published. Retailers would not be offered additional discounts on condition that they would buy their supply from dedicated distributors. Neither would BEW impose on non-dedicated distributors or retailers that bought their supply of BEW wrapped impulse ice-cream from non-dedicated distributors any obligation which would have the same effect as offering a conditional discount. Other undertakings included limiting remuneration to dedicated distributors, as well as certain performance-related discounts.

Other practices/findings:

- The Commission identified several 'interlocking' factors that it could not investigate owing to specific terms of reference but that it deemed to have an adverse impact on competition within the wrapped impulse ice-cream market. These related to the exclusivity arrangements with dedicated distributors and freezer exclusivity.

Table A4.1 (continued)

Date	Description
	• Further concerns were expressed on the revision of terms by BEW to its entire distribution network: during the course of the 1998 investigation but outside the period the Commission was allowed to investigate, BEW revised contractual and discount terms downwards. BEW did not want to 'over-reward distributors' (§5.116, p. 186). The changes placed greater emphasis on sales growth targets and performance-based incentive payments (PROMOTION). Over these incentives, dedicated distributors earned from accruals (PROMOTION) for central distribution and storage as well as related payments for achieving business plan targets. Cumulatively these pay-outs amounted to better terms than those offered to independent wholesalers, which accounted for only 10 per cent of BEW business.
	▫ Two of the 29 dedicated distributors chose to act as independent wholesalers following these contractual revisions (§2.16). In 1998 BEW extended the Barking operation to the Norfolk and Cambridgeshire areas following the decision by these two dedicated distributors not to renew their contracts.
	▫ BEW also further extended the operation in 1998/99 to cover the principal sales areas (Northampton and Bolton) of two dedicated distributors whose dedicated distributor agreements terminated during the period.
	• Of note is the Commission's suspicion that BEW might take its distribution in-house. These suspicions also seem to have been fuelled by the decrease in distributor earnings within a two-year period from 17.9 per cent in 1996 to 16.4 per cent in 1998.
	• Distribution remained a significant competitive arena, with the need for manufacturers and distributors to transact high volumes of products to achieve scale economies – the greater the number of units delivered and the greater the density of outlets served, the lower distribution costs would be. National and regional distributors ensured these goals and increased in importance.
	• Brand choice is shrinking. The 1998 survey found that some 44 per cent of smaller retailers stocked the products of only one manufacturer, and 35 per cent stocked only BEW's products.
	• The strength of a particular brand in terms of share and popularity was significantly important in the competitive arena.

25 November 1998
- BEW gave three months' notice to its dedicated distributors, terminating their contracts to establish a dedicated distribution system called Wall's Direct, effectively bypassing completely its earlier undertakings with the regulator.
- In summary, Wall's Direct was a 'contracted-out distribution system' consisting of a call centre, eight of the 29 former dedicated distributors that were successful in a tendering process, and a field sales force in addition to BEW's sales force. These contracts were signed directly with BEW. (The eight distributors will be referred to as Wall's Direct contractors, and the 21 other firms that either were unsuccessful in their tendering or outright decided to offer a wider range of brands are referred to as ex-dedicated distributors.) The M25 operation at Barking continued as before, but customer calls to either operation were channelled through a unique telephone number, that of Wall's Direct.
- According to the 2000 report, BEW seems to have already investigated an outsourced distribution network, and by 18 September 1998 invitations to tender were already developed.

22 December 1998
- The DGFT refers the case to the Commission. In his press release, the DGFT expressed his firm belief that BEW's undertakings would improve competition in impulse ice-cream. However, 'overall this was a problematic sector which required a thorough and wide-ranging review'. To this effect, the reference to the Commission was very broad, in contrast to earlier references that focused on a small number of practices by industry players.

January 1999
Ice-Cream World, a buying entity formed by some of BEW's ex-dedicated distributors in response to the termination of contracts by BEW, appears to have started during January.

1 March 1999
Wall's Direct starts operating.

Table A4.1 (continued)

Date	Description
May 1999	An issues letter was sent by the Commission to the major manufacturers describing its preliminary findings and inviting comments.
July 1999	The Commission sent suggested remedies to the major manufacturers, inviting comments.
September/ October 1999	A report was presented by the Commission to the DGFT.
January 2000	The report was published.

Notes:
1. The various marketing practices are classified by their topography as defined in Chapter 4 and are denoted in capitals.
2. The importance of the M25: according to the UK Highways Agency, the M25 or the London Orbital motorway is, at 117 miles, the world's longest city bypass (Highways Agency 2010). According to the Office for National Statistics (2002), the M25 appears to encompass the most heavily populated areas in the UK.
3. A complete list of the manufacturers making these undertaking is found in §3.3 of the 2000 report. The full undertakings are found in Appendix 3.1 to that report.
4. The report provides an extended description of the products that were considered – the definition was wider than that employed by the 1997 report to allow for a more far-reaching investigation and is described in Chapter 2, §2.20 to §2.31. For the purposes of the study, the most important product within the categories identified is wrapped (single) impulse ice-cream for immediate consumption.

A4.2   SEASONALITY

Seasonality played an important role in the UK ice-cream market, espe-cially in the three summer months, during which demand was (a) about five times higher than in the three winter months and (b) subject to large daily and weekly fluctuations. The unpredictability of the UK weather made it difficult to predict temperatures more than a few days in advance. The weather index is mapped in Figure A4.1 – the consumption of ice-cream was positively related to changes in weather, with warm (+100 in the index) seasons signalling greater probability and rate of approach by consumers to a given brand and, consequently, by retailers and distribu-tors and an increased volume of business, with resultant utilitarian and informational benefits generally offsetting the aversive consequences of manufacturing, stocking and trading.

As a direct consequence of seasonality and related unpredictability, a set of behaviours was emitted, including building stocks during winter and spring, stocking the perishable products (depending upon the ice-cream perishability, rates varied between 6 and 24 months) in central cold storage centres since retailers did not have adequate space for refrigeration and back-up freezers,[1] and varying production runs[2] in the late summer as necessary to cope with surges in demand.

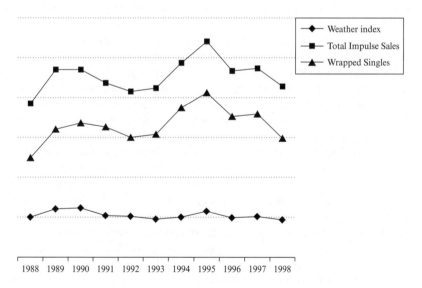

Source: Competition Commission (2000, p. 425).

Figure A4.1   Fluctuations of sales of ice-cream according to the weather

Warm seasons, for example, signalled the utilitarian and informational benefits of increasing the rate of sale of otherwise perishable products, including, naturally, higher sales volumes, longer production runs, higher volume purchases of raw materials, and quicker stock turn. Some aversive consequences were reduced, including the probability (informational) and cost (utilitarian) of perished stock and the cost (utilitarian) of holding a product in storage, which was 1.4p per unit. Longer production runs (informational) also signalled the related utilitarian savings from lower material purchase prices for larger volumes and a general decrease in per unit production cost, with the added incentive of not needing to store additional production when demand was particularly high (and inventory turnover was, therefore, higher). Increased demand brought utilitarian and informational benefits to distributors in the form of increased delivery sizes, reductions in per unit delivery costs and increased earnings (utilitarian) in the knowledge (informational) that distribution economies might accrue. Retailers benefited from increased purchase and consumption at their outlets. Warm summers were relatively more open settings where firms were vigorously involved in more marketing and production activities than bad summers. Some manufacturers, owing to their European-wide operations, were involved in exporting their production to warmer European countries, where summers are always hot, to mitigate the negative utilitarian and informational effects of this unpredictability and enjoy the derived benefits of more stable production runs and sales. BEW's mother company, Unilever, streamlined its wrapped impulse ice-cream packaging across the Union to weaken the impact of seasonality on its UK-based manufacturing operations. Further, BEW had out-of-season sales targets to mitigate the impact of seasonality on its own production – such targets were aimed at shaping distributor and retailer approach behaviour in the form of actively marketing impulse ice-cream outside the summer months through promotional and price (incentives and additional discounts) elements of the mix that supplemented the utilitarian benefits or reduced the aversive utilitarian consequences contingent on normal summer trade. Most manufacturers were also engaged in promotional activities (e.g. additional utilitarian benefits to increase the effectiveness of the brands as reinforcers – free stock offers promoted by Mars) to encourage distributors and retailers alike to order their pre-season stock fills.

A4.3   ROUTES TO MARKET

The maps in Figures A4.2 and A4.3 were provided to the Commission by BEW following research carried out by third parties and then amended

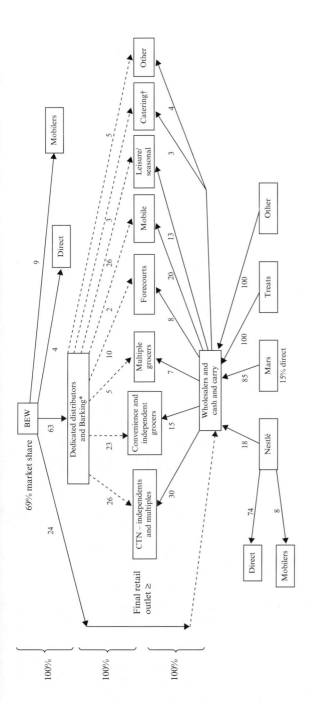

Notes:

* Dedicated distributors ceased in March 1999 and Wall's Direct was launched.
† Catering represens sales of wrapped impulse ice-cream to catering outlets. Ice-cream purchased as part of a meal is not included in the definition of impulse ice-cream.

Source: Competition Commission (2000, p. 144). Analysis of wrapped impulse ice-cream market shares at RSP, prepared by consultants for BEW, as modified by the Commission for Nestlé, Mars and Treats.

Figure A4.2   Routes to market for wrapped impulse ice-cream – percentage split of sales per distribution channel in 1998 for each major manufacturer

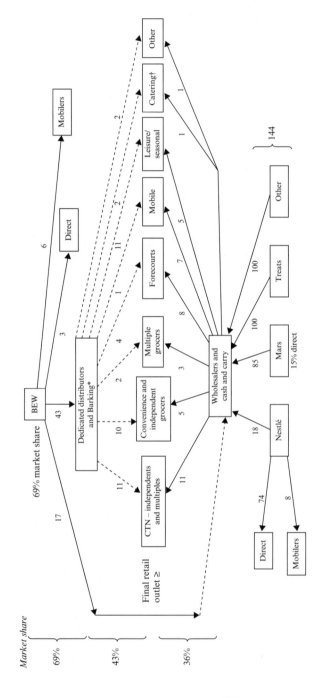

Notes:

* Dedicated distributors ceased in March 1999 and Wall's Direct was launched.

† Catering represents sales of wrapped impulse ice-cream to catering outlets. Ice-cream purchased as part of a meal is not included in the definition of impulse ice-cream.

Source: Competition Commission (2000, p.146). Analysis of wrapped impulse ice-cream market shares at RSP, prepared by consultants for BEW, as modified by the Commission for Nestlé, Mars and Treats.

Figure A4.3   Routes to market for wrapped impulse ice-cream – relative market shares per distribution channel in 1998

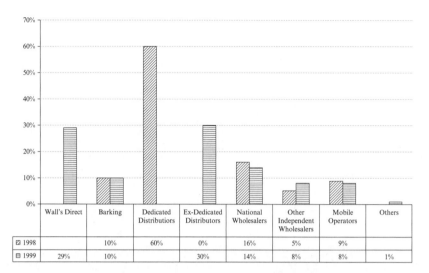

	Wall's Direct	Barking	Dedicated Distributiors	Ex-Dedicated Distributors	National Wholesalers	Other Independent Wholesalers	Mobile Operators	Others
1998		10%	60%	0%	16%	5%	9%	
1999	29%	10%		30%	14%	8%	8%	1%

Figure A4.4   Changes in radial distribution for BEW 1998–99

by the Commission to account for different information obtained directly from the firms portrayed in the map.

The Commission commented on the sheer scale of operations handled by dedicated distributors: approximately 17 per cent of the total distribution market, equivalent to 24 per cent of the total retail market share where legal title was held by them (see Figure A4.4). Their effective share was considerably higher (over 36 per cent of total retail market share) if one were to include the logistical services they provided to BEW to transport ice-cream which remained in the firm's legal title.

A4.4 MANUFACTURER BRAND MARKET SHARE ACROSS RETAIL

Table A4.2 Retail penetration percentages (market share) per manufacturer per retail outlet type

	All CTNs	Independent grocers	Forecourts	Other shops	Mobiles	Kiosks and cinemas	Catering
BEW (1998 market share)	75.30%	70.80%	63.60%	55.40%	74.80%	83.70%	85.40%
Nestlé	10.30%	12.30%	11.60%	11.00%	5.90%	6.70%	7.10%
Mars	11.30%	9.90%	19.10%	21.80%	2.10%	3.90%	3.20%
Treats	1.00%	1.80%	0.10%	2.20%	9.70%	0.80%	2.50%
Other	2.10%	5.20%	5.60%	9.50%	7.50%	4.90%	1.80%
Total	100	100	100	100	100	100	100
Sales of wrapped singles	£51,300,000.00	£47,400,000.00	£32,700,000.00	£40,500,000.00	£48,100,000.00	£20,200,000.00	£8,700,000.00
BEW (1997 market share)	77.20%	69.40%	69.30%	68.30%	69.00%	77.60%	74.70%
Nestlé	8.70%	14.90%	8.40%	9.60%	5.80%	10.30%	6.30%
Mars	10.90%	9.90%	18.50%	14.30%	1.80%	3.50%	8.80%

Treats	1.10%	1.60%	0.00%	1.10%	15.30%	3.70%	1.80%
Other	2.10%	4.20%	3.80%	6.70%	8.00%	4.90%	8.40%
Total	100	100	100	100	100	100	100
BEW (1996 market share)	76.30%	66.90%	66.60%	61.60%	64.20%	87.80%	67.90%
Nestlé	9.40%	15.20%	9.30%	11.20%	6.00%	2.70%	9.30%
Mars	11.60%	11.40%	20.60%	18.00%	6.70%	1.60%	10.40%
Treats	1.00%	1.80%	0.10%	1.60%	15.00%	3.00%	1.50%
Other	1.80%	4.80%	3.40%	7.60%	8.10%	4.90%	10.90%
Total	100	100	100	100	100	100	100

Note: CTN = confectioners, tobacconists and newsagents.

Source: Competition Commission (2000, p. 425). The Commission pointed out that figures may be subject to considerable error (§4.37, p. 109).

A4.5 SALES AT GROSS SALES VALUE AND ADVERTISING EXPENDITURE PER MANUFACTURER

Table A4.3 Sales and advertising expenditure per manufacturer in £ millions

	Manufacturer brand	1994 £ millions	1995 £ millions	1996 £ millions	1997 £ millions	1998 £ millions	Expenditure per brand (1996–98) £ millions
Nestlé	Kit Kat	N/A	N/A	£ 1.30			£ 1.30
	Fruit Pastille Lolly	N/A	N/A	£ 0.80	£ 0.80	£ 1.00	£ 2.60
	Mirage	N/A	N/A	N/A	£ 0.70	£ 1.10	£ 1.80
	Fab	N/A	N/A	£ 0.40			£ 0.40
	Mega Truffle	N/A	N/A			£ 2.00	£ 2.00
	Total wrapped impulse ice-cream Sales at GSV			£ 2.50 £25	£ 1.50 £24	£ 4.10 £23	£ 8.10
	Advertising as a percentage of GSV sales			10.00%	6.25%	17.83%	
Mars	Advertising	N/A	N/A	£ 1.00	£ 0.60	£ 1.10	£ 2.70
	Total wrapped impulse ice-cream Sales at GSV			£22	£23	£20	
	Advertising as a percentage of GSV sales			4.55%	2.61%	5.50%	

BEW						
Magnum	£ 2.70	£ 2.80	£ 1.70	£ 1.60	£ 2.70	£ 6.00
Solero	£ 0.60	£ 2.80	£ 2.10	£ 2.30	£ 1.30	£ 5.70
Calippo	£ –	£ –	£ 1.80	£ 1.40	£ 0.40	£ 3.60
Cornetto	£ 1.30	£ 0.10	£ 1.60	£ 1.40	£ 0.10	£ 3.10
Feast	£ 1.20	£ 0.80	£ 0.50	£ 0.10	£ –	£ 0.60
Winner Taco (started in 1998)					£ 1.50	£ 1.50
Others	£ –	£ 0.30	£ 0.20	£ 0.50	£ 1.10	£ 1.80
	£ 5.80	£ 6.80	£ 7.90	£ 7.30	£ 7.10	£ 22.30
Total wrapped impulse ice-cream Sales at GSV			£83.3	£160.8	£133.1	
Advertising as a percentage of GSV sales			9.48%	4.54%	5.33%	

A4.6 NESTLÉ AND MARS PROFITABILITY PERFORMANCE

Nestlé operated in a relatively more closed setting owing to its persistent losses (–33.9 per cent in 1995), which it managed to turn around in 1998 (3.1 per cent profit for a total of £700 000). The rules imposed by Nestlé SA (the UK operation's mother company) together with the physical presence of extreme losses signalled appropriate behaviour, including the shedding of excess capacity and the shutdown of its own-label ice-cream. Further, to achieve adequate profitability levels, Nestlé reduced both the margins payable to its retailers and distributors and its advertising activities in wrapped impulse ice-cream (the latter only until 1998). All Nestlé's distribution and retail channels lost money between 1996 and 1998 except its multiple retailer and confectionery, tobacco and newsagent sectors, which made some profit, and petrol station and forecourt sectors, which broke even. The available evidence suggests that Nestlé had a primary interest in reducing the heavy costs of its past investments and unprofitable operations, while increasing the effectiveness of its channel. However, the Commission failed to recognise the apparent inefficiency of Nestlé's operation as a factor that allowed BEW's unbridled growth. Sales were reported to be significantly lower than those of BEW, yet Nestlé increased its advertising sales as it focused its efforts further on the wrapped impulse ice-cream market.

Mars imported 95 per cent of its supply from its manufacturing facility in France, which ran at a loss and had excess capacity. Mars' performance followed a fate similar that of Nestlé, only breaking even in 1998 owing to a refocus on the take-home ice-cream market, where market conditions were significantly different from those of wrapped impulse ice-cream. This refocus increased sales significantly, with a consequent reduction in per unit production costs and a resultant decrease in transfer prices between France and the UK. The evidence demonstrates three important stimuli impinging on its managerial behaviour setting: (a) the importance of getting the French facility in the black to earn production economies, (b) the refocus on the take-home market, which would generate sales to fuel its production expansion plans for 2000–02, and (c) Mars' lack of adequate distribution facilities in contrast to Nestlé and BEW, especially after the loss of three of its distributors via acquisition by the latter firms. In 1997–98 Mars lost access to some of its direct retailers as well as national wholesalers. The evidence suggests that Mars' prime objective was to increase its sales revenues to improve market share and its ability to manufacture at a profit.

A4.7   THE CREATION OF WALL'S DIRECT

By mid-April 1998 BEW had commissioned a report (due in July 1998) from consultants to study 'a greenfield distribution system that would serve as a basis for direct distribution from manufacturer to ultimate retail customer' (Competition Commission 2000, p. 171), which would allow 'the maintenance of sovereignty' or what BEW defined as 'mechanisms to influence the service levels provided to its customers' (Competition Commission 2000, p. 173). BEW's board met in August to discuss the way forward following the publication of the Commission's report, as well as the completion of the consultants' report. The evidence shows that board members were in favour of creating an outsourced direct system of distribution for full control in a similar manner to what was occurring in the soft drinks and beer industry. Further, since the contracts of dedicated distributors would require six months notice, a very rapid agreement with the Office of Fair Trading was considered desirable. By September or October 1998 (although Unilever approved the plan in October, the actual proposal was sent to head office by BEW towards the end of November, underscoring the urgency and magnitude of the matter for both mother and subsidiary company), work had begun on setting up Wall's Direct, including an open-tender process for all areas where contractors would be required (call centre, sales, merchandising and logistics). In late November 1998, the BEW board presented a detailed proposal to Unilever for approval (see also Appendices 5.6 to 5.11 of the report) – the latter's policy that had to be followed was 'to maintain the strongest possible ice-cream business in the UK' (Competition Commission 2000, p. 450). The proposal stated that it resulted from the need to 'introduce a commercially viable alternative to the current [dedicated distributor] system as a result of the undertakings BEW gave earlier that month'. Further, the network would not be viable without the additional terms previously offered and therefore was going to be entirely disbanded. The alternative to replacing dedicated distributors was a reliance on wholesale distribution. This was considered unviable because (a) the channel was not sufficiently flexible to meet the needs of the wrapped impulse ice-cream market, and (b) most wholesalers were unable to respond to the highly unpredictable demand patterns generated by seasonality, or to deliver small quantities to marginal outlets or to maintain product quality throughout the supply chain. The 'reliance on wholesale distribution' alternative would amount to an unspecified loss in sales volumes and revenues. In the long term, a dedicated system could also be extended for use by other Unilever businesses in the UK. The proposal hinged upon the importance of a dedicated distribution system and spoke of how this system was an 'important pillar in BEW's strategy to grow the UK . . . market' (Competition Commission 2000, p. 452).

Wall's Direct was a viable commercial response to the 1998 undertakings that would allow control and ownership of the point of retail purchase and would allow BEW to build strong relationships with an existing 60 000 retail outlets as well as provide access to an additional 40 000 retail clients (not previously serviced by dedicated distributors). Wall's Direct, therefore, was specifically designed for strong expansion within the distribution network and overall company growth. Low/high estimates would mean that BEW would distribute 60 per cent/85 per cent of 1998 volumes during 1999, reaching growth by 2002. The fixed distribution costs were substantial and would generate the greatest burden if only the lower estimates were reached. Eventually, however, the heavy incidence of these costs on BEW's market flexibility would weaken, once 'full' volumes were reached. The call centre would initially focus on servicing existing customers, meaning that little time would be spent prospecting; however, once learning set in, the time saved would be refocused on prospecting. Wall's Direct aimed at providing a level of service superior to that provided by dedicated distributors by relying on a carefully chosen and manageable set of 'leading edge third party service providers', while it 'would focus on demand creation' (Competition Commission 2000, p. 457).

The proposal, among other details, also noted avoidance on the part of some of the ex-dedicated distributors – fewer were likely to be part of the final system than was originally assumed. The proposal reported their unwillingness to commit to a new business model in an environment of 'regulatory uncertainty', as well as moves from Mars to stimulate the interest of dedicated distributors in multi-brand wholesaling. This latter point further lends support to the earlier discussions regarding the importance of multi-product and multi-brand wholesaling to all distributors. Unfettered by constraints of exclusivity and threats by manufacturers that punished such behaviour, distributors might earn substantial utilitarian and informational benefits from distributing several brands and several products arising from scale economies. The proposal also outlined the effects on loss of volumes of these distributors, since the latter maintained a stronger relationship with their retailers. By combating these distributors through a superior level of service, lost volumes should be regained. In fact, the emphasis on the provision of superior service as *the sole* basis of differentiation with respect to retailers emerged very clearly from all the evidence provided by BEW relevant to the topic.

All in all, the aversive consequences (loss of market share, retail penetration and coverage) associated with abandoning some form of tight control on distribution to get closer to retailers appeared to far outweigh the aversive consequences of setting up and maintaining a new distribution system (transaction costs arising from the outsourcing contracts plus additional capital costs estimated to be well over £10 million) that would guarantee greater volumes in the medium to long term (two to three years). The new system was reported to go to profit by 2003. It should be noted that volume estimates included utilisation of wholesalers only until 2001. Subsequently, Wall's Direct would handle all business completely through this outsourced dedicated system. Only one of the Wall's Direct contractors was a wholesaler; the rest were involved in logistics provision, call centre and sales outsourcing services and central storage. One such organisation, Sunnyside Distribution, had been a dedicated distributor for BEW. However, with the formation of Wall's Direct, it refocused its business to provide central storage and logistics services under contract. The organisation commented how under the new undertakings it could not have continued trading as a distributor and would have wound up. These aversive consequences prompted a different, albeit related, internal (re)organisation.

In general terms, Wall's Direct operated as follows:

1. Any Wall's Direct contractor (including the ex-dedicated distributors) was required to use BEW's liveried vans in radial distribution, with a ban on carrying other manufacturer products or BEW products that were not ordered through Wall's Direct. This rule appears to have been contractually enforced. Perhaps one of the reasons some of the ex-dedicated distributors did not agree to this business model was because in so doing they would have been punished by the aversive consequences brought through not achieving target scale economies (drop size and density).
2. The call centre could only take orders for Wall's Direct, while the field sales force was to promote only BEW products regardless of where these were sourced. The utilitarian benefit of this was increasing the probability of retailer orders and the informational benefits arising from creating and increasing retailer awareness of the range of benefits accruing from the use of Wall's Direct.
3. Contractors were paid a management fee plus actual delivery costs with budgetary caps. This had the utilitarian benefit of keeping transaction costs relatively stable and the informational benefit of abiding by the 1998 undertakings.

The evidence demonstrates the severe constraints placed by the project within the managerial behaviour setting, with the prospect of heavy competition from Nestlé, Mars and other wholesalers (including ex-dedicated distributors) and consequent loss of business, with volume targets fixed by the board and Unilever, the heavy investment in the new system, the need to keep operating costs down to a minimum at least in the short term, the regulatory environment, the need to have enough human resources dedicated to the project, the loss of some of the dedicated distributors that had been instrumental in the growth of BEW, the pressures to maintain heavy consumer demand with the constraint that cutting marketing budgets on wrapped impulse ice-cream was the last resort, and other associated risks together with delivery capacity and project management. The Competition Commission correctly concluded that BEW had a deep vested interest in ensuring that Wall's Direct was a success. From an operant perspective, this is a specification of contingency relationships through a formulation of rules of behaviour – these rules identify possible outcomes of a variety of types of behaviour. If the arguments of consumer behaviour analysis were to apply, this is a clear example of firm deliberation:[3] the evidence shows a long process of verbal behaviour being carried out within the firm to identify a way forward. There are examples of instructions given by others (head office in the form of sales targets, and directions for keeping costs lean as well as maintaining mechanisms of control), a history of following the rules of head office, other self-rules in the firm's history of behaviour within the industry, the application of rules in unrelated settings (learnt from other areas) and other implicit self-rules that, in part, derive from the general rules of economics and commerce (e.g. moving towards economies of scale, resulting in increasing marginal returns).

All these stimuli hold a regulatory dimension, and at this planning stage (part of 'contingency planning'; Competition Commission 2000, p. 171) were purely informational – the indirect exposure to possible contingencies which would happen in future, if at all, and possible outcomes: pointing to possible relationships by establishing (assumed) relationships between stimuli and behaviour and behaviour and its outcomes (including possible losses, market gains and losses, etc.). Direct exposure to the contingencies would result, on average, in utilitarian consequences (there are such informational aspects as approval by head office or informational punishment if the DGFT regarded these as going against the undertakings).

In conclusion, the Commission highlights the actual impact of the creation of Wall's Direct as follows:

> following the 1998 report, BEW gave a number of undertakings . . . to the Secretary of State to supply wrapped impulse ice cream to dedicated distributors and to non-dedicated wholesalers on the same standard terms . . . and not to make discounts and bonuses available to retailers conditional on purchases from dedicated distributors. BEW remains subject to those undertakings. With the replacement of the dedicated distributors by Wall's Direct there is

no requirement on BEW to remunerate independent wholesalers on the same terms as Wall's Direct contractors. Nor is there any obligation not to discriminate with regard to discounts between sales by Wall's Direct and others. By terminating the contracts of the dedicated distributors BEW has undermined the purpose of the 1998 undertakings which concerned relativities between independent wholesalers and dedicated distributors, and deprived them of any real significance. (Competition Commission 2000, p. 24)

The creation of Wall's Direct to run in parallel with the Barking operation at the primary expense of its former distribution partners provided BEW with an opportunity to significantly extend its scale of operations and compete most effectively against the other major manufacturers at the retail rather than merely at the distribution levels.

A4.7.1 Aversive Effects of Wall's Direct on BEW's Distribution Shares

BEW estimated a reduction in volumes for the first year of operation of Wall's Direct but foresaw the recovery of at least 90 per cent of lost volumes by 2002 (i.e. 63 per cent of BEW distribution, with the balance being held by the Barking operation (*c.* 10 per cent) as well as other wholesalers). BEW assumed that in 1999 Wall's Direct would handle between 60 per cent and 85 per cent of the volume that would have otherwise been handled by the former dedicated distributors (40–50 per cent of all deliveries to retailers, depending on the number of the dedicated distributors that would form part of Wall's Direct). The same evidence shows that former dedicated distributors outside Wall's Direct would not contribute to business volumes in any way by 2002. The Commission calculated that on the basis of BEW's 1998/99 market share the volumes transacted by Wall's Direct and Barking would account for almost 50 per cent of the total distribution of wrapped impulse ice-cream by 2002 (BEW objected to this conclusion, stating that the evidence it presented was only estimates to its mother company). The Commission also stated that the investments in Wall's Direct would lead to substantial distribution cost savings. By September 1999, BEW reported the split of sales by distribution channel shown in Figure A4.5.

A4.8 LOSSES IN SALES BY THE EX-DEDICATED DISTRIBUTORS DURING 1999

The sales force of Wall's Direct launched an aggressive sales effort to win back the sales that had previously flowed to it through its dedicated distributors and which, post-Wall's Direct formation, continued to be

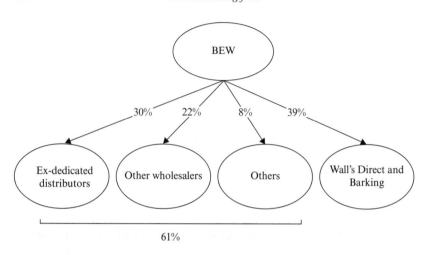

*Figure A4.5   Split of sales by BEW distribution channel nine months after
Wall's Direct was established*

transacted with the group of ex-dedicated distributors. BEW's efforts
were geared towards closing off sales opportunities to this tier of distribution. Whereas prior to the formation of Wall's Direct 60 per cent of BEW
business flowed through the dedicated distributors, between March and
August 1999 only 30 per cent flowed through that channel. BEW was also
claimed to have encouraged retailers to form buying groups to gain better
discounts. By the end of June 1999, total BEW sales handled by a sample
of 14 (out of about 22) of this group of distributors fell 42 per cent, with
an average decline of 21 per cent in indirect sales on which targets were
calculated and an average decline of 59 per cent in direct sales. Owing to
good weather, by the end of July 1999 the situation had improved, with
total sales losses in the BEW business averaging 35 per cent. The greatest
losses remained in direct sales. All in all, these distributors claimed difficulty in ever attaining the top-level bonuses, given the situation. The gains
this group made in selling the brands of other manufacturers (17 per cent
of ex-dedicated distributor sales) only partially offset their losses on BEW
products. However, given the element of fixed overheads in distribution it
appears highly unlikely that the ex-dedicated distributors of BEW could
adjust their costs in line with the falls in income, despite the increases in
sales from other manufacturer brands.

A4.9   BEW RETAILER TERMS

BOX A4.1   A TOPOGRAPHY OF BEW'S TERMS OF
SUPPLY TO RETAILERS, INCLUDING
STANDARD TERMS, AND FREEZER
AND OUTLET EXCLUSIVITY

General retailer terms of supply
BEW operates several categories of terms that operate in similar
fashion:

1. Negotiated terms which averaged 16.2 per cent in 1998 but in
    cases are up to 49 per cent of list price across all types of
    outlets including bonus payments, where:
    (a) BEW agrees with the retailer a discount off the list price
         (PRICE).
    (b) An additional discount or lump-sum rebate is paid
         (PROMOTION) if a certain level of sales is achieved.
    (c) Additional payments to the retailer are made on market-
         ing and promotional support and share of total freezer
         space (PLACE).
    (d) The terms of supply may be linked to other ice-cream
         products (PRODUCT, PLACE).
    Negotiated terms vary according to the type of outlet – BEW's
    negotiated discounts and bonuses average some 33 per cent
    to leisure/entertainment retailers, 27 per cent to catering, 23
    per cent to travel, 22 per cent to grocery retailers, and 13 per
    cent to CTNs and convenience stores. Terms also vary
    according to whether the outlet is exclusive to BEW.
2. Standard terms or non-negotiated terms (PRICE), which
    include a year-end bonus scale, which give a proportionately
    higher bonus over all annual purchases of ice-cream, the
    higher the volume of sales. Retailers without a BEW freezer
    earn richer bonuses (0–10 per cent versus 0–8 per cent for
    those with a BEW freezer). Bonus scales operate to lower the
    price at which retailers buy their BEW ice-cream – higher
    volumes mean higher bonuses. BEW maintains its scales in
    such a way that, if a competitor wants to buy into a share of
    the ice-cream sales of a given retail outlet, it would also have

to make additional bonus payments to cover any loss the retailer would inevitably suffer from not selling BEW ice-cream by taking on the rival offer. This increases the payments paid out to the retailer by the rival. The retailer is not punished for its avoidance of BEW by accepting a rival offer; on the contrary, it is the rival which is punished for approaching BEW's customers and for encroaching on its market share. To eliminate this disadvantage, the rival would have to buy into the entire BEW sales share of the outlet, which owing to the position of BEW is not likely to occur.

3. Standard terms for seasonal outlets similar to (2) above (up to 33.3 per cent to make up for these outlets being open only during peak season, and averaging total of 28.1 per cent including bonuses). In seasonal outlets the rival disadvantages (explained above) tend to be higher.

4. Mobile van operator franchising terms.

All bonuses are retrospective in that, when a particular level of purchases is realised, higher percentage bonuses are applied to the full value of purchases over the relevant period.

Franchise terms
Franchising payments:

- Business plan payments of up to 10 per cent of the previous year's net invoice value.
- Standard terms to wholesalers (except that the sales growth payment is paid on net invoice value rather than sales at list price).
- 2 per cent non-manufacturing discount from list price.
- Small franchisees with one liveried van and that are not wholesalers receive a 12.5 per cent rebate on wholesale list price, but do not receive the non-manufacturing deduction or the business plan payment.
- Mobile vans that are not franchisees do not receive bonuses.
- Cost of decorating the van.
- Franchisees are tied exclusively to BEW.

Exclusive outlets

- Negotiated terms of supply which, on average, are considerably higher than standard terms, reflecting more generous patterns of utilitarian reinforcement given in exchange for greater setting closure through full exclusivity of the entire retail space.
- Undisclosed off-invoice discounts on list price.
- Discounts and/or rebates paid on achieving certain sales levels. Sometimes a guaranteed discount or rebate is offered, which is not dependent on achieving given sales levels and consequently is similar to the discounts in (a).
- Payments by BEW (in money or in kind) to the retailer: these include promotional or marketing support, merchandising allowances and free provision of items, such as kiosks, tricycles and bins that BEW normally charges for. Promotional support may include sponsorship of visitor attractions at theme parks. Payments may be made either at the beginning of the contract or annually, with the annual payments made at the beginning, during or at the end of the year.
- BEW also normally provides free-on-loan freezers to the relevant shops.

Freezer exclusivity

- Freezers are loaned free of charge to retailers (Treats does not invest in the freezer but supplies the retailer with an amount of products equal in value to the freezer).
- Manufacturer pays for maintenance and rectifying mechanical breakdowns and other failures.
- Lump-sum payments (in some cases).
- Standard terms of supply which include bonus schemes. The bonus pay-outs to those retailers with exclusive freezers are less than the pay-outs to retailers without freezer exclusivity.
- Other terms and bonuses.

A4.9.1   Franchising of Mobile Van Operators

One special form of outlet exclusivity is the franchising (place, product and promotion) of mobile retailers. These are similar set-ups to exclusive outlets except that they are mobile retail outlets operating within a geographic territory. While BEW held about 6.1 per cent (370) of the *circa* 6000 mobile vans operating in August 1999, Nestlé covered under 1 per cent of the total as franchisees. Whereas tying the franchisor exclusively with the manufacturer amounts to setting closure, a variety of methods is used to manage the reinforcement patterns of the franchisee. Mutual reinforcement arises from the gains manufacturers derive from such arrangements.

A4.10 UTILITARIAN AND INFORMATIONAL REINFORCEMENT INHERENT IN FREEZER EXCLUSIVITY

Table A4.4 Utilitarian and informational reinforcement inherent in freezer exclusivity

	Utilitarian		Informational	
	Benefits	Aversive consequences	Benefits	Aversive consequences
Manufacturers	Guaranteed level of sales from particular outlet as a function of retailer take-up, duration of the contract period (the longer the better), store traffic, freezer placement, merchandising, number of secondary freezers, percentage of freezer allocated to brand/s, and brand popularity, consumer demand and market share. Resultant profits and faster product/ brand sales rates, at least, in the outlet that has an exclusive freezer. Related benefits	Depending upon the arrangement, the provision of a free or heavily subsidised freezer as a function of the extent of retailer take-up. Installation, maintenance and related breakdown costs as a function of the extent of retailer take-up. Related administration costs as a function of the extent of retailer take-up. Cost of merchandising and related support to retailers as a function of the extent of retailer take-up. The sheer investment in cabinets	Providing ice-cream at the required quality levels (the correct storage temperatures). Increased market penetration at retail level. Increased market share. Greater consumer awareness and brand visibility – the advantages of branding and advertising at the point of sale. Learning from deployed merchandising tactics. The contract period required for tie-in, which may last between one and five years depending upon arrangement. Faster	Book value on balance sheets as well as depreciation provisions in profit and loss accounts and maintenance schedules and administrative burdens as a function of the extent of retailer take-up. Retailers deciding to buy their own freezers, including industry freezers (freezers stocking a range of manufacturers' products) or taking up richer offers by rivals/ distributors. The degree of rival penetration signals the aversive consequences of either maintaining present level of exclusive

Table A4.4 (continued)

	Utilitarian		Informational	
	Benefits	Aversive consequences	Benefits	Aversive consequences
	from increased market penetration. Reduced incidence of discount/ bonus rates if the freezer is entirely subsidised by the manufacturer. The utilitarian advantages of branding and advertising at the point of sale. Freezer exclusivity allows a full range of a manufacturer's brands to be stocked even if some of the products have poorer sales than other manufacturers' products which cannot be stocked owing to exclusivity.	across the entire market depends upon the level of rival market penetration and freezer exclusivity arrangements.	sales rates. Improves the quality of availability of the product/brand at retail level.	freezer penetration or significantly increasing the number of freezers owned at a retail level. The financial resources to provide the critical mass of freezers required to compete effectively. Risks of not earning return on investment in possible adverse market conditions including poor season.
Distributors stocking retailers' exclusive freezers	Depending upon the degree of brand popularity, distributors may enjoy higher	Possibly reduce drop size if freezer is exclusive. Economies of scale may not be achieved if the	Informational benefits arising, including progress on bonus pay-outs, reaching agreed sales	Decrease in the ability of reaching distribution economies, especially if the brand chosen by the

	retail orders through the exclusive freezer, especially in peak season. This enables higher earnings in terms of discounts and bonuses. If the distributor holds close relationships with the manufacturer that supplied the freezer, then to an extent stocking the freezers is guaranteed sales.	retailer either has a limited range of frozen products on offer or does not offer the more popular brands. Higher per unit costs arising from the reduced ability of independent wholesalers to supply a complete range of impulse ice-cream products to outlets equipped with exclusive freezers.	target levels and general feedback on how well the distributor is faring. The financial resources to provide the critical mass of freezers required to compete effectively.	retailer is not popular. Attracts rivalry if distributor supplies own industry freezers. The financial resources to provide the critical mass of freezers required to compete effectively. Risks of not earning return on investment in possible adverse market conditions including poor season.
Retailers	Providing product range and brand range of preferred supplier. Earnings from space utilisation as a function of the manufacturer's brand popularity, consumer demand and market	Any portion of freezer supply, installation and maintenance costs that the retailer would have to pay. Reduced discount/ bonus rates if the freezer is entirely subsidised by the manufacturer. Running	Enhanced retail space utilisation. Better service provided to consumers. Merchandising and related support from manufacturer. Return on manufacturer's investment in the freezer installed	The contract period required for tie-in, which may last between one and five years depending upon arrangement. Possible delays in freezer removal or in maintenance. Selecting a manufacturer whose brand

Table A4.4 (continued)

	Utilitarian		Informational	
	Benefits	Aversive consequences	Benefits	Aversive consequences
Retailers	share. Depending upon arrangement, free freezer supply, installation and maintenance. Benefits are a function of the number of retail outlets owned by the retailer. Any related discounts. Fast-selling brands may earn significant returns if traffic is sufficient. The acquisition of own freezers meant retailers could generally purchase ice-creams at lower prices, reflecting extra bonus payments.	costs including power supply. The acquisition of own freezers meant that investment, installation and maintenance costs were at the retailer's expense.	at retailer site. Removes the risk that, if retailers acquire a freezer at their own expense, they may fail to earn a return owing to the effects of poor weather. The acquisition of own freezers allowed the retailers the choice of tying to a single or multiple brands.	popularity and consumer demand are lower than those of others. Book value on balance sheets as well as depreciation provisions in the profit and loss account, and maintenance schedules and administrative burdens.

A4.11 UTILITARIAN AND INFORMATIONAL REINFORCEMENT INHERENT IN OUTLET EXCLUSIVITY AND MOBILE RETAILER FRANCHISING ARRANGEMENTS

Table A4.5 Utilitarian and informational reinforcement inherent in outlet exclusivity and mobile retailer franchising arrangements

	Utilitarian		Informational	
	Benefits	Aversive consequences	Benefits	Aversive consequences
Manufacturers	Depending upon the retail outlet type and the consumer traffic volumes it attracts, an exclusive outlet is a method for generating as well as guaranteeing a certain volume of sales. If a sufficient critical mass of such exclusive outlets is created, there are significant advantages to be had from expanding the scale of operations and	The costs of maintaining and operating a number of these exclusive outlets. The cost of providing additional payments and services.	Contract duration provides manufacturer with predictability (in varying degrees depending upon contract length) of the relationship with the exclusive outlet. Provides very high visibility to retailer brands. Generates consumer awareness and a level of related promotional benefits, since the manufacturer brands now stand alone	Outlet exclusivity comes at the request of the retailer owing to the 1979 undertakings that set this rule in the setting.

Table A4.5 (continued)

	Utilitarian		Informational	
	Benefits	Aversive consequences	Benefits	Aversive consequences
	gaining significant economies. Related benefits from increased market penetration. Allows the full range of a manufacturer's brands to be stocked in the outlet without the hindrance of rival products that may be faster sellers. Benefits from improvement in how retail space is used directly derived from manufacturer marketing and promotional support.		without the chance of being compared to or substituted with rival brands – the advantages of branding and advertising at the point of sale. Increases degree of retail penetration and guarantees that rival manufacturers cannot sell their brands through specific outlets for the duration of the contract. Faster sales rates. Improves the quality of availability of the product/brand at retail level.	
Manufacturers engaged in franchising	Mobile vans are close to consumers and provide opportunities for impulse purchases.	Managing franchisee street territories. The cost of painting the van in brand livery.	Liveried vans increase visibility of brand and raise consumer awareness.	Choosing which franchisees are granted exclusive rights to sell the manufacturer's brand

Rival manufacturers

As franchisees are allowed only to sell the brands of the franchisor, mobile vans are a source of guaranteed sales within a territory given the volume of consumer demand within that territory. Sales and profits derived from the territory.

Charging/paying the franchisor discounts and bonuses.

Liveried vans signal the availability of a particular combination of utilitarian and informational reinforcement embodied in the brand within a given territory. Mobile vans signal convenience and may perhaps prompt impulse purchases, especially on warm days.

at manufacturer-organised special events. Organising, monitoring and policing franchisee street territories.

Outlet exclusivity comes at the request of the retailer owing to the 1979 undertakings that set this rule in the setting. Rival manufacturers are blocked out entirely of the retail outlet and need to wait until the contract expires for a counter-offer or pay the penalties to

Table A4.5 (continued)

	Utilitarian		Informational	
	Benefits	Aversive consequences	Benefits	Aversive consequences
Rival manufacturers				buy into the manufacturer's exclusive contract, with the possible consequence of litigation. Rivals are denied benefits that could have been derived had the retailer remained non-exclusively tied with one or more manufacturers, including expanding the scale of operations, lost sales from that retail outlet, and loss in brand visibility and consumer awareness together with other related promotional benefits that may accrue.
Retailers	Highly favourable terms including discounts, bonuses, payments and incentives allowances		Contract duration provides manufacturer with predictability (in varying degrees	(Longer) contract duration may be an aversive consequence if related sales levels are

	and free promotional items including kiosks and tricycles as well as vans and sponsorships. Some payments are made as an incentive to sign an exclusivity contract. Differential terms between exclusive and non-exclusive outlets. A free-on-loan freezer is also given. Marketing and promotional support to further optimise allocation of retail space.	depending upon contract length) of the relationship with the manufacturer.	poor or if terms and conditions are no longer sufficient to cover costs and renegotiation is not possible.
Franchisees	If the brands sold by the franchisee are popular, the franchisee is rewarded with higher volumes and faster brand sales. Exclusive territory for street trading is protected by the franchisor closing off the setting to other	The ownership and running costs of the van.	The brands sold may act as reinforcers in the sense that they signal reinforcement contingent upon the purchase and resale of those brands. The faster the rate of sales and the higher the consumer demand for such	Franchisees' limitation of not being able to sell the other brands may be a negative consequence depending upon the level of sales/profits attained within the territory and the popularity of the brands that cannot be sold. (Mobile)

Table A4.5 (continued)

	Utilitarian		Informational	
	Benefits	Aversive consequences	Benefits	Aversive consequences
Franchisees	franchisees with identical brands. Competition may exist from the presence of rival brands. Some franchisees are granted exclusive rights to sell the manufacturer's brand at manufacturer-organised special events guaranteeing sales especially during peak season. Franchisor pays the cost of painting the van in brand livery. Sales and profits derived from the territory and discounts and bonuses provided by the manufacturer.		brands, the greater the source of utilitarian and informational reinforcement derived from such activities. Exclusive territory for street trading that is protected by the franchisor closing off the setting to other franchisees with identical brands. The possibility of being granted exclusive rights to sell the manufacturer's brand at manufacturer-organised special events.	competition may exist from the presence of rival brands within the given territory.

NOTES

1. Ice-cream had to be maintained in its frozen state to preserve the product's quality for consumption. This means that any refrigeration units used had to keep the product at a constant −18°C (−64°F).
2. Chapter 5 of the report shows how changes in output may be very drastic owing to seasonality, for example, a 20 per cent increase in BEW's output in 1995, followed by a 10 per cent decrease in 1996, an 8 per cent increase in 1997 and a 16 per cent decrease in 1998.
3. Unlike consumer behaviour, however, such firm behaviour is not private in the sense that it occurs 'within the skin' but rather public behaviour, as may be seen from the various pieces of evidence presented by BEW, including the informal notes written by one member of staff during a meeting on the formation of Wall's Direct.

Appendix 5. Reflections on 'the marketing firm'

A5.1 MANAGERIAL BEHAVIOUR SETTING: MANUFACTURERS

- Legally binding undertakings imposed by regulator: for example, outlet exclusivity can only be requested by retailers.
- Sales, profit and growth rules set by mother company: for example, 33 per cent growth required by Unilever.
- Plans and objectives set by management as self-rules: for example, the entire deliberative process BEW passed through, including its plans and proposals to Unilever for the setting up of Wall's Direct. The report contains several appendices in this respect.
- Contractual rules, duties and obligations to distributors, retailers and other channel members. Terms and conditions of supply.
- Degree of retailer and distributor approach as a function of consumer demand/popularity, brand rates of sale, retail penetration and market share: for example, the theme underlying BEW's restrictive practices is the strengths of its brands and profitability.
- Patterns of consumer choice, seasonality and its impact on demand: related rules including winter and late summer production depending upon demand; centralised storage and springtime stocking behaviour; pre-season special offers to retailers to stock freezers early; the necessity of cold-chain storage and cold-chain delivery to maintain a quality product.
- Rules due to past consequences, for example, focus on other ice-cream markets by Mars in a bid to fill up otherwise idle capacity, on cost reduction by Nestlé, on retail, cabinet and distribution sovereignty by BEW and increasing Wall's Direct scale of operations.
- Sales revenues, profitability and other performance-related factors, including working capital for daily operations, as attested, for example, by the redefinition of direct accounts by BEW passing on the financial burdens to its ex-dedicated distributors.
- Transaction costs of operation, for example, marketing and selling costs, contracting costs, distribution and retail discounts, bonuses

and incentives, sourcing, production or importing costs, credit risks.

- Scale economies in (central and radial) distribution (where applicable), as well as in marketing and production.
- Rival action: deployment of stimuli to strengthen behaviour of consumer, retailer and distributor away, i.e. encroachment on consumer (brand), retailer and distributor share. The degree of mimicry present, which may suggest a degree of predictability in rival behaviour. Degree of anti-competitive and distortive behaviour. Dominance of one's brands versus those of rivals.
- Extent of distributor and retailer approach (exclusivity arrangements, greater focus on selling and distributing manufacturer brand rather than that of rivals).
- The nature and extent of barriers to entry and expansion.

A5.2 MANAGERIAL BEHAVIOUR SETTING: DISTRIBUTORS

- Legally binding undertakings imposed by regulator: for example, the 1998 undertakings prohibit BEW from discriminating on terms between dedicated distributors and independent wholesalers. Further, these terms must be published. This allows for a more open setting.
- Sales, profit and growth rules set by mother company (where applicable).
- Plans and objectives set by management as self-rules, including business model: for example, independent wholesaler versus exclusivity; logistics operator versus wholesaling.
- Geographic coverage: for example, in the case of BEW, no dedicated distributor is allowed to serve areas within the M25. BEW and Nestlé had distributors assigned according to their ability of geographic reach.
- Contractual rules, duties and obligations to manufacturers, retailers and other channel members. Terms and conditions of supply from manufacturers and to retailers. For example, the standard terms published by BEW for the 1999 season constrained the ex-dedicated distributors to use liveried vans, and these vans could be used only for orders made to Wall's Direct.
- Degree of retailer and manufacturer approach as a function of consumer demand/popularity, brand rates of sale, retail penetration and market share and geographic coverage/network density.
- Impact of consumer demand on manufacturer and retail business.

For example, during the 1997/98 season BEW distributors suffered from a decline in earnings because of the bad summer season.

- Sales revenues, profitability and other performance-related factors, including working capital for daily operations. For example, the redefinition of direct accounts created an added burden on ex-dedicated distributors of BEW working capital.
- Transaction costs of operation (marketing and selling costs, distribution costs).
- Scale economies in distribution. Capacity utilisation in terms of drop size, density, frequency of delivery, network coverage, product availability (inclinations towards multi-brand/multi-product wholesaling if economies of scale are to be had). Retail network size and growth.
- Rival actions where applicable. Degree of competitive, anti-competitive and distortive behaviour by various industry incumbents and effects on business.
- The nature and extent of barriers to entry and expansion.

A5.3　MANAGERIAL BEHAVIOUR SETTING: RETAILERS

- Legally binding undertakings imposed by regulator – outlet exclusivity may be requested rather than imposed by manufacturers.
- Sales, profit and growth rules set by retail management/controllers.
- Plans and objectives set by management as self-rules including business model (e.g. independent retailer versus exclusivity).
- Outlet type, for example, seasonal versus year-round and sector of operation.
- Contractual rules, duties and obligations to manufacturers, distributors and other channel members. Terms and conditions of supply from manufacturers and from distributors, including freezer and/or outlet exclusivity (partial/full).
- Degree of distributor and manufacturer approach as a function of consumer demand/popularity, brand rates of sale, retail penetration and market share. Also as a function of retail store location, sector and type.
- Impact of consumer demand on manufacturer, distributor and own business.
- Sales revenues, profitability and other performance-related factors, including working capital for daily operations.
- Transaction costs of operation (marketing and selling costs, sourcing costs).

- Retail capacity utilisation – appropriate use of retail space.
- Rival actions where applicable. Degree of competitive, anti-competitive and distortive behaviour by various industry incumbents and effects on business.

A5.4   APPROACH, AVOIDANCE AND ESCAPE

BOX A5.1   TOPOGRAPHY OF APPROACH/ AVOIDANCE IN MANUFACTURER↔DISTRIBUTOR RELATIONSHIPS

1.   Manufacturer approach and escape/avoidance behaviour in Manufacturer↔Distributor relationships

Structure of escape or avoidance behaviour by manufacturers away from distributors:

- Reducing importance of distribution channels by going direct to retailers (e.g. outlet exclusivity).
- Avoiding wholesale services entirely by vertical integration of radial distribution, including sub-contracting delivery services to non-wholesale specialists.
- The formation of Wall's Direct dedicated distribution system in direct competition with distribution tier. Any behaviour that generally undermines the position of the distributors.
- The refusal by BEW to accept Ice-Cream World as a buying entity, with the implied consequences of gaining advantage through volume discounts and related benefits.
  Discriminatory and predatory pricing and promotional incentives.
- The inability to negotiate further discounts to win retailer business. Although Mars and Nestlé allowed this, BEW maintained strict control on its prices and refused to negotiate. In these cases, sometimes BEW undercut the negotiations, going direct.
- Some distributors objected to dedicated distribution systems.

Structure of escape or avoidance behaviour by manufacturers away from ex-dedicated distributors:

- The formation of Wall's Direct, the proposed new business model under Wall's Direct contracting, and the disregard for previous relationships.
- In some cases, freezer and outlet exclusivity.

Structure of approach behaviour by manufacturers towards distributors:

- The provision of equitable and transparent terms and conditions that would enable distributors to achieve their sales and profit goals, including reduction of per unit delivery costs.
- Developing wholesale relationships further to allow for an economically viable tier of independent wholesalers.

2. Distributor approach and escape/avoidance behaviour in Manufacturer↔Distributor relationships

Structure of escape or avoidance behaviour by distributors away from manufacturers:

- Selling rival brands, especially in greater quantities.

Structure of escape or avoidance behaviour by distributors away from BEW:

- Importing BEW brands from overseas because there was a wider range of brands available and prices were considerably lower.
- Any behaviour that detracted from volumes that Wall's Direct could supply directly, including the trading of multiple rival brands, i.e. independent wholesaling (and independent retailing).
- Not signing or not acting as if within an exclusivity arrangement or not achieving levels of business volumes that exceeded £7.5 million.
- The formation of Ice-Cream World by ex-dedicated distributors.
- The provision of industry freezers.

Structure of escape or avoidance behaviour by distributors away from BEW's rivals:

- Change of business model by independent wholesalers to become a contractor of BEW to provide different services entirely – this reduces physical number of reinforcers in the setting.
- The provision of industry freezers in the context of BEW's dominance because these would be 'swamped' by BEW's products.

Structure of approach behaviour by distributors towards manufacturers:

- Selling adequate levels of own brands to achieve sales and profit goals.
- Approach to BEW was any distribution behaviour that involved significantly high-volume sales of BEW brands or the simple efficient provision of logistic services or allowed BEW control over the distribution tier in the market.

BOX A5.2   TOPOGRAPHY OF APPROACH/ AVOIDANCE IN MANUFACTURER↔RETAILER RELATIONSHIPS

1.   Manufacturer approach and escape/avoidance behaviour in Manufacturer↔Retailer relationships

Structure of escape or avoidance behaviour by manufacturers away from retailers:

- Threatened withdrawal of supply of the product.
- Delays in supplying the product, especially when demand is high.
- Inequitable terms that do not allow retail sales and profits. This also includes reduction in terms of supply (pricing and bonus discounts).

- Lower (unsatisfactory) levels of investment in market development, for example reductions in advertising spends, product development and innovation.

Structure of approach behaviour by manufacturers towards retailers:

- The provision of equitable and transparent terms and conditions that would enable retailers to achieve their sales and profit goals, including increasing return on retail capacity utilisation.
- Merchandising and related support to aid in the optimisation of retail space utilisation.
- Outlet and freezer exclusivity, to the extent that the Commission commented on how it most welcomed the practice.
- Appropriate levels of investments in market development to ensure consumer demand, adequate rate of brand sales, retail penetration and brand market shares.

2. Retailer approach and escape/avoidance behaviour in Manufacturer↔Retailer relationships

Structure of escape or avoidance behaviour by retailers away from manufacturers:

- Selling rival brands, especially in greater quantities.
- Exclusivity when such exclusivity is linked to rivals. In freezer exclusivity, where the primary freezer is of rivals and secondary freezers are placed in less prominent/visible areas or switched off during winter. Also where secondary freezers are swamped with rival brands, in particular those brands that are also stocked in primary freezers. Industry freezers stocked with rival brands.

Structure of escape or avoidance behaviour by retailers away from BEW:

- Selling multiple rival brands.
- Not signing or not acting as if within an exclusivity arrangement.

- Acquisition of industry freezers either through distributors or via own investment.
- Selling retail ice-cream share to rivals.
- Placing orders with distributors other than Wall's Direct, Barking or national wholesalers. Wall's Direct was to be most prominent.

Structure of approach behaviour by retailers towards manufacturers:

- Selling adequate levels of own brands to achieve sales and profit goals.
- To BEW, retailer approach is exclusively retailing BEW brands and placing orders from Wall's Direct or Barking.

A5.5 TOPOGRAPHY OF MARKETING MIX STIMULI

Marketing Mix Elements Deployed by Manufacturers Relevant to Distributors

Deployed by the manufacturer

Product stimuli

- Product and brand range.
- Product packaging.
- Product quality.
- Product innovation.
- Service levels for order taking, processing and fulfilment, including call centres.
- Legal title product.

Place/logistical stimuli

- Drop size, density, frequency and volume of orders to be delivered to retailer.
- Distance (and time) to travel from one destination to another on manufacturer business.
- Multiple brand and product (including those of rivals) drops.

- Ordering process, order fulfilment, order accuracy.
- Degrees of integration and distributor exclusivity and type of arrangements.
- Use of liveried versus non-liveried vans.
- Use of liveried vans for other manufacturer deliveries.
- Degree of outlet and freezer exclusivity.

Price stimuli

- Standard and negotiated terms of supply, including volume and performance-related discounts.

Promotional stimuli

- Standard and negotiated terms of supply, including incentives and bonus schemes.
- Additional incentive payments that cover transport and related costs.
- Terms/conditions to retailers, bonus payments and how these payments are settled with retailer.
- Sales force and call centre.
- Assignment of retail accounts.
- Marketing activities to develop the market.

Deployed by the distributor

Product

- Type of services offered, ranging from logistical services to fully fledged wholesaling activities.
- Service levels offered by distributors.
- Distributor innovation to maintain efficiency.

Place

- Distributor's geographic coverage/network density.

Promotion

- Investment and sales activities in building retail network.

Marketing Mix Elements Deployed by Manufacturers Relevant to Retailers

Deployed by manufacturer

Product stimuli

- Product and brand range.
- Product packaging.
- Product quality.
- Product innovation.
- Service levels for order taking, processing and fulfilment, including call centres.

Place/logistical stimuli

- Distributor exclusivity arrangements and coverage, order fulfilment and related aspects.
- Freezer provision, freezer type and size. Partial or full freezer exclusivity arrangements.
- Outlet exclusivity arrangements.

Price stimuli

- Standard and negotiated terms of supply, including volume and performance-related discounts and retrospective discounting.

Promotional stimuli

- Standard and negotiated terms of supply, including incentives and bonus schemes, sponsorships, special incentives, paid holidays, kiosk provision, provision of promotional material. Lump-sum payments and bonus payment frequency.
- Point-of-purchase displays and related promotional materials.
- Merchandising support.
- Sales force.
- Marketing activities to develop the market.

Deployed by the retailer

Place

- Outlet type and geographical location (with resultant consumer traffic) of retail space and general store outlay.

Promotion

- Negotiator in exclusivity discussions.
- Marketing to attract retail traffic.

References

Alchian, A.A. and Demsetz, H. 1972. Production, Information Costs, and Economic Organization. *The American Economic Review* 62(5), pp. 777–795.

Alhadeff, D.A. 1982. *Microeconomics and Human Behaviour: Towards a Synthesis of Economics and Psychology*. Berkeley: University of California Press.

Atkinson, P. and Coffey, A. 2004. Analysing Documentary Realities. In: Silverman, D. ed. *Qualitative Research: Theory, Method and Practice*. 2nd Edition. London: Sage Publications, pp. 56–76.

Babbie, E. 1990. *Survey Research Methods*. Belmont, CA: Wadsworth.

Barnes, J.G. 1994. Close to the Customer: But Is It Really a Relationship? *Journal of Marketing Management* 10, pp. 561–570.

Baum, W.M. 1994. *Understanding Behaviourism: Science, Behaviour and Culture*. New York: HarperCollins College Publishers.

Blois, K. 1972. Vertical Quasi-Integration. *Journal of Industrial Economics* 20, pp. 253–272.

Bryman, A. and Bell, E. 2007. *Business Research Methods*. Oxford, UK: Oxford University Press.

Buttle, F. 1984. Merchandising. *European Journal of Marketing* 18(6/7), pp. 104–124.

Churchill, G.A. 1979. A Paradigm for Developing Better Measures of Marketing Constructs. *Journal of Marketing Research* 16(1), pp. 64–73.

Coase, R.H. 1937. The Nature of the Firm. *Economica* 4(16), pp. 386–405.

Coase, R.H. 1960. The Problem of Social Cost. *The Journal of Law and Economics* 3(1), pp. 1–44.

Coase, R.H. 1974. The Economics of the First Amendment: The Market for Goods and the Market for Ideas. *The American Economic Review* 64(2), pp. 384–391.

Coase, R.H. 1988a. The Nature of the Firm: Influence. *Journal of Law, Economics and Organization* 4(1), pp. 33–47.

Coase, R.H. 1988b. *The Firm, the Market, and the Law*. Chicago, IL: University of Chicago Press.

Coase, R.H. 1988c. The Nature of the Firm: Meaning. *Journal of Law, Economics and Organization* 4(1), pp. 19–32.

Coase, R.H. 1988d. The Nature of the Firm: Origin. *Journal of Law, Economics and Organization* 4(1), pp. 3–17.

Commons, J.R. 1924. *The Legal Foundations of Capitalism*. Clifton, NJ: Augustus M. Kelley.

Competition Commission, 2000. *The Supply of Impulse Ice Cream: A Report on the Supply in the UK of Ice Cream Purchased for Immediate Consumption*. London: Competition Commission.

Creswell, J.W. 2003. *Research Design: Qualitative, Quantitative and Mixed Methods Approaches*. 2nd Edition. Thousand Oaks, CA: Sage Publications.

DairyReporter.com. 2003. *Ice Cream: The Perennial Snack*. Available at: http://www.dairyreporter.com/Industry-markets/Ice-cream-the-perennial-snack (accessed: 22 July 2010).

Delprato, D.J. and Midgely, B.D. 1992. Some Fundamentals of B.F. Skinner's Behaviourism. *American Psychologist* 47(11), pp. 1507–1520.

Demsetz, H. 1967. Toward a Theory of Property Rights. *The American Economic Review* 57, pp. 347–359.

Demsetz, H. 1995. *The Economics of the Business Firm: Seven Critical Commentaries*. Cambridge, UK: Cambridge University Press.

Dnes, A.W. 1992. *Franchising: A Case Study Approach*. Aldershot, UK: Avebury, Ashgate Publishing.

Dnes, A.W. 1996. *The Economics of Law*. London: International Thomson Business Press.

Douma, S. and Schreuder, H. 2008. *Economic Approaches to Organisation*. 4th Edition. Harlow, UK: Pearson Education.

Duxbury, N. 1995. *Patterns of American Jurisprudence*. Oxford, UK: Clarendon.

Easterbrook, F.H. and Fischel, D.R. 1991. *The Economic Structure of Corporate Law*. Cambridge, MA: Harvard University Press.

Eisenhardt, K.M. 1989. Building Theories from Case Study Research. *Academy of Management Review* 14(4), pp. 532–550.

Evans, D.S. 2001. *Payment Card Business: Chickens and Eggs and Other Conundrums*. Available at: http://www.ftmastering.com/mmo/mmo03_2.htm (accessed: 23 February 2004).

Evans, D.S. 2002. *The Antitrust Economics of Two-Sided Markets*. AEI–Brookings Joint Center for Regulatory Studies Publication 02(13), pp. 1–95.

Fagerstrøm, A., Foxall, G.R. and Arntzen, E. 2010. Implications of Motivating Operations for the Functional Analysis of Consumer Behavior. *Journal of Organizational Behaviour Management*, Special Issue: *Consumer Behaviour Analysis* 30(2), pp. 110–126.

Feyerabend, P. 1970. Consolations for the Specialist. In: Lakatos, I. and

Musgrave, A. eds. *Criticism and the Growth of Knowledge.* Cambridge, UK: Cambridge University Press, pp. 197–230.

Foss, N.J. and Klein, P.G. 2008. The Theory of the Firm and Its Critics: A Stocktaking and Assessment. In: Brousseau, E. and Glachant, J.-M. eds. *New Institutional Economics: A Guidebook.* Cambridge, UK: Cambridge University Press, pp. 425–442.

Foxall, G.R. 1981. *Strategic Marketing Management.* London: Routledge.

Foxall, G.R. 1988. Marketing New Technology: Markets, Hierarchies, and User-Initiated Innovation. *Managerial and Decision Economics* 9(3), pp. 237–250.

Foxall, G.R. 1990. *Consumer Psychology in Behavioural Perspective.* Washington, DC: Beard Books.

Foxall, G.R. 1992a. The Consumer Situation: An Integrative Model for Research in Marketing. *Journal of Marketing Management* 8(4), pp. 383–404.

Foxall, G.R. 1992b. The Behavioral Perspective Model of Purchase and Consumption: From Consumer Theory to Marketing Practice. *Journal of the Academy of Marketing Science* 20(2), pp. 189–198.

Foxall, G.R. 1994. Behavior Analysis and Consumer Psychology. *Journal of Economic Psychology* 15(1), pp. 5–91.

Foxall, G.R. 1996. *Consumers in Context: The BPM Research Program.* London: Routledge.

Foxall, G.R. 1997a. *Marketing Psychology: The Paradigm in the Wings.* Houndmills, UK: Macmillan Press.

Foxall, G.R. 1997b. The Emotional Texture of Consumer Environments: A Systematic Approach to Atmospherics. *Journal of Economic Psychology* 18(5), pp. 505–523.

Foxall, G.R. 1997c. The Explanation of Consumer Behaviour: From Social Cognition to Environmental Control. In: Cooper, C. and Robertson, I. eds. *The International Review of Industrial and Organizational Psychology.* Chichester, UK: Wiley, pp. 229–287.

Foxall, G.R. 1998. Radical Behaviourist Interpretation: Generating and Evaluating an Account of Consumer Behaviour. *The Behaviour Analyst* 21(2), pp. 321–354.

Foxall, G.R. 1999a. The Marketing Firm. *Journal of Economic Psychology* 20(2), pp. 207–234.

Foxall, G.R. 1999b. Putting Consumer Behaviour in Its Place: The Behavioural Perspective Model Research Programme. *International Journal of Management Reviews* 1(2), pp. 133–157.

Foxall, G.R. 1999c. Reply to Phil Reed. *Journal of Economic Psychology* 20(2), pp. 245–249.

Foxall, G.R. 2001. Foundations of Consumer Behaviour Analysis. *Marketing Theory* 1(2), pp. 165–199.

Foxall, G.R. 2002. Marketing's Attitude Problem – and How to Solve It. *Journal of Customer Behavioural Processes* 1, pp. 19–48.

Foxall, G.R. 2005. *Understanding Consumer Choice*. New York: Palgrave Macmillan.

Foxall, G.R. 2007. Explaining Consumer Choice: Coming to Terms with Intentionality. *Behavioural Processes* 75(2), pp. 129–145.

Foxall, G.R. 2009. *Interpreting Consumer Choice: The Behavioral Perspective Model*. New York: Routledge.

Foxall, G.R. 2010. Invitation to Consumer Behavior Analysis. *Journal of Organizational Behavior Management* 30(2), pp. 92–109.

Foxall, G.R. 2011. Brain, Emotion and Contingency in the Explanation of Consumer Behaviour. *International Review of Industrial and Organizational Psychology* 26, pp. 47–91.

Foxall, G.R. and Minkes, A.L. 1996. Beyond Marketing: The Diffusion of Entrepreneurship in the Modern Corporation. *Journal of Strategic Marketing* 4, pp. 71–94.

Foxall, G.R. and Schrezenmaier, T.C. 2003. The Behavioral Economics of Consumer Brand Choice: Establishing a Methodology. *Journal of Economic Psychology* 24(5), pp. 675–695.

Foxall, G.R., Oliveira-Castro, J.M. and Schrezenmaier, T.C. 2004. The Behavioral Economics of Consumer Brand Choice: Patterns of Reinforcement and Utility Maximization. *Behavioural Processes* 66(3), pp. 235–260.

Foxall, G.R., Oliveira-Castro, J., James, V.K. and Schrezenmaier, T. 2006. Consumer Behaviour Analysis: The Case of Brand Choice. *Revista Psicologia: Organizações e Trabalho* 6(1) January–June, pp. 50–78.

Foxall, G.R., Oliveira-Castro, J., Schrezenmaier, T. and James, V.K. eds. 2007. *The Behavioral Economics of Brand Choice*. Houndmills, UK: Palgrave Macmillan.

Gilbert, X. and Strebel, P. 1989. From Innovation to Outpacing. *Business Quarterly* 54(1), pp. 19–22.

Gronroos, C. 1994. Quo Vadis, Marketing? Towards a Relationship Marketing Paradigm. *Journal of Marketing Management* 10, pp. 347–360.

Guba, E.G. and Lincoln, Y.S. 1994. Competing Paradigms in Qualitative Research. In: Denzin, N.K. and Lincoln, Y.S. eds. *Handbook of Qualitative Research*. Thousand Oaks, CA: Sage Publishing, pp. 105–117.

Gummesson, E. 2000. *Qualitative Methods in Management Research*. Thousand Oaks, CA: Sage Publications.

Hakim, C. 2000. *Research Design: Successful Designs for Social and Economic Research*. Oxford, UK: Routledge.

Hammersley, M. and Gomm, R. 2000. Introduction. In: Gomm, R., Hammersley, M. and Foster, P. eds. *Case Study Method*. London: Sage Publications, pp. 1–17.

Hannan, M.T. and Freeman, J. 1989. *Organisational Ecology*. Cambridge, MA: Harvard University Press.

Hart, O. 1989. An Economist's Perspective on the Theory of the Firm. *Columbia Law Review* 89(7), pp. 1757–1774.

Hart, O. 1995. *Firms, Contracts and Financial Structure*. New York: Oxford University Press.

Hayes, L.J. and Chase, P.N. eds. 1991. *Dialogues on Verbal Behavior*. Reno, NV: Context Press.

Hayes, S.C. and Hayes, L.J. eds. 1992. *Understanding Verbal Relations*. Reno, NV: Context Press.

Hayes, S.C., Hayes, L.J., Reese, H.W. and Sarbin, T.R. 1993. *Varieties of Scientific Contextualism*. Reno, NV: Context Press.

Hayes, S.C., Hayes, L.J., Sato, M. and Ono, K. 1994. *Behavior Analysis of Language and Cognition*. Reno, NV: Context Press.

Herrnstein, R.J. 1997. *The Matching Law: Papers in Psychology and Economics*. Cambridge, MA: Harvard University Press.

Highways Agency. 2010. The MZS. Available at: http://www.highways. gov.uk/roads/18111. aspx (accessed: 2 August 2010).

Homans, C.G. 1974. *Social Behavior*. New York: Harcourt Brace Jovanovich.

Jensen, M.C. and Meckling, W.H. 1976. Theory of the Firm: Managerial Behavior, Agency Costs and Ownership Structure. *Journal of Financial Economics* 3(4), pp. 305–360.

Johnson, G. and Scholes, K. 2002. *Exploring Corporate Strategy: Text and Cases*. 6th Edition. Harlow, UK: Pearson Education.

Kagel, J.H. 1988. Economics According to the Rats (and Pigeons Too): What Have We Learned and What Can We Hope to Learn? In: Roth, A.E. ed. *Laboratory Experiments in Economics*. Cambridge, UK: Cambridge University Press, pp. 155–192.

Kearney, T., Kennedy, A. and Coughlan, J. (2007). Servicescapes: A Review of Contemporary Empirical Research, Conference papers, Paper 4 Dublin Institute of Technology, School of Marketing.

Kelemen, M. and Rumens, N. 2008. *An Introduction to Critical Management Research*. London: Sage Publications.

Klaes, M. 2000. The History of the Concept of Transaction Costs: Neglected Aspects. *Journal of the History of Economic Thought* 22(2), pp. 191–216.

Kotler, P. 1973. Atmospherics as a Marketing Tool. *Journal of Retailing* 49(4), pp. 48–64.

Kotler, P., Armstrong, G., Saunders, J. and Wong, V. 2001. *Principles of Marketing*. 3rd European Edition. Harlow, UK: Pearson Education.

Kuhn, T.S. 1962. *The Structure of Scientific Revolutions*. Chicago, IL: Chicago University Press.

Lee, V. 1988. *Beyond Behaviourism*. London: Erlbaum.

Leibenstein, H. 1966. Allocative Efficiency vs. X-Efficiency. *The American Economic Review* 56, pp. 392–415.

Macaulay, S. 1963. Non-Contractual Relations in Business. *American Sociological Review* 28, pp. 55–70.

Macneil, I.R. 1978. Contracts: Adjustment of Long-Term Economic Relations under Classical, Neoclassical and Relational Contract Law. *Northwestern Law Review* 72, pp. 854–905.

Marschak, J. 1950. The Rationale of the Demand for Money and of 'Money Illusion'. *Metroeconomica* 2, August, pp. 71–100.

Marshall, M.N. 1996. Sampling for Qualitative Research. *Family Practice* 13(6), pp. 522–525.

Mason, J. 2002. *Qualitative Researching*. 2nd Edition. London: Sage Publications.

Medema, S.G. 1994. *Ronald H. Coase*. London: Macmillan.

Michael, J. 1982. Distinguishing between Discriminative and Motivational Functions of Stimuli. *Journal of Experimental Analysis of Behaviour* 37(1), pp. 149–155.

Miles, M.B. and Huberman, A.M. 1994. *Qualitative Data Analysis: An Expanded Sourcebook*. 2nd Edition. Thousand Oaks, CA: Sage Publications.

Monteverde, K. and Teece, D. 1982. Supplier Switching Costs and Vertical Integration in the Automobile Industry. *Bell Journal of Economics* 13, pp. 206–213.

Morgan, R.M. and Hunt, S.D. 1994. The Commitment–Trust Theory of Relationship Marketing. *Journal of Marketing* 58, pp. 20–38.

Myers, M. 1997. *Qualitative Research in Information Systems*. Available at: http://www.qual.auckland.ac.nz/ (accessed: 10 December 2009).

Nightingale, P. 2008. Meta-Paradigm Change and the Theory of the Firm. *Industrial and Corporate Change* 17(3), pp. 533–583.

Office for National Statistics (UK). 2002. *Population Density, 2002: Regional Trends 38*. Available at: http://www.statistics.gov.uk/STATBASE/ssdataset.asp?vlnk=7662 (accessed: 2 August 2010).

Parkhe, A. 1993. Messy Research, Methodological Predispositions and Theory Development in International Joint Ventures. *Academy of Management Review* 18(2), pp. 227–268.

Patton, M.Q. 1987. *How to Use Qualitative Methods in Evaluation*. Newbury Park, CA: Sage Publications.

Patton, M.Q. 1990. *Qualitative Evaluation and Research Methods*. 2nd Edition. Newbury Park, CA: Sage Publications.

Payne, A. ed. 1995. *Advances in Relationship Marketing*. London: Kogan Page.

Penrose, E. 1959. *The Theory of the Growth of the Firm*. Oxford: Oxford University Press.

Perrien, J. and Ricard, L. 1995. The Meaning of a Marketing Relationship. *Industrial Marketing Management* 24, pp. 37–43.

Pierce, W.D. and Cheney, C.D. 2008. *Behaviour Analysis and Learning*. 4th Edition. New York: Psychology Press.

Pitelis, C.N. and Teece, D.J. 2009. The (New) Nature and Essence of the Firm. *European Management Review* 6(1), pp. 5–15.

Porter, M.E. 1980. *Competitive Strategy: Techniques for Analyzing Industries and Competitors*. New York: Free Press.

Posner, R.A. 1990. *The Problems of Jurisprudence*. Cambridge, MA: Harvard University Press.

Posner, R.A. 1992. *The Economic Analysis of Law*. New York: Little, Brown.

Potter, J.W. and Levine-Donnerstein, D. 1999. Rethinking Validity and Reliability in Content Analysis. *Journal of Applied Communication Research* 27(3), pp. 258–284.

Richardson, G.B. 1972. The Organisation of Industry. *Economic Journal* 82(327), pp. 883–896.

Rose, H. 1991. Case Studies. In: Allan, G. and Skinner, C. eds. *Handbook for Research Students in the Social Sciences*. Oxford, UK: RoutledgeFalmer, pp. 190–202.

Rosenberg, A. 1976. *Microeconomic Laws: A Philosophical Analysis*. Pittsburgh, PA: Pittsburgh University Press.

Silverman, D. 2010. *Doing Qualitative Research*. 3rd Edition. London: Sage Publications.

Skinner, B.F. 1953. *Science and Human Behaviour*. First Free Press Paperback Edition. New York: Free Press.

Skinner, B.F. 1974. *About Behaviorism*. London: Jonathan Cape.

Smith, L.D. 1986. *Behaviorism and Logical Positivism: A Reassessment of the Alliance*. Stanford, CA: Stanford University Press.

Stiglitz, J. 2010. *Freefall: Free Markets and the Sinking of the Global Economy*. London: Penguin.

Webster, F.E. 1992. The Changing Role of Marketing in the Corporation. *Journal of Marketing* 56(4), pp. 1–17.

Williamson, O.E. 1975. *Markets and Hierarchies*. New York: Free Press.

Williamson, O.E. 1985. *The Economic Institutions of Capitalism*. New York: Free Press.

Xiao, S.H. and Nicholson, M. 2010. Trick or Treat? An Examination of Marketing Relationships in a Non-Deceptive Counterfeit Market. *Journal of Organizational Behavior Management* 30(3), pp. 247–270.

Yani Soriano, M. and Foxall, G.R. 2002. A Spanish Translation of Mehrabian and Russell's Emotionality Scales for Environmental Consumer Psychology. *Journal of Consumer Behaviour* 2(1), pp. 23–36.

Yin, R.K. 2003. *Case Study Research: Design and Methods*. 3rd Edition. Thousand Oaks, CA: Sage Publications.

Yin, R.K. 2009. *Case Study Research: Design and Methods*. 4th Edition. Thousand Oaks, CA: Sage Publications.

Zuriff, G.E. 1985. *Behaviorism: A Conceptual Reconstruction*. New York: Columbia University Press.

Index

Alchian, A.A., 24, 29
Alhadeff, D.A., 8, 13, 14, 30, 54, 105
alpine, 249
approach behaviour, *see also* avoidance
   behaviour, escape behaviour
   and operational definitions and
   measures, 14, 32, 38, 52–3, 54–5,
   59, 60–62, 71, 74, 82, 88, 92, 97,
   104, 105, 111, 112, 117–18, 120,
   256, 289–93
a definition of, 59
as research propositions, 54–5
as response class, 59, 109
in consumer behaviour, 14, 32
in firm behaviour, 38, 52–3, 59,
   60–62
shaping and maintaining incidence
   of
   consumer behaviour approach,
      104, 112
   intermediary approach, 86, 105,
      111, 112, 114
   manufacturer aproach, 114
strength of, 71, 74, 88, 97, 105, 120
structure of approach
   manufacturer approach and
      escape/avoidance in
      manufacturer↔distributor
      relationships,
      structure of approach
         behaviour by
         manufacturers towards
         distributors, 290
   distributor approach and escape/
      avoidance behaviour
      by distributors in
      manufacturer↔distributor
      relationships,
      structure of approach behaviour
         by distributors towards
         manufacturers, 290

manufacturer approach and
   escape/avoidance behaviour
   in manufacturer↔retailer
   relationships,
   structure of approach behaviour
      by manufacturers towards
      retailers, 292
retailer approach and escape/
   avoidance behaviour in
   manufacturer↔retailer
   relationships,
   structure of approach
      behaviour by retailers
      towards manufacturers,
      293
topography of approach, *see*
   structure of approach
using the marketing mix to
   strengthen or encourage
   approach, 38, 54, 62
Armstrong, G., 36, 39, 57, 63
Arntzen, E., 31, 39, 103, 104, 118
Atkinson, P., 46
avoidance behaviour *see also* approach
   behaviour, escape behaviour
   and operational definitions and
   measures, 14, 32, 38, 52–3, 54–5,
   59, 60–62, 65, 92, 109, 111, 119,
   289–93
a definition of, 65
as research propositions, 54–5
as response class, 59, 109
in consumer behaviour, 14, 32
in firm behaviour, 37, 52–3, 59,
   60–62
proscription of avoidance, 105
structure of avoidance
   manufacturer approach and
      escape/avoidance in
      manufacturer↔distributor
      relationships,

structure of escape or
avoidance behaviour by
manufacturers away from
distributors, 289
structure of escape or
avoidance behaviour by
manufacturers away from
ex-dedicated distributors,
290
distributor approach and escape/
avoidance behaviour
by distributors in
manufacturer↔distributor
relationships,
structure of escape or avoidance
behaviour by distributors
away from manufacturers,
290
structure of escape or avoidance
behaviour by distributors
away from Birds Eye
Wall's, 290
structure of escape or avoidance
behaviour by distributors
away from Birds Eye Wall's
rivals, 291
manufacturer approach and
escape/avoidance behaviour
in manufacturer↔retailer
relationships,
structure of escape or
avoidance behaviour by
manufacturers away from
retailers, 291–2
retailer approach and escape/
avoidance behaviour in
manufacturer↔retailer
relationships,
structure of escape or avoidance
behaviour by retailers away
from manufacturers, 292
structure of escape or avoidance
behaviour by retailers away
from Birds Eye Wall's,
292–3
topography of avoidance, *see*
structure of avoidance
using the marketing mix to weaken
or discourage avoidance, 37,
54, 62

Babbie, E. 44
Barnes, J.G. 22
Baum, W.M. 2, 4, 30, 41, 42, 50, 57
behaviour analysis, *see also* consumer
behaviour analysis, firm behaviour
analysis, *and* case study, 41, 43,
45, 123
behaviour
as a physical natural event, 40
consumer behaviour, *see* consumer
behaviour *and* consumer
behaviour, an operant
interpretation
economic behaviour, *see* economic
behaviour *and* economic
behaviour, an operant
interpretation
marketing behaviour, *see* marketing
behaviour *and* marketing
behaviour, an operant
interpretation
proscription, 113
behaviour event *see* stimulus or event
behaviour settings,
a definition of, *see also* antecedent
stimuli *and* scope stimuli, 57
in conceptual and analytical
frameworks, 38, 53
in research propositions, 55–6
in the behavioural perspective model,
32–3
and operant classes of behaviour,
33
in sub-research questions, 132–5
scope and scope for behaving, 6,
9–13, 17–22, 23, 27, 37, 52, 54,
57, 94
characteristics of closed settings,
60–61
management, 15, 24, 62, 92, 119,
128, 136
qualification and management,
12, 28, 60–61, 64, 86, 109–13,
116, 118–20, 122
closed settings and setting
closure, 19, 25–7, 31, 34,
77, 80, 93, 94, 100–102,
105, 109, 117, 120, 174, 175
open settings, 32, 52, 60, 75,
100, 256, 287

types of behaviour settings
consumer behaviour setting, 9, 12,
18, 19, 27, 31, 32, 36, 37
managerial behaviour setting, 20,
37, 38, 53, 57, 74, 101, 102,
103, 117, 120, 121, 264, 267,
286–9
marketer behaviour setting, 20, 26,
38, 53
Behavioural Perspective Model (BPM),
4, 5, 7, 12, 31–3, 39, 52–3
and the three-term contingency,
52–3
marketer-controlled stimuli, 31, 111
operant classes of consumer
behaviour, 33
stimuli, learning history and a
specific physical context, 31–2,
51
Bell, E., 40, 42, 43, 50
bilateral contingency *see* relationships
as defined by the theory of the
marketing firm
and economic transactions, 18
relationships, 18, 19, 21, 126
Birds Eye Wall's, 47, 48, 66, 67, 68, 69,
70–110, 113, 114, 115, 116, 117,
119, 120, 123, 247–54, 256–7, 258,
259, 260–74, 285–92
Blois, K., 29
brand *see* marketing mix variables,
product
Bryman, A., 40, 42, 43, 50
Buttle, F., 33, 111

case evidence
antecedent stimuli
consumer demand, 84–5
manufacturer Performance
History, 75–8
market dominance of Birds Eye
Wall's, 74–5
regulatory intervention, 81
relationships as routes to market,
72–80
retail availability, penetration and
market share, 79–81
aversive effects of Wall's Direct on
BEW's distribution shares,
269

brand market share by manufacturer
across retail sector, 260–62
descriptive framework of empirically
verifiable firm relationships, 118
direct consequences of 1998
government intervention, 81–5
franchising of Mobile Van
Operators, 274
The 1999 investigation, 85–100,
269–93
distributor responses: Ice Cream
World, 100
freezer/outlet exclusivity retail
setting closure and managing
patterns of reinforcement,
92–9
losses in sales by the ex-dedicated
distributors, 269–70
managerial behaviour settings,
profitability opens the
managerial behaviour
setting, 75–6, 264, 286–8
topography of managerial
behaviour setting in
manufacturing firms,
286–7
topography of managerial
behaviour setting in
distribution firms, 287–8
topography of managerial
behaviour setting in
retailing firms, 288–9
managing distributor patterns of
reinforcement and setting
closure, 86–90
managing retailer reinforcement:
manufacturer terms to
retailers, 90–92
Nestlé and Mars performance, 264
retailer terms offered by Birds Eye
Wall's, 271–3
routes to market, 257–9
sales and advertising expenditure
per manufacturer in
£millions, 263
seasonality and its effects on ice-
cream consumption, 255–6
structure (topography) of
approach, avoidance and
escape, 289–93

timeline of events leading to
regulatory investigation in
1999, 247–54
utilitarian and informational
reinforcement inherent
in outlet exclusivity and
mobile retailer franchising
arrangements, 279–84
Wall's Direct, the creation of,
265–9

case study
and operant interpretations, 41–2
plausibility of interpretation,
40–42, 44, 113, 122
usefulness of interpretation, 40,
118
criteria for evaluation *see* case study,
evaluative criteria
data,
analysis, 48–9, 50, 52, 122, 123,
136–246
choice of dataset, 3, 43, 44–6, 50,
119
considerations, assumptions
and limitations, 44–6
use of secondary data, 3, 34,
44–6
coding, 48, 49, 52, 122
coding scheme used, 136–246
data reduction, 48
limitations of, 45–6
strategies and techniques for data
analysis, 48–9, 50
use of Nvivo in managing data
analysis, 50
within-case analysis and
conclusion drawing, 49
within-case sampling, 48–9
design and methodology, 42–50,
127–35
case study as reasearch design, 43
embedded units of analysis, 46–8,
50, 126
single case, 44, 45–6
strength of, 45
limitations of, 45–6
ethical considerations, 27–8, 50
evaluation of research carried out,
118–23

central concepts,
approach, avoidance and
escape, 120
economising on transaction
costs, 119
learning history and managerial
behaviour setting, 120–21
marketer control, extent of, 121
role of exchange, 119–20
rule-governed behaviour and
rule following, 121
significance of utilitarian
and informational
reinforcement, 121
use of scope and reinforcer
management, 118–19
usefulness of bilateral
contingency framework,
119
usefulness of four-term
contingency, 118
methodological limitations, 122–3
evaluative criteria of, 42
evidence, *see* case evidence
commentary presented as part of
the research, 65–102
supplementary commentary
presented by way of
appendix, 247–85
focus and bounds of the case, 46
generalisability, 42, 44, 50, 51, 122
outside the case study, 50, 122
statistical, 44
theoretical or analytical, 42, 122
methodology and design, 4, 40–51
methodology for analysing firm
behaviour, 52–3
philosophy of science assumptions,
40–41
protocol, 126–35
qualitative versus quantitative routes
to knowledge, 42–3
research objective *see also* case study
protocol, 3
research hypotheses, 43–4, 45
research propositions, *see also* case
study protocol, 53–6
the antecedents proposition, 53–4
discussion on evidence for,
103–6

the competition proposition, 56
  discussion on evidence for, 116
the Reinforcement Management
    Proposition, 54–5
  discussion on evidence for,
    109–16
the Scope Management
    propositions, 55
  discussion on evidence for,
    109–16
research questions *see also* case
    study protocol,
central question, 3–4
sub research questions, 127–35
role of theory in, 43–4
secondary data, the use of, 3, 43,
    44–6
statistical and theoretical
    significance *see* case study
    generalisability
statistical significance *see* case study
    generalisability
subjective interpretations and
    assessment, 46
triangulation, 45
units of analysis *see also* case study
    protocol, 3, 46–8
validity and reliability, 40–43, 48–50,
    122–3
Chase, P.N., 8
Cheney, C.D., 31, 41, 50, 56, 57, 58,
    60, 64
Churchill, G.A., 43
closed settings *see also* behaviour
    setting scope
characteristics of, 61–2
Coase, R.H., 1, 2, 5, 8, 9, 14, 15, 20, 23,
    24, 26, 28, 51, 54, 109
Coffey, A., 46
Commons, J.R., 15
Competition Commission, 3, 45, 46,
    47, 48, 51, 65, 70, 72, 77, 78, 80,
    81, 82, 83, 84, 88, 90, 92, 94, 100,
    101, 102, 103, 104, 105, 111, 115,
    117, 119, 122, 123, 126, 127, 247,
    248, 249, 250, 251, 252, 253, 254,
    255, 256, 257, 258, 259, 261, 264,
    265, 266, 268, 269, 292
competitive encroachment, 72, 91, 92,
    96, 99, 107, 118–20, 287

as a response class, 116
competitive isomorphism, 35
competitive mimicry, 35, 287
conceptual framework, 38
consequences of behaviour *see also*
    reinforcement *and* punishment, 2,
    10, 11, 16, 17, 18, 19, 20, 21, 22,
    23, 28, 30, 31, 32, 33, 34, 38, 41,
    52, 54, 56, 57, 58, 59, 60, 62, 64,
    70, 81, 82, 85, 86, 89, 90, 91, 92,
    95, 97, 99, 103, 104, 106, 110, 113,
    114, 121, 255, 256, 266, 267, 268,
    275–84, 286
a bifurcation of reinforcement and
    punishment, 33
and the probability of response, 32
as a focus of enquiry, 10
aversive consequencs of behaviour,
    11, 22, 28, 32, 33, 54, 58, 59, 60,
    62, 64, 70, 82, 85, 90, 91, 92, 95,
    97, 99, 103, 106, 114, 255, 256,
    266, 267, 275–84
benefits, positive or beneficial
    consequences of behaviour, 2,
    3, 11, 14, 15, 20, 21, 25, 26, 30,
    33, 58, 59, 60, 61, 62, 64, 65, 71,
    72, 73, 74, 75, 79, 81, 83, 84, 85,
    86, 87, 90, 91, 92, 94, 95, 96, 97,
    99, 100, 102, 104, 106, 114, 115,
    116, 121, 255, 256, 266, 267,
    275–84
influence of competitor behaviour,
    19
in economic transactions, 18–19, 21,
    20, 32
reinforcing and punishing
    consequences of consumer
    behaviour, 32
reinforcing and punishing
    consequences of firm behaviour,
    37
consequences of government
    intervention
direct consequences in 1998, 81–5
consumer behaviour *see also*
    Behavioural Perspective Model, 1,
    2, 3, 4, 5, 6, 7, 8, 9, 11, 12, 13, 14,
    18, 19, 20, 27, 28, 30, 31, 32, 33,
    34, 35, 36, 37, 38, 59, 93, 103, 111,
    115, 121, 268, 285

consumer behaviour analysis, 37, 38, 121, 268
consumer choice
and the BPM, 4, 27
and consumer-orientation, 9
defined, 11, 28
and marketer behaviour (marketing management) 12, 19
and marketing-orientated economic systems, 21, 26–7
commission's findings on, 111
importance of consumer choice in managerial behaviour setting, 286
consumer orientated management and consumer orientation, 6, 7, 8, 9, 13, 17, 21, 28
consumer situation, 12, 31–2
contingency shaped behaviour *see also* rule-governed behaviour, 58
Coughlan, J., 33
Creswell, J.W., 44

data analysis *see* case study data analysis
dedicated and non-dedicated distribution *see also* exchange relations *and* marketing relationships, 72, 103, 247, 248, 268, 289
the formation of Wall's Direct, 253, 269, 289
Birds Eye Wall's
dedicated distribution, 66, 68–9, 71–2, 82–4, 100–101, 104, 248–50, 252, 257–9, 265, 266, 268–70
termination of dedicated distribution contracts, 82, 84, 85, 87, 101, 105, 110, 252, 253, 258, 265, 267–9
discrimination among various levels of arrangements, 82–4, 104–6, 251, 268, 287
ex-dedicated distributors of, 47, 67, 84–90, 92, 94, 99, 100, 102, 106, 109, 114, 115, 117, 119, 121, 126, 253, 266, 267, 269, 270, 286–90

franchising *see* marketing mix variables place
non-dedicated arrangements, 72, 251
Delprato, D.J., 31, 40, 41, 51
Demsetz, H., 8, 15, 24, 28, 29
Director General of Fair Trading, 45, 83, 84, 101, 110, 253, 254, 268
distribution *see also* dedicated and non-dedicated distribution
radial *and* central, 66, 67, 70, 72, 267, 287, 289
discriminative function or stimulus, *see also* stimulus 10–12, 14, 15, 18–20, 22, 28, 31, 34, 38, 39, 52, 53, 57, 58, 64, 86, 103, 104, 111, 113
a definition of, 57
Dnes, A.W., 15, 43, 50
Douma, S., 1
Duxbury, N., 29

Easterbrook, F.H., 28
economic behaviour, 6, 8, 10, 11, 15–16, 24, 27, 30, 56, 62, 109, 113
an operant interpretation, 10–11, 56
exchange transaction as defining characteristic, 14
economic conditions for marketing to exist (and competition), 8–9
economic psychology, 6–7, 28, 39
and its contribution to marketing, 6–8
in explaining marketing behaviour and the theory of the firm, 7
economies of scale, 36, 37, 59, 64, 70, 71, 89, 116, 256, 266, 267, 268, 270, 287, 288
economic transactions *see* market and economic transactions
Eisenhardt, K.M., 43, 45
entrepreneurial function of the firm, 1, 8, 9, 18, 24, 25, 26, 27, 29
environmental stiumuls *see* stimulus
escape behaviour *see also* approach behaviour, avoidance behaviour *and* operational definitions and measures, 14, 32, 37, 52–3, 54–5, 59, 60–62, 65, 92, 109, 111, 119, 289–93
as research propositions, 54–5
as response class, 59, 109

in consumer behaviour, 14, 32
in firm behaviour, 37, 52–3, 59,
    60–62
structure of escape
    manufacturer approach and
        escape/avoidance in
        manufacturer↔distributor
        relationships
        structure of escape or
            avoidance behaviour by
            manufacturers away from
            distributors, 289
        structure of escape or
            avoidance behaviour by
            manufacturers away from
            ex-dedicated distributors,
            290
    distributor approach and escape/
        avoidance behaviour
        by distributors in
        manufacturer↔distributor
        relationships,
        structure of escape or avoidance
            behaviour by distributors
            away from manufacturers,
            290
        structure of escape or avoidance
            behaviour by distributors
            away from Birds Eye
            Wall's, 290
        structure of escape or avoidance
            behaviour by distributors
            away from Birds Eye Wall's
            rivals, 291
    manufacturer approach and
        escape/avoidance behaviour
        in manufacturer↔retailer
        relationships
        structure of escape or
            avoidance behaviour by
            manufacturers away from
            retailers, 291–2
    retailer approach and escape/
        avoidance behaviour in
        manufacturer↔retailer
        relationships
        structure of escape or
            avoidance behaviour
            by retailers away from
            manufacturers, 292

        structure of escape or avoidance
            behaviour by retailers away
            from Birds Eye Wall's,
            292–3
    topography of avoidance, *see*
        structure of escape
    using the marketing mix to bar
        escape, 62
essence of the existence of the
    marketing firm, 10
ethical considerations *see* case study
    ethical considerations
evaluative criteria see case study
    evaluative criteria
Evans, D., 114
exchange, 1, 2, 5, 6, 9–10, 14–21, 23–9,
    35–8, 47, 56, 59, 65, 68–71, 73,
    82–5, 89–91, 102, 106, 107, 108,
    109, 119, 120, 273
    an operant interpretation of
        exchange, 18–19
    econonic exchange, 2, 6, 14–18
    exchange theory, 16
    literal exchange, 5, 9, 15–17, 21, 23,
        26, 27, 35, 59, 70, 109
    market circumscription of
        economic exchange for
        predictability, stability and
        control, 3, 10, 23, 25, 37, 54,
        105, 120, 275–84
    market exchange, 6
exchange relations *see also*
    dedicated and non-dedicated
    distibution *and* marketing and
    market relationships, 17, 21,
    35–7, 47, 65, 69–73, 82–5, 102,
    108, 119
exclusivity arrangements *see also*
    dedicated and non-dedicated
    distribution, 65, 71–4, 80–81, 90,
    92–9, 101–2, 106–8, 110–12, 115,
    116, 118, 121, 247–51, 266, 271–9,
    281, 283, 286–90, 292–6
    freezer exclusivity, 65, 73, 74, 80, 92,
        94–9, 101, 107, 115, 248–51,
        273, 275–8, 292, 294, 295
    topograhy of utilitarian and
        informational reinforcement
        in freezer exclusivity
        arrangements, 275–8

outlet exclusivity, 65, 73, 74, 80, 92,
    93, 94–9, 102, 107–8, 112, 116,
    118, 247, 271, 274, 279, 281,
    286, 288–90, 295
  topograhy of utilitarian and
    informational reinforcement
    in outlet exclusivity
    arrangements, 279–84

Fagerstrøm, A., 31, 39, 103, 104, 118
Feyerabend, P., 7
firm behaviour analysis, 123
firm, defining characteristics, 8
firm, theory of, 5, 7, 8, 118, 120
Fischel, D.R., 28
Foss, N.J., 43, 119
four-term contingency, 118
Foxall, G.R., 1, 2, 3, 4, 5, 7, 8, 9, 28,
    29, 30, 31, 32, 33, 34, 35, 37, 38,
    39, 40, 41, 42, 49, 50, 52, 54, 56,
    57, 58, 59, 60, 61, 62, 64, 103, 104,
    106, 109, 111, 113, 116, 117, 118,
    121
function of the marketing firm, 9, 13,
    25, 28, 58
Freeman, J., 113
freezer exclusivity *see* exclusivity
    arrangements
function of marketing defined, 58
function of management, 26
function of managerial behaviour
    setting, 57
function of marketing mix, 63
function of reinforcement in human
    behaviour *see* reinforcement and
    punishment
function of response classes of
    behaviour, 56
functional analysis, 5, 8, 41, 109
  as distinct from topographical
    descriptions, 41
functional substitutability of brands,
    111

Gilbert, X., 39, 119
Glacier Foods Ltd, 142
Gomm, R., 42, 43
government intervention *see* regulatory
    and government intervention
Granada, 102

Guba, E.G., 3, 40, 42, 46, 49
Gummesson, E., 43

Hakim, C., 43
Hammersley, M., 42, 43
Hannan, M.T., 113
Hart, O., 8, 24, 28, 29, 33
Hayes, L.J., 8
Hayes, S.C., 8
Herrnstein, R.J., 115
Homans, C.G., 16
Huberman, A.M., 3, 40, 42, 43, 44, 45,
    46, 49, 51, 123
Hunt, S.D., 23

Ice-Cream World, 84, 100, 110, 148,
    184–5
induction versus deduction *see also*
    role of theory, 122
informational punishment defined *see
    also* consequences of behaviour
    and punishment, 59–60
informational reinforcement defined
    see also consequences of
    behaviour *and* reinforcement,
    59–60
intermediaries, 35, 39, 65, 70, 86, 87,
    105
  a marketing firm interpretation,
    35–6

James, V.K., 30, 111
James, William, 50
Jensen, M.C., 24, 29
Johnson, G., 35

Kagel, J.H., 11
Kearney, T., 33
Kelemen, M., 42, 51
Kennedy, A., 33
Klaes, M., 1
Klein, P.G., 43, 119
Kotler, P., 36, 39, 57, 63, 111
KPMG, 83
Kuhn, T.S., 7

learning history, 2, 14, 21, 31–2, 34, 35,
    36, 39, 41, 52, 57, 64, 104, 120, 268
  a definition of in consumer
    behaviour, 31–2

a definition of in firm behaviour, 57
and the internal organisation of the
    firm, 121
case evidence for managerial
    behaviour setting, topographical
    characterisation of, 74–8,
    286–9
    BEW's learning history, 74–8
    distributors, 287–8
    manufacturers, 286–7
    Nestlé and Mars' learning
        histories, 75–8, 264
    retailers, 288–9
in the Behavioural Perspective
    Model, 31–2
regulatory intervention timeline and
    events common to the learning
    histories of the ice-cream
    market incumbents, 81, 247–54
role of relationships in learning
    history, case evidence, 65–74
Lee, V., 10
Leibenstein, H., 20
Levine-Donnerstein, D., 42, 48, 49
Lincoln, Y.S., 3, 40, 42, 46, 49
literal exchange *see* exchange
long-term strategies
    cost leadership, 38, 119
    leadership through differentiation,
        38–9, 119
    outpacing, 38, 119
    and competitive interdependence,
        34–5
    strategic functions of firm behaviour,
        3
Lyons Maid, 77, 247, 248, 249, 250

Macaulay, S., 22
Mach, Ernst, 41, 50
Macneil, I.R., 22
management,
    essential functions of, 26
    of behaviour settings *see* behaviour
        settings, scope management
    of reinforcement and punishment
        see reinforcement and
        punishment, management of
    of reinforcers and punishers *see*
        reinforcement and punishment,
        management of

strategic scope of the organisation,
    29
managerial behaviour setting *see*
    behaviour settings
market and economic transactions, 2,
    8–10, 16, 18–23, 35
    exchange transactions within
        relationship boundaries, 88–9,
        109, 120
    market transactions and rules, 25
    market transactions as literal
        exchanges, 23
market-orientated societies, 10
market relationships *see* marketing and
    relationships
market transactions, 2, 8–10, 16, 23
marketer behaviour, 26, 40, 63
    setting *see* behaviour settings
marketer-orientated consumption, 21
marketing
    analysis of the marketing function,
        14–16
    a definition of, 5
    as the central purpose of business,
        8–10
    behaviour, 3, 6, 7, 30–32, 45, 56, 108,
        126
    costs *see also* transaction costs, 1, 21,
        23, 24
    firm *see* marketing firm
    functional analysis of, 5
    marketing management,
        an operant perspective, 12–13,
            14–27
        essence of, 27
        functions of, 58
        marketing-orientated
            management, 5, 7, 16, 21, 26,
                27, 28
        functions of marketing-
            orientated management, 5
    mix *see* marketing mix
marketing firm, 1–39, 42, 44–6, 48,
    50, 54–6, 58, 60, 62, 64, 70, 72,
    74, 78, 80, 82, 84, 86, 88, 90, 92,
    94, 96, 98, 100, 102–6, 109, 111,
    113–24
marketing management *see* marketing
marketing orientated management *see*
    marketing

marketing mix, 2, 3, 9, 13, 16, 17,
    21, 22, 23, 27, 28, 31, 34, 36, 38,
    53–7, 63–4, 93, 101, 111, 117, 118,
    127–36, 293–6
  operational definition of, 63–4
  topography of marketing mix
    stimuli, 293–6
  as deployed by manufacturers
    relevant to distributors
    product stimuli, 293
    place/logistical stimuli, 293–4
    price stimuli, 294
    promotional stimuli, 294
  as deployed by distributors
    relevant to manufacturers
    product stimuli, 294
    place/logistical stimuli, 294
    price stimuli, 294
    promotional stimuli, 294
  as deployed by manufacturers
    relevant to retailers
    product stimuli, 295
    place/logistical stimuli, 295
    price stimuli, 295
    promotional stimuli, 295
  as deployed by manufacturers
    relevant to manufacturers
    place/logistical stimuli, 296
    promotional stimuli, 296
  variables, 31, 55, 111, 118
    place *see also* dedicated and
      non-dedicated distribution,
      exchange relations, exclusivity
      arrangements *and* marketing
      and market relationships, 17,
      47, 63, 65–72, 82–4, 88–9,
      101, 104, 105, 107, 109, 112,
      120, 128, 129, 130, 132–5,
      147, 160–62, 164, 167, 182–5,
      188–90
  atmospherics *see* marketing mix
    variables, merchandising and
    atmospherics
  distribution *see* dedicated and
    non-dedicated distribution,
    exchange relations, exclusivity
    arrangements, marketing and
    market relationships
  franchising, 94, 113, 272, 274,
    279–84

freezer exclusivity *see* exclusivity
    arrangements, freezer
    exclusivity
  logistics, 65, 67, 69, 70, 82, 83, 84,
    85, 86, 89, 101, 107, 108, 259,
    265, 267, 287, 291, 293–5
  merchandising and atmospherics,
    63, 78, 79, 80, 91, 93, 95, 97,
    98, 108, 111, 112, 265, 273, 275,
    277, 292, 295
  outlet exclusivity *see* exclusivity
    arrangements, outlet exclusivity
  planograms, 79, 108
  retail, 3, 4, 13, 36, 38, 46, 47, 48,
    54, 55, 63, 65–102, 104, 106–9,
    111–21, 125–7, 129–31, 133,
    134, 247–52, 255–60, 264–83,
    286–96
  wholesale, 47, 65–73, 80, 82–4,
    86–90, 101, 103, 105, 107, 110,
    247–9, 251, 252, 257–9, 264,
    265, 267–70, 272, 277, 287,
    289–91, 293
  topography of place variables in the
    case evidence *see* marketing
    mix, topography of marketing
    mix stimuli
price and pricing, 2, 13, 16, 17, 21, 22,
    24, 25, 28, 31, 57, 63, 64, 71, 73,
    77, 86–9, 91–3, 102, 104, 105, 108,
    111, 118, 128–35, 249–51, 256,
    264, 271–3, 278, 289, 290, 294, 295
  Birds Eye Wall's and use of as an
    ability to discriminate between
    dedicated and non-dedicated
    distributors, 92, 109, 116
  shaping maintaining approach
    strength of through pricing and
    preferential terms, 71, 82, 86,
    87, 100
  topography of price variables in the
    case evidence *see* marketing
    mix, topography of marketing
    mix stimuli
product, 2, 13, 14, 17, 20–22, 31, 57,
    63–4, 70, 71, 73, 78, 79, 86, 89,
    92, 93, 95, 98, 99, 101, 111, 112,
    128–30, 132–5, 247, 249, 254, 256,
    265–6, 271, 274–7, 280, 285, 286,
    288, 291–5

brand, 2, 3, 13, 21, 32, 34, 36, 48,
        56–7, 64–5, 71, 73–4, 78–93,
        95–9, 104, 108, 110–12, 116,
        126, 247, 249, 250, 252, 255,
        260, 262, 266, 275–7, 280–84,
        286, 287, 288, 292, 293, 295
    availability, 80, 81, 98, 111
    functional substitutability of, 111
    multiple brand distribution and
        retailing, 71, 97, 99, 100,
        110–12, 266, 278, 288, 293
    operational definition, 56
    packaging, 57, 116, 256, 293, 295
    popularity, 65, 98, 108, 252, 275,
        276, 277, 278, 283, 286, 287,
        288
    preference, 78
    rates of sales, 29, 63, 79, 91, 92,
        93, 97, 98, 99, 108, 111, 117,
        283, 286, 287, 288, 292
    visibility, 80, 275, 282
    topography of product variables
        in the case evidence *see*
        marketing mix, topography
        of marketing mix stimuli
promotion, 13, 22, 31, 57, 59, 63,
        71, 73, 78, 86, 87, 89, 90, 91,
        92, 93, 95, 101, 111, 128, 129,
        130, 132, 133, 134, 135, 240,
        241, 242, 243, 248, 250, 251,
        252, 256, 271, 273, 274, 279,
        280, 282, 283, 289, 294, 295,
        296
    advertising, 13, 36, 59, 63, 78,
        79, 80, 93, 97, 111, 112,
        249, 250, 262, 263, 264,
        275, 276, 280, 292
    bonuses *and* bonus schemes, 71,
        72, 73, 87, 88, 91, 92, 95,
        97, 106, 116, 248, 250, 268,
        270, 271, 272, 273, 276,
        277, 278, 281, 282, 284,
        286, 291, 294, 295
    discounts, 63, 64, 71, 73, 87, 91,
        93, 95, 96, 97, 100, 102,
        106, 114, 250, 251, 256,
        268, 269, 270, 271, 273,
        277, 278, 281, 282, 284,
        286, 289, 291, 294, 295
    incentives, 59, 71, 87, 91, 95,

        106, 108, 252, 256, 282,
        287, 289, 294, 295
    point of purchase and point
        of sale, 31, 63, 79, 97, 250,
        275, 276, 280, 295
    topography of promotional
        variables in the case
        evidence *see* marketing mix,
        topography of marketing mix
        stimuli
marketing philosophy, 26
marketing and market relationships
    see also dedicated and non-
        dedicated distribution, exchange
        relations *and* exclusivity
    arrangments, 1–10, 13, 19, 21–31,
        33–9, 46, 47, 52–8, 65, 68–71,
        73–4, 82–5, 89, 92, 93, 97, 99, 101,
        102, 105–9, 112, 113, 116, 117,
        119–21, 125–7, 130, 131, 134, 266,
        268, 277, 289–92
    and exchange, 17, 21, 35–8, 47, 65,
        69–73, 82–5, 102, 108, 119
    bilateral contingency relationships,
        2, 3, 4, 18–19, 21, 23, 34, 46,
        106, 116, 119–20, 126, 128–9,
        131, 133, 135
    as defining characteristics of the
        firm, 8
    circumscribing of, 2, 3, 10, 20, 24,
        25, 29, 82, 83, 92, 93
    dedicated distribution and non-
        dedicated distribution *see*
        dedicated distribution and non-
        dedicated distribution
    definition of relationships in
        economics, 33
    definition of relationships in the
        theory of the marketing firm,
        33–6
    distinction between marketing
        relationships and relationship
        marketing, 22–3
    exclusivity arrangements *see*
        exclusivity arrangements
    management of relationships
        through strategic functions of
        the firm, 3, 10–14
    mutuality in marketing relationships,
        9, 13, 16–18, 22–3, 25–7, 35–8,

47, 56, 65, 68–71, 73, 82–6, 89,
102, 106–8, 116, 119, 120
mutuality and exchange in
marketing relationships,
35–6
non-exchange relationships, 17, 35,
109
non-marketing relationships, 21, 23
quasi-marketing relationships, 5,
9–10, 23, 26, 29
reciprocity and interdependence of
in, 2, 22, 26, 34, 35, 109, 113
relationship marketing, 5, 7, 9, 10,
21–3, 26–7
marketing strategies
a functional analysis, 37
marketing-orientated management *see*
marketing management
Mars, 47, 66, 67, 73, 76, 77, 78, 80,
81, 90, 94, 98, 99, 101, 102, 107,
108, 248, 249, 250, 256, 257, 258,
260, 261, 262, 264, 266, 267, 286,
289
Marschak, J., 1
Marshall, M.N., 48
Mason, J., 40, 42, 46
matching and melioration, 115
Meckling, W.H., 24, 29
Medema, S.G., 23, 24
Michael, J., 103
Midgely, B.D., 31, 40, 41, 51
Miles, M.B., 3, 40, 42, 43, 44, 45, 46,
49, 51, 123
Minkes, A.L., 29
Monteverde, K., 29
Morgan, R.M., 23
motivating operations (stimuli) and
motivational function, 31, 38, 39,
52, 53, 58, 103, 104, 105, 106, 111,
118, 122
mutual social interaction, 27
Myers M., 3, 42, 43

Nestlé, 47, 66, 67, 72, 73, 76, 77, 78,
80, 81, 90, 94, 96, 98, 99, 100, 101,
102, 107, 108, 248, 249, 250, 257,
258, 260, 261, 262, 264, 267, 274,
286, 287, 289
Nicholson, M., 34, 35, 54, 109, 116
Nightingale, P., 40

Oliveira-Castro, J., 30, 32, 111
Ono, K., 8
operant (behaviour)
a definition 56
operant behaviourism, 4, 7, 39–41, 50
a functional analysis
of behaviour, 8, 41, 109
of marketing, 5
as distinguished from
methodological behaviourism,
41, 46, 50
behaviour analysis *see* behaviour
analysis
consumer behaviour analysis *see*
consumer behaviour analysis
firm behaviour analysis *see* firm
behaviour analysis
operant analysis, 4, 11, 13, 27
operant methodology *see* behaviour
analysis *and* case study
operational definitions and measures,
56–64
definitions
approach, 59
antecedent stimuli, 57
avoidance, 59
behaviour as single event or
response chain, 56
behaviour setting, 57
brand, 57, 63–4
contingency-shaped behaviour,
58
consequential stimuli, 57–8
deprivation, 61
economies of scale, 59
environment and environmental
stimuli, 57
escape, 59
events as reinforcers or punishers,
58
function of marketing, 58
informational benefits or positive
consequences, 59–60
informational aversive
consequences, 59–60
learning history of the firm, 57
managerial behaviour setting, 57
marketer behaviour, 57
market information, 59
marketing mix, 63–4

negative punishment, 58
negative reinforcement, 58
operant, 56
outcomes of behaviour
classification,
patterns of reinforcement *see also*
patterns of reinforcement,
62
positive punishment, 58
positive reinforcement, 58
punishers, 58
punishing stimuli, 58
punishment, 56, 57
quality of reinforcers or punishers,
61–2
quantity of reinforcers or
punishers, 62
rate of responding, 56
reinforcement, 56, 57
reinforcer, 57
reinforcer or punisher
effectiveness, 61
reinforcing stimuli, 58
response class, 56
rule-governed behaviour, 58
sales and profits, 59
schedules of reinforcement
see also patterns of
reinforcement, 62, 64
stimulus, 57
stimulus class, 57
utilitarian aversive consequences,
59–60
utilitarian benefits or positive
consequences, 60
utilitarian informational negative
punishment, 60
utilitarian/informational positive
punishment, 60
utilitarian/informational negative
reinforcement, 60
utilitarian/informational positive
reinforcement, 60
measures, 56–64
behaviour setting management,
60–61
criteria for recognising open/
closed behaviour settings,
60–61
criteria for recognising the

availability and access
to reinforcement and
punishment, 60–61
criteria for recognising the
external control of the
situation, 61
events as reinforcers or
punishers, 58
function of marketing, 58
reinforcement management,
61–62
increasing the quality and
quantity of reinforcers
and/or punishers, 62
increasing the quality and
quantity of reinforcers
and/or punishers, 62
managing schedules of
reinforcement, 62
managing the effectiveness of a
reinforcer or punisher, 61
strategy used for specification and
interpretation, 52–3

Parkhe, A., 44
Patterns of reinforcement, 38, 52, 54–6,
61–2, 72–4, 79, 80, 86, 87, 89–7,
102–4, 106, 109, 111–13, 115, 116,
118, 119, 121, 122, 127, 265, 273,
274, 286
Patton, M.Q., 42, 48
Payne, A., 22, 26
Penrose, E., 36
Perrien, J., 23
Pierce, W.D., 31, 41, 50, 56, 57, 58, 60,
64
Pitelis, C.N., 119
place *see* marketing mix variables
Porter, M.E., 35, 39, 119
Posner, R.A., 15, 29
Potter, J.W., 42, 48, 49
price *see* marketing mix variables
product *see* marketing mix variables
promotion *see* marketing mix
variables
psychology
economic *see* economic psychology
operant *see* operant behaviourism
public interest, 45, 51, 123, 247, 248,
249, 251

punisher *see* operational definitions
    and measures
punishing stimulus *see* operational
    definitions and measures
punishment *see* operational
    definitions and measures *and*
    reinforcement

quasi-marketing relationships
    see marketing and market
    relationships
qualitative versus quantitative routes to
    knowledge *see* case study

Reese, H.W., 8
regulatory and government
    intervention, 30, 35, 45, 54, 65, 81,
    109, 110, 121, 125, 126
reinforcement *see also* operational
    definitions and measures
    deprivation of, 32, 61, 64, 88, 95, 97,
        99, 116
    function of reinforcement in
        human behaviour, 11, 57–8, 61,
        115
    patterns of reinforcement, 38, 52,
        54–6, 61–2, 72–4, 79, 80, 86,
        87, 89, 102–4, 106, 109, 111–13,
        115, 116, 118, 119, 121, 122,
        127, 265, 273, 274, 286
    reciprocal and mutual reinforcement,
        2, 10, 14–17, 23, 26–8, 35, 38,
        71, 73, 93, 119, 274
    schedules of, 13, 62, 64, 116, 248,
        275, 278
relationships *see* marketing and market
    relationships
response classes of behaviour *see*
    approach, avoidance, escape
    and operational definition and
    measures
retail *see* marketing mix variables,
    place, retail
role of theory in case study process *see*
    case study
Ricard, L., 23
Richardson, G.B., 3
Rose, H., 45
Rosenberg, A., 8
rules and rule governed behaviour,

rules, 20, 22, 24, 25, 28, 31, 32, 37,
    38, 49, 53, 57, 58, 59, 60, 61, 72,
    74, 86, 89, 91, 97, 101, 102, 103,
    104, 113, 121, 264, 268, 286,
    287, 288
    rules as stimuli *see also* stimulus
        regulatory stimulus, a definition
        of, 57
    rules in the consumer behaviour
        setting, 11, 31–2
    and setting scope, 11, 32
    consumer self-rules and
        deliberation, 32
    regulatory stimuli, 11, 31
    rule-following, 32
        history of, 32
        others' rules, 32
    rules in marketer behaviour
        setting, 20
    rules in the managerial behaviour
        setting,
        internal rules, 37
        profitability as a rule in the
            managerial behaviour
            setting, 75–6, 101, 264,
            286–8
        rule-following, 121
        rules in contracts, specifying
            contingencies, 58, 286–8
        firm self-rules, 37, 59, 286–8
        others' rules, 268
        topography of managerial
            behaviour setting *see*
            Managerial behaviour
            settings
    rule-based stimuli and regulatory
        dimension of stimuli, 37, 64,
        85
    rules of the market, 25
    rules of exchange, 20
    rule-governed behaviour *see also*
        contingency-shaped behaviour,
        58
    rule setting and rule following, the
        importance of, 121
Rumens, N., 42, 51

Sato, M, 8
Saunders, J., 36, 39, 57, 63, 111
scale economies, 36, 37, 59, 64, 70, 71,

89, 116, 256, 266, 267, 268, 270, 287, 288
setting *see* behaviour setting
setting scope *see* behaviour setting, scope
schedules of reinforcement *see* operational definitions and measures
Scholes, K., 35
Schreuder, H., 1
Schrezenmaier, T., 30, 32, 62, 111, 117
Secretary of State, 84, 127, 248, 251, 268
Silverman, D., 44
Skinner, B.F., 11, 40, 41, 50
Smith, L.D., 50
Smith, Adam, 20
social marketing, 7, 10, 16–17, 26, 27
Stiglitz, J., 124
stimulus or event *see also* marketing mix
   antecedent stiumuli or events *see also* behaviour setting, 10, 11, 28, 30, 31, 52, 53, 54, 57, 65, 103, 117, 125, 126
   the Antecedents Proposition *see* case study research propositions
   class, 57
   brands as a stimulus class *see also* marketing mix variables products, 57
   consequential stimuli or events, 33, 52–4, 57, 89, 103, 113, 119
   discriminative function or stimulus, 10–12, 14, 15, 18–20, 22, 28, 31, 34, 38, 39, 52, 53, 57, 58, 64, 86, 103, 104, 111, 113
   environmental,
   physical and spatial dimensions, 11, 12, 30, 31, 32, 37, 40, 57, 64, 66, 94, 103, 264
   regulatory dimensions *see also* rules and rule-governed behaviour, 12, 20, 31, 37, 57, 64, 85, 88 90, 101, 103, 125, 268
   regulatory stimulus, a definition of, 57

social dimensions, 11, 12, 20, 31, 33, 34, 37, 43, 50, 57, 64, 73, 85, 86, 101, 102, 103, 106
temporal dimensions, 11, 12, 20, 31, 37, 57, 64, 92, 103
management of *see* marketing mix topography *and* marketing mix variables
marketing mix elements as stimuli *see* marketing mix
stimuli *see* stimulus
strategic functions of firm behaviour, 3, 10–14
strategic scope of the organisation, 29
Strebel, P., 38, 119

Teece, D.J., 29, 119
theory of the firm
   analysis of consumer and marketing behaviour, 13
   the importance of consumer behaviour, 13
three-term contingency, 10–11, 30–31, 41, 52, 118, 122
topography of marketing mix stimuli *see* marketing mix
transactions *see* market and economic transactions
transaction costs, 1, 5, 15, 23, 24, 25, 37, 59, 70, 85, 87, 89, 109, 114, 116, 119, 120, 267, 286, 288
   Coase's marketing costs, 1, 23–4
treats, 47, 66, 67, 81, 94, 101, 107, 108, 249, 257, 258, 260, 261, 273
two-sided markets, 114

Unilever, 82, 83, 85, 86, 101, 105, 249, 256, 265, 268, 286
utilitarian reinforcement and punishment *see* consequences of behaviour, reinforcement *and* punishment

Wall's Direct, 47, 67, 72, 77, 82–90, 99, 100–106, 109–10, 115, 117, 119, 123, 126, 253, 257–9, 265–70, 285–7, 289, 290, 293
   events leading to the creation of, 265–9

Webster, F.E., 22
Williamson, O.E., 8, 23, 28
Wong, V., 36, 39, 57, 63, 111

Xiao, S.H., 34, 35, 54, 109, 116

Yani Soriano, M., 42
Yin, R.K., 40, 42, 43, 44, 45, 46, 48, 49, 50

Zuriff, G.E., 50